Y0-ASZ-508

Stanley G. Solomon
124 Crosby Hall
English 1-2A

COLLEGE HANDBOOK OF COMPOSITION

BY

EDWIN C. WOOLLEY

AUTHOR OF WOOLLEY'S HANDBOOK OF COMPOSITION

FRANKLIN W. SCOTT

FORMERLY HEAD OF THE DEPARTMENT OF ENGLISH
UNIVERSITY OF ILLINOIS

With the collaboration of

EVELYN TRIPP BERDAHL

THIRD EDITION

D. C. HEATH AND COMPANY

BOSTON NEW YORK CHICAGO
ATLANTA SAN FRANCISCO DALLAS
LONDON

PRINTED IN THE UNITED STATES OF AMERICA

PREFACE

The third edition of College Handbook of Composition, like earlier editions, is designed to be used by students of composition for reference, at the direction of the instructor, in case of errors in themes, and for independent reference by persons who have writing of any kind to do and who want information on matters of grammar, spelling, punctuation, paragraphing, manuscript-arrangement, or letter writing. The rules that make up the principal features of the book are much the same, for use has proved them to be fundamental and trustworthy guides to all who are engaged in writing.

But the rules have been adapted to such modifications in the use of English as have been established beyond question in the time since the second edition was published. These changes indicate a liberal attitude towards current usage as found in the recent practice of the best writers and take into account the several studies of English usage made in the past few years, as well as the latest editions of our American dictionaries and grammars. The Handbook offers, however, no departure from the general principle that the inexperienced should observe many rules of usage which may on occasion be ignored by accomplished writers.

The College Handbook may be used not only as a handbook of composition but also as an outline of the principles of rhetoric and composition so arranged as to present and illustrate the principles on which the rules are based. Those courses requiring only a minimum amount of rhetorical theory with a maximum of practice may therefore be based on this book without the addition of any other text. The rules are so grouped that together with brief statements of rhetorical principles they constitute a succinct but comprehensive treatment of unity, coherence, and emphasis as applied to the sentence, the paragraph, and the whole composition. In connection with the study of the sentence special attention should be directed to Appendix D, which presents a somewhat detailed study of connectives. Paragraph development is fully illustrated, and a section on outlining lays emphasis on the importance of careful organization in the whole composition. Diction and the qualities of style are given adequate attention.

Abundant examples illustrate widely varied applications of the rules and principles. Each principal rule and each section is followed by exercises, so placed that they are immediately accessible. Spelling, punctuation, grammar, and pronunciation are given the practical consideration shown by many years of experience to be most often needed by students.

Composition involves much more than the writing down of facts and ideas in orderly fashion. The gathering of material is often the most troublesome step in the preparation of compositions, troublesome to students, instructors, and librarians alike. To make this task as easy and effective as possible full directions are given for the use of the library, the taking of notes, the evaluating of sources, and the proper methods of documentation by means of footnotes. The directions for using the library, and especially the lists of reference books, are much fuller than in earlier editions. For those who aspire to get their writings into print directions are given for marking manuscript for the printer, and for reading and marking proof sheets — all the chores the writer must perform if he is to get his ideas decently in order on the printed page.

April, 1937

CONTENTS

CONTENTS IN DETAIL

[Numbers in boldface refer to sections or rules; other numbers refer to pages.]

RULES MOST OFTEN NEEDED

[Consult the full rule for corrective help.]

Diction

RULE	PAGE		
1	31.	Use English that conforms to the standard of good usage.	Good English
18	45.	Avoid jargon, vague, ambiguous, blanket words that cannot be precisely defined.	Jargon
23	51.	Do not be wordy.	Wordiness
30	54.	Avoid trite expressions.	Triteness
44–48	64–66.	Avoid awkward and needless repetition.	Repetition
49	66.	Vary your sentence diction and construction.	Variety

Sentence Unity

RULE	PAGE		
52	79.	Statements unrelated to each other should not be put in the same sentence.	Unconnected thoughts
53	80.	Avoid a long compound sentence made of statements linked by *and*'s and *but*'s.	*And's* and *but's*
55	85.	Avoid the excessive use of *so* as a connective.	*So's*
59	88.	Do not chop up the thought of one unified sentence into several short sentences.	Thought chopped up

Sentence Coherence

RULE	PAGE		
66–77	93–97.	A pronoun must refer unmistakably to its antecedent and should follow it closely.	Faulty reference
78	99.	Do not leave modifiers dangling with no particular word to modify.	Dangling modifiers
80–85	103–106.	Place modifiers as near as possible to the words they modify.	Position of modifiers
86	106.	Avoid awkward split constructions.	Split constructions
87–94	108–113.	Do not mix the construction in a sentence and thereby cause illogical agreement.	Mixed or illogical construction
103–107	117–120.	Do not omit words necessary to clarity.	Illogical omissions
108–117	122–128.	Sentence elements parallel in thought should be parallel in form.	Parallel construction

	RULE	PAGE	
Shifting voice, etc.	**118–123**	130–131.	Avoid unnecessary shifting of subject, voice, mood, tense, number, and person.
Connectives	**124**	132.	Use connectives that express the exact relationship intended.
			SENTENCE EMPHASIS
Important positions	**129**	135.	Put important words in the important positions in a sentence: first or last.
Proper subordination	**134**	137.	Put principal ideas into principal clauses; subordinate ideas into subordinate clauses.
			GRAMMAR
Subject and verb	**200**	203.	A verb must agree in number with its subject.
Pronoun and antecedent	**201**	206.	A pronoun must agree with its antecedent in number.
Object	**206**	209.	The object of a verb or of a preposition is in the objective case.
			PUNCTUATION
Period fault	**236**	232.	Do not use a period after a fragment.
Comma fault	**247**	241.	A comma is not sufficient punctuation between coördinate principal clauses not joined by a pure conjunction.
Series	**249–253**	243–245.	Words, phrases, and clauses used in a series are separated by commas.
Non-restrictive modifiers	**259a**	248.	A non-restrictive modifier should be set off by commas; a restrictive modifier should not be set off by commas.
Introductory sentence-elements	**261–265**	250–252.	An introductory sentence-element is usually followed by a comma.
Punctuation consistent	**266**	253.	Coördinate sentence-elements should be punctuated alike.
So, therefore, however	**268**	254.	Use a semicolon between clauses of a compound sentence that are joined by conjunctive adverb, *so, therefore, hence,* etc.
Indiscriminate use of dashes	**281**	262.	Do not use dashes indiscriminately in place of commas, semicolons, or periods.
Apostrophe and pronouns	**304**	278.	Never use an apostrophe with the possessive case of the personal pronouns.

COLLEGE HANDBOOK OF COMPOSITION

THE USE OF THE LIBRARY

GENERAL INFORMATION REGARDING THE LIBRARY

Card catalogue

The college student, who is frequently required to write papers or to make a special investigation of some subject, should learn how to use his library. He should, first of all, know how to use the card catalogue, which is the index of the library. It lists on 3 × 5-inch cards every book contained in the library. These cards are filed alphabetically according to author, title, and subject in a cabinet of small drawers which are labeled to indicate their contents. (In some libraries there are separate catalogues for the author cards, for the title cards, and for the subject cards, but they are usually combined into a single catalogue.) Thus nearly every book in the library is listed at least three times: under its author's name, under its title, and finally under its subject.

An author card has as its heading the surname of the author. (A heading is the word, phrase, or name at the top of the card by which the card is filed.) An author card is made for every book the author of which is known, whether the authorship is individual or group. An exception occurs in the case of a work by so many different authors that their number is prohibitive for entry.

A title card has as its heading the title of the book and is filed according to the first word of the title not an article. Works with titles likely to be remembered, anonymous works, and periodicals have title cards.

A subject card has as its heading the name of the subject treated in the book. For instance, *Oils, Fats*

Card catalogue

and Fatty Foods by E. R. Bolton, has as its subject heading: *Vitamines.* (The headings for subject cards in most libraries are in red type.) When a student is looking for a book by an author with a common surname, whose forename he does not know, he will save time by looking under the subject of the book rather than under the author's name, for there may be many cards by authors of the same surname. As a rule all works, with the exception of fiction, plays, and poetry, have subject cards.

In addition a work may be entered not only under author, title, and subject, but also under the name of the editor, translator, or compiler.

A catalogue card is reproduced below:

104
Sa5c Santayana, George, 1863–

Character & opinion in the United States, with reminiscences of William James and Josiah Royce and academic life in America, by George Santayana . . . New York, C. Scribner's sons, 1920.

1 p. 1., v–ix, 233 p. 21½ cm.
Printed in Great Britain.

Contents. — The moral background. — The academic environment. — William James. — Josiah Royce.—Later speculations.—Materialism and idealism in American life. — English liberty in America.

1. U. S. — Civilization. 2. James, William, 1842–1910. 3. Royce, Josiah, 1855–1916. I. Title.

20–26993

Library of Congress B945.S23C5

In the top left-hand corner of this card is the call number that indicates where the book can be found on the library shelves. Next comes the author's name and the date of his birth. On the line below appears the title of the book, the author's name with the first name first, the place of publication, the publisher, and the date of publication. The line that follows explains that at the beginning of the book there are one printed page, an empty page, then some pages numbered with Roman numerals, that there are 233 pages in the body of the book, and that it is $21\frac{1}{2}$ centimeters high. After a summary of the contents, which may aid the student in determining whether the book will be of value to him, comes a list of subject headings under which the book may be found in the card catalogue. Thus in many libraries this book will be indexed five times: once under the author's name, once under its title, and three times under different subject headings. The rest of the information on the card is of special interest to librarians.

Call slip

When the student has found the card for a book he desires, he should write on the call slip furnished by the library: the call number, the author's name, the title, and the volume number if the work is in several volumes. (A separate slip should be made out for each book.) The slip should then be presented at the loan desk.

REFERENCE BOOKS

Reference books

A reference book is a book that contains a great deal of information in a small space and is so planned that the facts can be found quickly. Dictionaries and encyclopedias are typical reference books. These books are as a rule kept together in a separate room and cannot be taken from the library.

One of the best ways to begin the study of a subject is to consult a good encyclopedia. Here one may get a preliminary or general survey of a large subject or a brief article on a limited subject, and also a list of books on a subject. By consulting the index volume of an encyclopedia, the student may find additional articles bearing on his subject. For example, under *sun spots* in the *Encyclopædia Britannica*, he is referred to supplementary articles under these headings: *spectroheliograph*, *climate*, *corona*, *trade cycle*, etc.

The following lists include important reference books:

ENCYCLOPEDIAS

Encyclopedias

Encyclopædia Britannica. 14th edition, 1929. 24 vols. Vol. 24, Atlas and index.

Encyclopedia Americana. 1931–1932. 30 vols.

Americana Annual. 1923–. Annual supplement to the *Encyclopedia Americana.*

New International Encyclopedia. 1922–1930. 27 vols.

New International Year Book. 1907–. Annual supplement to the *New International Encyclopedia.*

DICTIONARIES

Dictionaries

New Century Dictionary. 1927–1933. 2 vols.

New English Dictionary. 1888–1933. 10 vols. and supplementary vol. (Also referred to as *Murray's Dictionary* or the *Oxford Dictionary.*) Especially valuable for derivations and the changes in the meanings of words.

New Standard Dictionary. 1935.

Webster's New International Dictionary (Second Edition). 1935.

SPECIAL DICTIONARIES

Special dictionaries

Allen, F. S. *Allen's Synonyms and Antonyms.* 1921. Words characterized as "affected," "bookish," "rare," etc. No definitions.

Century Cyclopedia of Names, a pronouncing dictionary of names in geography, biography, mythology, history . . . 1911.

Crabb, George. *Crabb's English Synonyms.* 1917. Distinctions in meaning given.

Craigie, Sir William and Hulbert, James R. *A Dictionary of American English on Historic Principles.* 1936–. Comparable to the *New English* (*Oxford*) *Dictionary.* To be completed in 20 parts, of which Part I was issued in 1936.

Fernald, J. C. *English Synonyms and Antonyms.* 1931. Distinctions in meaning given. Use of prepositions.

Fowler, H. W. *A Dictionary of Modern English Usage.* 1926.

Henderson, I. F. and Henderson, M. A. *Dictionary of Scientific Terms.* 1929.

Roget, P. M. *Thesaurus of English Words and Phrases.* 1933. Valuable for enlarging the vocabulary.

SMITH, WILLIAM G. *Oxford Dictionary of English Proverbs.* 1936.

VIZETELLY, F. H. *A Desk-book of 25,000 Words Frequently Mispronounced* . . . 1929.

REFERENCE BOOKS FOR SPECIAL SUBJECTS

Agriculture

Special reference books

Agricultural Index. 1919–.

BAILEY, L. H. *Cyclopedia of American Agriculture.* 1908–1909. 4 vols.

Publications of the United States Department of Agriculture. For example, the *Yearbook* and the *Experiment Station Record.*

Allusions, Proverbs, Quotations

ALLIBONE, S. A. *Poetical Quotations from Chaucer to Tennyson.* 1891.

—— *Prose Quotations from Socrates to Macaulay.* 1889.

APPERSON, G. L. *English Proverbs and Proverbial Phrases.* 1929.

BARTLETT, JOHN. *Familiar Quotations.* 1914.

—— *New and Complete Concordance . . . of Shakespeare.* 1894.

BENHAM, W. G. *Book of Quotations, Proverbs and Household Words.* 1929.

BREWER, E. C. *Dictionary of Phrase and Fable.* 1931.

—— *Reader's Handbook* of famous names in fiction, allusions, references, proverbs, plots, stories, poems. 1911.

CRUDEN, ALEXANDER. *Complete Concordance to the Old and New Testament.* 1930. A good desk concordance.

GERWIG, HENRIETTA. *Crowell's Handbook for Readers and Writers.* 1925.

HOYT, J. K. *New Cyclopedia of Practical Quotations.* 1922.

SMITH, W. G. *Oxford Dictionary of English Proverbs.* 1935.

STRONG, JAMES. *Exhaustive Concordance of the Bible.* 1894.

WALSH, W. S. *International Encyclopedia of Prose and Poetic Quotations from the Literature of the World.* 1908.

Anthropology and Ethnology

Peoples of All Nations. 1922–1924. 7 vols.

RIPLEY, W. Z. *Selected Bibliography of Anthropology and Ethnology of Europe.* 1899.

Architecture

Special reference books

FLETCHER, SIR BANISTER. *History of Architecture on the Comparative Method.* 1931. An excellent reference book, but not a history of architecture.

KIMBALL, S. F. and EDGELL, G. H. *History of Architecture.* 1918.

RATHBUN, S. H. *A Background to Architecture.* 1926.

SIMPSON, F. M. *History of Architectural Development.* 1905–1911. 3 vols.

STURGIS, RUSSELL. *Dictionary of Architecture and Building.* 1901–1902.

STURGIS, RUSSELL and FROTHINGHAM, A. L. *History of Architecture.* 1906–1915. 4 vols.

Art

American Art Annual. 1899–.

Ars Una. A general history of art. 1909–1928. 7 vols., now issued.

Art Index. 1930–.

CHAMPLIN, J. D. and PERKINS, C. C. *Cyclopedia of Painters and Painting.* 1892. 4 vols.

FIELDING, MANTLE. *Dictionary of American Painters, Sculptors, and Engravers.* 1927.

PIJOAN, JOSÉ. *History of Art.* 1927. 3 vols. Many excellent photographs. Discussion includes architecture, painting, sculpture, and the minor arts and crafts.

REINACH, SALOMON. *Apollo.* An illustrated manual of the history of art throughout the ages. 1924.

Biography

Appleton's *Cyclopædia of American Biography.* 1888–1900. 7 vols. Supplementary volumes compiled by the New York Press Association. Vols. 8–11.

Dictionary of American Biography. 20 vols. 1928–1936. Includes only persons no longer living.

Dictionary of National Biography. 1885–1901. 63 vols. Supplements: 1901, 3 vols.; 1912, 3 vols.; 1927, 1 vol.

National Cyclopedia of American Biography. 1892–1935. 24 vols. Current loose-leaf volumes. Includes living persons only.

THOMAS, JOSEPH. *Universal Pronouncing Dictionary of Biography and Mythology.* 1930.

Special reference books

Who's Who; Who's Who in America; Wer Ist's; Qui Êtes-Vous? etc. Separate books containing brief accounts of living men and women. Issued more or less regularly in the various countries.

Botany

Botanical Abstracts. Monthly publication containing abstracts and citations. 1918–1926. Merged with *Biological Abstracts.*

BRITTON, N. L. and BROWN, A. *Illustrated Flora of the Northern United States, Canada* . . . 1913. 3 vols.

Chemistry

BOLTON, H. C. *Select Bibliography of Chemistry.* 1899–1904.

Chemical Abstracts. American Chemical Society. 1907–.

THORPE, SIR THOMAS. *A Dictionary of Applied Chemistry.* 1922–1927. 7 vols. Supplement, 1934–1935. 2 vols.

Classical Antiquities

PECK, H. T., editor. *Harper's Dictionary of Classical Literature.* 1897.

SANDYS, SIR JOHN. *Companion to Latin Studies.* 1925.

WALTERS, H. B. *A Classical Dictionary of Greek and Roman Antiquities.* 1916.

WHIBLEY, LEONARD. *Companion to Greek Studies.* 1931.

Commerce, General Business, Economics, Statistics

CHISHOLM, G. G. *Handbook of Commercial Geography.* 1932.

CLARK, V. S. *History of Manufactures in the United States.* 1929. 3 vols.

Encyclopedia of the Social Sciences. 1930–1935. 15 vols.

FREEMAN, W. G. and CHANDLER, S. E. *The World's Commercial Products.* 1907.

MULHALL, M. G. *Dictionary of Statistics.* 1903.

Newark, N. J. Free Public Library. 2400 business books and guide to business literature. 1921.

—— Business books: 1920–1926. 1927.

Publications of the United States Department of Commerce. For example, *Commerce Yearbook; Survey of Current Business; Statistical Abstract.* Contains tables covering all fields in which statistics are usually needed, such as population, vital statistics, etc.

Special reference books

United States. Bureau of the Census. *Census.* 1790–

WEBB, A. D. *The New Dictionary of Statistics.* 1911.

WHITAKER, JOSEPH. *An Almanack.* 1869–. Statistics for the British Empire.

World Almanac. Annual. 1868–.

Current Events and Progress

American Year Book. 1910–1919. 1925–.

Congressional Record. 1873–. Published daily during sessions of Congress. Contains presidents' messages, congressional speeches and debates in full, and record of votes.

Europa. With which is incorporated *Europa Yearbook.* 1930–. European *Who's Who.*

New York Times Index. 1913–. Subject index to the *Times.* Forms an outline of current history.

Public Affairs Information Service. 1915–.

Statesman's Year Book. 1864–.

Times (London) *Official Index.* 1906–.

World Almanac. 1868–.

Customs and Holidays

BRAND, JOHN. *Observations on the Popular Antiquities of Great Britain.* 1888–1890. 3 vols.

CHAMBERS, ROBERT. *Book of Days.* 1914. 2 vols.

HAZELTINE, M. E. *Anniversaries and Holidays.* 1928.

HAZLITT, W. C. *Faiths and Folklore.* 1905. 2 vols.

SCHAUFFLER, R. H. *Our American Holidays.* 1907–1933. 12 vols.

WALSH, W. S. *Curiosities of Popular Customs . . .* 1898.

Education

Education Index. 1930–.

MONROE, PAUL, editor. *Cyclopedia of Education.* 1911–1913. 5 vols.

Engineering

Engineering Index. 1884–.

Gazetteers and Atlases

Cambridge Modern History. Vol. 14, Atlas. 1912.

Hammond's New-World Loose Leaf Atlas. 1920. New maps distributed from time to time.

Lippincott's New Gazetteer. 1931.
Putnam's Historical Atlas, Mediaeval and Modern. 1927.
Rand, McNally's Commercial Atlas. 1935.
Times Survey Atlas of the World. 1920–1922.

Special reference books

General Science

International Catalogue of Scientific Literature. 1902–1919.
THOMSON, J. R. *The Outline of Science.* 1922. 4 vols.

Geology

Bibliography of North American Geology. 1931–1934. 2 vols.
Publications of the United States Geological Survey. For example, *World Atlas of Commercial Geology; Geological Atlas of the United States.*

History

Cambridge Ancient History. 1923–. Vols. 1–10. Vols. 1–4, Atlas.
Cambridge Mediaeval History. 1911–. Vols. 1–8.
Cambridge Modern History. 1902–1926. 14 vols. Vol. 14, Atlas.
CHANNING, EDWARD, HART, A. B., and TURNER, F. J. *Guide to the Study and Reading of American History.* 1912.
Guide to Historical Literature. Edited by G. M. Dutcher and others. 1931.
LARNED, J. N. *Literature of American History,* a bibliographical guide. 1902.
New Larned History for Ready Reference. 1922. 12 vols.
Pageant of America; a pictorial history of the United States. 1925–1929. 15 vols.
Writings on American History. 1904–1933. Covers the years 1902–1903, 1906–1930.
See also references under *Current Events and Progress.*

Home Economics

PLANCHÉ, J. R. *Cyclopædia of Costume.* 1876–1879. 2 vols.
ROBERTSON, A. I. *Guide to Literature of Home and Family Life.* 1924.

Industrial Arts

Industrial Arts Index. 1913–.

Law

Special reference books

BLACK, H. C. *Law Dictionary.* 1933.

BOUVIER, JOHN. *Law Dictionary and Concise Encyclopedia.* 1929.

Corpus Juris. 1914–.

Index to Legal Periodicals. 1908–.

United States. Library of Congress. *State Law Index.* 1925–. 1929–.

Literature

A.L.A. Booklist, a guide to new books. 1905–.

A.L.A. Catalog, 1926; an annotated basic list of 10,000 books. Supplement, 1926–1931, an annotated list of approximately 3000 titles. 1933.

BAKER, E. A. *Guide to the Best Fiction.* English and American, including translations from foreign languages. 1932.

—— *Guide to Historical Fiction.* 1914.

Book Review Digest. 1905–.

Cambridge History of American Literature. 1917–1921. 4 vols.

Cambridge History of English Literature. 1907–1927. 15 vols.

CLARK, B. H. *British and American Drama of Today.* Study outlines, biographies, and bibliographies. 1921.

—— *Continental Drama of Today.* 1914.

COUSIN, J. W. *A Short Biographical Dictionary of English Literature.* 1925.

CROSS, T. P. *A List of Books and Articles, Chiefly Bibliographical, Designed to Serve as an Introduction to the Bibliography and Methods of English Literary History.* 1932.

Dramatic Index. 1910–.

FIRKINS, INA. *Index to Plays, 1800–1926.* 1927. Supplement, 1927–1934. 1935.

—— *Index to Short Stories.* 1923. Supplement, 1929. 2 vols.

GAYLEY, C. M. and SCOTT, F. N. *Methods and Materials of Literary Criticism.* Vol. I. GAYLEY and SCOTT, 1899; Vol. II. GAYLEY and KURTZ, B. P., 1920.

GHOSH, J. C. and WITHYCOMBE, E. G. *Annals of English Literature, 1475–1925.* 1936. Principal publications of each year together with alphabetical index of authors.

GRANGER, EDITH. *Index to Poetry and Recitations.* 1918. Supplement, 1929.

HARVEY, SIR PAUL. *Oxford Companion to English Literature.* 1932.

Special reference books

HEFLING, HELEN and RICHARDS, EVA. *Index to Contemporary Biography and Criticism.* 1934.

KELLER, H. R. *Reader's Digest.* 1931.

LOGASA, HANNAH and VER NOOY, WINIFRED. *Index to One-act Plays.* 1924–1932. 2 vols.

MACKERROW, R. B. *Introduction to Bibliography for Literary Students.* 1927.

MANLY, J. M. and RICKERT, EDITH. *Contemporary British Literature.* Bibliographies and study outlines. 1935.

—— *Contemporary American Literature.* 1929.

Modern Humanities Research Association. Annual bibliography of English language and literature. 1920–.

MOULTON, C. W., editor. *Library of Literary Criticism of English and American Authors.* 1901–1905. 8 vols.

SHARP, R. F., compiler. *Biographical Dictionary of Foreign Literature.* 1935.

U. S. Catalog; books in print. 1900–. The four editions and their supplements, including the *Cumulative Book Index,* record practically all material printed in the United States since 1898. Since 1931 it has included British publications of importance.

Who's Who among Living Authors of Older Nations. 1928–.

Who's Who among North American Authors. 1921–.

Medicine

Quarterly Cumulative Index Medicus. 1927–. Formed by the union of the *Index Medicus* and the *Quarterly Cumulative Index to Current Medical Literature,* the latter covering material from 1916 to 1927.

STEDMAN, T. L. *Practical Medical Dictionary.* 1934.

Music

GROVE, SIR GEORGE. *Grove's Dictionary of Music and Musicians.* 1928. 6 vols.

KOBBÉ, GUSTAV. *The Complete Opera Book.* 1935.

The Oxford History of Music. 1929–1934. 7 vols.

Mythology

EDWARDES, MARIAN. *Dictionary of Non-Classical Mythology.* 1912.

GAYLEY, C. M. *Classic Myths in English Literature and in Art.* 1911.

Special reference books

GRAY, L. H., editor. *Mythology of All Races.* 1916–1932. 13 vols.

See also references under *Classical Antiquities.*

Natural History

Nature Library. 1905–1912. 17 vols. By several authors, treating such subjects as animals, birds, shells, butterflies, trees, etc.

Philosophy and Psychology

BALDWIN, J. M. *Dictionary of Philosophy and Psychology.* 1928. 3 vols.

MURCHISON, C. A., editor. *A Handbook of General Experimental Psychology.* 1934.

—— *A Handbook of Social Psychology.* 1935.

Psychological Abstracts. 1927–.

Psychological Index. 1894–.

RAND, BENJAMIN, compiler. *Bibliography of Philosophy, Psychology, and Cognate Subjects.* 1905. 2 vols.

Physics

GLAZEBROOK, SIR RICHARD, editor. *A Dictionary of Applied Physics.* 1922–1923. 5 vols.

Political Science

Encyclopedia of the Social Sciences. 1930–1935. 15 vols.

The League of Nations from Year to Year. Information section, Secretariat of the League of Nations. 1927–.

MCLAUGHLIN, A. C. and HART, A. B. *Cyclopedia of American Government.* 1914. 3 vols.

MYERS, D. P. *Handbook of the League of Nations.* World Peace Foundation Publications. 1935.

Political Handbook of the World. 1927–.

Student's Guide to Materials in Political Science. Prepared by L. Burchfield. 1935.

See also references under *Current Events and Progress.*

Religion and Ethics

Catholic Encyclopedia. 1907–1922. 17 vols.

FRAZER, SIR J. G. *The Golden Bough.* 1925–1930. 12 vols.

HASTINGS, JAMES, editor. *Encyclopædia of Religion and Ethics.* 1911–1927. 13 vols.

Jewish Encyclopedia. 1901–1906. 12 vols.

SCHAFF, PHILIP. *The New Schaff-Herzog Encyclopedia of Religious Knowledge.* 1908–1912. 13 vols.

Sociology

Encyclopedia of the Social Sciences. 1930–1935. 15 vols.
HANKINS, F. H. *Introduction to the Study of Society.* 1929.
Social Work Year Book. 1935. A description of organized activities in social work and in related fields.
See also references under *Current Events and Progress; Debate Material; Commerce, General Business, and Statistics; Political Science.*

MISCELLANEOUS

Debate Material

Miscellaneous reference books

FOSTER, W. T. *Argumentation and Debating.* 1932.
The Handbook Series. 1914–. The former *Debater's Handbook Series* is now incorporated with this. Bibliographies; reprints from books, magazines, etc.; briefs.
Intercollegiate Debates. 1909–. A yearbook of college debating with records of questions and decisions, specimen speeches, and bibliographies.
PHELPS, E. M. *Debaters' Manual.* 1929. Articles selected from authorities on debating. Bibliographies.
Reference Shelf. 1922–. Pamphlets on current topics.
University Debaters' Annual. 1915–. Constructive and rebuttal speeches delivered in debates of American colleges and universities. Briefs and bibliographies.
See also references under *Current Events and Progress; Commerce, General Business, and Statistics.*

United States Public Documents

BOYD, A. M. *United States Government Publications.* 1918.
SWANTON, W. I., compiler. *Guide to United States Government Publications.* 1918.
Various catalogues and price lists covering United States public documents, 1789–.

GUIDES TO REFERENCE BOOKS AND TO THE USE OF THE LIBRARY

Reference guides

ARNETT, L. D. *Elements of Library Methods.* 1925.
HUTCHINS, MARGARET, JOHNSON, ALICE, and WILLIAMS, MARGARET. *Guide to the Use of Libraries.* 1936.

MINTO, JOHN. *Reference Books.* 1929. Supplement, 1931. Especially valuable for English publications.

MUDGE, I. G. *Guide to Reference Books.* 1936.

MAGAZINES

Magazines

Magazines are the principal sources of information on the subjects of current interest. In the better class of magazines the student will often find articles of permanent value. Every year or six months, or at other convenient periods, the numbers of a magazine are bound together in a volume and are thus available for reference use in a convenient form. The following list gives a few of the standard magazines which are of importance for general reading, current history, and book reviews:

GENERAL

American

American Mercury
Atlantic Monthly
Foreign Affairs
Forum and Century
Harper's Monthly
Living Age
National Geographic
North American Review
Scientific American
Scribner's Magazine
Virginia Quarterly Review
Yale Review

English

Contemporary Review
Criterion
Fortnightly
London Mercury
Nineteenth Century and After

CURRENT EVENTS

American

Congressional Digest
Current History Magazine
Literary Digest
Nation
New Republic
News Week
Review of Reviews
Survey
Time
New York Times (Sunday) Section 4. *Review of the Week.*

English

New Statesman and Nation
Spectator
Saturday Review

BOOK REVIEWS

American

Books
Saturday Review of Literature
New York Times Book Review
Virginia Quarterly Review

English

Saturday Review
Spectator
Times (London) *Literary Supplement*

GREGORY, WINIFRED, editor. *Union List of Serials in the Libraries of the United States and Canada.* 1927. Supplements, 1931–1933.

PERIODICAL INDEXES

Periodical indexes

Periodical indexes are invaluable as an aid in locating material scattered through a vast number of periodicals. These indexes list alphabetically every article of importance by author or subject, generally both, and also frequently by title. Most of the indexes appear monthly and at frequent intervals are cumulated; that is, all the material in the separate numbers is combined into a single alphabet.

Poole's Index to Periodical Literature. 1802–1907; 1887–1908. Subject index only.
Reader's Guide to Periodical Literature. 1900–. Alphabetical list under author, title, and subject.
International Index to Periodicals. 1920–. Devoted chiefly to humanities and science.
See also special indexes under subjects above.

USE OF REFERENCE BOOKS

Judging the value of books for reference

In judging the value of books as sources for reference material, the student should consider certain points:

Evaluating sources

a. He should first of all develop a critical attitude; he should not accept all that he sees in print. He should ask these questions:

(1) Can the accuracy of the statements in the book be depended upon? Is the author an authority on his subject? Some information regarding the author may often be found on the title page of the book. His name is frequently followed by the degrees he has received from universities, by the names of other books that he has written, or by the names of learned societies, institutions, etc., to which he belongs. Additional information regarding the author may be found in biographical dictionaries, such as *Who's Who*, etc. More confidence can be placed in magazine and encyclopedia articles if they are signed by the person writing them, for that person assumes responsibility for the accuracy of the statements. In using statistics, the student should note whether they are based on official or other reports, and whether exact reference is made to their sources. Greater confidence can be placed in a book published by a reputable firm than in others.

(2) Might the author be biased? Might he have political, religious, national, or racial prejudices?

b. He should distinguish between primary and secondary material; that is, between original documents or texts and someone's interpretation of that document or text. For example, the Declaration of Independence and the Constitution of the United States are primary material; Carl L. Becker's *The Declaration of Independence; a Study in the History of Political Ideas* (New York, 1922), and James M. Beck's *The Constitution of the United States; a Brief Study of the Genesis, Formulation, and Political Philosophy of the Constitution of the United States* (New York, 1922) are secondary material. Both secondary and primary material are of value to the student: the secondary often furnishing an analysis or interpretation of the primary material; and the primary not only presenting information, but also serving as a check for inaccuracies of fact or of interpretation in the secondary material.

c. The date of the book should be noted. (The date usually appears on the title page; if not, on the copyright page.) In many subjects, such as those on which the information changes rapidly with time, the value of the material depends directly upon the date. The student should also note, in examining the card catalogue, whether there is a "revised edition" or an "enlarged edition" of the book he is to use.

d. Reference books that give bibliographies, that is, lists of books on the same subject, are of value. These bibliographies are usually placed at the end of an article or a chapter or at the end of a book.

e. The scope of the book should be considered. One work may give a detailed analysis of the subject for the specialist; another may give only a summary. If the student is to write a short paper, he would find a summary treatment in one chapter of a book of more value to him than a three-volume treatise.

Use of books for reference

In order to decide whether a book contains material bearing on his subject, the student will need to become acquainted with the contents without having to read the book through. The title page may often give him information regarding the subject treated, the field covered, the class of readers for whom the book is intended, or the point of view of the author. The preface usually states these facts, and often gives the author's reasons for writing and the names of those to whom he is indebted for assistance in the work. By a study of the table of contents, which may give only the chapter headings or may include a detailed analysis of the chapters, the student will gain an idea of the material in the book. Many works contain introductory chapters which give a general survey of the subject, preparing the reader for the matter to follow. In the opening and concluding paragraphs of a chapter, the student may find summaries of the chapter. At the end of the book there may be a summarizing chapter. The index at the end of a work is an alphabetical list of topics, persons, places, events, etc., appearing in the book. From the index, the student can quickly find out whether a particular subject is treated in the work; from the table of contents, however, he will get an outline of the whole work.

Taking library notes

Before the student takes any notes, he should first read hastily the whole article, chapter, or book, as the case may be, in order to get the author's main point and his development of that point. The student will then be better able to judge just what material he needs. In a second reading, he should note down the main point and the vital steps in the development of that point. The number of less important details to be noted down will depend upon the length of his paper and the relative importance of the material to him. If the article is to furnish him background matter, he may need to note only the main point. The shorter the notes the better, of course; yet enough of the context should be taken so that the idea cannot be misinterpreted. The student is under a moral obligation to the author, whose ideas he is using, to give the reader a correct understanding of these ideas. Also the notes should be full enough to be intelligible when "cold."

The notes may be in the form of a direct quotation or of a paraphrase or a summary in the student's own words. Direct quotations are especially valuable when the points are very important, when they might be

Taking library notes

questioned, or when they are aptly stated. The student must be very careful in his notes to enclose direct quotations in quotation marks; otherwise later he might allow borrowed phrases to appear in his paper as his own. Also when he is summarizing someone else's material, he must in his notes give credit to the author. (See *Footnotes*, pp. 24–30.)

The following suggestions on the form of notes may be helpful:

a. Take notes on cards or slips of paper of a uniform size. Library card size, 3 × 5, is convenient, but a larger size may be used.

b. Write on one side only and do not crowd the writing.

c. State the subject in the upper left-hand corner.

d. State on each card the exact source, noting the author, the work, and the page. (The bibliography at the end of the student's paper will give fuller information regarding the source. See *Bibliography*, pp. 20–24.)

e. Put each point upon a separate card; if more than one card is needed for one point, note the subject and the name of the book on each new card. Number these cards and clip them together.

f. Put quotation marks around material that is exactly quoted. If parts are omitted, elision marks (. . .) should be used where the omission occurs. (See Rules 241 and 289*e*.) Brackets should enclose words which are not part of the quotation, but which are written within the quotation marks. (See Rule 285.) Do not use quotation marks for paraphrases or summaries.

g. Always quote exactly, even to the punctuation marks and the spelling. If there is an obvious error in the text, insert after it the word *sic* in brackets, which indicates that the quotation is exact. (See Rule 285, Note.)

h. Formulate a system of abbreviations and follow it consistently. For instance, if the word *Renaissance* occurs frequently in the text, abbreviate it to *Ren.* Use *w.* for *with,* etc. As a rule, in a summary omit the articles, copulas, and connectives.

After the notes are taken, they may be arranged alphabetically according to the subject in the left-hand corner and filed in a tray or pasteboard box into which they fit. Guide cards may be used to indicate the divisions of the subject. The student then has his notes in a convenient form for writing his paper. (For the proper form for footnotes see pp. 24–30.)

These same directions may be followed in note-taking for "outside" reading. Since such notes do not, as a rule, have to be rearranged as do the notes for a paper, they may be more conveniently taken on loose-leaf notebook paper and may be included with the student's class notes.

BIBLIOGRAPHY

Making a bibliography

In the preparation of a paper, the student should not limit himself to one or two references for his material; he should consult as many as his library and his time permit. An early step in the preparation of his report should be the tentative listing of books and articles that might bear on his subject. This list is his bibliography. Later from this list he may drop those books that upon examination prove to be of no help to him.

The following sources may be of value to the student in gathering his bibliography:

a. The card catalogue of the library. (1) Listed under subject headings he will find the books in his field. (2) Also at the end of the file on his subject, he will often find a "see also" card, listing related subject headings that may lead him to additional books.

Using card catalogues

Example:

> Vocational education, see also
> Professional education
> Technical education

(3) He should look under the subject headings listed at the bottom of the library cards. For instance, if he were looking under *Neutrality*, these subject headings on a card would be found: (*a*) International law and relations. (*b*) World politics. (*c*) U. S. foreign relations. (*d*) Sea power. (*e*) Economic policy. (*f*) Sometimes under a subject heading he will find a subdivision devoted to bibliographical cards. A bibliographical subdivision occurs under *Vocational education* with one bibliography listed thus:

> Vocational education — Bibliog.
> Bennett, Wilma, *comp.*
> Occupations and vocational guidance, a source list of pamphlet material.

b. Bibliographies. The student should consult the bibliographies published by the Library of Congress (see Swanton's *Guide to Government Publications*) and by the American Library Association (the *A.L.A. Index*, the *A.L.A. Catalog*, the *A.L.A. Booklist.*)

c. Encyclopedias. At the end of articles lists of books are given.

d. Periodical and government indexes. (See *Periodical Indexes*, p. 15.)

e. Textbooks and articles. In footnotes, at the ends of chapters, etc., bibliographies are often given.

Noting references

As soon as the student finds a book or an article which he thinks will be of help to him, he should make a note of it. Each reference should be written down on a separate library card or slip of paper (3 × 5 inches). With only one title on a card, the student may quickly arrange his bibliography in alphabetical order. Enough information regarding the book should be copied down so that the book may be identified easily. As a rule, the following points should be included:

a. Name of author in full, surname first.

b. Title of book or article.

c. For a book: edition, if other than the first; place of publication; publisher if desired; date of publication; number of volumes, if more than one.

d. For an article: title of periodical; volume number; page number; date of issue of the periodical (month, day, and year).

Specimen Bibliography Card

881
A 8 po.Yco

Cooper, Lane

The Poetics of Aristotle, its meaning and influence
Boston: Marshall Jones and Company, 1923.

Bibliography pp. 154–157.

Additional information, not to be included in the final bibliography, may be noted on the card; as, for example, the library call number, the scope of the book, bibliography included in the book, the source of the reference, etc.

Form of finished bibliography

When the student has completed his report, he can copy his bibliography from his cards on sheets of paper and place it at the end of his manuscript. The following models will illustrate forms for various kinds of books and articles.

1. Books
   (*a*) By one author
   PARRINGTON, VERNON LOUIS. *Main Currents in American Thought.* New York: Harcourt, Brace and Company, 1927.
   (*b*) By two authors
   BEARD, CHARLES AUSTIN and BEARD, MRS. MARY. *The Rise of American Civilization.* New York: Macmillan, 1927.
   (*c*) By more than three authors
   SIZER, THEODORE and others. *Aspects of the Social History of America.* Chapel Hill: University of North Carolina Press, 1931.
   (*d*) Without an author
   Congressional Record. Washington, D. C.: Government Printing Office. Vol. 80, no. 22, p. 1343. Jan. 31, 1936.
   (*e*) An edited text
   WORDSWORTH, WILLIAM. *The Prelude.* Edited from the manuscript with introduction and textual and critical notes by Ernest De Sélincourt. Oxford: The Clarendon Press, 1926.
   (*f*) A translation
   GREGORY OF TOURS. *The History of the Franks.* Translated by O. W. Dalton. Oxford University Press, 1927. 2 vols.
   (*g*) A book in a series
   GREENE, EVARTS BOUTELL. *Provincial America. 1690–1740.* New York: Harper and Brothers, 1905. (The American Nation: A History, edited by Albert Bushnell Hart.)
   (*h*) An anthology or book of readings
   UNTERMEYER, LOUIS, editor. *Modern American Poetry:* a critical anthology. 4th revised edition. New York: Harcourt, Brace and Company, 1930.

2. Articles
   (*a*) Magazine article
      FARR, CLIFFORD H. "The Philosophy of Growth." The *Atlantic Monthly*. CXXXVI : 508–517. Oct., 1925.
   (*b*) Encyclopedia article
      COLE, G. D. H. "Socialism: Principles and Outlook." *The Encyclopædia Britannica*. 14th edition. XX : 888–895.
   (*c*) Essay in a collection
      NEILSON, WILLIAM ALLAN. "Burns in England." In *Anniversary Papers* by colleagues and pupils of George Lyman Kittredge. Boston: Ginn and Company, 1913.

3. Government Publications
      "Trend toward Apartment-house Living in America." *Monthly Labor Review*. Vol. XXIV, no. 6, pp. 1–18. June, 1927. Washington, D. C.: United States Government Printing Office.

Arrangement of bibliography

The bibliography is usually arranged alphabetically according to the last name of the author. If the author's name is not known, the book or article is generally placed alphabetically according to the title. If the bibliography is long, it may be advisable to classify it; as, for example, according to subject matter, or according to primary or secondary sources.

FOOTNOTES

Acknowledgment of sources

It is permissible and often desirable for a student to use another's material in his paper. He must, however, give the author credit for this borrowed material. He is borrowing not only when he copies word for word, but also when he puts the ideas of another into his own words.

The following paragraph, a direct quotation from an article by H. S. Canby in *Harper's Magazine*, February, 1936, could not be handed in as the student's own work. If used in a paper, it must be enclosed in quotation marks.

Acknowledgment of sources

Our tendency was, therefore, to make the college into another and better competitive America. We did not want to think about it, we wanted to be it. In the nineteen thirties we have been taught to consider that expansionist age in terms of great forces wielded by builders, wreckers, pirates, who were quite unconscious that they were working for anything but their own wealth and power. We of the college were quite innocent of such speculations, and thought of the magnates, when we thought of them at all, only as men who had made good. But of the fierce competitions in which they were the captains and the kings we were of course not unaware, being acutely conscious that success in our collegiate world would seat us on the great American bandwagon.

The following paragraph borrows from the preceding paragraph the ideas and some of the phrasing. It should not be handed in as the student's own work.

Students in my father's time modeled their college life upon the America of the nineties, a highly competitive society. Inside and out of college it was an exciting game. We students of the nineteen thirties see that time as an expansionist age with vast forces in the hands of builders, wreckers, pirates working only for their own wealth and power. But to my father's generation these magnates were men who had made good against great odds. And so in their undergraduate days these students had to take part in the fierce competition in college to be prepared for the fight afterward. Success in their collegiate world would seat them on the great American bandwagon.

The following paragraph paraphrases the first paragraph and acknowledges its indebtedness by the use of quotation marks and by citing the author.

The students of the nineties, as Mr. Canby says in a recent article in *Harper's,* modeled their college life upon the America of their time, a highly competitive society. We of the nineteen thirties, as Mr. Canby points out, have come to regard that time as an expansionist age with vast forces in the hands of "builders, wreckers, pirates, who were quite unconscious that they were working for anything but their own wealth and power." But the college students of the nineties were "innocent of such speculations." What they were aware of when they did think about the matter, was that the magnates had made good in a fiercely competitive world. And as Mr. Canby says, what they were acutely conscious of was that success in their collegiate world would seat them on the great American bandwagon.

It is not necessary to acknowledge the sources of proverbial expressions or of familiar quotations such as those from the Bible or of facts and ideas that are common property.

Biblical quotation in sentence: Again I remind you that they who sow the wind, they shall reap the whirlwind.

Accepted fact: The Treaty of Versailles was signed in 1919.

Fact regarding the accuracy of which there might be some difference of opinion: According to Mr. Hotson, Shakespeare's *Merry Wives of Windsor* was played for the first time in April, 1597.

The acknowledgment of credit due an author may be made in the text as in the paragraph above or may be made by listing the author with the book or article in the bibliography, but more specific acknowledgment with the exact pages used should be made in a footnote on the page on which the quotation or reference occurs. (See *Text with footnotes*, p. 28.)

Use of footnotes for explanatory material

Footnotes may also be used for additional explanatory material that if put into the text might interrupt the thought, or that may be too remotely connected with the text or too long to be placed within parentheses in the text.

Example: They were to regain youth as had old Æson.[1]

Place

Footnotes should be placed at the bottom of the page on which the borrowed material occurs, and not

[1] Allusion to the myth of Medea and Æson in which Medea through her sorceries restores Æson's youth.

at the end of the paper. (Page 28.) In manuscript prepared for the printer, the footnote may be placed immediately below the word or passage to which it refers, and separated from the body of the text by lines across the page above and below it.

The following points should be noted: **Form**

a. To indicate the reference of the footnote, numbers are to be preferred to asterisks or other symbols. However, in some cases, such as statistical tables where numbers might be misleading, it is better to use asterisks, daggers, etc.

b. It is preferable in a manuscript to number the footnotes consecutively on the page, but not consecutively throughout the manuscript, for the reason that additional footnotes may be inserted without a complete renumbering. In books, footnotes are usually numbered consecutively through each page or chapter.

c. The index number should be placed after the word or passage to which the footnote refers, and at the beginning of the footnote. (Page 28.)

d. The first reference to a work should contain the following details in this order: (1) author's surname with initials; (2) title (of a book or periodical, underscored; of an article, quoted); (3) number of edition, if more than one; (4) place of publication, if desired; (5) name of publisher, if desired; (6) date of publication; (7) volume and page numbers. When both volume and page numbers are given, the abbreviations *vol.* and *p.* may be omitted. When the page number stands alone, it is better to use the abbreviation *p.* Usually Roman numerals are used for volume numbers, and Arabic for page numbers. (For customary punctuation in footnotes, see p. 28.)

e. If the reference is the same as the one immediately preceding, the abbreviation *ibid.* (Latin *ibidem,* "in the same place") may be used, with the volume and page reference if they are different. (Page 29.)

f. If the footnote refers to a work previously mentioned, but not immediately preceding, the name of the author and the abbreviation *op. cit.* (Latin *opere citato,* "the work cited") may be used. This abbreviation can only be used when one work of an author has been cited. The entire reference must be repeated if several works have been cited.

g. If the author's name is given in the text in connection with the quotation, it will not be necessary to give the name again in the footnote.

h. If the author's name and book are well known, it is sufficient to give merely the author's surname, usually in the possessive case.

Example: Spenser's *Faerie Queene,* Canto V, Stanza 1.

Text with footnotes

The following example will illustrate the proper use of footnotes:

Various claims of American citizens upon Mexico had been a matter of difficulty and negotiation between the two governments since 1836,[1] and were still largely unsettled. The President now hit upon these claims as the "aggravated wrongs" which should be the basis for the complaints against Mexico,[2] although "many of the claims were exorbitant and some of them fraudulent."[3] Meanwhile, General Taylor, who had been sent to occupy the disputed territory beyond the Nueces River, had advanced to a position opposite Matamoras where a strong Mexican force was located, and Polk seemed to think there was some hope of a collision in the near future,[4] which would give him more satisfactory ground for his war message.

[1] Reeves, J. S., *American Diplomacy under Tyler and Polk,* Baltimore, 1907, pp. 76–108.

[2] *The Diary of James K. Polk during his Presidency, 1845–1849.* Edited by M. M. Quaife, Chicago, 1910, I : 363–382.

[3] Reeves, *op. cit.,* p. 86.

[4] *Diary of James K. Polk,* I : 380.

For some time, however, no hostilities occurred; the President became impatient of delay, and on May 9 the Cabinet agreed that a message recommending war should be prepared and submitted by the following Tuesday (May 12), whether the Mexican forces had committed any act of hostility against Taylor or not. Buchanan, the Secretary of State, had already drawn up a statement of the causes of complaint; the President had decided to substitute practically the precise language he himself had used in dealing with the Mexican claims in his annual message of the year before; then suddenly the situation was changed by the receipt of news that same evening from Taylor that the Mexicans had attacked and hostilities had begun. The Cabinet was immediately summoned again, and it was agreed that a message should be sent recommending vigorous and prompt measures to enable the Executive to prosecute the war.[5]

Abbreviations used in footnotes, etc.

The following words and abbreviations are used in footnotes, bibliographies, and references. The foreign words and abbreviations in this list are usually printed in italics.

a.a.O. (*am angeführten Orte*). At the place quoted.
ad loc. (*ad locum*). At the passage cited.
art., *plural*, arts. Article.
c. or ca. (*circa*). At or near a given date.
cf. (*confer*). Compare or consult.
ch. or chap., *plural*, chaps. Chapter.
col., *plural*, cols. Column.
et al. (*et alii*). And others.
et seq. (*et sequens*). And following.
f., *plural*, ff. Page following.
Fig., *plural*, Figs. Figure.
ibid. (*ibidem*). The same reference as the one immediately preceding. The volume, page, etc., may be the same or may be different.
id. or idem. The same.
infra. Below.
l., *plural*, ll. Line.
loc. cit. (*loco citato*). The same passage as that just cited.
n., *plural*, nn. Note.
no., *plural*, nos. Number.

[5] *Ibid.*, pp. 384–386.

Abbreviations used in footnotes, etc.

op. cit. (*opere citato*). The same work as one previously mentioned. To be used only when there has been but one work of an author cited. The entire reference must be repeated if several works have been cited.

p., *plural*, pp. Pages. Pp. 6–8, pages 6 to 8 inclusive. Pp. 6 f., page 6 and the page following. Pp. 6 ff., page 6 and the pages following.

passim. Here and there.

ps., *plural*, pss. Psalm.

sec., *plural*, secs. Section.

sic. So, thus. Sometimes inserted in brackets within quoted matter after an erroneous work or date, etc., to indicate that the quotation is exact. "I saw neather [*sic.*] one."

st. Stanza.

supra. Above.

v. or vid. or vide. See.

v.s. (*vide supra*). See above.

vol., *plural*, vols. Volume.

v. Verse.

THE WORD

GOOD USAGE

1. Use good English, English that conforms to the standard of good usage. Although this standard cannot be absolute, for language is living and growing, yet it is sufficiently definite at any one period to serve as a trustworthy guide. Good usage may be defined as the usage that is current, that is understood throughout the nation, and that is employed in the speech of well-educated people and in the writing of the best modern authors. **Good usage defined**

To determine whether a word is in good usage, consult the latest edition of an unabridged dictionary. Here words that are not in good usage will be labeled by such terms as the following: *archaic*, *colloquial*, *cant*, *dialectal*, *foreign*, *obsolescent*, *obsolete*, *poetic*, *provincial*, *rare*, *slang*, *technical*, *vulgar*, etc. If none of these qualifying terms follows a word in the dictionary, one can conclude that the word is in good usage. (See Rule 13.)

NATIONAL USAGE

2. Avoid provincialisms; that is, words peculiar to certain parts of the country, not used by the nation as a whole. The following are provincialisms: *allow* or *expect* for *think* or *suppose; tote* for *carry; you all* for *you; piece* for *short distance; out of kilter* for *out of repair; to be partial to* for *like* or *prefer* as in *I am partial to dark meat* for *I prefer dark meat; want in* or *want out* for *want to come in* or *want to go out.* **Provincialisms**

PRESENT USAGE

3. Avoid obsolete, obsolescent, and archaic words in prose. An obsolete word is one no longer in use; an **Obsolete, obsolescent, archaic words**

obsolescent word, one going out of use; an archaic word, one too old-fashioned for general use. These words used by an inexperienced writer often fail to give the humorous or quaint or elegant effect that he desires to produce. Such words are *anent, in sooth, mayhap, methinks, oft, swain, thou,* etc.

New words and phrases

4. Avoid newly coined words until they are adopted by the best writers and speakers. (See also Rule 9.)

> Bad: We plan to auto through the mountains.
> Improved: We plan to drive through the mountains.
> Incorrect: She enthuses about her work.
> Correct: She is enthusiastic about her work.

Extempore formations

5. Avoid, except as a humorous device, the use of words of your own coining. There are instances when a new coining may be effective and therefore excusable.

> Effective: He owns a shy deprecating smile (complete with dimple) and a tentative manner of speaking, both tending to obscure the fact that his mind has a sharpness and an *unbluffability* quite remote from that of the conventional college graduate.

REPUTABLE USAGE

Reputable usage

6. Use reputable English, English used by the best writers and speakers. The right of an author to rank among the best English and American authors can be determined only by the general judgment of scholars and critics, as well as of the reading public, and only after that judgment has endured long enough to become established. A single instance of the use of a word, even by one of the best authors, does not establish the word as good English. The word must be shown to be in general use among such authors.

Reputable English is the diction suitable for formal or semiformal writing. One might use *swell* or *snappy* or *cuckoo* (*crazy*) in everyday familiar conversation, but a good writer would not use them in formal material such as an article on Renaissance Gardens or on the Diesel Engine or an address on National Sovereignty. There is a broad general diction used in the good newspapers, magazines, and books, and suitable for all ordinary writing, which is not pompous or elegant or pedantic, and which on the other hand is not colloquial, slangy, vulgar, or illiterate. (Colloquialisms, etc. may be used in dialogue to characterize the speakers.)

NOTE. — It is not always possible to make clear distinctions among colloquialisms, barbarisms, improprieties, slang, vulgarisms. Some dictionaries will label a word as a colloquialism, others as a barbarism, others as slang.

7. Avoid colloquialisms in formal writing. A colloquialism is an expression used in common conversation and in familiar letters and presumes a close relationship between the writer or speaker and his readers or listeners. Colloquialisms at times give vigor to one's writing, and in some such instances their use is permissible. More often, they contribute nothing and give the impression that the writer is too slipshod to search for the fitting word or phrase. (See Appendix A.)

Colloquialisms

a. **Note the following colloquial expressions:**

Colloquial: I do not take any stock in his reforming.
Improved: I do not have any faith in his reforming.

Colloquial: With his usual assurance he fixed things up to suit himself.

Improved: With his usual assurance he arranged things to suit himself.

NOTE. — *Fix* meaning *to arrange, to set to rights, to repair* is colloquial; but *fix* meaning *to make firm* or *fast* is not colloquial, as in: *His heart is fixed, trusting in the Lord.*

Colloquial: The swamps were just beautiful with iridescent mists of fast-evaporating moisture.

Improved: The swamps were very beautiful with iridescent mists of fast-evaporating moisture.

Contractions

b. **Avoid contractions in formal writing.** The common contractions are *don't, isn't, haven't, won't, I'll, we'll,* etc.

Abbreviations

c. **Avoid colloquial abbreviations in formal writing.** Many of these abbreviations belong to campus life. Some of them are understood and are acceptable in familiar conversation; as, for example, *exam,* which is recognized by the *New English Dictionary* as a word and is marked *colloquial.* But others are not generally intelligible and should be avoided; as, for example, *con* for *condition, pro* for *probation.* Avoid such abbreviations as *movies, Jap, phone, auto, gent.*

Incorrect use of one part of speech for another

8. Avoid improprieties. An impropriety is the use of a legitimate word in a wrong sense, a word used to fulfill the office of a part of speech to which it does not belong. (See Rule 14, the chapter on Grammar (especially Rule 215), and Appendix A.) For example:

1. Nouns used as verbs: *to suicide; to suspicion.*
2. Nouns used as adverbs:

   Wrong: That is plenty good enough.
   Wrong: Hide it some place *or* any place.
   Right: Hide it somewhere *or* anywhere.

3. Adjectives used as nouns: *a canine, a feline, a drunk.*
4. Adjectives used as adverbs:

   Wrong: I am real lonesome.
   Right: I am very lonesome.

   Wrong: I am some better.
   Right: I am somewhat better.

   Questionable: Have you read this far *or* that far?
   Right: Have you read so far as this *or* so far as that *or* thus far?

   Wrong: I did good in the examination.
   Right: I did well in the examination.

   Wrong: He has improved considerable.
   Right: He has improved considerably.

   Wrong: I sure am glad.
   Right: I am surely glad.

5. Adverbs used as adjectives:
   Wrong: I feel badly about her leaving.
   Right: I feel bad about her leaving.
6. Verbs used as nouns: *a combine* (*a combination of persons* or *organizations*), *an invite, a steal, eats, a good buy*.
7. Prepositions used as conjunctions:
   Wrong: Do like she does.
   Right: Do as she does.
   Wrong: He will not go except *or* without you go too.
   Right: He will not go unless you go too.

9. Avoid barbarisms in diction. Barbarisms are current words coined without authority from words in good standing. Typical barbarisms are the following: *to enthuse* (see Appendix A), *to burglarize, to jell* for *to jelly, tasty* for *tasteful, homey* for *homelike, newsy, musicianly, complected* (see Appendix A), *preventative* for *preventive, illy* for *ill, overly* (see Appendix A), *irregardless* for *regardless, broadcasted* for *broadcast.* Other examples may be found in Appendix A.

Unauthorized formations

NOTE. — The standing of a word depends, not on the nature of its formation, but solely on its acceptance or non-acceptance by good usage (see Rule 1). *Baseballist* and *cheesery* are bad English, though they are formed after the analogy of *pianist* and *creamery,* which are good English.

Analogy not a safe guide

10. Avoid the language of advertising, which often commits gross errors in diction. Note the following objectionable expressions:

Advertising lingo

Personalize your shirt by having your initials embroidered upon it.
We especially *feature* clothes for large women.
This spring you *ensemble* your suit yourself, a coat of one color, a skirt of another.
If you want a job, he is the man *to contact.*
We begin our selling campaign by making people *shoe-conscious.*

Visit our new *sleepwear* department.
It is time *to clock* the kitchen.
Smith *sold himself* to his employer by his ready wit.
He always *puts* his *sales talk across.*

H. L. Mencken in *The American Language* (4th edition) notes some of the sonorous names the American business man has invented for his trades: *mortician* for *undertaker; realtor* for *real estate agent; electragist* for *electrical contractor; aisle manager* for *floorwalker; beautician* for *hairdresser.*

Slang

11. In formal writing and speaking use slang with great caution. Be certain that the idea could not be just as vigorously and exactly expressed by words in good standing. (Slang includes improprieties, barbarisms, and other vulgar and inelegant expressions. See Rules 8 and 9.)

NOTE. — Slang has these good points:

a. It may be vigorous and refreshing.

b. It may express an idea very briefly and succinctly.

c. It may more aptly fit special needs than any other word. Many such words have been adopted permanently into our language; for instance, *cad, mob, banter, sham, lynch,* etc. A. W. Read says regarding the adoption of slang: "Slang becomes something else when used by the best people. Slang is no longer slang, but a legitimate part of our language when it is used by such writers as Mark Twain. But some slang never ceases to be slang."

Note the effective use of slang in this sentence:

> This book is so beautiful, so intelligently constructed, so perfectly styled, so really acute at moments — and so *phoney.*

Slang is objectionable for these reasons: Slang

a. It may be out-of-tone in formal writing and speaking. For instance:

> We, the undersigned students, are not *crabbing* about the disciplinary measures drawn up by the Council; we are *crabbing* because we are not represented on that Council.

b. It may be unintelligible to many readers. For instance:

> He is a *lug.*

c. It often fails to express an exact idea. A slang phrase may become a rubber-stamp expression used in infinite repetition by people too lazy or too illiterate to state their thoughts with precision. For instance, *grand, keen, smooth* may be applied to almost anything to express approval. There is no particularization, no identification. These words when used to describe a girl give no definite idea of her appearance, her manners, or the traits of character that make her attractive.

d. It may soon go out of fashion. By overuse it will lose what vivid and original qualities it may have had when first used. For instance: *kick the bucket; nifty; peacharino; spifflicated; regular guy; rubberneck; buttinski; believe me, kiddo* are no longer fashionable slang words.

12. Use idiomatic expressions, for they show the writer's familiarity with the language and add vigor and individuality to his style. Idioms

An idiom is an expression peculiar to the language. For instance, in English one says, "How do you do?" or "How are you?" in German, literally translated into English, "How goes it?" or "How do you find yourself?"; in French, literally translated, "How do you carry yourself?" Idioms, which often violate the rules of grammar and logic, as, for example, the phrases *many a year* and *a few friends*, are, however, based upon well-established usage. (As a guide to good usage, one should consult the best unabridged dictionaries. See Rule 13.) Since idioms do not comply with the rules of logic and grammar, they may have to be learned individually.

Idiomatic use of prepositions

a. **Idiom requires that some words be followed by arbitrarily fixed prepositions.** Note the following correct use of prepositions:

agree *to* (a proposal); *with* (a person)
angry *at, about* (a thing); *with* (a person)
argue *with* (a person); *for* or *against* or *about*, not *on* (a measure)
correspond *to* or *with* (a thing); *with* (a person)
differ *from* expresses unlikeness; differ *with* expresses divergence of opinion

> This book differs from the other in giving more details.
> I differ with you about the importance of athletics.

different. The preposition sanctioned by American usage is *from*. The use of *than* and *to* can be supported by good British usage.
independent *of*, not *from*
interest *in*, not *for*
listen *to*, not *at*
possessed *by* or *with* (an idea); *by* (a spirit); *of* (goods)
with regard to, or *as regards*, not *with regards to*, or not *in regards to*
with respect to, not *in respect of*
stay *at* home, not stay *to* home
superior *to*, not *than*
try *to*, not try *and*
wait *on* (a customer); *for* (a person or thing); wait *at* (a place)

> I will wait for you as long as I can (not on you).

b. **Idiom demands that certain words be followed by infinitives, others by gerunds.** For instance:

Idiomatic use of infinitives and gerunds

Infinitive	*Gerund*
able to go	capable of going
like to go	enjoy going
eager to go	cannot help going
hesitate to go	privilege of going

c. **Idiom is violated when two or more sentence-elements are limited by a single modifying phrase or clause that is not idiomatically adapted to both.**

Modifiers in double capacity

Wrong: He had no love or confidence in his employer.

Right: He had no love for, or confidence in, his employer. [Correct, but awkward. Better: He had no love for his employer and no confidence in him.]

Wrong: I shall always remember the town because of the good times and the friends I made there.

Right: I shall always remember the town because of the good times I had and the friends I made there.

Wrong: He acquired a knowledge and keen interest in chess.

Right: He acquired a knowledge of chess and a keen interest in it.

d. **Avoid the following expressions used for idioms:**

Idiomatic expressions

Inferior	*Preferred*
cannot help but remember	cannot help remembering
have got to	have to *or* must
near enough that I could see it	near enough for me to see it
seldom or ever	seldom if ever
there is no doubt but {that / what}	there is no doubt that
very interested	very much [1] interested

[1] To express an absolutely high degree of a quality, we place *very* before the positive of the adjective: '*very sick, very pleasing, a very distressed* look.' But instead of saying 'I was *very much pleased, very greatly distressed*,' many incorrectly say 'I was *very pleased, very distressed*,' feeling *pleased* and *distressed* as adjective rather than as verbal forms, which they are. Similarly, we should use *too much, too greatly* before verbal forms, not simple *too:* 'I was *too much* (or *too greatly*) discouraged by this failure to try again.' — G. O. Curme, *Syntax*.

Exercise

Idioms

What violations of English idiom do you find in the following sentences?

1. You needn't to go to all that trouble.
2. Military training has been made compulsory to all able-bodied men between the ages of eighteen and forty.
3. He gave us an inspiring talk in regards to what was expected of us.
4. The author states of how beautiful the countryside is.
5. He has been to work at the barn all morning.
6. She took the occasion to complain about the tough meat.
7. He did not make the mistake of aspiring at a lofty style.
8. I was very disgusted with his speech.
9. I read the newspapers as a sort of a duty and not for pleasure of reading.
10. They are in great need for help.

LEARNING GOOD USAGE

Means of learning good usage

13. In order to learn what is good English, the student should cultivate the habit of prompt reference to books on grammar, rhetoric, and composition, and to good dictionaries. The best dictionaries are the unabridged editions of *Webster's New International Dictionary*, (second edition) the *Standard Dictionary*, and Murray's *New English Dictionary*. Recent editions should be consulted. Note, for instance, these differences between the 1930 and the 1935 editions of *Webster's New International Dictionary*. In the 1930 edition *to film* with the meaning *to photograph for the moving pictures* is not given; it is given with that meaning in the 1935 edition as an expression in good usage. *To taxi* is not given in the earlier edition; it is in the later as an expression in good usage. *To broadcast* in the earlier edition has only the meaning of *disseminating widely;* in the later edition it can also mean *to* *broadcast a program over the radio.* In the earlier edition *cad* is labeled as a colloquial word; in the later edition there is no label; hence it is a word in good usage.

14. Students should by careful use learn how much information about a word is given in an unabridged dictionary. For example, the student can learn the syllabication of a word (the division of the word into syllables, information that he needs when he wishes to divide a word at the end of a line); he can find out whether an expression containing two originally separate words is to be written as one word, as a compound word with a hyphen, or as two separate words; he will find the pronunciation; the part of speech to which the word belongs; the plural of nouns; the various verb forms, such as the present infinitive, preterit, past participle, and the present participle; the etymology or derivation of the word; the definition; the usage; synonyms; and illustrative sentences showing how words are actually used.

Information in unabridged dictionaries

There are also many short dictionaries, such as *Webster's Collegiate Dictionary*, the *Desk Standard Dictionary*, the *Student's Standard Dictionary*, which omit much material given in the unabridged dictionaries. These short dictionaries are far inferior, for the purposes of a student of English, to an unabridged dictionary.

Abridged dictionaries inferior to unabridged

Exercise

Consider the italicized words in the following sentences. Some of these words themselves, or the special sense in which they are used, or their grammatical construction in the sentence might be questioned. Would you sanction their use in good writing or in good speech?

Good usage

1. *Doc,* I cannot get *shut* (or *shet*) of my cold.
2. Will you give me a small paper *sack?*
3. *Come by* for me at eight o'clock.

Good usage

4. We did not *get to* go on a vacation this summer.
5. *Tell him* good-by for me.
6. She *went to* go downstairs and caught her heel.
7. I *went to* open my suitcase and found that the lock had been forced.
8. Do *come back* sometime.
9. We *like to* died laughing at his stories.
10. I *am about to* freeze in this cold room.
11. I *don't hold by* any of those old superstitions.
12. Will you *be by* for me in time for the game?
13. There is *church* tonight.
14. I feel *like* I swallowed a lot of bubbles full of happiness. They make me feel *like* I was laughing all the time.
15. It seems *like* I never get my work done.
16. Let's play *like* we are on a boat.
17. It looks *like* Oscar ought to win.
18. You work just *like* your brother.
19. You are treating me *like* a fool.
20. She is *all of* six feet high.
21. We had *all sorts* of fun.
22. They took *all of* our share too.
23. I ache *all over*.
24. He is an *all-around fellow*.
25. You can go *for all of me*.
26. If you insulate your house properly, you won't be heating *all outdoors*.
27. He is *so all-fired* honest.
28. They went *right along* talking during the concert.
29. He got *along* by himself.
30. I was not *along* when it happened.
31. It happened *along back* about 1920.
32. Traveling *around* the way I do, I meet many strange people.
33. Come *around* sometime.
34. We *haven't* enough to go *around*.
35. She is just able *to be around*.
36. He is always hanging *around* the pool hall.
37. I'll be there *around* three o'clock.
38. She gave us *a lot of flapdoodle* about how we should treat the boys.
39. Some poor *sucker* is always *falling for her line*.
40. Are you going to wear your *tux* tonight?
41. She is buying new *drapes* for her room.

42. He *got so balled up* on the *exam* that he couldn't answer a question.
43. His *gum shoe* tactics are often successful.
44. You cannot *hog* all the credit.
45. She is the *spit and image* of her father.
46. An *unwealthy* boy cannot be happy in those surroundings.
47. Isn't it cold *though?*
48. Have a *try* at it.
49. Will you *chauffeur* us to the play tonight?
50. The boys are going *to bach it* this summer.
51. I have *vacuumed* the rugs.

CLEARNESS

15. Use words that will make the meaning immediately clear. A writer must choose his words with precision. The speaker, in conversation or even on the platform, if he sees that his meaning is not clear, can try again to make his listeners understand. The writer, however, with only one opportunity to make himself understood, must choose his words with the greatest care.

Precise word

16. Distinguish between words of similar meaning. Find the word that will precisely express the thought. Note the distinction in meaning between these words: *rebellion, revolution, revolt, insurrection, mutiny.*

Words of similar meaning

"*Rebellion* is open, organized, and armed resistance to constituted authority; *Revolution,* as here compared, implies the overthrow of one government and the substitution of another; as, Jack Straw's *Rebellion,* the Great *Rebellion* (1642–1652); the *Revolution* of 1688; the American *Revolution;* the French *Revolution.* But the two words are often used of the same event, according to the point of view of the user. *Revolt* and *Insurrection* denote an armed uprising against authority which does not attain the extent of a *rebellion; Mutiny* commonly denotes an insurrection against military or naval authority . . ." — *Webster's.*

Mala-
propisms

17. Do not confuse words similar in spelling but different in meaning. For example, distinguish between *allusion* and *illusion, conscience* and *conscious, deceased* and *diseased, formerly* and *formally, respectfully* and *respectively, flaunted* and *flouted.* (For the definitions of these and other words often confused, see the list of words commonly misspelled under Rule 338 and in Appendix A.)

Exercise A

Precise
word

Note the italicized words in the following sentences. The writer has not said exactly what he meant to say. Substitute the precise word.

1. The principal of our high school always *identified* himself with the football team.
2. You certainly *inferred* that I was not telling the truth.
3. I am *prepared* to help you if you will do your part.
4. Her whole interest in life centers *around* her son.
5. He had always impressed me as cold and *foreboding.*
6. The *personalities* from left to right are: Julian Lewis, defendant; Harry Cramer, cab driver; and John Waldman, defendant.
7. Her parents have sacrificed everything for her; her friends are always coming to her rescue; but she is *oblivious* of all this.
8. She always makes her health her *alibi* for her failures.
9. I *understand* that you are going to Europe this summer.
10. These children will have *hygienic* surroundings.

Clear the ambiguity in these sentences:

1. Roof with beauty for the last time. (Advertisement of roofing material.)
2. In his new book the eminent zoölogist discusses the question: "Which is more superior in point of sex, man or woman?"

Exercise B

Words of
similar
meaning

Consult an unabridged dictionary for the distinctions in meaning between the members of each of the following groups of words:

Duty, obligation; displease, offend, vex; great, grand, sublime; govern, rule, regulate; government, constitution; liberty, freedom, license; faith, creed; deceit, deception; both, pair, twain, two; beautiful, fine, handsome, pretty.

18. Avoid jargon, which is defined by Quiller-Couch as "vague omnibus words, round-about official circumlocutions." **Jargon**

a. **Avoid vague, ambiguous, blanket words, words that cannot be precisely defined.** Writers who do not know what they wish to say, or who are too lazy to search for the exact word use such words as the following: *factor, case, asset, basis, proposition, slant, instance, thing, condition, nature, line, character, element, field, situation, world* as in *business world, professional world, religious world,* etc. Lord Tweedsmuir, speaking of jargon, says: "Take that awful word 'reaction,' which is particularly rampant among our friends in the United States. I do not know how many letters I have received from Americans asking what my 'reaction' was to something or other. I supposed the writers meant what I thought about it. Why could they not say that?" Note the following sentence quoted by the *Times* (London) as an illustration of jargon:

> The unity of view of the participants in the conversations has been established regarding the exceptional importance at the present time of an all-embracing collective organization of security on the basis of indivisibility of peace.

Exercise

Try to improve the following sentences by making substitutions for the jargon:

1. The *outstanding thing* in her life is her devotion to her invalid sister.
2. *In the last analysis* we find that the economic motive *plays an important part* in men's actions.

Jargon

3. In time we hope *to do away with* all the slums in the city.
4. Her inspiring talks always give us a *new slant* (or a *new angle*) on life.
5. His love of sports *predominated* in his college years.
6. From 1912 to 1920 the Democratic Party had a *monopoly on legality*.
7. Your letter is *at hand* and we *beg to state* that your order was filled on October 16.
8. My first job was *along educational lines.*
9. There in that dusty, bad-smelling factory the wonders of the modern *industrial world were unfolded* before me.
10. One of the fascinating *factors* of football is *bodily contact*. Most boys seem to get more delight out of this kind of exercise than from other types despite the fact that the bodily injury *element* is *ever in evidence.*
11. Many men who are respected by a few are not receiving their just share of respect. The cause for this *seemingly backward apportionment* of respect lies in the fact that true respect is rare.
12. One of the most important *elements* that most people object to in the Ford car is the *idea* of a V-motor.
13. The so-called smooth person could be divided into two *types.*
14. The valley is *composed* mostly *of* natives who are ignorant and quarrelsome.
15. My inability to learn mathematics soon *brought itself to the surface.*
16. I should not like to *come into contact with* his displeasure.

Technical words

b. **Avoid technical words in non-technical writing.** If it is necessary to use technical expressions because no others are available, their meaning should be made clear to the non-technical reader. For the reader not familiar with sport, these athletic terms might need explanation: *fly, spiral, grounder, line drive, battery.* Note the obscurity of the following sentences:

The book gives an elaborate account of the construction and validation of the English placement tests for college freshmen, with a study of the predicative significance of this examination, and also discusses the adequacy of bases for the homogeneous grouping in freshman English.

It would seem also that the point of view of objective dematerialization ("abstractionism") generally tends to develop into subjective dematerialization (mysticism, solipsism, introversion) just as, in the case of individualism, we noted that "naturalistic individualism" developed into "subjective individualism," and for similar reasons. — Quoted in the *Manchester Guardian* as illustrating the use of technical jargon.

19. Avoid foreign words and phrases. A writer who uses foreign expressions freely may not be understood and may give the impression of attempting to display his knowledge. A foreign phrase is occasionally permissible when there is no English equivalent to convey the exact meaning. English equivalents are to be preferred to: *entre nous, faux pas, nouveau riche, terra firma, sub rosa.*

Foreign words and phrases

EFFECTIVENESS

20. Use specific and concrete words, as a rule, rather than general and abstract words. General and abstract words express indefinite, inclusive ideas; specific and concrete words express definite and limited ideas, often appealing directly to the senses. For example, *animal* is a general word and *cat* or *dog* is specific; *beauty* is an abstract idea and *an apple tree in full bloom* may be a concrete expression of the idea of beauty. (Specific and concrete words may in turn become general and abstract when compared with words of more limited application.) General and abstract words may be used to advantage when the writer or speaker wishes to summarize, or when he wishes to state his ideas very briefly without particular emphasis. The difficulty is, however, that general and abstract words are overused because the writer's thoughts are often too vague and hazy for specific or concrete words, or because the

General, specific, abstract, concrete words

writer is too timid or too lazy to state exactly what he has in mind. Specific and concrete words are often effective in stirring the reader to form a definite and vivid picture. Note in the following passage how the concrete details serve to impress upon the reader's mind the opening abstract statement:

Sovereigns die and Sovereignties: how all dies, and is for a time only; is a "Time-phantasm, yet reckons itself real!" The Merovingian Kings, slowly wending on their bullock-carts through the streets of Paris, with their long hair flowing, have all wended slowly on, — into Eternity. Charlemagne sleeps at Salsburg, with truncheon grounded; only Fable expecting that he will awaken. Charles the Hammer, Pepin Bow-legged, where now is their eye of menace, their voice of command? Rollo and his shaggy Northmen cover not the Seine with ships; but have sailed off on a longer voyage. The hair of Towhead . . . now needs no combing; Iron-cutter . . . cannot cut a cobweb; shrill Fredegonda, shrill Brunhilda have had out their life-scold, and lie silent, their hot life frenzy cooled. . . . They are all gone; sunk, — down, down, with the tumult they made; and the rolling and the trampling of ever new generations passes over them; and they hear it not any more forever. — CARLYLE.

Concreteness may be overdone; it may become tiresome and may give the impression that the writer is striving to produce an effect. He may be so fulsomely concrete with details that he will obstruct the main point or impression that he wishes to make.

EXERCISE

Specific and concrete words

Give several specific or concrete words for each general or abstract word. For instance: *cloth: velvet, satin, mohair, taffeta, organdy*, etc.

Verbs: *to look, to walk, to talk, to say, to laugh*
Nouns: *girl, fruit, vehicle, show, bird, goodness, gentility*
Adjectives: *pleasant, bright, dark, cold, young*

Denotation and connotation

21. Consider the associated meanings of words. Besides their literal meaning or denotation, words have connotation or additional meanings, associations, overtones. *House* denotes a structure used for human habitation. *Home* denotes a house, a dwelling place, but in addition it has rich emotional associations. It suggests family life, affections, warmth, protection, safety, and also a place that one owns and belongs to, as one's native land. None of these overtones surrounds the words *house, domicile, dwelling place.* Use words that will contribute to the effect that you wish to produce.

Also many words may by their connotation be definitely fitted for certain surroundings. Words may be vulgar, poetic, pompous, homely, humorous, etc. (See Rules 1–12.) *Kid* and *young child,* in popular usage, have the same denotation: but *kid* is a vulgarism and is out of place in formal writing. *Telephonic communication* is pompous; *telephone call* is preferable. *Job* is suitable when used to denote manual work; *position* is used for work of other kinds. If one is doubtful regarding the connotation of a word, he can find information in the distinctions between synonyms and the illustrative sentences given in an unabridged dictionary. The various books of synonyms may be of assistance. (See p. 4.)

Exercise A

Denotation and connotation

Discuss the denotation and the connotation of the following words: *cross* (noun), *king, mother, forest, storm, liberty, night*

What difference in connotation is there to you between the words in each group: *violin, fiddle; sailor, mariner; soldier, warrior; horse, steed; epistle, letter; load, burden; garret, attic; infant, baby; donate, give; commence, begin; proceed, go*

Exercise B

Denotation and connotation

For commonplace words such as *boy, man, woman, food, money, house, dog, horse* try to find substitutes that would fit under the following headings. (Consult dictionaries of synonyms, especially Roget's *Thesaurus*.) For example:

Commonplace	*Vulgar, derogatory*	*Colloquial, slang, etc.*	*Elevated, poetic*
girl	slut	skirt	maiden
	hussy	jane	damsel
		flapper	damoiselle

Forceful predicate verbs

22. Use forceful predicate verbs. *Appear, be, seem* are weak, lifeless verbs. Prefer the active voice to the passive voice.

Weak: A mountain was seen looming up in the distance.
Stronger: A mountain loomed up in the distance.

Weak: There is a horse eating grass in our yard.
Stronger: A horse is eating grass in our yard.

NOTE. — The use of forceful verbs may be overdone:

Her angry words pounced out upon him.
He heaved, "Great day, this."
In her haste her hands raced about among the papers.

Onomatopoeic words should be used with caution. Too frequent use of such words as *buzz, chug, hiss, purr, sizzle, whir, whine,* etc., makes one question the writer's sincerity and resourcefulness.

EXERCISE

Substitute forceful verbs in place of the weak verbs:

1. He appeared to flinch slightly as the rapidly revolving circular saw bit into the log with a loud screech.
2. A wild turkey was almost caught by the little boy with his bare hands.
3. Occasionally there were deer that could be seen drinking at the lake.
4. Foxes and other animals were hunted by the Neelys, but the wily raccoon seemed most to allure both men and dogs.
5. It was found by him that channel catfish bite best in swift, shallow water in the early part of the night.
6. Great clouds of smoke piling above the tree tops were seen by them.

ECONOMY OF WORDS

23. Do not be wordy. Wordiness

Wordy: Yesterday I had occasion to be the witness of a very interesting incident.

Improved: Yesterday I saw an interesting incident.

Wordy: At midnight the physician made a statement, saying that the governor was better.

Improved: At midnight the physician stated that the governor was better.

Wordy: I call your attention to the fact that you have overdrawn your account.

Improved: I remind you that you have overdrawn your account.

24. Avoid clumsy circumlocutions such as *there is,* etc., *along the lines of, of the nature of, of the character of, the reason why . . . is because,* etc. Clumsy circumlocutions

Wordy: There were two hundred students who went.

Improved: Two hundred students went.

Wordy: The reason why I went is because I wished to see her.

Improved: I went because I wished to see her.

25. Do not repeat the same idea in different words unless repetition is necessary for clearness or for emphasis. Redundancy

Redundant: If I had abundant wealth and plenty of resources, I should travel the rest of my life.

Improved: If I had abundant wealth, I should travel the rest of my life.

Redundant: The cottage was cozy, snug, and comfortable.

Improved: The cottage was cozy.

Redundant: They both dress alike.

Improved: They dress alike.

Redundant: Will you please repeat that again?

Improved: Will you please repeat that?

Redundant: The autobiography of my life.

Improved: My autobiography.

Redundant phrases: In any shape or form, of any sort or kind, in this day and age, in this country of ours.

Consider also: united in marriage, new recruit, widow of the late James Brown, Easter Sunday, incarcerated in jail, present incumbent, scalded by hot water.

Redundant *up, out, of,* etc.

26. Omit unnecessary *up*, *out*, *of*, etc. as in *settle up; end up; lift up; rise up; rest up; pay out; lose out; fall down; fall off of; remember of; meet up with; to be at*, as in *where are you at?*

Unnecessary independent predication

27. Avoid unnecessary independent predication. Do not use a compound sentence if a simple sentence with a compound predicate will serve. Avoid a series of primer sentences; unite them, putting subordinate thought into subordinate form. (See Rule 53.)

Wordy compound sentence: We canoed down the river and we returned by train.

Improved: We canoed down the river and returned by train.

Primer style: As you approach the island from the west, you get a view of a high cliff. This cliff is about six miles in length. It is of sandstone, and rises almost perpendicularly from the water. Numerous cracks and crevices can be seen in the cliff. . . . 45 words.

Predication reduced: Approaching the island from the west, you get a view of a high, sandstone cliff about six miles in length, rising almost perpendicularly from the water, its face seamed with cracks and crevices. . . . 33 words.

Subordinate clause to phrase or word

28. Reduce subordinate clauses containing unimportant material to phrases or to single words. (See Rule 137.)

Wordy: In the house in which we used to live when we were in Winstead was a large playroom, which was located just at the head of the stairs.

Clauses reduced to phrases: Just at the head of the stairs in our house in Winstead was a large playroom.

Wordy: My grandfather, who was a shipbuilder and who lived in Salem, made frequent trips to China.

Clauses reduced to appositive and to participial phrase: My grandfather, a shipbuilder living in Salem, made frequent trips to China.

Exercise

Revise the following wordy sentences:

Economy of words

1. She went to work and upset all my plans.
2. I should like to check up on my grades.
3. Let's us go right away.
4. I should like to try it out first.
5. I always have to rest up after my vacation.
6. I sat in back of him at the concert.
7. All of my relatives will be there.
8. They beat him up after the game.
9. When one enters the university, he has the problem to solve concerning his roommate. In behalf of the solution to this problem concerning my own roommate, I rented a room that was to be shared with me by a boy from Illinois. Naturally I wondered at various times if our ideals, likes, dislikes would be similar. In short, would we have habits and actions that would be satisfactory to each other?
10. Football was his favorite sport. When he came to high school, he went out for the team. Not long afterward he made the first squad. He was much larger than the average boy of his age. Later on he became one of the most popular of the boys in school. This did not turn his head. He said that he was just as human as the rest of us.
11. All of his fraternal brothers promised to vote as he had asked them to.
12. I kept the chickens until they matured in size.
13. It was one of those warm sultry days after a rainstorm. The particular day of which I am speaking was Saturday. I had postponed some necessary shopping until the last minute. I was lucky enough to get a ride down town.
14. When you have heard the true facts, you will understand.
15. We must repeat that exercise over again.

16. Refer back to page ten.
17. The horse ran for the stable because he feared that some other horse would eat his feed, or probably thought that his stall partner would eat more than his share of hay. Whatever it was that made him hurry back to the stable, I do not know, but whatever it was, it must have been very important; at least he acted as though it were.

SINCERITY AND NATURALNESS

OVEREMPHASIS

Over-emphasis

29. Avoid overemphasis. Use intensives and superlatives sparingly; they tend to weaken rather than to strengthen a statement. A writer who because of indolence or a limited vocabulary resorts to such words to attract attention might better use effective nouns and verbs that do not need to be bolstered with intensifying adjectives and adverbs. Note the following overworked intensives: *so*, *very*, *literally*, *terribly*, *horribly*, *frightfully*, *perfectly*, *exceedingly*, *awfully*, *never*, *always*.

TRITENESS

Overworked formulas

30. Avoid trite rhetorical expressions. They compel the reader to doubt the writer's sincerity, his interest in his subject, or his capacity for original thought or expression. Of the following list of phrases, many were originally inappropriate and others have lost their force through frequent repetition:

all too soon
sigh of relief
beat a hasty retreat
the commercial world, the social world, etc.
favor with a selection
render a vocal solo
rendition
discourse sweet music
untiring efforts
all in all
it goes without saying
bolt from a clear sky *or* bolt from the blue
someone has said
specimen of humanity
had the privilege *or* had the opportunity

Overworked formulas

hungry as bears
repast
do justice to a dinner
toothsome viands
sought his downy couch
vast concourse
never in the history of
news leaked out
dull, sickening thud
those present
in evidence *or* much in evidence
abreast of the times
was the recipient of
everything went along nicely
the student body
doomed to disappointment
was an impressive sight
made a pretty picture
completed the scene
nestled among the hills *or* among the trees
like sentinels guarding
sumptuous repast
all nature seemed
all nature clothed in a robe
each and every
on this particular day
long-felt want
it seems (in narrative)
working like Trojans
herculean efforts
wended their way
enjoyable occasion
in a pleasing manner
replete with interest
undercurrent of excitement
last sad rites
tonsorial parlor
checkered career
last but not least
tired but happy
cheered to the echo
breathless silence
speculation was rife
tiny tots
along . . . lines (*e.g.*, along agricultural lines)
along the line of *or* along these lines
as luck would have it
the proud possessor
in touch with
social function
in the last analysis
waited in breathless suspense
order out of chaos
those with whom we come in contact
imbued with
mother earth
breakneck speed
passed away
made his escape
eye witness
consumed by the flames
in a dazed condition
tendered his resignation
brought death to
in a dying condition

Hackneyed quotations, allusions, and proverbs

31. Avoid hackneyed quotations, literary allusions, and proverbs, such as the following:

The light fantastic toe
Truth is stranger than fiction
Teach the young idea how to shoot
Method in his madness
Sadder but wiser

Cupid has been busy
Variety is the spice of life
The best laid plans of mice and men, etc.
All work and no play, etc.
Never put off till tomorrow, etc.
Make hay while the sun shines
All is not gold that glitters
When ignorance is bliss, etc.
Music hath charms, etc.

Newspaper mannerisms

32. Certain hackneyed newspaper mannerisms are especially to be avoided. These have arisen through the effort of writers to adorn their style where no ornament was needed, or to introduce a forced humor, or to avoid repetition of the same word. Repetition of the same word is to be preferred to the invention of artificial epithets. (See Rule 46.) Very undesirable:

Nicknames of states and cities

a. **The designation of states and cities by their nicknames,** as, *the Buckeye State, the Sunflower State, the Gopher State, the Cream City,* etc.; and the dragging in of these nicknames where no name at all is needed.

Bad: He arrived in Boston yesterday. Many citizens of the Hub were gathered to meet him.
Improved: He arrived in Boston yesterday. Many citizens were gathered to meet him.

Current newspaper rhetoric

b. **The regular employment of verbal ornaments,** such as *fatal affray, fistic encounter, struggling mass of humanity, scantily attired, knights of the pen* (for *reporters*), *the officiating clergyman, equines* (for *horses*), *canines* (for *dogs*), *felines* (for *cats*), *fair sex, well-known clubman, breakneck speed, city bastile, milady.*

Straining for novelty of phrase

c. **Obtrusive straining for novelty of phrase.**

Bad: The football Warriors of the Badger State will play the Windy City's squad of pigskin chasers this afternoon.
Improved: The Wisconsin football team will play the Chicago team this afternoon.

Bad: The guests spent the evening in doing the "light fantastic" act.

Improved: The guests spent the evening in dancing.

Bad: Indefatigable knights of the pen dogged his steps as far as the hostelry.

Improved: Reporters followed him to his hotel.

AFFECTATION

33. Do not use high-flown language for plain things. Straining for high-sounding expressions to replace plain English makes a style weak rather than strong. For instance, say *leg*, not *limb; letter*, not *kind favor; house*, not *residence; body*, not *remains; flowers*, not *floral offerings; funeral*, not *obsequies* or *last sad rites; I went to bed*, not *I retired; I got up*, not *I arose.* Such attempts at "fine writing" are in bad taste.

High-flown language

Bad: To keep the horse healthy you must be careful of his environment.

Improved: To keep the horse healthy you must be careful of his stable.

The inexperienced writer often loses force and vigor by failing to use idiomatic phrases, which, he fears, will detract from the correctness and dignity of his style. (See Rule 12.)

Stiff: His criticism is something to which I cannot become accustomed.

Improved: His criticism is something I cannot get used to.

Stiff: If you want them to obey, you must speak more loudly.

Improved: If you want them to obey, you must speak louder.

34. In prose avoid the use of words suited only to poetry. Examples are *dwelt, oft, oftentimes, ofttimes, morn, amid, 'mid, 'midst, o'er, 'neath, 'tis, 'twas. Heretofore, therein, thereof, thereby* are awkward substitutes in good natural writing for *before this event, in it,* and *of it.*

Poetic and legal diction

The historical present

35. In narrative relating past events, prefer the past tense to the so-called "historical present." The latter is a device intended to produce the effect of strong emotion, but is more likely to seem affected than to create the impression desired. (For awkward shifting of tenses in narrative, see Rule 177.)

Affected: He shouted to attract her attention, but she went on toward the danger, not heeding his warning. Lashing his horse and riding swiftly toward her, he shouted again. This time she hears. She stands still and awaits him. He lifts her to his saddle and rides frantically toward the hut. [Throughout this passage the past tense should be used.]

Initials and blanks in place of names

36. Designate persons, places, and dates in a story by complete names and dates. The custom of using initials and dashes, and of representing dates in a similar manner, is obsolete; it suggests affectation.

Objectionable: In the year 18—, when my father was a young man in the little town of B——, he formed a strong friendship with a wealthy farmer, Mr. M——.

Preferable: In the year 1892, when my father was a young man in the little town of Bristol, he formed a strong friendship with a wealthy farmer, Mr. McManus.

Names for characters in a story

NOTE. — In narrative composition, definiteness, clearness, and smoothness are gained by calling the characters by name as soon as they are introduced.

Awkward: One afternoon this winter two friends of mine called at my home and suggested that we go ice-boating. Now one of these men had never ridden in an iceboat. The other man was warmly dressed for the occasion, but the man who had never had the experience, as it afterwards turned out, was dressed rather less warmly than usual. When we reached the lake, the first friend and I were busy getting up the sail, and did not notice that the teeth of the other man had begun to chatter as soon as the chilly breeze struck him. It happened, moreover, that this man who was dressed so lightly was selected to sit on the end of the runner-plank, while my first friend and I managed the tiller and the sheet.

Improved: One afternoon this winter two friends of mine called at my home and suggested that we go ice-boating. Now one of these men, Tom Lamont, had never ridden in an ice-boat. The other man, Bert Pryor, was warmly dressed for the occasion, but Tom, as it afterwards turned out, was dressed rather less warmly than usual. When we reached the lake, Bert and I were busy getting up the sail, and did not notice that Tom's teeth had begun to chatter as soon as the chilly breeze struck him. It happened, moreover, that Tom, in spite of his thin clothing, was selected to sit on the runner-plank, while Bert and I managed the tiller and the sheet.

The writer and we for I

37. In mentioning yourself, avoid the expressions *we* and *the writer*. Use *I*, *my*, and *me*, and guard against unnecessary reference to yourself. The use of *we* in an editorial which purports to be the utterance of a board of editors is entirely proper, but as designating an individual speaker or writer it is an affectation.

Bad: We have selected for our text the second verse of the Epistle of Jude.

Right: I have selected for my text, etc.

Exercise

Sincerity and naturalness

How would you improve the following sentences?

1. With your coöperation we expect to make progress by leaps and bounds.
2. She has pinched every penny to make ends meet.
3. In this great country of ours there is a chance for everybody.
4. We expect to put over our drive in a big way.
5. In this day and age women have an opportunity for a full life.
6. We are literally soaked to the skin.
7. She is perfectly wild about tennis.
8. My erstwhile chum has left his native heath and gone to the great metropolis to live.

9. Despite the whimsical appellation of "Baby Face," John is a fine, manly youth.
10. Courthouse Knob rises from the prairie, a spectacular pinnacle, devoid of all vegetation. There it stands, towering above all else, a worthy goal for any ambitious climber to attempt to scale.

What comments would you make regarding the following sentences from a student's letter to a teacher, requesting the use of the teacher's name as a reference? Suggest revisions.

> There is a time in the life of everyone when his circumstances are such that in order to reach the height to which his ambition urges, he needs a little pull by those who are in power and by those who have a fair knowledge of his ability. As regards the teaching vocation, I feel that no one is in a better position to know the intellectual ability and the general character of a person than his teachers . . . Be advised that the favor will be highly appreciated by me and that I shall, when placed in a responsible position, be mindful of my conduct. It pleases me to have the honor to remain, Most sincerely yours, . . .

FIGURES OF SPEECH

Figures of speech

38. A figure of speech is a comparison between things of different classes, essentially unlike except in some striking particular or particulars, as, for example: *His mind works like a machine.* Figures of speech, if used with care, may give clearness, vigor, aptness, and beauty to one's style. These cautions should, however, be observed:

Originality

a. **Figures of speech must be fresh and original.** Do not use trite phrases. (See Rule 30.)

Spontaneity

b. **Figures of speech should seem spontaneous.** Those comparisons that flash upon the mind in moments of emotion will more surely carry with them elements of truth than figures that are artificially and laboriously constructed.

c. **Comparisons suggested by figures should be in good taste.** (See Rule 33.) Do not compare commonplace things with lofty things. Use figures sparingly in the discourse of ordinary life.

Good taste

Bad: This soap will be a blessing to you in the darkest hours of Monday morning.

Bad: The empty stalls of the barn were like a desolate garden in late November.

d. **Figures of speech should be essentially true;** there should be a possible basis for comparison. Observe the straining for an effect in these figures. (See Rule 32 *c.*)

Truth

Bad: The whitewashed fence around the old schoolhouse was like the collar of a pilgrim father.

Bad: His feet flapped across the floor like angry pancakes.

Bad: The little lake, like a tired child, snuggled down among its hills and went to sleep.

e. **Figures of speech should not be used too frequently.** They may become confusing or tiresome.

Overuse of figures

Bad: We sat around the fire which leaped like a thousand sprites. The cool air was as intoxicating as a draught of old champagne, and the occasional breeze was a soft caress. Now and then across the lake, which was as level as a mirror, came the call of the whippoorwill, as lonesome as that of a lost soul.

f. **A prolonged figure of speech worked out in detail may divert the reader's attention from the subject matter which the figure aims to ornament or make clear.**

Detailed figures of speech

Too detailed: The body politic is like the human body. Both begin as germs, and develop into complex structures. The sovereign power of the state is the head of the individual; the laws and customs are the brain; the judges and magistrates are the will and the sense; commerce, agriculture, and industry are the mouth and stomach which prepare and digest the food; the public finances are the blood which by the heart is distributed throughout the organism.

Incongruity with what precedes

39. Do not use a figure of speech which is incongruous with the expression preceding.

Incongruous metaphor: The officers must enforce discipline among the raw material.

Right: The officers must enforce discipline among the new men.

Incongruous metaphor: We got some oil for the wheel at a farmhouse, and thus our hotbox was nipped in the bud.

Right: At a farmhouse we got some oil for the wheel and thus prevented a hotbox.

Incongruous metaphor: He must conduct his business on an honest foundation.

Right: He must conduct his business in an honest manner; [or] He must build his business on an honest foundation.

Bad: The probe of the Fond du Lac grand jury has netted five corrupt officials.

Right: The probe of the Fond du Lac grand jury has revealed five corrupt officials; [or] The dragnet of the Fond du Lac grand jury has caught five corrupt officials.

Bad: With his fortune blown to the four winds, all his ambition was crushed.

Right: All his ambition was, like his fortune, blown to the four winds; [or] In the ruin of his fortune his ambition was crushed.

Figures not carried out

40. When a figure of speech has been used, the expression following it should carry out the figure — should not (1) embody an incongruous figure or (2) be incongruously literal.

Bad: The freshman algebra course is a rocky and difficult road to travel. But whether we like it or not we are required to wade through it. [The figure embodied in *rocky road* is not carried out by the figure embodied in *wade through*.]

Right: The freshman course in algebra is a rocky and difficult road to travel. But whether we like it or not, we are required to travel it.

Inferior: It made a deep impression on my mind which I shall never forget. [The figure embodied in *impression* is not carried out by the literal expression *forget.*]

Right: It made a deep impression on my mind, which will never be effaced.

Exercise

Figures of speech

What comments would you make upon the following figures of speech? What changes would you suggest?

1. A welter of guesses swelled along the diplomatic fronts when it was reported that the Archduke Otto was near the Austrian border.
2. He is as vile an insect as ever crawled across the page of time.
3. The book is written from a slant upon which truth can never walk.
4. The Gadsden Purchase was but a drop of land in the ocean of the vast continent.
5. The publishers used the rotary printing press as a weapon to cut each other's throats.
6. The Roman toga was seen upon the barbarian's back, and the Roman tongue, though mutilated and mangled, was found within his mouth.
7. A flood of cheap books poured forth until the field was overcrowded.
8. He remained as mum and inactive as a Boston oyster stranded on the beach in the month of August.
9. These bluffs are comparable to an exquisitely carved, antique jewel set amid the shallow glitter of the paste diamonds of civilization.
10. The autumn winds have blown against the tree of time, and the tree of time has lost all of its leaves — all except one which still clings, even today, on the uppermost branch, flinging its challenge to all the world. That is what my mountain means to me.
11. He displays a kindly heart of gold hidden beneath an exterior of rough granite.
12. Her Dresden china beauty has withstood the acid test of time.

GRACE OF STYLE

Euphony

41. Choose your words with regard to the pleasantness of their sound. Avoid verse formations in prose, awkward repetitions of words, and clumsy constructions. Read your sentences aloud in order to detect these faults.

Rhyme, rhythm, alliteration, etc.

42. In prose avoid rhyme, a regular rhythm, alliteration, over-repetition of the same consonant or vowel sounds.

Objectionable rhyme: Then came the time for heart-breaking leave-taking.

Objectionable repetition and rhyme: The fountains were kept playing night and day to keep up the display.

Objectionable rhythm: He bowed his head in grief before the picture of his child.

Objectionable alliteration: He braced himself against the bitter blasts blowing with cutting force.

Objectionable alliteration: The ship flew fearlessly forward into the fury of the storm.

Objectionable repetition of vowel sounds: The old home was sold over and over before the former owner could buy it back.

NOTE. — This rule is not intended to discourage the sparing use of the patterns of poetry in prose as a means of increasing the force of passages designed to produce an emotional appeal. Note, for instance, these effective words from Carlyle: "Slowheaving Polar ocean over which the great Sun hangs low and lazy."

Cacophony

43. Avoid cacophony, or harsh combinations of sound which are difficult of pronunciation. Note that cacophony occurs where the end of one word and the beginning of the next have the same sound.

Bad: He grasped the inexplicable situation with his usual analytical skill.

Repetition of words

44. Avoid awkward and needless repetition of a word or phrase. This fault, which gives the impression of carelessness or paucity of vocabulary, may be corrected by a judicious use of pronouns or synonyms, by omitting words, or by recasting the sentence. (For repetition of ideas, see Rule 25.)

Bad: He said that the orders said that uniforms must be worn.

Improved: He said that the orders required the wearing of uniforms.

Bad: After the work on the tappets has been done, the mechanic again goes under the car. This time the mechanic goes under the car to take apart the bearings so that he can lift out the piston.

Improved: After the work on the tappets is done, the mechanic again goes under the car, this time to take apart etc.

45. Intentional repetition may be used to gain clearness and force. (See Rule 138.)

Repetition for emphasis: Harriet came to spend the last week in May with us. And strange to say, George also arrived for a visit that last week in May.

46. Prefer repetition to labored and awkward avoidance of it. **Awkward avoidance of repetition**

Awkward: If it has this effect on a healthy skin, it will have a worse result on an inflamed cuticle.

Preferable: If it has this effect on a healthy skin, it will have a worse effect on an inflamed skin.

Straining for synonyms

Note. — A constant straining for conspicuous synonyms to replace words previously used is a characteristic mannerism of newspaper writers. (See Rules 2 and 32.) Avoid this practice; repeat the noun, or else choose an inconspicuous synonym.

Bad: At the faculty meeting yesterday the question of football was again discussed. Those of that learned aggregation who opposed the gridiron game succumbed at the final vote.

Improved: At the faculty meeting yesterday the question of football was again discussed. The opponents of the game were defeated at the final vote.

Bad: The extremely warm weather of the past several weeks has not exactly been conducive of producing record-breaking scores at the Y.M.C.A. bowling alleys. In fact it has almost been too warm for even the most ardent lovers of the tenpin game, and enthusiasm has for some time been at a rather low ebb.

Improved: The extremely warm weather of the past several weeks has discouraged the production of high scores at the Y.M.C.A. bowling alleys. It has been almost too warm for even the most enthusiastic bowlers, and the general interest in the game has been slight.

Careless repetition of the conjunction *that*

47. Guard against the repetition of the conjunction *that*, when *that* is separated by intervening words from the subject and predicate which it introduces.

Wrong: It is pleasant to reflect that after all this work has been done and all these difficulties have been conquered, that we shall get a good rest.

Right: It is pleasant to reflect that after all this work has been done and all these difficulties have been conquered, we shall get a good rest.

Repetition with a change of meaning

48. Avoid using the same word with different meanings in the same sentence or in close sequence.

Bad: Since several years passed since the death of his wife . . .

Improved: Several years having passed since the death of his wife . . .

Bad: I couldn't get up courage to get up and investigate.

Improved: I couldn't summon courage to get up and investigate.

Repetition of similar sentence construction

49. Vary your sentence construction. Do not make many sentences coming close together noticeably alike in construction. This principle is often violated (*a*) by beginning many sentences near each other with *after, then, next, this, there is, there are;* (*b*) by using with noticeable frequency a compound sentence with two members of about equal length joined by *and* or *but;* (*c*) by using participial phrases with noticeable frequency; and (*d*) by the habitual use of *so* as a connective. (See Rule 55.)

50. Absolute phrases are often a useful aid to proper subordination and to smoothness of style. But there are two kinds of absolute phrases which, being conspicuously awkward, are best avoided; *viz.* Absolute phrases:

a. **Absolute phrases in which the substantive is a pronoun.** Absolute pronoun

Clumsy: He gave up the task, it being too difficult.
Better: He gave up the task as too difficult.

Clumsy: I being unacquainted with the road, my party got lost.
Better: Since I was unacquainted with the road, my party got lost.

NOTE. — An absolute phrase in which the pronoun refers to the subject of the sentence is especially objectionable. In such cases wordiness is added to awkwardness, since the pronoun is superfluous.

Bad: I made a trip to Catalina Island in 1922, I being then in my tenth year.
Better: I made a trip to Catalina Island in 1922, being then in my tenth year.

Bad: The furnace could not be repaired immediately, it being red-hot.
Better: Being red-hot, the furnace could not be repaired immediately.

b. **Absolute phrases in which the substantive is modified by a perfect participle, especially a passive perfect participle.** Such phrases are clumsy, unidiomatic, and suggestive of elementary Latin exercises. Latinistic phrases

Clumsy: His horse having been fed, Macy continued his journey.
Better: When his horse had been fed, Macy continued his journey.

Exercise

Euphony Study the following passage for euphony. How is a euphonious effect obtained? Do you find rhyme, a regular rhythm, alliteration, repetition of vowel and consonant sounds? If so, what comments would you make regarding their use in this prose passage?

And this is how I see the East. I have seen its secret places and have looked into its very soul; but now I see it always from a small boat, a high outline of mountains, blue and afar in the morning; like faint mist at noon; a jagged wall of purple at sunset. I have the feel of the oar in my hand, the vision of the scorching blue sea in my eyes. And I see a bay, a wide bay, smooth as glass and polished like ice, shimmering in the dark. A red light burns far off upon the gloom of the land, and the night is soft and warm. We drag at the oars with aching arms, and suddenly a puff of wind, a puff faint and tepid and laden with strange odors of blossoms, of aromatic wood, comes out of the still night — the first sigh of the East on my face. That I can never forget. It was impalpable and enslaving, like a charm, like a whispered promise of mysterious delight. — Joseph Conrad.

Exercise

Repetition Revise such of the following sentences as you think need revision. Give your reasons for changing the sentences or for leaving them as they are.

1. He puts his feet up on the desk, pulls his pipe from the desk drawer. Slowly he fills the pipe; slowly he tamps the tobacco; slowly he lights it. His hand cupped around the bowl of the pipe, he chews on the stem.
2. The following directions for the process of being disagreeable are not directed, of course, toward those who already have the process well in hand.
3. The ideal instructor is not always the easiest instructor. The ideal instructor, of course, must always be well informed on his subject. He should be able to talk about his subject as related to present-day topics. He should have a knowledge of other subjects besides the one that he is teaching. He should explain

his assignments so that every student in his class will understand.

4. Every boy likes to fish, and being no exception to the rule, I am very fond of fishing. However, every time that I am reminded of going fishing, I think of one unsuccessful fishing trip that I took.
5. I was always certain that in spite of the petty crimes that he committed as a boy that he was made of good stuff.
6. I wish I could repeat her words about you. I wish I could give you some idea of her admiration for you.
7. While he does not like to be interrupted while he is grading papers, perhaps he will not object to this interruption.
8. I am sorry to write that I need more money again. I seem always to be financially embarrassed.
9. The flashing signal light disclosed the ledge of sandbags piled along the levee. Beyond the gray and soggy mass of sandbags was the gray river washing against its bank.
10. She could speak no English, and I was unable to be articulate in German, but that did not prevent us from carrying on a conversation.
11. He now views his past and present and sees clearly a course through which his ship, guided by hope, will set a course.
12. It was Class Day — the day of days for our graduating class; the day when we made speeches, told jokes on one another, and related the history of our high-school adventures.

Exercise

Absolute phrases

If necessary, recast these sentences containing absolute phrases.

1. Ella being what she is, you cannot expect any more from her.
2. It having rained excessively, the farmer was unable to prepare his soil until the middle of May. The time being very short, it was necessary that he work day and night to get the crops planted.
3. The weather being unbearably hot, it was impossible to use the horses for field work.

4. I had to do most of the housework, I being the only girl in the family.
5. I trudged down twenty-eight flights of stairs, I being certain that the elevators had stopped running.

EXERCISES ON THE WORD

I. INFORMATION FROM DICTIONARIES

Exercise 1

Abbreviations

Consult the table of abbreviations in the front part of a dictionary so that you may understand information that is often given in abbreviated form. For example, what do the following abbreviations mean: *OF.*, *Oxf.*, *E.D.*, *colloq.*, *at. wt.*, *AS.*, *ff.*, *p. a.*, *pr. var.*, *d.*, *e.g.*?

Exercise 2

Unabridged dictionaries superior to abridged

Look up each of the following words both in an unabridged dictionary and in an abridged one, and write a report showing how much more discriminatingly and clearly the larger volume explains the use of each word than the smaller one does: *idealism*, *Bible*, *liberal*, *court*, *Christian*, *color*, *moral*, *law*, *evolution*, *catholic*. State the exact title, the date, and the publisher of each of the dictionaries consulted.

Exercise 3

Etymology

How may the etymologies given by the dictionary help one in remembering the meaning of the following words? (Note that when a series of words have the same etymology, the etymology may be given only once with the first word of the series.) *Incarnation*, *egregious*, *cruciform*, *umbrageous*, *entrepreneur*, *risibility*, *legerdemain*, *dénouement*, *metempsychosis*, *agnostic*, *contiguous*, *incunabula*, *cant*, *factitious*.

Exercise 4

Verb transitive or intransitive?

Look up the following verbs in a dictionary. State whether each verb is transitive or intransitive, and illustrate the correct use of each verb: *propose*, *purpose*, *sit*, *set*, *frighten*, *scare*, *learn*, *teach*, *isolate*, *derogate*, *desiccate*, *elicit*, *elide*, *simulate*, *ricochet*, *limn*, *synthesize*, *instigate*, *apprehend*, *envisage*, *castigate*, *interdict*, *genuflect*, *deploy*, *collude*.

Exercise 5

Definition

In consulting a dictionary about the use of a word, try not merely to get a general idea of the meaning of the word, but to discover within what *limits of meaning* the word is confined. To this end read the definition *as a whole;* do not pick out a single synonym and suppose that this and the word defined are interchangeable. *Cut* is defined thus: "To separate the parts of with, or as with, a sharp instrument; to make an incision in; to gash; to sever; to divide." To pick out the last synonym ("to divide") and reason that since *cut* means *divide,* one may say "I will cut the money among them" would be absurd. What *cut* means is ascertained not from one synonym taken separately but from the definition read *as a whole.*

Look up the following words in an unabridged dictionary; read each definition, and read the examples; write sentences illustrating the correct use of each word:

unction	microcosm	crass	misanthropy
sabotage	macrocosm	cynosure	philanthropy
shibboleth	polyandry	sententious	meticulous
antiphony	immanent	sophistication	opprobrious
stentorian	imminent	ubiquity	ostentatious
mordant	eminent	chicane	ineluctable
travesty	harbinger	denizen	peccadillo
seismograph	panegyric	duress	precocious
neologism	mundane	colloquial	sycophant
adjudicate	nepotism	hedonist	syllogism
impugn	innocuous	hegemony	sinecure
contumacy	voodoo	misogyny	recalcitrant
retroactive	anomalous	misogamy	increment
anachronism			

Exercise 6

Inflectional forms

Find out from a dictionary whether all of the following forms are correct:

1. *I dove,* or *I dived.* 2. *No trump was bid,* or *no trump was bidden.* 3. *It is proved,* or *it is proven.* 4. *I wakened,* or *I woke,* or *I waked.* 5. *I swang,* or *I swung.* 6. *He was drownded,* or *he was drowned.* 7. *The ship sank,* or *the ship sunk.* 8. *The dress shrank,* or *the dress shrunk.* 9. *She wrang the clothes,* or *she wrung the clothes.*

II. GOOD USAGE

Exercise 7

Good usage

Determine from an unabridged dictionary the suitability or unsuitability of the following words in ordinary formal discourse: *hired girl, babe, bogus, varsity, swain, whilst, sport* (a person), *walkout* (noun), *high-brow, josh, come across, get by with, put one over on, get it across, renig, pants* (clothing), *ofttimes, brainy, clean up* (to make money), *depot* (railway station), *dope* (information), *electrocute, fix you up, galore, foot the bill, gent, lief, a whole lot, minus* (without), *opine, orate, overly, photo, right away, holdup, homey, faze, domicile, hodgepodge, up-to-date, wire* (verb), *nonce, blues.*

Exercise 8

Part of speech

Find out from an unabridged dictionary what part of speech each of the following italicized words is. Is each correctly used for ordinary formal discourse?

1. She plays tennis *first-rate.*
2. We stopped at a *near-by* house to inquire.
3. She is doing *uplift* work in the slums.
4. He hopes to get a *raise.*
5. I am going, *providing* the trip is not expensive.
6. Can you give me a *recommend?*
7. I am studying *voice.*
8. *Most* everyone had heard the news.
9. I cannot give *that* much money to the stadium fund.
10. We are going to *vacation* in the West.

Exercise 9

Good usage

Consult an unabridged dictionary and decide upon the good usage for ordinary formal discourse of the italicized words or phrases in the following sentences:

1. Put the book *right* there.
2. John is a *likely* lad.
3. I cannot say *as* I am glad to go.
4. All are glad of the return to *normalcy.*
5. *I'll be back in an hour.*
6. We had *pretty* cold weather.
7. This is *all the farther* I can go.

8. When I was a boy on the farm, I *devoted most of my efforts* to taking care of the cows and pigs. Good usage
9. You *favor* your father in looks.
10. *Immediately* you hear him call, you must run to him.
11. There were *lots* of people at the meeting.
12. She *certainly* got a good *fit* on your coat.
13. It is *handy* to have the grocery store near you.
14. Will you *wait on* me at the corner?
15. I am *mighty* glad that you came.
16. You had better *doctor it up* before you hand it in.
17. You *mayhap* will be ready to leave then.
18. She looked very *distingué.*
19. My mother was *pernickety* about the books we read.
20. We are in a *tremendous* hurry.
21. I am going *anyhow,* even if he says I cannot.
22. I *appreciate* your feeling as you do about your own brother.
23. It will cost us *around* fifty dollars.
24. She could not help me *any.*
25. Any one of our gowns will give you *chic.*
26. It makes no more *difference* to me *than* it does to you.
27. The fog was so heavy that we *couldn't hardly* see.
28. She has been *ill from* typhoid fever.
29. We had a pleasant evening *reminiscing* about the *little old burg in days long gone by.*
30. We saw a good *show* last night.
31. They are *as good as* engaged.
32. That was a *curious* coincidence.
33. She *failed* her examination.
34. I *never can seem* to do it well.
35. The President had expressly committed the United States to the active *support and participation in* a league or association of nations.
36. Modern children are not taught to *mind.*
37. Even though it rained all of the time, we had *quite* a pleasant visit.
38. He was too *impractical* to succeed in business.
39. You should *patronize* your neighborhood grocer.
40. Make it *snappy.*
41. He has handled the characters in his story in a *past-masterly* fashion.
42. Italy now *devaluates* the lira.
43. Our new athletic *publicator* has arrived.

Exercise 10

Idiomatic construction

Find out, either from explicit statements in the definitions or from examples, what idiomatic construction — especially what preposition — is required with each word; and write sentences illustrating the correct use of each word: *compare, angry, infer, talk* (verb), *agree, surrounded, suspected, speak, vary, variance, contrast, deserving, affinity, consist, amuse, accused, accountable, admission, anxious, discouraged, eager, exult, concerned, impatient, look, necessary, necessity, opposed, opportunity, inquire, oblivious.*

III. CLEARNESS

Exercise 11

Distinctions in meaning

Consult the dictionary for the distinctions in meaning between the members of each of the following pairs of words: *neglect* and *negligence; ingenuous* and *ingenious; fewer* and *less; admit* and *confess; instinct* and *intuition; contagious* and *infectious; hygienic* and *sanitary; wit* and *humor; criticize* and *censure; farther* and *further.*

Exercise 12

Precision

Substitute precise words for the italicized words:

1. I have three *aughts* in my answer to the problem.
2. *Beside* being a mathematician, he is also a musician.
3. The decadent Roman civilization was a *feminine* civilization.
4. Much *literature* has been published about the use of limestone on farm lands.
5. Her charming innocence is *childish.*
6. We have much to learn from *heathen* cultures such as the Greek and Roman.
7. Careful management is necessary to keep farm earnings *continuously* above the average.
8. Transporting passengers and mail by airplanes has proved to be not only possible but *practical.*
9. I am quite *jealous* of your opportunity to study in Europe.
10. After supper you can have that *snug* place by the fire.
11. She was so *decisive* in her manner that people have always given in to her.
12. The wreck was due to an *error* of the switchman.

13. It would be almost an impossibility to write a *comprehensible* paper on the economics of man when volume after volume has been written without exhausting the subject.
14. If we give your class all of these privileges, we shall no doubt be establishing *precedence* which may be unwise. (Notice the pronunciation.)

Exercise 13

Find the precise meaning of each word in the following groups, and write sentences to illustrate that meaning. **Precision**

1. Mental, intelligent, intellectual.
2. Abandon, desert, forsake.
3. Hate, detest, abhor, abominate, loathe, despise.
4. Great, large, big.
5. Give, bestow, grant, confer, present.
6. Silent, reserved, uncommunicative, reticent, taciturn.
7. Last, latest, final, ultimate, extreme.
8. Stay, stop, tarry, linger, remain, sojourn, abide, live, dwell.
9. Work, labor, toil, drudgery.
10. Memory, remembrance, recollection, reminiscence.

Exercise 14

For the jargon phrases in these sentences try to find substitutes that will make the meaning clear. **Clearness**

1. This book is written *on the order of* a biography.
2. Beauty is one of the many essential *steps* in becoming a cultured person.
3. If you recommend me for this position, I shall appreciate the *fact*.
4. Building a concrete foundation in that racing current was a hard *proposition*.
5. Football in the United States *commands a predominating* interest.
6. They gave a large *affair* in the Masonic Hall.
7. You are always a great *asset* to a party.
8. They told us of a *case where* a man was struck by lightning.
9. There are many *factors* in business that I like.
10. History is out of my *line;* my major is chemistry.

IV. EFFECTIVENESS

Exercise 15

Effectiveness

Improve, if necessary, the diction in these sentences. State the specific rule that applies to the changes made.

1. À propos and en passant, it might be worthy of note that Jake Schmidt, kicker and passer on the football team, is learning the lay of the land in the Chicago office of the World Life Insurance Company.
2. I greatly admire the slow, soft drawl of the Southern people, for it gives an impression of culture and refinement that the rapid-fire speaking of the Northerners does not portray.
3. The benefits from Sunday sports would be of two natures; namely, the mental and the physical.
4. A good swimmer finds enjoyment in cutting through the water with long firm strokes that cause the water to have the appearance of boiling as he ends each stroke.
5. His ridicule of human nature is nevertheless peppered with pity.
6. For the spectators on the beach, the swimming races, motorboat races, and dashes in the sand prevent boredom from entering at any time.
7. I think that Mother Nature is at her best in the early spring.
8. Life as a beach guard is not all a bed of roses, but there are thorns in every path we choose to follow in life.
9. Preservation of his own life is a man's only thought, and he will gladly risk another's life in order to gain his own purpose.
10. The edges of the sky raveled off into rain.
11. Nothing is so despicable as a bowing, smirking person trying to act a gentleman while he has a hypocrite's heart behind his smiling mask.
12. My chief enjoyment and pleasure in life has been, and still is, the pursuit of my studies in music.
13. Then I found the dark side of the picture called Life. Life was ofttimes not all sunny and bright, but there were rough edges which sorely tried the youth that I was.
14. Thus what had been an interesting ball game suddenly

was turned haywire and some nice, timely hitting by Williams and Lehman was turned to no account. Effectiveness

15. After surviving the rush for tickets, one is herded into a stuffy car. After all available seats have been filled, the passengers have to sit on their baggage in the aisles.
16. The deflated holdings of inexperienced investors resulting from the recent stock market crash have greatly revived the belated hopes of questionable promoters who sense a growing desire on the part of the gullible public to recoup their heavy losses by making a lucky strike in a speculative venture.
17. The oculist suggested that if these new glasses did not help my eyes that I had better go to a specialist.
18. Our meat is prepared and packed by machinery and thus is untouched by the human hand.
19. When the last match has been struck, the proud possessor of the cigarette lighter with a grand flourish brings the treasured piece of mechanism from his vest pocket, and with a nonchalant flip of the lever, he proceeds to light his cigarette, but to his wonder and amazement, there is no ignition.
20. The keen intellect of the Greeks could not have reached such heights of development had not the great masters lived at a time when the stage was set for tremendous strides in the realms of thought.
21. The whole appearance of this Jersey cow is very striking. She has a soft skin. As you stroke her, it rolls smoothly between the fingers. Her hair is a rich cream color, soft and glossy. It gives her the appearance of being a well-cared-for animal.
22. Her eyes were shaded by long, black lashes, curving backward in a very peculiar way, and these matched in hue her eyebrows, and the tresses that were tossed about her tender throat and were quivering in the sunlight.
23. She shielded her face with a moody hand.
24. The mountains, with their forever-changing contours, seem to move in a slow dance calculated to allure him. There are young and sprightly peaks of fantastic shapes like dancing fauns; there are smoothly rounded and maternal ranges; there are hoary oldsters whose crowns are forever white with snow.

Effectiveness

25. The sand deserts of New Mexico and Arizona are very large. They give a conception of slow death and destruction; then close by, the Grand Canyon splits the earth open as if it would swallow the whole universe.
26. Like the big apples in a barrel hauled in a wagon over rough country, Joseph Kennedy has come to the top. The trip along the highway of life here has thrown him up and now out to greater fields of endeavor.
27. In conformation of the traditions of the University Concert and Entertainment Board, the Star Course is proud to present for your approval the coming season's program of attractions.
28. Our sorority has been particularly careful of the way it takes care of the doors and windows which might be entered.
29. He brags on his popularity with the girls.

THE SENTENCE

UNITY

51. A sentence should express a single complete thought. (See Rule 64 and discussion under Rule 236.) If it contains two or more statements, these should be so related as to express a single thought. Conversely, a sentence should contain at least one complete statement.

General principle

52. Statements that lack connection with each other should not be put in the same sentence. Defects in unity may be corrected in several ways:

Statements unconnected in thought

a. **By placing the unrelated statements in different sentences.**

Unity secured by division

Bad: Mathematics is my hardest subject, and comes at eleven in the morning.

Improved: Mathematics is my hardest subject. It comes at eleven in the morning.

Bad: Ruskin was a famous English critic, and was born in 1819.

Improved: Ruskin was a famous English critic. He was born in 1819.

Bad: I have received your letter of May 6, and the shirts referred to were shipped yesterday.

Improved: I have received your letter of May 6. The shirts referred to were shipped yesterday.

b. **By subordinating one statement to another.**

Unity secured by subordination

Unified: Mathematics, my hardest subject, comes at eleven in the morning.

Unified: Ruskin, the famous English critic, was born in 1819.

Unified: The shirts referred to in your letter of May 6 were shipped yesterday.

Bad: I was visiting my grandfather last winter in Vermont and I went to a maple sugar camp.

Improved: When I was visiting my grandfather last winter in Vermont, I went to a maple sugar camp.

Bad: There were cars ahead of us and behind us for several blocks and we could not move out of the line.

Improved: We could not move out of the line, because there were cars ahead of us and behind us for several blocks.

Unity secured by filling up gaps in thought

c. **By filling up the gaps in thought.**

Bad: Engineering has always interested me, but last winter I heard a talk by a famous engineer. Then I decided to take an engineering course.

Improved: Although engineering has always interested me, I did not decide to take up an engineering course until I heard a talk last winter by a famous engineer.

Bad: The scenery along the banks is very pretty, but the river is too shallow to be navigated by large boats.

Improved: The scenery along the banks is very pretty, but few people have seen it, because the river is too shallow to be navigated by boats large enough to carry passengers.

Bad: The operation of an incubator is simple, but no machine will work well unless it is watched.

Improved: An incubator is simple in operation, but, like any other machine, it will not work well unless it is watched.

Statements strung together with *and* and *but*

53. Avoid a long compound sentence consisting of statements strung together with *and's* and *but's*. Break the sentence into shorter sentences or put subordinate ideas into a subordinate form; *i.e.*, subordinate clause, phrase, or single word. The untrained writer does not perceive differences of importance between ideas, but places each in an independent clause and joins them by *and*, *but*, or *or*. The skilled writer endeavors to express these differences by the exactness and variety of subordination.

Overuse of *and* and *but*

Bad: The aircraft production program was badly delayed, and a good many people think we did nothing in building airplanes, but the government reorganized the work, and put capable production specialists in command, and these men corrected the faults in the planes and increased production, and before the end of the war they were turning out planes faster than the government could supply pilots to man them.

Improved: It is true that the aircraft production program was badly delayed, so that it is no wonder many people think we accomplished nothing in building airplanes. As a matter of fact, however, after the government reorganized the work and put capable production specialists in command, not only were the faults in the planes corrected, but production was increased. Before the end of the war, airplanes were being turned out faster than the government could supply pilots to man them.

Inferior: [First clause overemphasized.] I came into class and found I was five minutes late.

Predication reduced: [Subordinate clause.] When I came into class I found I was five minutes late; [or, participial phrase] On coming into class I found I was five minutes late.

Inferior: There were three big maple trees beside the house, and under them in the shade was a sand pile, and in this we children used to play.

Predication reduced: Beside the house in the shade of three big maples was a sand pile, in which we children used to play.

Inferior: It was a fine frosty morning and two seniors were walking toward college.

Predication reduced: One fine frosty morning two seniors were walking toward college.

Bad: The time comes, and the student is unprepared to choose a major study, but yet he must choose.

Predication reduced: When the time comes, the student must choose a major study, even though he is unprepared to make the choice.

Note. — Avoid the excessive use of *and* and *also* at the beginning of sentences. Practice the use of a variety of connectives, and note that it is often better to place them within the sentence rather than at the beginning. (See Rule 132.)

Exercise

Unity

Revise such of the following sentences as you find ununified. Give your reasons for changing sentences or for leaving them as they are.

1. She sat across from me, and the light from the candles was not kind to her.
2. He is a rather small man with sandy hair and soft brown skin, and his voice is smooth and quiet.
3. Brownie's job is to care for the cuts, bumps, and bruises of the football players, and he performs his tasks with a never-ending cheerfulness and good nature.
4. I would sit on the doorstep of the old farmhouse, and I would hear again the mournful cry of the whippoorwill and the whoo-whooing of a watchful owl; and once more the stories of eventful coon-hunts would lull me to peace with the world.
5. Many times I have been very fond of people, but I have often been jolted into a realization of my gullibility.
6. During the past summer I found employment on a large country estate, and I became acquainted with what I liked to think of as summer symphonies. These symphonies I would divide into two distinct classes. There are those that are produced by such animate things as birds, men, and animals, and in the other class are those sounds produced by inanimate things such as windmills, machinery of all kinds, wind, and rain.
7. For the first time it occurred to me that I had never earned enough money to buy my clothes and my father was in business as a very young man.
8. It is not a question of what to order since the student's purse hardly ever allows more than a "coke," and "dates" usually ask you what flavored "coke" you would like, but what really takes the time is deciding what kind of "coke" is wanted.

Straggling sentences

54. Avoid long, straggling sentences written without grammatical plan and covering either too many ideas or too many periods of time to make a definite impression on the reader's mind.

Narrative

Bad: That night we camped near the outlet, and the next morning we packed our equipment and took down the tents and put them into the canoes and started down the outlet with our canoe in the lead, but we had not gone more than a few miles when we came to a fallen tree right across our way, and as the banks were soft mud it would be hard to carry around it, so we held a council of war and decided to cut through the trunk, which was not very large, so after much splashing and nearly upsetting the canoe we succeeded in disposing of the obstacle, after which we proceeded on our way.

Improved: That night we camped near the outlet. The next morning, after stowing our tents and equipment in the canoes, we started down the stream, our canoe leading. After we had paddled a few miles, we came to a tree which had fallen right across our way. As the banks were soft mud, to carry around the tree would have been difficult; accordingly, holding a council of war, we decided to cut through the trunk, which was not very large. After much splashing, and nearly upsetting the canoe, we succeeded in disposing of the obstacle, and proceeded on our way.

Summary

Bad: Tennyson's poem *Lady Clara Vere de Vere* is the speech of a young country fellow to a young lady of high birth who is beautiful but a heartless coquette, having attempted to ensnare the young man and then cast him off merely to amuse herself, as she has done with a number of other young fellows, one of whom, as the young man who is speaking reminds her, committed suicide from grief at her cruelty, which makes the young man who is speaking despise the lady, for he tells her that he cares neither for her beauty nor for her high birth, since she has no goodness of heart, and he solemnly tells her she ought to cease amusing herself by her coquetry and to "pray Heaven for a human heart."

Improved: Tennyson's poem *Lady Clara Vere de Vere* is the speech of a manly young country fellow to a beautiful but heartless young lady of high birth, who has attempted to amuse herself by breaking his heart — a speech expressing disdain for charms beneath which there is no goodness of heart, and contempt for hereditary rank the possessor of which lacks true virtue and honor; reminding the lady of the suicide of another country lad, whom she had enticed by feigned affection and then cruelly repudiated; and solemnly adjuring her to cease her unworthy and injurious diversion, to turn her leisure to some good end, and to "pray Heaven for a human heart."

Note. — A sentence may be long without violating unity. The first of the two foregoing sentences violates unity because it is straggling, lacking grammatical plan. The second does not violate unity; it has a definite organization of which parallelism is an important factor. (See Rule 108.) This parallelism may be made clear by the following diagram:

Tennyson's poem . . . is . . . a speech	1. expressing	*a.* disdain *b.* contempt
	2. reminding her 3. adjuring her	*a.* to cease *b.* to turn *c.* to pray

Exercise

Straggling sentences

Study the following sentence. Is it straggling, without grammatical plan? Does it lack unity? Could the reader's attention be better held if the sentence were divided? If so, what changes would you make?

We think that there is footloose in society, in the enthusiasms with which people become missionaries for the various things in which they take a deep personal interest, a great capacity for helping the other fellow along, and we believe that any leisure-time service should consider its function not alone to be the promotion of specific activities, such as athletics or the arts, but that we should consider as a leisure-time field, in which a great many will find happy outlets for their energies, the pursuit of information or of intellectual culture, not as a matter of schooling but as a matter of post-school avocational interest, and that others can only be served by affording organized outlets for their own leisure enjoyment, in being helpfully identified with causes and movements which are appealing to them, in capacities of service to their group as individuals, or to society at large. — *Youth . . . Leisure for Living*, published by the *U. S. Office of Education.*

55. Avoid the excessive use of *so* as a connective between the verbs of a compound predicate and between clauses. In place of *so*, substitute a more precise connective (see *so* in Appendix D), or recast the sentence, subordinating the less important element. *And so* is to be preferred to *so*. (For punctuation with *so*, see Rule 268.)

The *so* habit

Inferior: He was only one among many so was not observed.

Preferable: Being only one among many, he was not observed; [or] He was only one among many and so was not observed.

Inferior: His wife thought he would be thirsty; so she brought a pitcher of water.

Preferable: His wife, thinking he would be thirsty, brought a pitcher of water.

Inferior: The people were opposed to him for some unknown reason; so he had to accomplish his purpose through secret agents.

Preferable: Since the people were, for some unknown reason, opposed to him, he was compelled to accomplish his purpose through secret agents.

Inferior: I decided it was high time we camped, for it would soon be dark, so I turned the canoe toward shore.

Preferable: I decided it was high time we camped, for it would soon be dark; so [or, *accordingly*] I turned the canoe toward shore.

56. Avoid the excessive use of *then* as a connective between the verbs of a compound predicate and between clauses. Substitute other connectives (see Appendix D), or recast the sentence, subordinating the less important element. *And then* is to be preferred to *then*. (For punctuation with *then*, see Rule 268.)

Use of *then*

Inferior: I paddled the boat for a while, then fell into a reverie.

Preferable: After paddling the boat for a while, I fell into a reverie; [or] I paddled the boat for a while, and then fell into a reverie.

Exercise

So and *then*

Revise the following sentences:

1. I heard a doorbell ringing, louder and closer, but in the dark. Then I opened my eyes; then with difficulty I focused them upon a circle of playmates looking down upon me. I assured my companions that I was uninjured; then I skated away a trifle unsteady. Later when I picked up the evening paper, I saw the letters printed there; then they dimmed and blurred. I held the paper away from my face; then I held it close.
2. After dinner comes a rest period; then comes the afternoon scoutcraft activities period; then the boys go swimming.
3. I am in no hurry; so I'll wait for you.
4. We telegraphed; so we ought to hear tonight.
5. This was my first visit to Paris; so I went on all the sight-seeing trips planned for us.
6. I remembered that you had met him; so I thought you would be interested in hearing about him.
7. I made my deliveries before school in the morning; so I had to be up very early.
8. We could not find what we wanted at the first shop; so we continued to search in the other shops.
9. My grandmother likes to do her own marketing; so every morning she starts forth with her basket.
10. The room was very stuffy; so I opened a window.

Two *but's* or *for's*

57. Two consecutive statements should not both be introduced by *but* or *for*. (See Rule 58.) This fault may usually be corrected by omitting the first *but* or *for*.

Bad: Iago became fond of Desdemona but she paid no attention to him but seemed to favor Cassio.

Improved: Iago became fond of Desdemona. She paid no attention to him but seemed to favor Cassio.

Bad: He suddenly paused, for it seemed wonderful that he could speak so easily, for usually he was bashful.

Improved: He suddenly paused; it seemed wonderful that he could speak so easily, for usually he was bashful.

58. Do not put a series of similar clauses or a series of similar phrases in an overlapping construction, — *i.e.*, with the second depending on the first, the third on the second, the fourth on the third, etc. Recast the sentence. (See Rule 57.)

Overlapping dependence

Awkward: I never knew a man who was so ready to help a friend who had got into difficulties which pressed him hard.

Improved: I never knew a man so ready to help a friend who found himself hard pressed by difficulties.

Misleading: He is a blunt, manly fellow, who admires a soldier and despises an effeminate fop, who struts about affectedly and dresses daintily.

Clear: He is a blunt, manly fellow, who admires a soldier and despises an effeminate, affected, daintily dressed fop.

Awkward: I was so uncomfortable that I rolled up my sleeves so far that my arms got sunburned, so that I could hardly sleep that night.

Improved: Feeling very uncomfortable, I rolled up my sleeves so far that my arms got badly sunburned. The pain of my smarting skin kept me awake most of that night.

Awkward: This was the first of the entertainments of the senior girls of the dormitory.

Improved: This was the first entertainment given by the senior girls of the dormitory.

Note, however, that a series of similar clauses or phrases all depending on the same sentence-element gives rise to no awkwardness. (See Rules 54, note, and 108.)

Right: I rise to nominate a man who has ever been stanch in his loyalty, who has long been a trusted counselor in the policies of our party, who has demonstrated his fitness for his office by the efficiency of his administration in others, whose honor has never been assailed save by calumnious envy, whose fame is destined to echo down the coming ages, who . . . etc.

Right: His face has come down to us marked with all the blemishes put on it by time, by war, by sleepless nights, by anxiety, perhaps by remorse.

Exercise

Overlapping dependence

Revise such of the following sentences as need revision. Give your reasons for changing the sentences or for leaving them as they are.

1. Why do I like my girl? When I talk at great length about my courses, when I explain to her the construction of a new bridge, when I hold forth about my religious views, when I tell my best funny stories, what does she do? She hangs on every word.
2. Recently I met George Hunt, who was introduced to me by his roommate whom I have known for many years.
3. She is so much pleased with her new dress that we are giving a party so that she can wear it.
4. She was related to the banker of our town, who was the son of wealthy Kentucky parents who owned more than a section of land in our community, which he inherited at the death of his father.
5. A furious wind began to blow, which all but swept our car from the highway which was flanked on both sides by deep ditches.

Thought chopped up

59. Do not chop up the thought of one unified sentence into several short sentences. Put the thought into one sentence with proper subordination and reduced predication. (See Rule 28.)

Bad: Two friends were to meet me in a neighboring town. We were to go to my home. They were to visit with me. We were then going to college together.

Improved: Two friends, who were to meet me in a neighboring town, were to go home with me for a visit before we went to college.

Bad: My best friend in high school was our coach. His name was John Everett. He coached our football and basketball teams.

Improved: My best friend in high school was our football and basketball coach, John Everett.

Exercise

Revise such of the following sentences as need revision. Give your reasons for changing the sentences or for leaving them as they are.

Thought chopped up

1. A crow has a reputation for wisdom. I studied its habits for months. I decided that the wisdom of these birds is surpassed by that of no other creature of the woods.
2. There is one good thing that can be said for the crow. That is the great service he does in eating all kinds of harmful insects. Insects are his staple food. In ridding the fields of them, he does the farmer a great service.
3. The Drive is an animate picture. Automobiles roll along. Tires sing over smooth concrete. The occupants are smug and comfortable in their wrapping of sleek furs. Under the Drive, where the American Masters of Finance never look, live the forgotten men of the city. These are Chicago's unemployed. They sleep against pillars. In the winter the stinging river wind whips them. They wrap their shivering bodies in newspapers and burlap sacks.
4. I have spent almost a year now in a liberal arts course. I do not feel that I have gained much. I have received moderately good grades. I have had a passably good time. But I am not seriously interested in the course I am taking.
5. The state prison is about a mile outside the limits of the city. It is located so that escaping convicts would have to go through the city or along a highway. This highway leads directly to a small town. This town is practically a lookout station under the direction of the prison.

The run-on sentence

60. Do not attach the last part of a sentence to the following sentence that introduces a new thought. Either put it back into the preceding sentence or make it independent.

Bad: At the first meeting of my classes, I was very nervous. I made an absolute failure of everything I tried, and I noticed that the answers of many of my fellow freshmen were wrong.

Improved: At the first meeting of my classes, I was so nervous that I made an absolute failure of everything I tried. I noticed that the answers of many of my fellow freshmen were wrong.

Bad: In the tree we had what we called a four-story house and on the top floor, which was rather large, we had high cloth walls. No one could see us from below and it was here that I smoked my first pipeful of tobacco.

Improved: In the tree we had what we called a four-story house and on the top floor, which was rather large, we had cloth walls so high that no one could see us from below. It was here that I smoked my first pipeful of tobacco.

Run-on sentence

Revise the following sentences. Give your reasons for making changes.

1. The old crow will imitate perfectly the weak caw of its young. This is in order to lure the hunter from the neighborhood of the nest, and almost all traps set for these black vandals are studiously avoided.
2. In the spring the orchard was filled with pink and white blossoms. They sent their spicy fragrance over the neighborhood, and in the fall the apples hung heavy.
3. The majority of American high school teachers are young women who have plans for matrimony. If they have no plans, they wish they had, and they have no intention of spending their lives teaching.
4. Through the window came shouts and cheers from the vacant lot next door. There a ball game was in progress and Ralph sank deeper into gloom.

Frequent use of parentheses

61. Avoid the frequent use of parentheses. The parenthetic material may be subordinated, or may be put into separate sentences, or may be omitted.

Bad: My cousin (he is the one that you met when you visited me two years ago) has just returned from the East where he saw many important football games (especially the Yale-Harvard and the Army-Navy games).

Improved: My cousin, whom you met when you visited me two years ago, has just returned from the East, where he saw the Yale-Harvard, the Army-Navy, and other important football games.

62. Do not run two sentences together into one by using a comma between them instead of a period. Comma fault

Wrong: He was present at all athletic contests with his word of cheer for the losers and congratulations for the winners, in this manner he made many friends.
Right: He was present at all athletic contests with his word of cheer for the losers and congratulations for the winners. In this manner he made many friends.

Wrong: When the game begins, the two teams line up much in the same manner as in a football game, the center forward of the team stands in the middle of the field on the 50-yard line, facing the goal.
Right: When the game begins, the two teams line up much in the same manner as in a football game. The center forward of the team stands in the middle of the field on the 50-yard line, facing the goal.

NOTE. — If the clauses are so related in thought that they may be put into one sentence, they should be separated by a semicolon rather than by a comma.

63. Do not run two sentences together into one with no punctuation between them. The comma fault is not cured by omitting the comma but by substituting for it either a semicolon or a period. This and the preceding rule concern matters of sentence sense; but since punctuation is involved, see Rule 237c, also. "Comma fault" made worse

Wrong: He said he would not attend the dance I don't know why not.
Right: He said he would not attend the dance; I don't know why.
Right: He said he would not attend the dance. I don't know why.

64. Subordinate sentence-elements should not be capitalized and punctuated like complete sentences. (See Rule 236.) Period fault

Wrong: It offers a course for those who wish to study painting. At the same time affording opportunity for literary study. [Participial phrase lacking subject and predicate.]

Right: It offers a course for those who wish to study painting, at the same time affording opportunity for literary study. [Or,]

Right: It offers a course for those who wish to study painting. At the same time it affords opportunity for literary study.

Wrong: Among her suitors were two she favored most. One a college student, the other a capitalist. [Phrases in apposition with *suitors.*]

Right: Among her suitors were two she favored most; one a college student, the other a capitalist. [Or,]

Right: Among her suitors were two she favored most. One was a college student, the other a capitalist.

Wrong: Constant practice and perseverance are necessary. When one is trying to master the Australian Crawl. [Subordinate clause introduced by *when.*]

Right: Constant practice and perseverance are necessary when one is trying to master the Australian Crawl.

Exercise

Comma fault; period fault

Analyze the following sentences, showing why there are comma and period faults. Correct these mistakes.

1. The kick in the Australian Crawl is almost a replica of the motion of the propeller on a motorboat, the knees must not be bent at any time during the stroke.
2. The kick must be perfectly timed with the movement of each arm to produce a steady pace, most great swimmers kick the feet three times to each arm movement.
3. The American pioneer has always been very wasteful and ruthless as he pushed into the wilderness to find a home, he has dissipated more of the resources than he has used.
4. The passenger pigeon was a large, beautiful, varicolored bird, sixteen to seventeen inches long. With a graduated tail nearly as long as the wings.
5. He was a gregarious bird. Living either in the wooded uplands or swamps and constantly migrating in search of food.
6. Long before the lazy January sun had crept forth behind the snowy tops of the mountain range of the

Schwabische Alb, we were on our way to the Neuffen. One of the most beautiful peaks in the entire range.

7. At noon we reached the shelter on the top of Neuffen. This shelter was close to the old ruin of the castle of the lords of Neuffen. Which now looked as bright and mysterious to us as only the castles of fairy-tale days could have looked.
8. We spent a long time on top of the peaks and enjoyed the beautiful sight from there. As well as a meal which we prepared at a quickly started fire.

COHERENCE

65. Coherence requires that the parts of a sentence be so worded and arranged that they will stick together. General principle

REFERENCE

66. Do not use a pronoun instead of a noun if there might be doubt about its antecedent. This fault may be avoided by repeating the antecedent, by using an equivalent noun, or by recasting the sentence. Uncertain or ludicrous reference

Uncertain: Geraint followed the knight to a town, where he entered a castle.

Clear: Geraint followed the knight to a town and there saw him enter a castle.

Uncertain: He told his father he would soon get a letter.

Clear: He said to his father, "You will [or I shall] soon get a letter."

Not immediately evident: The ghost of his old partner appeared to Scrooge. He told him he must reform.

Clear: The ghost of his partner appeared to Scrooge and admonished him to reform.

Ludicrous: Whistling for Rover, my cousin put a pail in his mouth and we started.

Clear: Whistling for Rover, my cousin put a pail in the dog's mouth, and we started.

NOTE. — Avoid using a plural pronoun referring to a singular noun preceding; make the pronoun singular or repeat the noun in the plural.

Bad: The incubator is a modern device for hatching chickens. All poultrymen who do business on a large scale use them.

Improved: The incubator is a modern device for hatching chickens. All poultrymen who do business on a large scale use it; [or] . . . use incubators.

Vague reference of *this* and *that*

67. Avoid the vague reference of the pronouns *this* and *that*. This fault may often be corrected by changing the pronoun to a demonstrative adjective and inserting a noun after it.

Weak reference: He asked where Cary was. I could not answer that.

Improved: He asked where Cary was. I could not answer that question.

Weak reference: We do oppose the bill; if we did not, we should not publish this.

Improved: We do oppose the bill; if we did not, we should not publish this article.

Remote reference

68. Do not use a pronoun to refer to a noun that is widely separated from it; repeat the noun.

Undesirable: Once there was a very old orchard across the street from our house. The apple trees were ancient and gnarled and bent from many years of heavy fruit-bearing. In the spring it was filled with pink and white blossoms.

Improved: . . . In the spring the orchard was filled . . .

Reference to a noun not prominent

69. Avoid reference of a pronoun to a noun decidedly subordinate in thought or syntax. Some more prominent noun is likely to be mistaken for the antecedent. Repeat the noun or recast the sentence.

Bad: Mrs. Bloodgood appeared at Powers's Theatre in Fitch's play, *The Girl with the Green Eyes*. This piece was written by *him* especially for Mrs. Bloodgood.

Improved: Mrs. Bloodgood appeared at Powers's Theatre in Fitch's play, *The Girl with the Green Eyes*. This piece was written by Mr. Fitch especially for Mrs. Bloodgood.

Bad: In Miss Howerth's story of her life she relates this incident.

Improved: Miss Howerth in the story of her life relates this incident.

Allowable: Tom's happiness was a joy to see; he literally danced on the pavement. [*Tom* is subordinate in syntax but not in thought.]

70. Avoid using a pronoun or a pronominal expression to refer to a word or phrase that has not been directly expressed. Either repeat the antecedent instead of using a pronoun or provide a word or expression to which the pronoun will refer.

Reference to a word not expressed

Bad: The cadet must keep his hands out of his pockets; *that* would be very unsoldierly.

Improved: The cadet must keep his hands out of his pockets; to put them there would be very unsoldierly.

Bad: Marx is a violinist, the study of *which instrument* he began when a boy.

Improved: Marx is a violinist. He began the study of the violin when he was a boy.

Bad: Mink skins are valuable, because *these animals* are now scarce.

Improved: Mink skins are valuable, because minks are now scarce.

71. Avoid using the relative pronoun *which* to refer to a whole statement if that statement contains nouns which might be mistaken for the antecedent.

Reference to a whole statement

Undesirable: He did not hear her cry which was due to his deafness.

Better: He did not hear her cry because of his deafness. [Or,] Because of his deafness he did not hear her cry.

Undesirable: Unless you steer carefully, the boat may crash into the wharf, which may result in serious damage to the hull.

Clear: Unless you steer carefully, the boat may crash into the wharf, seriously damaging the hull.

Clear: Unless you steer carefully, you may run the boat into the wharf and seriously damage the hull.

Antecedent in parentheses

72. Avoid the awkward device of explaining an ambiguous pronoun by repeating its antecedent in parentheses; use the antecedent alone or recast the sentence.

Awkward: If Davis treated Dixon discourteously, there is no objection to his (Dixon's) decision.

Improved: If Davis treated Dixon discourteously, there is no objection to Dixon's decision; [or] Dixon is not to be blamed for his decision if he was treated discourteously by Davis.

Indefinite *you*

73. Avoid the use of indefinite *you* in formal composition. The fault may be corrected by using either the passive voice or the pronoun *one*, or by substituting the noun or pronoun which is really intended. (For the fault of shifting from *you* to *one* and to *we*, see Rule 178.)

Undesirable: You should not use *they* indefinitely.

Improved: *They* should not be used indefinitely; [or] One should not use *they* indefinitely.

Indefinite *they*

74. Avoid using *they* indefinitely; use the passive voice, or recast the sentence.

Vague: They make bricks in Fostoria.

Improved: Bricks are made in Fostoria.

Vague: They had a collision on the electric road.

Improved: There was a collision; [or] A collision occurred (more formal).

Vague: They don't have redbirds in Wisconsin.

Improved: There are no redbirds in Wisconsin; [or] Redbirds are not found in Wisconsin (more formal).

Indefinite *it*

75. Except in impersonal expressions, such as *it rains*, *it seems*, *it is cold*, etc. do not use *it* without an antecedent; recast the sentence.

Undesirable: In the notice on the bulletin board it says the drill is held at four.

Improved: The notice on the bulletin board says the drill is held at four.

Undesirable: In Garland's *Life among the Corn Rows* it gives a description of life among the farmers.

Improved: Garland's *Life among the Corn Rows* gives a description . . .; [or] In Garland's *Life among the Corn Rows* there is a description . . .

Undesirable: Does it say *Fair Oaks* on that car?

Improved: Is that car marked *Fair Oaks?*

Note. — The habit of beginning sentences with *it is* or *it seems* makes a weak style and often leads to confusion of pronouns. (See Rule 66.)

76. Avoid the confusion of having in the same sentence both an indefinite *it* and an *it* with an antecedent.

Indefinite *it* and definite *it* in the same sentence

Bad: Radium gives out heat enough in an hour to raise its own weight of water from the freezing to the boiling point; yet it wastes away so slowly that it has been estimated that it would require fifteen hundred years for it to lose half its weight.

Improved: Radium gives out heat enough in an hour to raise its own weight of water from the freezing to the boiling point; yet it wastes away so slowly that according to estimates, in fifteen hundred years it would lose only half its weight.

77. The use of a demonstrative adjective (especially *that* or *those*) without the relative clause necessary for clearness is a colloquialism. (For vague reference of *this* and *that*, see Rule 67.)

Indefinite *that* and *those*

Not clear: I observed that the building was one of those rambling old mansions.

Clear: I observed that the building was a rambling old mansion; [or] . . . one of those rambling old mansions that one often sees in New England towns.

Exercise

Correct any faults in reference that you may find in the following sentences.

Reference

1. I spent my Christmas vacation hunting rabbit, quail, and coon, which I think is ideal.
2. Although the British ship never captured the *Bounty,*

Reference

they captured several mutineers on the island and they were taken to England where they were tried for mutiny.

3. Of recent years so many young people have gone to college and prepared to teach that it has overcrowded the profession.
4. On the Byrd expedition, a transport plane was used to carry him and his instruments over the South Pole. They also use them for experimentation, such as weight-lifting, endurance flying, and racing.
5. No one ever takes notice nowadays when an airplane passes overhead. They know it is there, but they do not know what type it is or what makes it function.
6. As I enter these headquarters of one of the greatest universities of the world, I am amazed at the complete lack of decoration or of any attempt whatsoever to make it at all impressive or even attractive.
7. It is one of those sentimental movies.
8. Primary children are not the only ones who cheat; it is even true of high-school and college students.
9. With so many courses in physical education offered, it seems as though it should be a simple task to fit one of them into each schedule. But this does not appear to be true.
10. It cannot be denied that there are newspaper editors in the profession solely for its monetary gain and with no thought for the public's welfare.
11. The ideals that he has learned on the mat will carry over into his life as a citizen and will help him to do his part in its work.
12. We arrived at the airport a bit early, but I did not mind that. This enabled me to look around.
13. When the first few warm spring days come and make us somewhat drowsy, many take advantage of it and say that they have spring fever.
14. She is a senior and a physical education major. This occupies all of her time.
15. We took a wheel off his wagon and rolled it down the road with us in hope that we might make some use of it later, which we actually did.
16. While Allen was very young, his father died, which left the burden of the family upon his mother.

17. The cold air makes outdoor activities a pleasure, which encourages participation in sports.
18. If he executes his commands out of time with the beat of the drums, it gives the band a ragged appearance.

DANGLING MODIFIERS

78. Avoid the use of dangling modifiers. A modifier dangles when it is attached to no word in the sentence, or may be attached to the wrong word. (The modifiers that dangle are participial, gerund, and infinitive phrases, and elliptical clauses.) This fault may be remedied either by supplying the noun or pronoun that the construction logically modifies, or by changing the dangling construction to a complete clause. **Dangling modifiers**

1. Dangling modifiers at the beginning of the sentence. Almost always these constructions should modify the subject of the main clause.

(*a*) **Dangling participial phrases** — **Dangling participial phrases**

Dangling: Having come of age, I took my son into partnership with me.

Improved: When my son came of age, I took him into partnership; [or] Having come of age, my son entered into partnership with me.

Dangling: There we landed, and having eaten our lunch, the boat departed.

Improved: There we landed, and after we had eaten our lunch, the boat departed; [or] There we landed, and having eaten our lunch, we saw the boat depart.

Dangling: Coming around the curve, the house was seen.

Improved: As we came around the curve, we saw the house; [or] Coming around the curve, we saw the house.

(*b*) **Dangling gerund phrases** — **Dangling gerund phrases**

Dangling: In talking to Smith the other day, he told me about the race.

Improved: As I was talking to Smith the other day, he told me about the race; [or] In talking to Smith the other day, I learned about the race.

Dangling: After pointing out my errors, I was dismissed.
Improved: When he had pointed out my errors, I was dismissed; [or] After pointing out my errors, he dismissed me.

Dangling: After flunking three times, the professor reproved me.
Improved: When I had flunked three times, the professor reproved me; [or] After flunking three times, I was reproved by the professor.

Dangling: After singing hymn 523, Mr. Barnes will lead in prayer.
Improved: After we have sung hymn 523, Mr. Barnes will lead in prayer; [or] After singing hymn 523, we shall be led in prayer by Mr. Barnes.

Dangling infinitive phrases

(*c*) **Dangling infinitive phrases** —

Dangling: To enjoy a walking trip, the feet should be in good condition.
Improved: To enjoy a walking trip, take care that your feet are in good condition.

Dangling: To appreciate pictures, they should be studied.
Improved: To appreciate pictures, study them; [or] If pictures are to be appreciated, they should be studied.

Dangling elliptical clauses

(*d*) **Dangling elliptical clauses.** (An elliptical clause is a clause from which the subject and predicate are omitted; e.g., *while going* for *while I was going*, *when a boy* for *when he was a boy*.)

Dangling: When six years old, my grandfather died.
Improved: When I was six years old, my grandfather died.

Dangling: While visiting in my home town, the city hall burned down.
Improved: While I was visiting in my home town, the city hall burned down.

Elliptical clauses in titles

Note. — Avoid dangling elliptical clauses in titles. The construction is frequently awkward.

Awkward: *An Accident while Hunting*
Improved: *An Accident in a Bear Hunt*

Awkward: *Things Learned while Canvassing*
Improved: *Things Learned by a Canvasser*

2. Dangling modifiers at the end of the sentence. The most common of these dangling constructions is the participial phrase of result beginning with *thus* or *thereby*.

Participial phrases of result (*thus* or *thereby*)

Bad: He was well acquainted with the best literature, thus helping him to become an able critic.
Improved: He was well acquainted with the best literature; this helped him to become an able critic; [or] so that he was helped.

Bad: He has to stand still until the rod man comes up, thus giving him no chance to move about and keep warm.
Improved: He has to stand still until the rod man comes up; thus he has no chance to move about and keep warm; [or] so that he has no chance.

Bad: The little ship was very light, causing it to ride the waves easily.
Improved: The little ship was very light; thus it rode the waves easily; [or] so that it rode the waves easily.

79. An exception to Rule 78 may be made in the case of participial, gerund, or infinitive constructions which designate general action, not the action of any specific doer or receiver of the action. Regarding this matter Fowler says, ". . . there is a continual change going on by which certain participles or adjectives acquire the character of prepositions or adverbs, no longer needing the prop of a noun to cling to . . . The difficulty is to know when this development is complete." The following participles are frequently used in an unobjectionable dangling construction: *speaking*, *allowing*, *coming*, *counting*, *failing*, *granting*, *talking*, *using*, *supposing*, *assuming*, *considering*, *taking*, *leaving*, *turning*, etc.

Allowable dangling modifiers

Right: Generally speaking, he is a careful workman.
Right: Taking everything into consideration, the decision was a fair one.
Right: In swimming, the head should not be lifted too high.

Exercise

Dangling participles

Correct all dangling constructions. For sentences 28–33, consult Appendix A regarding *due to*, etc.

1. Besides earning enough spending money for my first year in college, my summer's work taught me responsibility.
2. I believe that by employing younger teachers it would improve the standards of teaching in our schools.
3. While carrying on a conversation, people listen attentively, for he always has something important to say.
4. After draining the oil from the car, the oil pan is loosened from the block. When loosening the bolts, they should be loosened at opposite angles from each other.
5. Now at the age of twelve my wish had been fulfilled.
6. Being very hot in the day coach, his coat was folded over his arm.
7. After spending the night in camp, the automobiles took them on to the next town.
8. Gradually I became accustomed to walking on the ties. It was fortunate that I did, considering what occurred in the next few minutes.
9. Walking carefully across the trestle, high above the rest of the world, thrills chased up and down my back.
10. Stopping suddenly and turning toward me, I heard George shout, "It's a train whistle!"
11. Coming around the curve at the end of the bridge toward which we were walking, I heard a faint whistle.
12. Granting his willingness to work, he has, however, refused three jobs in the last week.
13. Generally speaking, minors are not allowed in the Casino.
14. Not wishing to be caught with the treasure on board when he landed in New York, the little ship put in at an isolated port.
15. Keeping our plans to ourselves, it was not until our adventure was all over that the other gang heard of it.
16. She scrubbed the pan with steel wool, thus causing it to leak.
17. When firmly set, you remove the soufflé from the oven.

18. To meet the entrance requirements, it is necessary to have four years of Latin.
19. At the age of fifteen, my uncle took me to Europe.
20. To be blended properly, the barrels should be sealed a year.
21. She cleaned her clothes in gasoline, thereby causing an explosion.
22. Considering the condition of the roads, it is a wonder that we reached home that night.
23. Before pouring the juice into the bottles, they should be placed in hot water.
24. According to all I hear, she is a very attractive person.
25. There are many ways of selecting pictures, considering price, color, design, and size.
26. When on parade, a uniform is generally worn, but is not necessary for learning drum majoring.
27. After tramping over fields through brush and brier, a piece of steaming hot rabbit pie is a dish to revive you.
28. Owing to his father's illness, it was necessary for him to take his father's place at the mill.
29. He had left due to a telegram from his father.
30. He could not stay due to the lateness of the hour.
31. Due to your foresight, we had plenty of food.
32. Our train was late due to a wreck on the track.
33. We cannot come owing to the heavy floods.

ORDER OF MEMBERS

Position of modifiers: general rule

80. Every modifier should be so placed that the reader connects it immediately with the member it modifies, and not with some other member. A phrase or a clause that modifies the main clause may very often be placed with advantage at the beginning of the sentence.

Bad: The storm broke just as we reached the shore with great violence.

Improved: Just as we reached the shore, the storm broke with great violence.

Bad: The ball is thrown home by a player stationed in the middle of the square called the pitcher.

Improved: The ball is thrown home by a player called the pitcher, who is stationed in the middle of the square.

Ambiguous: He closely associated himself with the church, every day becoming more and more useful in the community.

Clear: He closely associated himself with the church, which every day became more and more useful in the community; [or] Closely associating himself with the church, he every day became more and more useful in the community.

Position of the adverbs *only*, *almost*, etc.

81. As a rule, place the adverbs *only*, *merely*, *just*, *almost*, *ever*, *hardly*, *scarcely*, *quite*, *nearly*, next to the words they modify, not elsewhere. If they are to modify only a part of the predicate, place them before that part.

Colloquial: I only want three.
Better: I want only three; [or] I want three only.

Colloquial: Do you ever expect to go again?
Better: Do you expect ever to go again?

Colloquial: It is the handsomest vase I almost ever saw.
Better: It is almost the handsomest vase I ever saw.

Colloquial: I never remember having met him.
Better: I do not remember ever having met him. [*never* = *not ever*.]

Colloquial: I nearly ate the whole dozen.
Better: I ate nearly the whole dozen.

Misplaced clauses

82. A modifying clause should not be so placed that a verb following it may, in reading, be erroneously joined with the verb of the clause instead of with the verb preceding the clause. Observe that in some instances the difficulty is remedied by placing the time modifier first.

Ill arranged: I walked out into the night as the moon rose and wandered through the grounds.

Clear: As the moon rose, I walked out into the night and wandered through the grounds.

Ill arranged: He sprang to the platform on which the dead man lay and shouted.

Clear: Springing to the platform on which the dead man lay, he shouted.

83. As a rule, arrange a sentence containing a relative clause so that the clause immediately follows its antecedent. Position of relative clauses

Awkward: I had many pleasant experiences while I was there, some of which I shall always remember.

Better: While I was there, I had many pleasant experiences, some of which I shall always remember.

Awkward: The correspondence began just one month later which led to the surrender.

Better: The correspondence which led to the surrender began just one month later.

Note. — If a sentence containing a relative clause cannot be arranged according to the foregoing rule, use two separate sentences or two coördinate clauses.

Bad: The police are looking today for the persons last in company with Clara Belinfant, the daughter of Abraham Belinfant, a rich New York merchant, who has been missing since July 18.

Better: The police are looking today for the persons last seen in company with Clara Belinfant, the daughter of Abraham Belinfant, a rich New York merchant. The girl has been missing since July 18.

84. Do not place between two members of a sentence a modifier applicable to either member. Do not trust to punctuation to show the application of the modifier; recast the sentence. Squinting modifiers

Defective: The person who steals in nine cases out of ten is driven to do so by want.

Improved: In nine cases out of ten, the person who steals is driven to do so by want.

Defective: Since a canoe cannot stand hard knocks when not in use it should be kept out of the water.

Improved: Since a canoe cannot stand hard knocks, it should be kept out of the water when not in use.

Defective: The jury which has been investigating the death of the girl today brought in a verdict of suicide.

Improved: The jury which has been investigating the death of the girl brought in today a verdict of suicide.

Separation of coördinate modifiers

85. Two phrases or clauses modifying the same sentence-element and of parallel form and function should not be placed one before and one after that element; they should be put together.

Awkward: When he has once made up his mind, you may be sure he will never draw back when he has got fully started.

Improved: When he has once made up his mind and got fully started, you may be sure he will never draw back.

Split constructions

86. Avoid awkward split constructions. Prefer the split construction, however, to an ambiguous or artificial substitution.

Split infinitive

a. **Split infinitive.**

Awkward: I went there in order to personally inspect it.
Improved: I went there in order to inspect it personally.

Awkward: It is impossible to in any way remove them.
Improved: It is impossible in any way to remove them.
Improved: It is impossible to remove them in any way.

Acceptable: We expect in the coming year to more than double our holdings.

Acceptable: Every effort must be made to stanchly defend the party principles.

The passive or the perfect infinitive with an adverb inserted cannot be considered a split infinitive.

Passive infinitives: I wish to be clearly understood.
Perfect infinitive: She seems to have just heard the news.

Split comparison

b. **Split comparison.**

Awkward: He is as tall as, if not taller than, you.
Improved: He is as tall as you, if not taller.

Split prepositional phrase

c. **Split prepositional phrase.**

Awkward: He submitted to, though he did not fully approve of, the rules.

Better: He submitted to the rules, though he did not fully approve of them.

NOTE. — Such a construction may be used, for the sake of brevity, in statutes, contracts, and the like, in which smoothness of style is of little consequence.

> The Congress shall have power to dispose of, and make all needful rules and regulations respecting, the territory . . . belonging to the United States.
> — *The Federal Constitution.*

Except in such a context, the harshness of the construction more than offsets the gain in compactness.

d. **Split subject and predicate.**

Split subject and predicate

Awkward: He, instead of acting as my guide, followed me. [False emphasis on *he*.]
Improved: Instead of acting as my guide, he followed me.

Awkward: Fishing was not good, and they, becoming impatient, decided to quit. [False emphasis on *they*.]
Improved: Fishing was not good, and becoming impatient they decided to quit.

EXERCISE

When necessary, change the order in these sentences.

Order of numbers

1. To adequately develop the subject of war, one would probably have to write a book.
2. We just had finished when he came in.
3. I never remember such a hot summer.
4. Coming through the woods we nearly were lost.
5. I hardly can understand what she says.
6. Do you ever suppose we shall hear from them again?
7. It was the worst swearing I almost ever heard.
8. I don't think that I can go this evening.
9. I stood at sunset when a strong wind was beginning to blow on the top of a bluff looking down at the harbor.
10. The idea of our Ruby Secret Society had grown out of a book as most of my ideas did in which the ruby seal meant lips sealed to all secrets.
11. Although she at first improved slowly she became weaker.
12. I, seized with a sudden longing for ice cream, snatched my purse and ran for the counter.
13. I settled back on the uncomfortable bench, vacated

kindly and hurriedly by the old gentleman, for a long wait.

14. You have only been in bed about fifteen minutes.
15. The present studies in animal husbandry, initiated by John E. Lathrop and completed since Professor Lathrop's death by his associates, are of the second type.
16. Through an error a baby boy was born on Wednesday to Mr. and Mrs. Thomas Browne of 76 Locust Street instead of to Mr. and Mrs. T. W. Brown of East Washington Avenue.
17. I dislike to continually use the first person.
18. Rawdon Crawley is best remembered for the great scene in which he strikes down the profligate Lord Steyne in defense of his honor.
19. I should like to die there when the time for me to go, comes.
20. A terrible wind and thunder storm visited the Fourth Regiment camp Thursday night, shortly after taps were sounded, playing havoc on all sides.

LOGICAL AGREEMENT OF SENTENCE-MEMBERS

Logical agreement of sentence-members

87. Every sentence-element should be in logical accord with the rest of the sentence. (See Rules 91 and 93; also *Subject*, *Cause*, and *Reason* in Appendixes.)

Illogical: Of these names sixteen were chosen to be members. [*Sixteen* (*names*) does not agree logically with *were chosen to be members.*]

Improved: Of the persons named, sixteen were chosen to be members.

Illogical: The life of a hod carrier is sometimes happier than a prince. [*The life* does not agree logically with *is happier than a prince.*]

Improved: The life of a hod carrier is sometimes happier than that of a prince.

Illogical: He hated to submit to the rules — *viz.*, church attendance and not smoking. [Church attendance and abstinence from tobacco are not rules.]

Improved: He hated to submit to the rules — namely, those requiring attendance at church and abstinence from smoking.

Illogical: A fireman seldom rises above an engineer. Logical agreement

Improved: A fireman seldom rises above the position of engineer.

Illogical: The comedy *Love's Labour's Lost*, written by Shakespeare, is supposed to have occurred in Navarre.

Improved: The events related in Shakespeare's comedy *Love's Labour's Lost* are supposed to have occurred in Navarre.

Illogical: Nothing looks more untidy than to see an expensive motor coming out of the garage covered with mud.

Improved: Nothing looks more untidy than an expensive motor covered with mud coming out of the garage.

Illogical: As a question of economy, it is advantageous to use water power.

Improved: For the sake of economy, it is advantageous to use water power.

Illogical: He had to choose between signing away his inheritance or being hanged.

Improved: He had to choose between signing away his inheritance and being hanged.

Illogical: There is no place to hang it only in the hall.

Improved: There is no place to hang it except in the hall; [or] The hall is the only place in which to hang it.

Illogical: I sat on the opposite side from which Charlie was sitting.

Improved: I sat opposite Charlie; [or] I sat on the side opposite to the one on which Charlie was sitting.

Illogical: Coffee seeds are selected from the coffee plants with desirable characteristics, are then planted in a nursery or in a field where the mature plants are to grow, and come into bearing in their second or third year. [Last predicate not consistent with subject.]

Improved: Coffee seeds are selected from the coffee plants with desirable characteristics, and are then planted in a nursery or in a field where the mature plants are to grow. The plants come into bearing in their second or third year.

88. Do not leave a subordinate clause logically unattached to its sentence. Unattached clauses

Illogical: The resonator responds in a manner analogous to that *which* one tuning fork responds to another.
Improved: The resonator responds in a manner analogous to that *in which* one tuning fork responds to another.

Illogical: There were some people whom I could not tell whether they were English or American. [*Whom* has no construction.]
Improved: There were some people whom I could not distinguish as English or American.

Sentences or sentence-elements left uncompleted

89. Do not leave a grammatical construction unfinished.

Illogical: The fact that I had never before studied at home, I was at a loss what to do with vacant periods. [The noun *fact* with its appositive modifier *that . . . home* is left without any construction.]
Improved: The fact that I had never before studied at home made me feel at a loss as to what to do with vacant periods.

Illogical: The story tells how a young German, who, having settled in Dakota, returns to Wisconsin and there marries an old schoolmate. [The clause beginning *how a young German* is left unfinished; *German* (modified by the clause *who . . . schoolmate*) has no construction.]
Improved: The story tells how a young German, having settled in Dakota, returns to Wisconsin and marries an old schoolmate.

Illogical: Any man who could accomplish that task, the whole world would think he was a hero. [*Man*, with its modifier *who . . . task*, is left without any construction.]
Improved: Any man who could accomplish that task the whole world would regard as a hero.

Illogical: That's all I want, is a chance to test it thoroughly. [*Is* has no subject.]
Improved: That's all I want — a chance to test it thoroughly [see Rule 278]; [or] All I want is a chance to test it thoroughly.

90. Do not add to a relative clause a predicate that cannot be a part of that clause nor one that is not clearly an additional predicate of the main clause. As a test of the coherence of this kind of predicate, see whether it can be placed immediately after the subject of the relative clause, or immediately after the subject of the main clause. Violations of this rule may be corrected by (*a*) making the predicate following the relative clause into another predicate of the relative clause, (*b*) changing the relative clause into an independent assertion, (*c*) omitting the *and*, *but*, or *or*, and changing the predicate following the relative clause into a subordinate element, or (*d*) making the predicate following the relative clause into another relative clause by itself. Unrelated predicate

Illogical: In this river are some large fish which the people regard as sacred and allow no one to catch them. [Test: *which the people allow no one to catch them;* [or] *in this river are some large fish allow no one to catch them.*]

Improved: (*a*) In this river are some large fish, which the people regard as sacred and allow no one to catch; [or] (*b*) In this river are some large fish. The people regard these as sacred, and allow no one to catch them.

Illogical: It is subjected to severe strains, which it must withstand and at the same time work easily and rapidly. [Test: *which it must work easily and rapidly;* [or] *it is subjected to severe strains at the same time work easily and rapidly.*]

Improved: (*b*) It is subjected to severe strains; it must withstand these, and at the same time must work easily and rapidly; [or] (*c*) It is subjected to severe strains, which it must withstand, at the same time working easily and rapidly.

Possible: Next day I went to Cleveland where I stayed for a week and then returned home. [Test: *where I then returned home;* [or] . . . *I went to Cleveland and then returned home.*]

Preferred: (*b*) Next day I went to Cleveland. There I stayed a week, and then returned home.

Possible: I met many people there whom I had seen before but did not know their names. [Test: *whom I did not know their names;* [or] *I met many people there but did not know their names.*]

Preferred: (*d*) I met many people there whom I have seen before but whose names I did not know.

Sentence as subject or predicate complement

91. Do not use a sentence (except a quoted sentence) as the subject of *is* or *was*.

Illogical: I was detained by business is the reason I am late.

Improved: I was detained by business; that is the reason I am late.

A similar fault is the use of a sentence (except a quoted sentence) as a predicate substantive after *is* or *was*. This fault may be corrected by changing the substantive clause.

Illogical: The difference between them is De Quincey is humorous and Macaulay is grave.

Improved: The difference between them is that De Quincey is humorous and Macaulay is grave.

Quotation coherent part of a sentence

92. When a part of a quoted sentence is incorporated into another sentence, it must be a coherent part of that sentence.

Illogical: Jane Austen pictures Elizabeth Bennet as intelligent, frank, independent, impulsive, and "more quickness of observation and less pliancy of temper than her sister."

Improved: Jane Austen pictures Elizabeth Bennet as intelligent, frank, independent, impulsive, with "more quickness of observation and less pliancy of temper than her sister."

When or *where* clause for predicate noun

93. Do not use a *when* or *where* clause in place of a predicate noun; use a noun with modifiers. This error is likely to occur in definitions. (See also Rule 87.) A definition should state the class to which an object belongs and should enumerate traits that distinguish it from other members of its class.

Illogical: Cribbing is where you copy somebody's answer in an examination.

Improved: One form of cribbing is copying somebody's answer in an examination.

Illogical: Intoxication is when the brain is affected by the action of certain drugs.

Improved: Intoxication is a state of the brain, caused by the action of certain drugs.

Exercise

Define each of the following in one sentence. **Definitions**

Baseball and football terms: *strike, ball, base on balls, hit, run, goal, kickoff, forward pass, referee.*

Political terms: *boss, machine, rotten borough, dark horse.*

94. Avoid the use of a *because* clause as a noun clause. It is correctly used as an adverbial clause. (See *Cause* and *Reason* in Appendix A.) *Because* clause as a noun clause

Undesirable: The reason why I failed was because I had not studied my lesson.

Improved: The reason why I failed was that I had not studied my lesson.

Undesirable: Because I did not write to her was no reason for her being angry with me.

Improved: The fact that I did not write to her was no reason for her being angry with me; [or] Because I did not write to her, she had no reason for being angry with me.

Exercise

Correct any incoherencies in the following sentences: **Logical agreement of sentence-members**

1. She is one of those persons whom you never can be sure whether she likes you or not.
2. That's what I heard was the trouble.
3. The fact that I had won in the oratorical contest in high school, I had the courage to compete in the college contest.
4. He has a scholarship is the reason he is going to the state university.
5. The difficulty is you are too young.
6. Because I have driven a truck for two years is the reason I got the job.

Logical agreement

7. The chief cause for the higher price of wheat is due to the drought.
8. It is as important for the man to know the right kind of food that he should eat as the woman.
9. In this golf lesson the shoulders and hips can be explained together since they are similar.
10. Similar to the plight of other students, he was not a wealthy boy.
11. To satisfy the opinion of the public and of the press, many leaders are forced to act against their own principles.
12. The horse power that is advertised is the power that can actually be developed in proportion to the speed of the car. This means that the "99 horse power" car is the power that is developed in speed.
13. I think that undertaking is a very fine profession, and I hope sometime to become one.
14. The first time that I read a book by myself was when my mother was away for the winter.
15. It being Children's Day combined with very warm weather brought close to six thousand persons to see the fair.
16. At the end of this round he does not throw away his clubs or give up, but he thinks of the next time out how he will correct the mistakes he made this time.
17. The question whether alcohol is a food or not has not reached agreement by medical authorities.
18. The reason I locked the door was because there have been robberies in the neighborhood.
19. The first time that she came to see us was when I was six years old.
20. We were in Europe is the reason why I did not graduate with my class.

COMPARISONS

Logical comparisons

95. Compare only things that can logically be compared. Do not compare a part or quality of a thing with a whole thing.

Illogical: His tread is as stealthy as an Indian.
Improved: His tread is as stealthy as an Indian's; [or] as that of an Indian.

Illogical: The students in European universities seem much more mature than American universities.
Improved: The students in European universities seem much more mature than those in American universities.

96. Avoid ambiguities in comparisons. Supply words that will make the meaning clear. Ambiguities in comparisons

Ambiguous: I like Mary as much as Jane.
Clear: I like Mary as much as I like Jane.
Clear: I like Mary as much as Jane does.

Ambiguous: My home is nearer John's home than yours.
Clear: My home is nearer to John's home than yours is.
Clear: My home is nearer to John's home than it is to yours.

97. When comparing a thing to other members of its own class, exclude from the group the thing compared by adding *other* or *else* or an equivalent word. Do not compare the thing with itself. *Other* or *else* in a *than* or *as* clause

Illogical: Lead is heavier than any metal.
Logical: Lead is heavier than any other metal.
Logical: Lead is heavier than iron.

Illogical: Shakespeare is greater than any English poet.
Logical: Shakespeare is greater than any other English poet.

98. When comparing a thing to the members of a class to which it does not belong, do not exclude the thing from that class. That is, do not restrict the standard of comparison by *other* or *else* or an equivalent word. Illogical use of *other* or *else* in *than* or *as* clause

Illogical: That little word *home* means more to me than any other word of twice its length.
Logical: That little word *home* means more to me than any word of twice its length.

Note the following logical comparisons:

New York is larger than Chicago.
New York is larger than any other city in the United States.

New York is larger than any city in Europe.
New York is the largest of all the cities in the United States. (See 99 *c*.)

The *of* phrase limiting a superlative

99. In the *of* phrase limiting an adjective or an adverb in the superlative degree —

a. **The object of *of* should be a plural noun or a collective noun, not a noun designating an individual person or thing.**

Illogical: He is the tallest of any man in the regiment.
Logical: He is the tallest of all the men in the regiment; [or] He is the tallest man of the regiment.
Logical: He is taller than any other man in the regiment.

b. **The object of *of* should designate a class to which the subject of comparison belongs, not a class to which it does not belong.**

Illogical: The Germans make the most beautiful toys of all countries.
Improved: Of all nationalities, the Germans make the most beautiful toys.

c. **The object of *of* should not be restricted by *other* or *else* or any equivalent word.**

Illogical: Shakespeare is the greatest of all other English poets.
Logical: Shakespeare is the greatest of all English poets.

Than and *as* clauses in double comparison

100. When *than* and *as* are used in a double comparison, name the second person or thing in the comparison after the first occurrence of the adjective.

Illogical: Fostoria is as large, if not larger, than Delaware.
Logical: Fostoria is as large as Delaware, if not larger.
Illogical: He is bigger and fully as strong as Buck.
Logical: He is bigger than Buck and fully as strong.

Place of noun with *one of the . . . if not the*

101. When a superlative is used in the expression *one of the . . . if not the*, place the noun modified by the superlative immediately after the first occurrence of the adjective.

Illogical: One of the greatest, if not the greatest, generals of America.

Logical: One of the greatest generals of America, if not the greatest.

102. In making comparisons, do not leave the standard of comparison unindicated or only vaguely implied; let the standard be definitely stated or implied. Omission of standard of comparison

Incomplete: Manufacturers have come to see the greater economy of the electric motor.

Complete: Manufacturers have come to see the greater economy of the electric motor as compared to steam power.

EXERCISE

Make the following comparisons logical. Illogical comparisons

1. I think that Florence is the most fascinating of all other cities in the world.
2. John Reed was one of the greatest, if not the greatest, football players on the All-American team.
3. This rug is longer and as wide as that one.
4. She was the most popular of any of the girls in our class.
5. People are learning to appreciate modern art more.
6. The wool in my blanket is a better quality than hers.
7. Our little city has more amusements for its young people than any other city twice its size.
8. John is taller than any boy in school.
9. He is the youngest of any man in the Senate.
10. She is more of a student, but she is good company.
11. Is Chicago nearer New Orleans than New York?
12. The footprints in the dusty road were as broad as a bear.
13. His shoulders are as strong as an ox.
14. His parents are beginning to have a greater influence in his life.
15. Our team is as heavy if not heavier than theirs.

ILLOGICAL OMISSIONS

103. Avoid the incorrect use of words in a double capacity. A word or a combination of words may be correctly used in a double capacity if it is fitted for both the offices it serves. For example, in the sen- Words used in a double capacity tence, *I can do it as well as you*, *can do it* serves as the predicate of both *I* and *you*, and does so correctly, since it agrees grammatically with both pronouns. But there are various ways of using words in a double capacity that are incorrect; these are indicated in the following rules:

Auxiliaries and copulas in a double capacity

a. **Avoid the use of an auxiliary or a copula in a double capacity if the same form is not grammatically proper in both parts of the sentence; write the proper form with each part.**

Bad: The fire was built and the potatoes baked.
Improved: The fire was built and the potatoes were baked.
Bad: He was a patriot, but all the rest traitors.
Improved: He was a patriot, but all the rest were traitors.

NOTE. — The omission of an auxiliary is likely in most cases to produce an awkward sentence, even when there is no violation of the foregoing principle. As a rule, it is better to repeat the auxiliary.

Awkward: Light was seen through the opening, and the voice of my rescuer heard.
Better: Light was seen through the opening, and the voice of my rescuer was heard.

Be as both principal and auxiliary

b. **Do not make a single form of the verb *be* serve both as a principal and as an auxiliary verb.**

Bad: At first the drill was interesting and liked by most of the men.
Better: At first the drill was interesting and was liked by most of the men.

Principal verbs in a double capacity

c. **Avoid the use of a principal verb in a double capacity if the same form is not grammatically proper in both parts of the sentence; write the proper form for each part.**

Bad: He did what many others have and are doing.
Better: He did what many others have done and are doing.

Bad: We ate such a dinner as only laborers can.
Better: We ate such a dinner as only laborers can eat.

Other modifiers in a double capacity

d. **Two sentence-elements should not be limited by a single modifying phrase or clause unless that modifier is idiomatically adapted to both.** (See Rule 12 *c*.)

To (in *as to*, *in regard to*, etc.) used in a double capacity

e. **When *as to*, *in regard to*, or *in respect to* is used as a single preposition to govern a clause, the *to* should not be made to govern a substantive within the clause.**

Illogical: A dispute arose *as to* [= *concerning*] whom the honor should belong.
Improved (awkward): A dispute arose *as to* [= *concerning*] whom the honor should belong to.
Preferable: A dispute arose *as to* [= *concerning*] who should receive the honor. (See Rule 203 *b*.)

Omission of *that*

104. Do not omit the subordinating conjunction *that* when it is needed to make the meaning clear. *That* is often necessary in order to bind together elements of the subordinate clause which it introduces, especially when there is a possibility that the subject of the *that* clause might be mistaken for the object of the verb of the principal clause. It is also needed when the *that* clause stands first in the sentence.

Clear: I thought they would like each other.
Slightly misleading: I forgot the old man had been left alone.
Immediately clear: I forgot that the old man had been left alone.
Slightly misleading: Silas Marner was brought back to church interests because he felt to do the right thing by Eppie he must have her christened.
Immediately clear: Silas Marner was brought back to church interests because he felt that to do the right thing by Eppie he must have her christened.
Clear: That he is coming tomorrow seems incredible.

NOTE. — For the faulty omission of *that* after *so*, see Appendix A.

Omission of completing clauses

105. Avoid, except in light conversation, the use of *so*, *such*, *that*, *those*, etc. without completing clauses. *So* and *such* suggest that they should be followed by result clauses. The writer probably means *very* when he uses *so* or *such.*

Incomplete: I am so tired.
Complete: I am so tired that I cannot go.
Complete: I am very tired.

Incomplete: She is such a kind person.
Complete: She is such a kind person that we can count upon her help.
Complete: She is a very kind person.

Incomplete: She has that pink and white complexion.
Complete: She has that pink and white complexion that one associates with English women.
Complete: She has a pink and white complexion.

Omission of articles and possessives

106. As a rule, repeat an article or a possessive adjective before each noun in a series, unless all the nouns designate the same thing, or unless they are unmistakably different individuals or things.

Illogical: She watched her grandmother, aunt, and mother sewing.
Preferred: She watched her grandmother, her aunt, and her mother sewing.

Illogical: I asked what were the names of her puppies and kitten.
Preferred: I asked what were the names of her puppies and her kitten.

Right: For that summer I was day clerk, night clerk, bellboy, and porter, all in one.

Right: The cup and saucer are mine.

Right: He is my friend and teacher. [One person.]

Right: My friend and my teacher are coming together. [Two persons.]

Omission of prepositions

107. Prepositions are often omitted in phrases indicating time, place, and manner. The omission may be idiomatic and therefore acceptable in the best usage, or it may be colloquial and to be avoided in formal writing.

Omission of prepositions

Time: The preposition is often omitted in phrases expressing time at which or duration of time.

Idiomatic: They are coming next Tuesday.
Idiomatic: They will stay two months.
Informal: The armistice was signed the eleventh of November.
More formal: The armistice was signed on the eleventh of November.

Place: The preposition is often omitted in phrases expressing destination.

Idiomatic: He is safe home at last. [Arrival at a place.]
Idiomatic: Home is the sailor, home from sea,
And the hunter home from the hill. — *Stevenson.*
Undesirable: He is home. [Location in a place.]
Correct: He is at home.

Undesirable: He is living some place in Arizona.
Correct: He is living somewhere in Arizona.
Correct: He is living in some place in Arizona. [See Appendix A.]

Undesirable: You may sit any place you wish.
Correct: You may sit anywhere you wish.
Correct: You may sit in any place you wish.

Manner

Colloquial: Friendships made that way will never last.
Preferred: Friendships made in that way will never last.

Exercise

Illogical omissions

Fill in any omissions in the following sentences.

1. She spends a fortune on clothes as the women of her class always have, and are still.
2. She was very young and pushed beyond her strength.
3. The water was so calm.
4. He has been home two years now.
5. He is that gentle, inoffensive kind of person.
6. If you knew what I know, you would hurry as fast as I am.

7. My dress is pressed and the dishes washed.
8. I found it some place in England.
9. You cannot answer him that way.
10. I saw John was not listening.
11. We can give you no information with regard to the person you refer.
12. He was a liberal, but all the rest reactionary.
13. Here is the book you asked for.
14. That child is such a nuisance.
15. They swam and dived as only swimmers of long experience can.
16. For Friday and Saturday night "dates" and church Sunday, one needs several silk dresses.

PARALLELISM

Parallel thoughts in parallel form

108. Sentence-elements that are parallel in thought should, as a rule, be made parallel in form. *And, or, but* should join like elements; *i.e.*, if one is an infinitive, the other should be; if one is a relative clause, the other should be; if one is an appositive, the other should be; if one is a verb in the active voice, the other should be.

Bad: The crowd began to wave handkerchiefs and shouting good-byes. [*To wave* and *shouting*, both objects of *began*, are awkwardly dissimilar in form: *to wave* is an infinitive; *shouting* is a gerund.]

Improved: The crowd began to wave handkerchiefs and to shout good-byes. [The two objects are made parallel; both are infinitives.] [Or] The crowd began waving handkerchiefs and shouting good-byes. [The two objects are made parallel; both are gerunds.]

Bad: I delight in a good novel — one which portrays strong characters and in reading the book you are thrilled. [The two qualifiers of *one* are awkwardly dissimilar in form; the first (*which portrays strong characters*) is a relative clause, the second (*in reading the book you are thrilled*) a sentence.]

Improved: I delight in a good novel — one which portrays strong characters and which thrills the reader. [The two qualifiers are made parallel; both are relative clauses.]

Parallel thoughts in parallel form

Bad: Two courses are open to us: first, to have the missionary society transfer to us a missionary now in the field; second, one of our own members has volunteered to go, and we may send him. [The two appositives to *two courses* are awkwardly dissimilar in form; the first (*to have . . . field*) is an infinitive phrase, the second (*one of our own members . . . him*) a sentence.]

Improved: Two courses are open to us: first, to have the missionary society transfer to us a missionary now in the field; second, to send one of our own members, who has volunteered to go. [The two appositives are made parallel; both are infinitive phrases.] [Or] Two courses are open to us. First, we may have the missionary society transfer to us a missionary now in the field; second, we may send one of our own members, who has volunteered to go. The two appositives are made parallel; both are sentences.]

Bad: I have lived in many states, some for only a short time, while in others I have lived a year or more. [The two qualifiers of the main clause are awkwardly dissimilar in form; the first (*some for only a short time*) is an incomplete modifier of *lived*, the second (*while . . . more*) a complete subordinate clause.]

Improved: I have lived in many states — in some for only a short time, in others for a year or more. [The two qualifiers of the main clause are made parallel; both are prepositional phrases modifying *lived*.]

Bad: I was asked to contribute to the church, Christian Association, and to the athletic fund. [The three modifiers of *contribute* are awkwardly dissimilar in form; the first is a complete phrase, the second a noun with both the preposition and the article lacking, the third a complete phrase.]

Improved: I was asked to contribute to the church, to the Christian Association, and to the athletic fund. [The three modifiers of *contribute* are made parallel in form; each is a complete phrase.] [Or] I was asked to contribute to the church, the Christian Association, and the athletic fund. [*To* is made to govern three objects parallel in form, — each consisting of *the* and a noun.]

Bad: The gun barrel is then sent to be chambered and slots to be cut in. [The two modifiers of *is then sent* are awkwardly dissimilar in form; the first is an infinitive, and the second a predicate.]

Improved: The gun barrel is then sent to be chambered and to have slots cut in it. [The two modifiers of *is then sent* are made parallel; both are infinitives.]

And which

109. Avoid joining a relative clause to its principal clause by *and*, *but*, or *or*. Since these conjunctions are coördinating, they should connect elements grammatically coördinate. It is true that the *and which* construction can be found in the best writing. An author who is master of his material and his style may purposely use this construction to gain emphasis. The tyro, however, should be cautious in its use. His *and which* constructions are usually due to his lack of knowledge of the difference between main clauses and subordinate clauses. An undesirable *and which* construction can be corrected by (*a*) omitting the conjunction, (*b*) changing the relative clause to a principal clause, or (*c*) inserting a relative clause before the conjunction.

Undesirable: He came home with an increase in weight, but which hard work soon reduced.

Improved: He came home with an increase in weight, which, however, hard work soon reduced.

Improved: He came home with an increase in weight, but hard work soon reduced it.

Undesirable: On the way we met a Mr. Osborn from the neighborhood of Denver and who had the typical Western breeziness.

Improved: On the way we met a Mr. Osborn from the neighborhood of Denver, who had the typical Western breeziness.

Improved: On the way we met a Mr. Osborn, who came from the neighborhood of Denver, and who had the typical Western breeziness.

110. For the sake of clearness, coördinate sentence-members that are long or complex should be introduced in a similar or identical manner. Otherwise the reader may associate the wrong members.

Clearness of coördination: general principle

Obscure coördination: Then I learned how he had run away from his father, a gypsy vagabond who professed to be a horse trader and was in reality a thief, dressed in some clothes that he found on a scarecrow in a cornfield, learned the way to my home through the map in an old railway timetable, and come all the way on foot. [This sentence is well constructed; its defect is that the relation between the coördinate members is not shown by similar beginnings.]

Clear coördination: Then I learned *how* he had run away from his father, a gypsy vagabond who professed to be a horse trader and was in reality a thief; *how* he had dressed in some clothes that he found on a scarecrow in a cornfield; *how* he had learned the way to my home through the map in an old railway timetable, and had come all the way on foot.

The foregoing principle has many different applications. The four following are worthy of special mention:

111. A subordinating conjunction introducing several coördinate clauses should be repeated if the clauses are long and the coördination of those assertions would otherwise not be immediately clear. Repetition is especially important with clauses in indirect discourse introduced by *that.*

Repetition of subordinating conjunctions

Obscure coördination: The registrar told him that he could not have credit for his half year of German and he must be put on probation because of his poor grades in English.

Clear coördination: The registrar told him *that* he could not have credit for his half year of German and *that* he must be put on probation because of his poor grades in English.

Obscure coördination: When they saw the excellent structure which, though handicapped by the strike and the difficulty of getting materials, he had yet completed in less than the required time, and considered how valuable such a man would be to them, they gave him a permanent position.

Clear coördination: *When* they saw the excellent structure which, though handicapped by the strike and the difficulty of getting materials, he had yet completed in less than the required time, and *when* they considered how valuable such a man would be to them, they gave him a permanent position.

NOTE. — When the coördinate clauses are very short, repetition of the conjunction is usually not necessary; *e.g.:*

Right: He seems to be pretty well, though he takes no exercise and neglects his diet.

Repetition of auxiliary verbs

112. An auxiliary verb belonging with several verbs should be repeated if the coördination of these verbs would otherwise not be immediately clear. When other verbs intervene between the coördinate verbs, clearness usually demands repetition of the auxiliary.

Obscure coördination: The captain must be quick to see just what movement will get his company out of close quarters and give the order clearly.

Clear coördination: The captain *must be quick* to see just what movement will get his company out of close quarters and *must give* the order clearly.

NOTE. — When the verbs stand close together, repetition is usually unnecessary; *e.g.:*

Right: You must line up quickly and march downstairs.

Right: The sheep may stray and be lost.

Repetition of prepositions

113. A preposition governing several objects should be repeated if the construction of the objects would otherwise not be immediately clear. Repetition is usually desirable when the objects are separated by intervening modifiers. When the objects stand close together, repetition is usually unnecessary; *e.g.:*

Clear: He had lived in Cuba, Panama, and Barbadoes.

Clear: It was exposed to the wind, the rain, and the scorching sun.

Not immediately clear: The place is often visited by tourists who are fond of rugged scenery, and especially amateur photographers.

Clear: The place is often visited *by* tourists who are fond of rugged scenery, and especially *by* amateur photographers.

114. An infinitive-sign (*to*) introducing several coördinate infinitives should be repeated with each infinitive after the first, when the construction of those infinitives would otherwise not be immediately clear. Repetition of the infinitive-sign

Not immediately clear: Here nature has done her best to enchant those that can see and feel, and make them her lifelong worshipers.

Clear: Here nature has done her best *to enchant* those that can see and feel, and *to make* them her lifelong worshipers.

NOTE. — When the infinitives stand close together, repetition of the *to* is usually not necessary; *e.g.:*

Clear: Has he learned to dance, converse, and make himself agreeable?

115. Correlative conjunctions should be followed by coördinate sentence-elements; if a predicate follows the first, a predicate should follow the second; if a modifier the first, a modifier the second; and so on. Correlatives

Undesirable: They would neither speak to him nor would they look at him. [*Neither* is followed by an infinitive; *nor* by a subject and complete predicate.]

Improved: They would neither speak to him nor look at him. [The correlatives are each followed by infinitives completing *would.*]

Undesirable: He is not only discourteous to the students but also to the teacher. [*Not only* is followed by an adjective, *but also* by a phrase modifying the adjective.]

Improved: He is discourteous not only to the students but also to the teacher. [The correlatives are each followed by a phrase limiting *discourteous.*]

Illogical parallelism

116. Do not use the parallel form for sentence-elements that are not parallel in thought.

Bad: The story tells of the bravery and promotion of a private. [*Bravery* designates a quality, *promotion* designates an experience.]

Improved: The story tells of a private's bravery and of his promotion.

Bad: He tells in vivid language how dangerous to a vessel is the breaking loose of a cannon on wheels, and how a ship's gunner captured an escaped cannon. [The substantive clause *how dangerous to a vessel is the breaking loose of a cannon* designates a general truth; the substantive clause *how a ship's gunner captured an escaped cannon* designates a specific event.]

Improved: He tells in vivid language how a cannon on wheels broke from its fastenings on a ship (explaining the perils that attend such an accident), and how it was captured by a gunner.

Series form for dissimilar elements

117. Avoid the use of the formula *a*, *b*, and *c* for sentence-elements not coördinate. Violations of this rule may be corrected (1) by inserting *and* between *a* and *b*, (2) by conforming *c* to *a* and *b*, or (3) by taking *c* out of the series.

Bad: He was tall, slim, and wore a black coat. [Here *a* and *b* are adjectives, and *c* is a verb.]

Improved: (1) He was tall and slim, and wore a black coat; [or] (3) He was tall and slim, and he wore a black coat.

Bad: We denounce the act as cruel, barbarous, and sincerely regret that it occurred. [Here *a* and *b* are adjectives and *c* is a verb.]

Improved: (1) We denounce the act as cruel and barbarous, and sincerely regret that it occurred; [or] (3) We denounce the act as cruel and barbarous, and we sincerely regret that it occurred.

Bad: She is young, well-educated, and has an aggressive manner. [Here *a* and *b* are adjectives and *c* is a predicate.]

Improved: (2) She is young, well-educated, and aggressive.

Exercise

Give parallel structure to elements parallel in thought. **Parallel construction**

1. Mussolini intends to make use of the great store of natural resources, which are at the present time untouched, and thus benefiting Italy.
2. The Indians slashed each other until one had his head split open and blood squirting all over.
3. Rickenbacker appeared to be of middle age, stood as straight as an arrow, and his speech was very seldom, but usually carried some weight.
4. Many times that caged animal is thinking of wide rolling prairies, rabbit hunts, and just to be free.
5. All the boys rush to the lake for a dip, or outside for setting-up exercises and then washing at the row of faucets over the long sink in the washroom, and they are ready to march to the mess hall for breakfast.
6. During my leisure hours I played the piano, tennis, swam, and read.
7. We play hockey, participate in skiing, coast, and toboggan.
8. The really genuine girl will not look for wealth and social advantage in her friends, but the ideals and behavior of her friends.
9. I think this book should be in our library. It would change one's view toward Greenland and would be educational as well as a good story book.
10. What our actions are now, the tastes which we form now, determine the kind of men and women we shall be.
11. Now place the second half of the tire on the wheel, and pushing the two sides together at the top, thus causing the tire to drop into the groove of the wheel.
12. I can hardly decide whether the strongest emotions of my life were experienced the night my favorite girl quit me, or was I more shaken the day the horse kicked me on the head.
13. We not only followed his advice in business matters, but also he was our moral guide.
14. I developed an interest in automobiles through necessity rather than having pleasure in them.
15. In our new paper we will print the news, history, financial, business, social, and current events.

16. You can make your years in college enjoyable as well as producing good grades and learning a profession.
17. Beauty is found in everything the human eye can see, the ear can hear, and in imaginary thought. If a person wishes to enjoy beauty, he must learn to use his imagination and concentrate on art.
18. My people are hard-working, thrifty, and they are ambitious.
19. He drank two glasses of my grandmother's blackberry brandy and which is very powerful stuff.
20. He made a vast fortune in Nevada but which he soon lost on Wall Street.

UNNECESSARY SHIFTING

Shifting of subject

118. Avoid unnecessary shifting of subject. (See Rule 119.)

Bad: We passed over the road quickly and soon the camp was in sight.

Improved: We passed over the road quickly and soon saw the camp.

Bad: The wars in the Balkan states had renewed old rivalries between Austria and Russia and a general European conflict speedily resulted.

Improved: The wars in the Balkan states had renewed old rivalries between Austria and Russia and speedily resulted in a European conflict.

Shifting of voice

119. Avoid unnecessary shifting of voice. The change of voice almost always involves a change of subject. (See Rule 118.)

Bad: He had for years professed himself a democrat, and his belief in the sovereignty of the people was frequently proclaimed.

Improved: He had for years professed himself a democrat, and frequently proclaimed his belief in the sovereignty of the people.

Bad: I wrote my theme, translated my French, and in a few minutes my algebra problems were done.

Improved: I wrote my theme, translated my French, and in a few minutes did my algebra problems.

120. Avoid unnecessary shifting of mood. Shifting of mood

Bad: First stir in the flour and then you should add the butter and salt.

Improved: First you should stir in the flour and then you should add the butter and salt; [or] Stir in the flour first and then add the butter and salt.

121. Avoid unnecessary shifting of tense. (See Rules 177 and 220–223.) Shifting of tense

Bad: The creature opened the door and then comes clanging up the stairs.

Improved: The creature opened the door and then came clanging up the stairs; [or] The creature opens the door and then comes clanging up the stairs.

122. Avoid unnecessary shifting of the number of nouns and pronouns. (See Rule 201.) Shifting of number

Possible: Each one knew that their chances for escape were very slight.

Preferred: Each one knew that his chances for escape were very slight.

Possible: Nobody had yet received their orders.

Preferred: Nobody had yet received his orders.

123. Avoid unnecessary shifting of person. (See Rule 178.) Shifting of person

Bad: The more we walk, the more we go hill-climbing, the more powerful do the muscular engines of one's heels become.

Improved: The more we walk, the more we go hill-climbing, the more powerful do the muscular engines of our heels become.

Bad: One should spend the morning hours, not on trivial matters, but on work requiring mental effort, for your mind is freshest during those hours.

Improved: One should spend the morning hours, not on trivial matters, but on work requiring mental effort, for one's mind is freshest during those hours.

Exercise

Unneces-sary shifting of subject, voice, etc.

Correct shifts in subject, voice, mood, tense, number, and person in the following sentences:

1. The best moccasins are handmade, and if possible have an Indian make them for you.
2. David, even as a child, was a keen observer and precociously intelligent. He has many troubles and sorrows, especially during his childhood, but his high spirits and sound common sense always bring him through his difficulties.
3. Everyone likes to do business with him because he will always give them a square deal.
4. Our parents are our sponsors and benefactors, and often very real sacrifices have been made by them for us.
5. Everyone must wait their turn.
6. Many people fail to realize that the party in power is greatly influenced by the number of votes that are cast for them.
7. A person always seems to understand and to do a thing better if they like it and are interested in it.
8. An experienced skier will always examine a slide before using it because they know the dangers involved in skiing.
9. Before repeal, anyone fairly well acquainted with a saloonkeeper could buy liquor from him regardless of their age.
10. Many very satisfactory schedules have to be changed completely so that a physical education requirement could be met.
11. One can always count on her if you give her plenty of time.
12. First shrink your material; then you are ready to cut out your dress.

CONNECTIVES

Coherence gained by connectives

124. A sentence may often be made coherent by the insertion of the precise connectives that will indicate the relationship of its parts. (See Rule 52 *b* and *c* and Appendix D.)

Incoherent: The owners of these Colonial houses were ordinarily well-to-do men and they had enough money to live in a pleasant and generous manner, but they could not afford any extravagances, but they built substantially and they were obliged to build economically.

Improved: The owners of these Colonial houses were ordinarily well-to-do men, who had enough money to live in a pleasant and generous manner, but who could not afford any extravagances; consequently, although they built substantially, they were obliged to build economically.

125. A sentence may often be made coherent by the insertion of summarizing or recapitulating words. (See Appendix D.)

Coherence gained by summarizing words

Note the italicized summary words in the following sentences:

And to set forth the right standard, and to train according to it, and to help forward all students towards it according to their various capacities, *this* I conceive to be the business of a University. — NEWMAN.

Broad quadrangles, high halls and chambers, ornamented cloisters, stately walks, or umbrageous gardens, a throng of students, ample revenues, or a glorious history, *none of these things* were the portion of that old Catholic foundation; *nothing in short* which to the common eye sixty years ago would have given tokens of what it was to be. — NEWMAN.

126. A swift, staccato, journalistic style tends to dispense with connectives. This style, with its quick succession of clipped clauses, may be very expressive; it should not, however, be used by an inexperienced writer unless he is certain that the coherence of his ideas will be immediately clear to his reader, and that the staccato style is appropriate to his material and his purpose.

Omission of connectives

As an illustration of this journalistic style, note the following passage:

A special guard in red uniforms and 50 private detectives standing by every entrance were not enough last week for the opening of the Henry Clay Frick art collection on Manhattan's Fifth Avenue. Dynamic Miss Helen Clay Frick sent for the bomb squad from police headquarters and a special detail of a precinct captain, a sergeant, and twelve patrolmen. Only then were the doors opened and New York's bluest bloods admitted to a museum to which, in the will of its donor, "the entire public shall forever have access subject only to reasonable regulations."

Grandson of Distiller Abraham Overhold, Henry Clay Frick laid the foundation of his great fortune in Pittsburgh coke ovens. Shrewd little Andrew Carnegie bought an interest in Frick Coke Co., made Frick a Carnegie partner in 1889. The partners never liked each other. It was not until 1900 that they broke in what was to be one of the classic feuds of U. S. industry. When Partner Carnegie tried to force Partner Frick to sell out on his own terms, Partner Frick chased him down the office building corridor. Thereafter both men were more or less free to indulge their hobbies: Carnegie, the Great Philanthropist; Frick, the Art Collector. . . . — *Time*.

OMISSION OF UNNECESSARY WORDS

Omission of unnecessary words

127. A sentence may be made coherent by the omission of unnecessary words. (See Rules 23–26.)

Bad: About my grandfather, there are several stories that I should like to relate concerning him.

Improved: There are several stories that I should like to relate concerning my grandfather; [or] I should like to relate several stories concerning my grandfather.

Bad: There were many of us left before the meeting was over.

Improved: Many of us left before the meeting was over.

EMPHASIS

General principle

128. Various devices may be used to impress a certain part of the sentence idea upon the reader's mind. But emphasis must not be gained at the expense of coherence.

129. Emphasis may be gained by placing the important words in the important positions in a sentence: either at the first of the sentence or at the last, especially the last. Important words in important positions

Weak: Then he would return to work, whistling a merry tune all the while.

Better: Then he would return to work, all the while whistling a merry tune.

Weak: He said nothing, but kept looking at my neck for some reason or other.

Better: He said nothing, but for some reason or other kept looking at my neck.

NOTE. — Sentences ending with prepositions are by no means incorrect; such sentences are frequently found in good literature. The question is not one of correctness, but of effectiveness. A sentence with a preposition at the end is often far more emphatic than the stilted sentence with the preposition buried within it. When the preposition is at the end, the stress does not fall upon the preposition but upon the word preceding. Sentence ending with a preposition

Emphatic: There is the girl that I am in love with.

Stilted: There is the girl with whom I am in love.

Emphatic: I refuse to be made a fool of.

130. Transforming a loose sentence into a periodic sentence — one in which the main clause is not completed until the end — is an effective means of securing emphasis. A periodic sentence is not always to be preferred to a loose sentence. By far the larger number of sentences in English are loose. Periodic sentences

Loose: We were drenched to the skin in spite of our rubber coats before we had gone a hundred yards through the wet grass and underbrush that covered the hillside.

Loose but satisfactory: Before we had gone a hundred yards through the wet grass and underbrush that covered the hillside, we were drenched to the skin in spite of our rubber coats.

Periodic: Before we had gone a hundred yards through the wet grass and underbrush that covered the hillside, we were, in spite of our rubber coats, drenched to the skin.

Climactic order

131. A series of words noticeably varying in strength should be placed in climactic order, unless the writer intends to make an anticlimax for the sake of humor.

Weak: I think that the characters are well drawn, that the diction is stately and beautiful, and that the plot is very interesting.

Improved: I think that the plot is very interesting, that the characters are well drawn, and that the diction is stately and beautiful.

Weak: He proved himself to be mercilessly cruel at times, unforgiving, and discourteous.

Improved: He proved himself to be discourteous, unforgiving, and at times mercilessly cruel.

Transitional words, parenthetic expressions within the sentence

132. If possible place transitional words, parenthetic expressions, etc. within the sentence, preferably near the beginning so that their effect is soon felt.

Less emphatic: His master was always very kind to him. However, his master's wife was altogether too parsimonious.

Better: His master was always very kind to him. His master's wife, however, was altogether too parsimonious.

Less emphatic: The study of birds is fascinating. It requires a great deal of patience, however.

Better: The study of birds is fascinating. It requires, however, a great deal of patience.

Less emphatic: There is another use for this machine, I think.

Better: There is, I think, another use for this machine.

Less emphatic: If you still hesitate after all that has been said, I despair of persuading you.

Better: If, after all that has been said, you still hesitate, I despair of persuading you.

Transposition

133. Emphasis may be gained by putting words out of their usual order, which in English is subject, predicate, object.

Emphatic: Greater love hath no man than this, that a man lay down his life for his friends.

Emphatic: Understand her you cannot.

NOTE. — Transposition should be used sparingly in prose. Because it is a violation of the usual English order, its frequent use gives the effect of artificiality.

134. Do not put a logically principal statement in a subordinate clause and the logically subordinate statement in the principal clause unless there is some good reason for such inversion. Upside-down subordination

Bad: I was walking down State Street yesterday when I came upon a crowd of people gathered about a horse that had fallen down.

Improved: As I was walking down State Street yesterday I came upon a crowd of people, etc.

Bad: The thoughts of the engineer turned toward the home he was approaching when suddenly he saw the glare of fire on the track ahead.

Improved: The thoughts of the engineer turned toward the home he was approaching. Suddenly he saw the glare of fire on the track ahead.

Bad: Having finished their work, they began to talk about former good times when one of the fellows suggested that they hound Nicholson.

Improved: Having finished their work, they began to talk about former good times. Presently one of the fellows suggested that they hound Nicholson.

135. Emphasis may be gained by using the balanced sentence. (See Rule 108.) Balanced sentence

Emphatic: Then the eyes of the blind shall be opened, and the ears of the deaf shall be unstopped.

Emphatic: He is patient, forbearing, and resigned, on philosophical principles; he submits to pain, because it is inevitable, to bereavement, because it is irreparable, and to death, because it is his destiny. — NEWMAN.

NOTE. — Antithesis or contrast may be used for emphasis.

Emphatic: The Puritans hated bear-baiting, not because it gave pain to the bear, but because it gave pleasure to the spectators. — MACAULAY.

Emphatic: The *Sun* made vice attractive in the morning; the *Post* made virtue dull in the evening.

Proportion

136. Emphasis may be gained by proportion. Greater space should be given to the more important part of the sentence idea. More effective use may be made of proportion in larger units of discourse, however, than in the sentence.

Emphasis upon less important details: Then came my first glimpse of the Pacific Ocean — a sight I should never have had except for my uncle's thoughtfulness and generosity in asking me to join him and his family on their trip to the coast.

Excision

137. Emphasis may be gained by cutting out unnecessary words. (See Rules 23–26 and 44.)

Unemphatic: The happiest memories that I retain from my childhood are the memories that center about the summers that I spent on my grandfather's farm. (24 words)

Improved: My happiest childhood memories are of the summers spent on my grandfather's farm. (13 words)

Repetition

138. Emphasis may be gained by the repetition of important words. (See Rules 45–46.)

Emphatic repetition: When I was a child, I spake as a child, I understood as a child, I thought as a child: but when I became a man, I put away childish things.

Fairly emphatic: I am not afraid of the dark, nor of high places; nor am I frightened by animals. I dread a monster more intangible than any of these — Fear of Fear.

Emphatic: I am not afraid of the dark, nor of high places; nor am I afraid of animals. I am afraid of a monster more intangible than any of these — Fear of Fear.

Exercise

Emphasis

a. Make the following sentences more emphatic.

1. Is that the dog of which you are afraid?
2. I have known most of the tragedies of boyhood, I think. My beloved dog was run over and killed, my pet rabbit escaped, and there were other tragedies.

3. Between rapid puffs of smoke, Wally outlined his opinion of college professors as slave drivers, in no uncertain terms.
4. The rain continued until our little creek became a raging, swift river.
5. I insisted that a player-piano was the last thing I wanted.
6. If you had listened to us, you would never have been in this mess, it seems to me.
7. She is absolutely unsophisticated, gentle, and kind.
8. The story of the buried treasure had been preserved by the cabin boy, the only one of the crew to survive, according to the old fisherman.
9. As the mail train thundered by, I used to think of the letters that it carried: letters of blackmail, of love and hate; letters of dear ones who were soon to be together again; letters from a boy in the great city to his mother back home; letters from one great business firm to another.
10. At first I found it very difficult to concentrate with several radios turned on constantly. However, by the end of my freshman year, I had learned to study regardless of the noise.

b. Why are the following sentences emphatic?

1. Like all young people, I thought I was going to set the world on fire. But as the years go by, I am beginning to learn that I am not going to set anything on fire.
2. The theater is still a wonder to me: it is a strange, hallowed world apart.
3. My job in the mouse trap factory was to put on the catch, fling the trap into a basket, and repeat the performance, time after time, hour after hour, day after day.
4. During the fall of 1929 when the country went insane over the stock market crash, when factories closed and banks shut their doors, when some men used revolvers and others walked out of tenth-story windows, the people of Hoffwasser calmly talked of butchering hogs if the weather stayed cold.
5. Next to me in zoölogy laboratory sits Emery. For every five drawings that the rest of the students

make, he produces about three. I envy Emery, the failure, the joke of the class. He has the scientific spirit of investigation; and that seems to be just the reason why it may take him double time to pass the course. His soul is serene. No one can hurry him. He knows what he wants from the course, and it perturbs him not one whit that his scholastic rating is low. His work is its own reward. I seldom find the time to locate under the microscope even the minimum that is required of us, for our drawings must be handed in on time if one wants a high grade. I work for the grade, and that's all I get — the grade.

EXERCISES ON THE SENTENCE

Exercise 1

Unity

Revise such of the following sentences as you find ununified, stating in each case the rule that applies. State also your reason for considering any sentence unified.

1. Our greatest adventure was our participation in the World War, which we brought to a successful conclusion and prevented the Germans from subjugating Great Britain and France and ultimately our own country, at a cost of billions of dollars and great suffering and hardship to our soldiers, to whom the country will always be grateful, and is now providing generously for the disabled, and will provide for all when time and conditions permit.
2. Among the average herd of Jersey cattle, she will appear to be small. She weighs about seven hundred and fifty pounds and is seven years old.
3. There were several other boys whom I knew much better than Carl, and no lasting friendship has resulted from them.
4. In the center of the field, a team was practicing. One player was knocking flies and grounders. His teammates were fielding them. Their uniforms were gray and their socks banded in gold.
5. Near the benches, which were placed on either side of the field, were rows of bats and managers were keeping them in order.

6. The typical cowboy is not (although there are but few left) extinct as yet, but contrary to public opinion they are not ignorant, but good-natured and well-educated boys. Unity
7. The fine manners of a Southerner are known the world over because he will not tolerate discourtesy to any lady.
8. The number of people attending universities is gradually increasing, people are beginning to put into practice their beliefs that more money can be earned with the aid of an education.
9. "Next," called the dean's assistant in a foreboding tone. My turn was drawing near. I tied another knot in my handkerchief. I wriggled restlessly to the edge of the bench that guarded the door to a little office marked "Dean of Women" in straight black letters. I was waiting for a conference that I had not requested. There was no denying it, I was nervous.
10. Gray persistent rain beat down unceasingly from the cheerless leaden sky overhead. A dogged beating, beating rain, which had drenched all outdoors.
11. There is the man who is a racing fanatic who will bet his own clothing on a horse race.
12. The island is far from the mainland so it is seldom visited by tourists.
13. I have made many friends this first year in college, but none of them has been such a good friend as John, but of course I have known him for ten years.
14. Despite the fact that this cow has soft, gentle eyes, she has a bad disposition. When she is slightly disturbed, she becomes very wild. When she is in this mood, she seems to be more like a tiger than a dairy cow.
15. He fought the sea monsters as though they were mice. Although this was easy to do, for he had armor on and a sword in his hand.
16. Most of my classmates in high school had no ambition to get a better education, so they wondered why I wanted to go to college.
17. No two people think alike or reason in quite the same way; from childhood we all form likes and dislikes;

we establish opinions on religion, on politics, on society, on peace and war, and on all types of human relationships.

18. In such a world of affairs as we live in, almost everyone has need for an extensive knowledge of business principles, and should I decide, upon finishing college, if I ever do so, not to follow the line of business, I should not consider my energies at all wasted, for I should be better fitted to carry on my own private affairs and dealings with my fellow beings and to conduct more intelligently any work either private or public which I might undertake.
19. The town had hoped he would leave his five hundred thousand dollars for the building of a new gymnasium, for our high school is very old and was erected before athletic games were considered as essential as they are now.
20. As the argument continued, more girls drifted into our room. Each one adding her thoughts on the subject, all of them trying to help.
21. Better not smoke now, he thought. There had always been trouble about his smoking. She had hated the smell. Hated to have ashes scattered around. Now that he was home again, he had better be civilized. No use trying to sneak, for she'd be sure to smell the smoke.
22. The townspeople are discouraged about raising the money, for a large percentage of the citizens are farmers who cannot donate to the fund, for they are heavily burdened with debts.
23. One evening I came home very much elated because I had had a most enjoyable evening because I was certain that I had made a good impression on my hostesses.
24. I think that the question of allowing Sunday sports is of special interest in the spring, because it is so easy on wintry Sundays to sit all day by the fireplace with the latest scandal sheet and a box of candy, lazily patting yourself on the back for not having to go outdoors to play under stormy skies.
25. In that family the husband rules, and the wife stays at home and does the housework and takes care of the children. Which is as it should be.

26. This new ruling will force many fraternity men to seek more expensive lodgings when they had planned on living as cheaply as possible when forced to attend the summer session because of a system of scale grading that flunked them in perhaps only one course. Unity
27. If then the power of speech is a gift as great as any that can be named — if the origin of language is by many philosophers even considered to be nothing short of divine — if by means of words the secrets of the heart are brought to light, pain of soul is relieved, hidden grief is carried off, sympathy conveyed, counsel imparted, experience recorded, and wisdom perpetuated — if by great authors the many are drawn up into unity, national character is fixed, a people speaks, the past and the future, the East and the West are brought into communication with each other — if such men are, in a word, the spokesmen and prophets of the human family — it will not answer to make light of literature or to neglect its study; rather we may be sure that, in proportion as we master it in whatever language, and imbibe its spirit, we shall ourselves become in our own measure the ministers of like benefits to others, be they many or few, be they in the obscurer or the more distinguished walks of life — who are united to us by social ties, and are within the sphere of our personal influence. — JOHN HENRY NEWMAN.

EXERCISE 2

Rewrite the following sentences to make them coherent. State in each case the rule that applies. Coherence

1. When a school is composed of the best students only, everyone would require the same training, making it an easier task to educate them.
2. An earthen pot was found by the head of everybody buried in the graveyard, and they varied in size according to the size of the person.
3. While excavating among the mounds in this burial ground, many articles were found.
4. The country around the mounds is rather hilly and wild, which makes it a natural place for Indians to live.

Coherence

5. The water is warm this beautiful morning, and followed by a cool shower imparts a rosy glow and a feeling of unconquerable strength.
6. Soon after putting the coal into the stove, the flames began shooting out of all the cracks in the old stove.
7. Southerners are a very healthy people which is due to the outdoor life that they lead.
8. I daring to aspire to be a botanist, and with one line of my ancestors coming from Berlin and the other from Dublin, I am studying French.
9. If these ladies really did good in the right way, instead of meeting to gossip about this unfortunate family, they would ask their husbands to find the man a job, and, instead of visiting the wife for an opportunity of looking over her house, they would help her organize her household so that she could find some time to rest.
10. I know a student who was on probation every semester that he was in school. He just managed to get by, but he spends much effort and energy doing it. He always takes his limit of cuts the first two weeks, and then if he oversleeps or wants to go out of town for a week end, he will spend hours trying to convince the doctors that he was ill.
11. Harley is sitting beside me writing a letter to his family whose purpose is also to make the same request that I am making of you.
12. We only want to stay away three months.
13. Everything that he does is done with an eye on convention and etiquette — which is a good thing when not carried to extremes.
14. When the fact that instructors and apparatus must be provided for each course, and that therefore the greater the number of courses the greater the expense to the community is, is considered, it becomes obvious that the curriculum of the junior college will be small.
15. Nothing was done to prevent the factory owners from hiring labor at extremely low rates, which they proceeded to do.
16. He was very fond of reading, his mind was keen, and he had formed the habit of learning apt phrases.

17. A golf course full of hazards has nothing on cutting a lawn full of lawn ornaments. Coherence
18. Looking about a mile westward, the first big object which we see is the international railway bridge.
19. I believe that the reason why Socrates was condemned to death was because during his trial he did not appeal to the people to be forgiven.
20. There is no doubt that everyone is busy earning money, and not much time is spent in the study of the fine arts.
21. Here everyone registers, pays their fees, and finds out where they are to stay.
22. Because of his old age, that is why Socrates preferred death to exile.
23. I think that we should build there because most of the sororities have or are going to build there.
24. I was forced to go outside the first boat to get around, and in doing so, the boat directly behind me cut me off.
25. He believed that a student should be taught his hardest subjects first and mastering one subject at a time before beginning another.
26. As an illustration that aërodromes can be made to be profitable is told by A. H. Abel in the March issue of the *Airway Age.*
27. He was determined to again try to find out where the knock came from.

Exercise 3

Revise any of the following sentences that lack emphasis. Give your reasons for changing sentences or for leaving them unchanged. **Emphasis**

1. The enjoyment that I have in swimming is highly spiced with thrills, for there is usually some sort of excitement to be had.
2. He could never resist the temptation to be clever, no matter whose expense his cleverness might be at.
3. Seeing my father draped in a long black judge's robe and perched up behind the bench like a lollipop in a display case furnished me with so much amusement that I usually did not mind having to wait a long time for him before his case was brought to a close so that he might take me out to lunch.

Emphasis

4. It was a gloomy day, the gentle rain and the dark clouds overhead casting an appearance of depression and dejection upon all terrestrial objects.
5. My ideal of a gentleman is a man of culture, refinement, fine feelings, and good manners.
6. They had saved for years when suddenly they lost everything in the bank failure.
7. In October, 1793, Marie Antoinette was executed in Paris, after a trial in which false and atrocious charges were urged against her in addition to the treasonable acts of which she had been guilty.
8. I could carry only my blue china pig bank, my flowered parasol, and a ruffled net handkerchief, I found.
9. When the temple was finished, a debasing, almost wild ceremony was held, we are told.
10. You think that college has changed since you attended an institution of higher learning.
11. He was hated by those opposed to his religious beliefs, and he was almost always misunderstood.
12. The geographical topography of the land upon which my home town is built and the region immediately surrounding it is very level.
13. He had a heart of gold, and generosity seemed to be always first with him.
14. Giant workmen, stripped to the waist, were exerting their powerful strength in handling the three-ton buckets of white-hot metal.
15. A man can be engaged in almost any occupation and be a gentleman: he can be a football player and a real fellow and still be such a man.
16. There have been many recent criticisms directed toward the present generation in regard to the light in which they hold the idea of good manners.
17. It was only in my senior year that I considered such a thing as a profession. Therefore, when my high-school days were over, I was still in a state of indecision as to the course in which I should enroll.
18. His fat, pudgy fingers barely stretched five white keys from *c* to *g*, and as he played, his head came down in accent, a suggestion of a tongue struggled in the corner of his mouth, and he kept his feet swinging free under the piano bench, moving back and forth in time with the music and his bobbing head.

19. When you have true wisdom, you can see at once the cloud and the sun, the shadow and the light; you can compare the height of the church spire with that of the factory smokestack; the whole course of the stream will be clear to you. Emphasis

THE PARAGRAPH

MECHANICAL MARKS OF A PARAGRAPH

Indention: Of ordinary paragraphs

139. In manuscript the first line of every paragraph should be indented at least an inch. (See Plate II, line 1, p. 317.)

Of numbered paragraphs

140. No exception to the foregoing rule should be made when paragraphs are numbered.

Wrong:

I. What power has Congress to punish crimes?
II. State in what cases the Supreme Court has original jurisdiction.
III. How are presidential electors chosen? Would it be constitutional for a State legislature to choose them?

Right:

I. What power has Congress to punish crimes?

II. State in what cases the Supreme Court has original jurisdiction.

III. How are presidential electors chosen? Would it be constitutional for a State legislature to choose them?

Uniform indention

141. The first lines of all paragraphs should begin at the same distance from the margin; do not indent the beginning of one paragraph an inch, that of another two inches, that of another half an inch, etc.

Incorrect indention

142. Only the first line of a prose paragraph should be indented, except for special reasons. (See also Rule 362.)

Incorrect spacing out

143. After the end of a sentence do not leave the remainder of the line blank unless the sentence ends a paragraph; begin the next sentence on the same line. This rule is violated in Plate I, line 4, page 316.

DIVISION INTO PARAGRAPHS

PARAGRAPHING AS AN AID TO CLEARNESS

144. Parts of a composition that are distinct in topic may also by paragraphing be made distinct to the eye — an effect that promotes clearness. Paragraphing, if properly employed, gives the reader as much assistance in understanding a whole composition as punctuation gives him in understanding a sentence. For instance, suppose a brief essay on Queen Elizabeth discusses three topics: (*a*) Elizabeth's personal character, (*b*) her character as a ruler, and (*c*) her popularity with her subjects. To treat each topic in a separate paragraph makes evident at once the beginning and the end of each topic, and thus enables the reader to grasp without effort the structure of the essay.

The fundamental principle

The number of paragraphs in a composition does not by any means always correspond with the number of main topics. (See Rules 153 and 154.) The number of paragraphs is a relative matter, depending upon the extent to which the subject is developed. In a very brief treatment, each main topic might be completed in a paragraph. But if the subject is developed at length, then each topic may require many paragraphs, each one of its subtopics or smaller units receiving a paragraph.

145. A passage entirely distinct in topic from what precedes and follows should be written as a separate paragraph.

(i) Paragraphing of distinct parts

Thus, suppose an essay on gasoline engines presents —

a. An explanation of the operation of gasoline engines.
b. An estimate of gasoline engines as compared with other kinds of engines.

Parts *a* and *b* should be embodied in separate paragraphs.

Suppose a story tells —

a. The hero's visit to the bank and his transactions there.
b. What was happening meanwhile at the hero's factory.

Parts *a* and *b* should be embodied in separate paragraphs.

Paragraphs of introduction and conclusion

146. A passage that serves as an introduction or a conclusion to a composition consisting of several paragraphs may, for the sake of clearness, be paragraphed separately, even if it consists of only one or two sentences. For example:

> The large body of recent State legislation compelling railway companies to reduce passenger fares, though it probably sprang from good intentions, is likely to have three unfortunate consequences.
>
> [*The main body of the essay consists of three paragraphs, each discussing one of the three unfortunate consequences.*]
>
> One cannot foretell, of course, how many years will elapse before these three results of the recent railway legislation will work themselves out; it may be five years, or it may be a dozen. But that they will sooner or later work themselves out seems, in the light of history, practically certain.

Paragraphs of transition

147. A passage that serves merely to make a transition from one group of paragraphs to a following group may, for the sake of clearness, be paragraphed separately. For example:

> [*The achievements of Macaulay as a man of letters are discussed for several paragraphs.*]
>
> Macaulay's political achievements, though less distinguished than his literary achievements, are worthy of a somewhat detailed notice.
>
> [*Several paragraphs follow, dealing with Macaulay's political career.*]

Note. — A brief transition sentence may often be included in the paragraph which develops the new topic; it should not be tacked on to the paragraph preceding. For example:

[*The need for audacious accuracy as a desirable quality in speech has been discussed for several paragraphs.*]

Such audacious accuracy, however, distinguishing as it does noble speech from commonplace speech, can be practiced only by him who has a wide range of words. Our ordinary range of words is absurdly narrow. It is important, therefore, for anybody who would cultivate himself in English to make strenuous and systematic efforts to enlarge his vocabulary . . . — G. H. PALMER.

[*Then follow three paragraphs discussing range of vocabulary.*] (Note that the transition sentence is included in the first paragraph on the new topic, *range of vocabulary.*)

148. In narratives, as a rule, any direct quotation, together with the rest of the sentence of which it is a part, should be paragraphed separately. Paragraphing of direct quotations

Right:

There were no takers. Not a man believed him capable of the feat. Thornton had been hurried into the wager, heavy with doubt; and now that he looked at the sled itself, the concrete fact, with the regular team of ten dogs curled up in the snow before it, the more impossible the task appeared. Mathewson waxed jubilant.

"Three to one," he proclaimed. "I'll lay you another thousand at that figure, Thornton. What d'ye say?"

Thornton's doubt was strong in his face, but his fighting spirit was aroused — the fighting spirit that soars above odds, fails to recognize the impossible, and is deaf to all save the clamor for battle. He called Hans and Pete to him . . .

149. In dialogue, each speech, regardless of length, should be paragraphed separately in order to make immediately clear each change of speaker. Dialogue

Wrong:

"When did you arrive?" I asked. "An hour ago," he answered. "Didn't you get my letter?" "No." "Strange," he said.

Right:

"When did you arrive?" I asked.

"An hour ago," he answered. "Didn't you get my letter?"

"No."

"Strange," he said.

Indention after a quotation

NOTE. — In order to paragraph an isolated quotation separately (as is done in the example under Rule 148), the line following the quotation must be indented.

Indention in the midst of a sentence

150. A quotation may by paragraphing be detached from the introductory expression (*e.g.*, *he said*) if the quotation closes the sentence.

Right:

Mr. Peggotty looked around upon us and nodding his head with a lively expression animating his face said in a whisper,

"She's been thinking of the old 'un." — DICKENS. [Quotation closes the sentence.]

Wrong:

Thinking I could stand it if my friend could, I called out to him,

"Come on. Who's afraid?" and started into the house. [Quotation does not close the sentence.]

Wrong:

Thinking I could stand it if my friend could, I called out to him,

"Come on. Who's afraid?"

and started into the house. [Quotation does not close the sentence.]

Right:

Thinking I could stand it if my friend could, I called out to him, "Come on. Who's afraid?" and started into the house. [Quotation does not close the sentence.]

(ii) Grouping of related parts

151. When several consecutive short passages present slightly different topics, yet collectively form a larger division of a composition, the distinctness and unity of the whole division should be made apparent, rather than the individuality of its parts. Hence these

short passages should not be written each in a separate paragraph, but should be combined into one paragraph. Grouping of related parts

Thus in an essay on a steel factory, describing —

a. The process of sheet-rolling,
b. The process of rail-rolling,
c. The process of casting,

part *b* should not be written as follows:

Steel ingots six feet long and six inches square were heated to a white heat in a large oven.

When sufficiently hot, an ingot was removed and taken on an endless chain to the first set of rollers.

These rollers were eighteen inches in diameter. When the ingot had been passed through them, it was a bar of steel ten feet long and five inches thick.

Then the bar of steel was put on another endless chain and taken to a second pair of rollers.

This process was continued, the bar being passed successively through five or six pairs of rollers.

It came from the last pair a red-hot rail of standard size.

It was next bent slightly so that the base was convex. This was to allow for unequal contraction in cooling.

The rail was now left to cool.

When cold, it was taken to the cold rollers and rolled perfectly straight.

The foregoing passage should be written as a single paragraph; and so should part *a* and part *c* of the same essay unless their treatment is long and complicated.

152. Do not mislead the reader by paragraphing when there is no change of topic or other clear reason. (But see Rule 153.) Paragraphing where there is no change of topic

The paragraphing in the following passage, for example, is illogical and therefore misleading.

The beauty of Fra Angelico's character has been the admiration of all who ever studied the life of that devout and gentle artist. He might have lived in ease and comfort, for his art would have made him rich; instead, he chose the cloister life. Fra Angelico was gentle and kindly to all.

He was never seen to display anger and if he admonished his friends, it was with mildness. . . .

In this passage, the discussion of the gentleness of Fra Angelico begins in the sentence *Fra Angelico was gentle*, etc.; the sentence *He was never*, etc., continues the discussion of this topic — does not introduce a new topic. Hence, the sentence *He was never*, etc., should follow without a paragraph break.

LENGTH OF PARAGRAPHS

Paragraphs too long

153. Extended composition or passages in the text with no paragraph-breaks may strain the reader's attention; shorter paragraphs give him more frequent opportunity to summarize the thought. A passage more than 300 words long, even if it constitutes a single unit of composition, should usually not be written as a single paragraph, but should be divided into two or three paragraphs of convenient length (*i.e.*, not longer than 200 words).

Thus, an essay on Lincoln, presenting —

a. A narrative of his life (350 words)
b. An estimate of his greatness (100 words)

should not be written as two paragraphs corresponding to the two main divisions of the material, but should be paragraphed in some such way as the following:

¶ Events of life up to 1860 (200 words)
¶ Career as president (150 words)
¶ Estimate of his greatness (100 words)

Over-frequent paragraphing

154. Overfrequent paragraphing indicates either a lack of development or a failure to see the relationship of the thoughts. Hence, a composition no longer than 150 words should usually be written without any paragraph divisions.

155. A sentence or a short passage which the writer wishes to make especially emphatic may be paragraphed separately. Sentences made conspicuous by detachment

Thus, in the following passage the italicized part, although it does not begin a new subject, may properly be set apart for emphasis.

Indefinite narrative should not be entirely avoided; it is useful, and for some purposes is preferable to concrete narrative. Parts of a story that are not of dramatic interest, speeches that are of no interest or importance, — these may properly be conveyed by indefinite rather than by concrete narrative. But remember this:

Actions occurring at important points of a story should be related by concrete, not indefinite narrative.

Exercise

Paragraph the following:

The conversation began: "I met you once before, General Lee," Grant said in his normal tones, "while we were serving in Mexico, when you came over from General Scott's headquarters to visit Garland's brigade, to which I then belonged. I have always remembered your appearance, and I think I should have recognized you anywhere." "Yes," answered Lee quietly, "I know I met you on that occasion, and I have often thought of it and tried to recollect how you looked, but I have never been able to recall a single feature." Mention of Mexico aroused many memories. Grant pursued them with so much interest and talked of them so readily that the conversation went easily on until the Federal was almost forgetting what he was about. Lee felt the weight of every moment and brought Grant back with words that seemed to come naturally, yet must have cost him anguish that cannot be measured. "I suppose, General Grant," he said, "that the object of our present meeting is fully understood. I asked to see you to ascertain upon what terms you would receive the surrender of my army." Grant did not change countenance or exhibit the slightest note of exultation in his reply. "The terms I propose are those stated substantially in my letter of yesterday — that is, the officers and men surrendered to be paroled and disqualified from taking up Paragraphing

arms again until properly exchanged, and all arms, ammunition and supplies to be delivered up as captured property."
—D. S. FREEMAN, *R. E. Lee.*

UNITY

Unity of a paragraph

156. A paragraph by its very form, its separation from what precedes and follows, suggests that its contents should be on one division of a subject. Therefore material that is not a unit should not be given the form of unity. If the paragraph can be summarized completely in one unified sentence, then the paragraph is unified.

Ununified:

Snow tonight swept across many Big Ten gridirons. Illinois worked out strenuously for Ohio State, hoping to find the Buckeyes in a relapse after their keying for Michigan. A victory would enable Illinois to finish with a single loss. Ohio State regards the Michigan victory by one point as a bad break, the memory of which they hope to erase at Urbana Saturday.

Ununified:

History tells us that not many years ago, men, women, and children left their happy homes and wended their way across the plains and over the Rocky Mountains to the little streams of California in search of the precious metal, gold. Who of us, though, have ever heard of men making a rush for iron ore? Iron ore is found in many places in the United States; in fact it can be found in some quantity, whether small or large, in almost every state. The greatest deposit of iron ore is to be found in the Lake Superior region. Here the metal lies close to the surface while in almost all of the other regions the ore runs in small deep veins.

Unified:

The House and Senate are naturally unlike. They are different both in constitution and character. They do not represent the same things. The House of Representatives is by intention the popular chamber, meant to represent the people by direct election through an extensive suffrage, while the Senate was designed to represent the states as political units, as the constituent members of the Union. The terms of membership in the two houses, moreover, are different. The two chambers were unquestionably intended to derive their authority from different sources and to speak with different voices in affairs; and however much they may have departed from their original characters in the changeful processes of our politics, they still represent many sharp contrasts to one another, and must be described as playing, not the same but very distinct and dissimilar rôles in affairs. — WOODROW WILSON.

157. A paragraph often contains a sentence that summarizes all the material in the paragraph. This sentence, the topic or thesis sentence, is frequently placed at the beginning of the paragraph. (Note the first sentence in the unified paragraph quoted under Rule 156.) **Topic sentence**

EXERCISE

In the following unified paragraph, do you find a topic sentence? If not, make one. Show how each sentence develops the topic sentence. **Unity**

The democratic rule that all men are equal is sometimes confused with the quite opposite idea that all men are the same and that any man can be substituted for any other so that his differences make no difference. The two are not at all the same. The democratic rule that all men are equal means that men's being different cannot be made a basis for special privilege or for the invidious advantage of one man over another; equality, under the democratic rule, is the freedom and opportunity of each individual to be fully and completely his different self. — H. M. KALLEN.

COHERENCE

158. The sentences in a paragraph should be so arranged that the thought progresses in logical sequence. **Arrangement of sentences**

Incoherent:

When I was a child, I was lured to water by an uncontrollable instinct. One day a friend and I set out in a canoe to paddle down the small river which flowed through our town. The movement of the water pressing steadily on and urging on our light boat fascinated me. We paddled for hours until we reached a part of the river that was unfamiliar to us. We had obtained a wonderful canoe, which fairly leaped over the water. At each turn of the bank of the stream, we craned our necks to see what was coming. As the world drifted by us, we stared at the unfamiliar sights. We had a wonderful trip, but of course we suffered for our fun when we reached home. The canoe had been taken without the owner's permission.

Improved:

When I was a child, I was lured to water by an uncontrollable instinct. One day a friend and I set out in a canoe, which we had borrowed without the owner's permission, and paddled down the small river flowing through our town. I was fascinated by the movement of the water pressing steadily on and urging on our light boat. The canoe, a good one, fairly leaped over the water. At each turn of the bank of the stream, we craned our necks to see what was coming. As the world drifted by us, we stared at the unfamiliar sights. We had a wonderful trip, but, of course, we suffered for our fun when we reached home.

Transitional words and phrases

159. The relationship between the sentences in a paragraph may be made clear by the use of transitional words. (See Appendix D.)

Coherent:

That the state of nature, at any time, is a temporary phase of a process of incessant change, which has been going on for innumerable ages, appears to me to be a proposition as well established as any in modern history. Paleontology assures us, *in addition*, that the ancient philosophers who, with less reason, held the same doctrine, erred in supposing that the phases formed a cycle, exactly repeating the past, exactly foreshadowing the future, in their rotations. *On the contrary*, it furnishes us with conclusive reasons for thinking that, if every link in the ancestry of these humble indigenous plants had been preserved and were accessible to us, the whole would present a converging series of forms of gradually diminishing complexity, until at some period in the history of the earth, far more remote than any of which organic remains have yet been discovered, they would merge in those low groups among which the boundaries between animal and vegetable life become effaced.

— T. H. HUXLEY.

160. A paragraph may sometimes be made coherent by filling in a gap in the thought. **Filling in a gap in thought**

Incoherent:

The university, if it is to be a real exponent of a liberal education, must resist vigorously the modern tendency toward extracurricular activities of one kind or another. Athletics, literary societies, homecomings, foundation days have their place in college life and are valuable. Our stadium, costing about $2,000,000, seating about 70,000 persons, and rising from the prairie as a huge architectural monstrosity, is now for several months of the year the center of university thought and activity. Vast throngs are attracted to our community, but no one of these has any thought for the real function of the university. There are wild demonstrations of loyalty for the team and the institution, but little or no interest in academic work. A university must be built on something more substantial than college songs, class cheers, and sentimental loyalty.

Improved:

The university, if it is to be the real exponent of a liberal education, must resist vigorously the modern tendency toward extracurricular activities of one kind or another. Athletics, literary societies, homecomings, foundation days have their place in college life and are valuable *within certain limits, but they ought not to become the center of interest.* Our stadium, costing about $2,000,000, seating about 70,000 persons, etc.

161. Coherence may be gained by the repetition of words at the close of one sentence and at the beginning of the next sentence. **Repetition of words**

Coherent:

. . . His conduct has, indeed, on some questions, been so Whiggish, that both those who applauded and those

who condemned it have questioned his claim to be considered a *Tory*. But his *Toryism*, such as it is, he has held fast through all changes of fortune and fashion . . .
— MACAULAY.

Ordering a sentence with reference to the preceding sentence

162. Coherence may be gained by arranging the members of a sentence so as to form close connection with the preceding sentence.

Inferior: He wished to examine the planet Mars, then in the western part of the sky. He began to turn the telescope in order to do this.

Better: He wished to examine the planet Mars, then in the western part of the sky. In order to do this, he began to turn the telescope.

Parallel construction

163. Coherence may be gained by using sentences parallel in form, for when the same form is maintained, the reader immediately catches the relationship of the ideas. Note that in the following paragraph the parallel sentences keep the reader aware that the author is naming coördinate details, each developing his topic sentence.

Coherent:

. . . The weakness of the modern Romantic poet is that he must keep himself aloof from life, that he may see it. He rejects authority, and many of the pleasures, along with the duties, of society. He looks out from his window on the men fighting in the plain, and sees them transfigured under the rays of the setting sun. He enjoys the battle, but not as the fighters enjoy it. He nurses himself in all the luxury of philosophic sensation. He does not help to bury the child, or to navigate the schooner, or to discover the Fortunate Islands. . . .
— Sir WALTER RALEIGH.

EXERCISE A

Coherence

In the following paragraph, point out all the devices for securing coherence:

That the boom period between 1920 and 1930 was the most spectacular period of our sporting history, the end of the biggest and greatest, the period of the super-champion when the United States not only led the world but admitted it, is beyond question. That it was the boom period of sport in this country is not, however, true. There was more noise and shouting, more exaggeration and hyperbole, more space in the newspapers devoted to sports or what passed at the time for sports; but there were fewer persons actually playing games. The space in the press was devoted to the super-champions, not to the second-raters who play golf and tennis all over the land. No, if we are not yet in the boom period of American sport, we are approaching it. To-day there is a more intelligent appreciation of the values of real sport, there are more persons of average ability competing, there are more participants who are interested in the game for the game's sake, more people playing than ever before in our history. Not merely is this a greater period for athletes than the era of the super-champion, but there is every likelihood of greater times ahead. — J. R. Tunis.

Exercise B

Write pairs of sentences linked with the following transitional words: *Furthermore, and then, therefore, hence, nevertheless, in fact, accordingly, on the other hand, still, besides.* Coherence

Note this illustration: Shakespeare wrote for a stage that had practically no scenery. He *therefore* had the characters in the play describe the settings in order to help the audience imagine them.

EMPHASIS

164. Emphasis may be placed upon the important idea in the paragraph by giving it more space than is given to the less important ideas. Proportion

Emphatic:

In this sense, silly folk and dullards *think*. The story is told of a man in slight repute for intelligence, who, desiring to be chosen selectman in his New England town, addressed a knot of neighbors in this wise: "I hear you don't believe I know enough to hold office. I wish you to understand that I am thinking about something or other most of the time." Now reflective thought is like this random coursing of things through the mind in that it consists of a succession of things thought of;

but it is unlike, in that the mere chance occurrence of any chance "something or other" in an irregular sequence does not suffice. Reflection involves not simply a sequence of ideas, but a *con*sequence — a consecutive ordering in such a way that each determines the next as its proper outcome, while each in turn leans back on its predecessors. The successive portions of the reflective thought grow out of one another and support one another; they do not come and go in a medley. Each phase is a step from something to something — technically speaking, it is a term of thought. Each term leaves a deposit which is utilized in the next term. The stream or flow becomes a train, chain, or thread. — JOHN DEWEY.

Position

165. Emphasis may be placed upon the important ideas in the paragraph by putting them at the beginning and at the end of the paragraph. Coherence, however, must not be sacrificed for the sake of emphasis.

Emphatic:

Pepys has, indeed, had full reward for all his pains. Since the appearance of his Diary in the first abbreviated form which printed scarcely half of its contents, much learned and loving labor has been spent on its elucidation. The ingenuity and industry of successive editors has enlarged our knowledge and understanding of the work; the two original volumes, what with inclusion of the parts at first suppressed and a great bulk of comment, have increased to ten. One editor has retranscribed the manuscript, another has compiled a book on Pepys and the world he lived in; the family genealogy has been unearthed and a study made of one of its members as "a later Pepys"; so far has the reflected glory shone. The diarist's early life has been laid bare; his letters published, with his will; his portraits reproduced; a whole book on Pepys as a lover of music has appeared; an essay on the sermons that he heard; even the medical aspects of his married life have been explained by a physician-author. Essayists and bookmakers still find in him an ever-fertile subject for their pens; no biographical dictionary or encyclopedia is without a full account of the great diarist; and rising finally to the full stature of a real biography, few names to-day in English literature are better known, few classics more widely read or more enjoyed. — W. C. Abbott.

166. Emphasis as well as coherence may be gained by using sentences parallel in form. (See Rule 163.) Parallel construction

Exercise

By what means is emphasis gained in this paragraph? Emphasis

The most fascinating type of hunting to them was the "coon" hunt. The Neelys loved to swing along through the dense forests on a winter night, lanterns, saws, and guns at their sides, and a pack of well-trained dogs sniffing the trail ahead. They loved to hear those dogs bay and run and finally tree the quarry, to see the pair or pairs of eyes shining far up in an old oak, and to make their saws sing through that oak. Sometimes the chase, after the dogs first scented the raccoon, raced on for many miles up and down the river; but an entire night of work, even if no reward resulted, only made the hunt more attractive because of its variety and difficulty. The men also hunted foxes and other animals, but the wily raccoon seemed most to allure men and dogs.

PARAGRAPH DEVELOPMENT

167. Develop the central thought of the paragraph as fully as is necessary for a clear understanding of the idea. A paragraph may be developed by the use of: (*a*) definition, (*b*) illustration or example, (*c*) comparison or contrast, (*d*) generalization based upon particular facts and details, (*e*) repetition, (*f*) elimination, (*g*) relation of cause and effect, (*h*) combination of methods. The choice of method should of course depend upon one's material and purpose. Methods of development

a. Definition

Well, what I mean by Education is learning the rules of this mighty game. In other words, education is the instruction of the intellect in the laws of Nature, under which name I include not merely things and their forces

Methods of development

but men and their ways; and the fashioning of the affections and of the will into an earnest and loving desire to move in harmony with those laws. For me education means neither more nor less than this. Anything which professes to call itself education must be tried by this standard, and if it fails to stand the test, I will not call it education, whatever may be the force of authority, or of numbers, upon the other side. — T. H. HUXLEY.

b. Illustration or example

With the single exception of Falstaff, all Shakespeare's characters are what we call "marrying men." Mercutio, as he was own cousin to Benedick and Biron, would have come to the same end in the long run. Even Iago had a wife, and, what is far stranger, he was jealous. People like Jacques and the Fool in *Lear*, although we can hardly imagine they would ever marry, kept single out of a cynical humour or for a broken heart, and not, as we do nowadays, from a spirit of incredulity and preference for the single state. For that matter, if you turn to George Sand's French version of *As You Like It* (and I think I can promise you will like it but little), you will find Jacques marries Celia just as Orlando marries Rosalind. — STEVENSON.

c. Comparison or contrast

See the exquisite contrast of the types of mind! The pragmatist clings to facts and concreteness, observes truth at its work in particular cases, and generalizes. Truth, for him, becomes a class-name for all sorts of definite working-values in experience. For the rationalist it remains a pure abstraction, to the bare name of which we must defer. When the pragmatist undertakes to show in detail just *why* we must defer, the rationalist is unable to recognize the concretes from which his own abstraction is taken. He accuses us of *denying* truth; whereas we have only sought to trace exactly why people follow it and always ought to follow it. Your typical ultra-abstractionist fairly shudders at concreteness: other things equal, he positively prefers the pale and spectral. If the two universes were offered, he would always choose the skinny outline rather than the rich thicket of reality. It is so much purer, clearer, nobler. — WILLIAM JAMES.

d. Generalization based upon particular facts and details

Methods of development

The want of serious and sustained thinking is not confined to politics. One feels it even more as regards economical and social questions. To it must be ascribed the vitality of certain prejudices and fallacies which could scarcely survive the continuous application of such vigorous minds as one finds among the Americans. Their quick perceptions serve them so well in business and in the ordinary affairs of private life that they do not feel the need for minute investigation and patient reflection on the underlying principles of things. They are apt to ignore difficulties, and when they can no longer ignore them, they will evade them rather than lay siege to them according to the rules of art. The sense that there is not time to spare haunts an American even when he might find the time, and would do best for himself by finding it.

— JAMES BRYCE.

e. Repetition

With all this in mind, I have often been tempted to put forth the paradox that any place is good enough to live a life in, while it is only in a few, and those highly favored, that we can pass a few hours agreeably. For, if we only stay long enough, we become at home in the neighborhood. Reminiscences spring up, like flowers, about uninteresting corners. We forget to some degree the superior loveliness of other places, and fall into a tolerant and sympathetic spirit which is its own reward and justification. Looking back the other day on some recollections of my own, I was astonished to find how much I owed to such a residence; six weeks in one unpleasant country-side had done more, it seemed, to quicken and educate my sensibilities than many years in places that jumped more nearly with my inclination.

— STEVENSON.

f. Elimination (Note how the author first tells what peace is not meant, and then what peace is meant.)

The proposition is peace. Not peace through the medium of war; not peace to be hunted through the labyrinth of intricate and endless negotiations; not peace to arise out of universal discord fomented, from

Methods of development

principle, in all parts of the empire; not peace to depend on the juridical determinations of perplexing questions, or the precise marking of the shadowy boundaries of a complex government. It is simple peace; sought in its natural course, and in its ordinary haunts. It is peace sought in the spirit of peace, and laid in principles purely pacific. I propose, by removing the ground of the difference, and by restoring the former unsuspecting confidence of the colonies in the Mother Country, to give permanent satisfaction to your people; and (far from a scheme of ruling by discord) to reconcile them to each other in the same act and by the bond of the very same interest which reconciles them to British government. — EDMUND BURKE.

g. Relation of cause and effect

Those who accepted the traditional views of the world and of religion, and opposed change, were quite justified in suspecting that scientific investigation would sooner or later make them trouble. It taught men to distrust, and even to scorn, the past which furnished so many instances of ignorance and gross superstition. Instead of accepting the teachings of the theologians, both Catholic and Protestant, that mankind through Adam's fall was rendered utterly vile, and incapable (except through God's special grace) of good thoughts or deeds, certain thinkers began to urge that man was by nature good; that he should freely use his own God-given reason; that he was capable of becoming increasingly wise by a study of nature's laws, and that he could indefinitely better his own condition and that of his fellows if he would but free himself from the shackles of error and superstition. Those who had broadened their views of mankind and of the universe came to believe that God had revealed himself not only to the Jewish people but also, in greater or less degree, to all his creatures in all ages and in all parts of a boundless universe where everything was controlled by his immutable laws.

— J. H. ROBINSON and C. A. BEARD.

h. Combination of methods

Nature seems to have apportioned the voices of many of her creatures with sensitive regard for their environment. [Generalization.] Sombre voices seem fittingly to be associated with subdued light, and joyous notes with the blaze of sunlit twigs and open meadows. [Repetition, contrast.] A bobolink's bubbling carol is unthinkable in a jungle, and the strain of a wood pewee on a sunny hillside would be like an organ playing dance-music. [Illustration, contrast.] This is even more pronounced in the tropics, where, quite aside from any mental association on my part, the voices and calls of the jungle reflect the qualities of that twilight world. [Repetition.] The poor-me-one proves too much. He is the very essence of night, his wings edged with velvet silence, his plumage the mingled concentration of moss and lichens and dead wood. [Illustration.]

— William Beebe.

Exercise

Paragraph development

Bring to class paragraphs illustrating as many of these methods of development as you can find.

EXERCISES ON THE PARAGRAPH

Exercise 1

Paragraph division

Apply the principles of paragraph division to the following passages. Give the reasons for your paragraph division.

1. "Peggotty," says I suddenly, "were you ever married?" "Lord, Master Davy," replied Peggotty. "What's put marriage in your head?" She answered with such a start that it quite awoke me. And then she stopped in her work, and looked at me, with her needle drawn out to its thread's length. "But *were* you ever married, Peggotty?" says I. "You are a very handsome woman, an't you?" I thought her in a different style from my mother, certainly; but of another school of beauty, I considered her a perfect example. There was a red velvet footstool in the best parlour, on which my mother had painted a nosegay. The groundwork of that stool and Peggotty's complexion appeared to me to be one and the same thing. The stool was smooth, and Peggotty was rough, but that made no difference. "Me handsome, Davy!" said Peggotty. "Lawk, no, my dear! But what put marriage in your head?" "I don't know! You mustn't

Paragraph division

marry more than one person at a time, may you, Peggotty?" "Certainly not," says Peggotty, with the promptest decision.

— Dickens.

2. "Dear Sister, I haven't had much time to write. But the news is that Dad got a contract out at Alder Point. Jim Usher and I went out to Bridgeville with Dad. When Dad was surveying, we target-practiced. How are you getting along? Please send me some foreign stamps. The place is as dead as a door-nail; so I cannot tell you very much. Love, Frank Green. P.S. Don't forget the stamps." There it was again — stamps! They were his latest interest when I left home in September. He could not even write a letter without bringing in stamps! And I had a suspicion that that was his object in writing the letter — to get stamps. So he was still at it. I could close my eyes and see a room full of boys, and stamps. Stamps everywhere: stamps on the table, on the couch, on the chairs, and on the floor. Every floor in the house was covered with them. And no one dared sweep them up. Heavens, no! Why, some of them were worth a thousand dollars! Why didn't he sell them, then, if he could get so much as that for them? Well, for cat's sake, a fellow couldn't sell them till the c'lector came around, could he? Where was the collector and when was he coming? Oh, he was somewhere and he'd be along some day. Gee, girls were a nuisance, always asking questions. Stupids! Never could understand anything, anyway. So the nuisance found it better not to interfere; and the stamps remained unmolested. Every night the bunch would come trooping in, and gather in the den with their stamps and stamp albums. "Hey, Green, I'll trade you a Guatemala for that Santo Domingo. You've got two of them anyway." "Well, I hope to tell you I won't! What are you trying to pull? Guatemalas only market for five dollars, and I can get ten for this, any old day, and I don't mean maybe." Sometimes the argument became so heated as to necessitate a little interference from the nuisance. The battle would subside for a time and then break out afresh, rising higher and higher, until the nuisance would decide it was time for intervention again. I didn't send any stamps, and neither have I received another letter. It was almost nine months ago that the stamp hobby was in full swing; so I suspect that it is over now. I shall be glad if it is, but I am not letting myself become too elated. One cannot with a thirteen-year-old brother.

Exercise 2

Decide whether each of the following paragraphs is unified. If it is unified, you should find in the paragraph, or be able to formulate, a topic sentence. (See Rule 157.)

Paragraph unity

1. Blessed is he who has found his work; let him ask no other blessedness. He has a work, a life-purpose; he has found it, and will follow it! How, as a free-flowing channel, dug and torn by noble force through the sour mud-swamp of one's existence, like an ever-deepening river there, it runs and flows; — draining-off the sour festering water, gradually from the root of the remotest grass-blade; making, instead of pestilential swamp, a green fruitful meadow with its clear-flowing stream. How blessed for the meadow itself, let the stream and its value be great or small! Labor is Life: from the inmost heart of the Worker rises his god-given Force, the sacred celestial Life-essence breathed into him by Almighty God; from his inmost heart awakens him to all nobleness, — to all knowledge, 'self-knowledge' and much else, so soon as Work fitly begins. Knowledge? The knowledge that will hold good in working, cleave thou to that; for Nature herself accredits that, says Yea to that. Properly thou hast no other knowledge but what thou hast got by working: the rest is yet all a hypothesis of knowledge; a thing to be argued of in schools, a thing floating in the clouds, in endless logic-vortices, till we try it and fix it. 'Doubt, of whatever kind, can be ended by Action alone.' — Carlyle.

2. Life is filled with many hard and discouraging days, but I am convinced that the most discouraging of days are those when my rhetoric assignment book reads, "March 3, (Wed.) — Theme 5; 450–600 words on a subject arising from the essays on education." Would that Montaigne and Milton, who are really the instigators of this crime, could but know my resentment! I am one of those unfortunate persons who are unable to sit down and conscientiously scratch off a six-hundred-word theme in the length of time that it takes to write out each of those four thousand and six hundred letters that go to make such a theme. What I am striving to prove to my reader is that I am in a class of students in this university from whose brains it is no more possible to wring words than to tap syrup from a maple tree unless the words and the maple syrup happen to be there. Now, it goes unsaid that the only time one can get the maple syrup from the

maple tree is in the early spring of the year — the right season for tapping trees. As with the tree, so with my head. I cannot get theme matter from my block of wood if it is the wrong season. I have "crabbed" to instructors about the limited number of theme subjects until, if they do not deem me as being temperamental, they must believe me to be another one of those anything-for-an-excuse persons. But if they could only know how, when an assigned subject happens to "hit home," I fairly itch to get to the old pen and paper to sketch off that theme before I lose the inspiration. It seems to me that the only way in which I can account for my trouble and the trouble of the others is that we are temperamental. Until now I have always held that only geniuses are temperamental. Manifestations of genius in my young life were Willie Potter, who could play "The Rosary" on the xylophone when he was only in the eighth grade, and little Mary Dalton, who studied in Chicago every summer at the Glenn Dillard Gunn School of Music before she reached her teens. "Ah, they are geniuses!" people remarked, but I thought that they were peculiar — peculiar in the sense that they were not quite bright in their studies and received their high-school diplomas for what should have been pay-checks for winning silver cups for the school in state high-school musical contests. How our senior class snickered when our geniuses received their diplomas on graduation day, but we have to take back a little, for I read in the home town *Gazette*, which was around my clothes in last week's laundry kit, that little Mary Dalton is being presented to Chicago musicians by Glenn Dillard Gunn himself next Tuesday night. So much for temperamental geniuses who can get through life playing pianos without having to write six-hundred-word themes that have to be in at nine o'clock on a Wednesday morning.

Paragraph unity

3. The college, if it is to be a real exponent of a liberal education, must resist vigorously the modern tendency toward extracurricular activities of one kind and another. Athletics, literary societies, college journalism, homecomings, all of them have their place, all are valuable within limits; but they must never be permitted to be substituted for what President Wilson called the "main show" of education. I am fully convinced that university athletics as now organized is detrimental to education and scholarship. Our own stadium, costing about $2,000,000, seating about 70,000

persons, is for several months of the year the center of university interest and activity. Vast throngs are attracted to our little community, but no one in the crowds has any thought for the real function of the university. The wildest demonstrations of loyalty for the team and for the institution are aroused, but not a spark of intellectual curiosity. A college must be built on something more substantial than college songs, class cheers, and sentimental loyalty.

Exercise 3

Unity, coherence, and emphasis

(*a*) State the topic sentences for the following paragraphs. (*b*) Show how the material in the paragraphs is made coherent and emphatic. (*c*) Point out the various methods by which the paragraphs are developed.

1. The American people, more than any other people, is composed of individuals who have lost association with their old landmarks. They have crossed an ocean, they have spread themselves across a new continent. The American who still lives in his grandfather's house feels almost as if he were living in a museum. There are few Americans who have not moved at least once since their childhood, and even if they have stayed where they were born, the old landmarks themselves have been carted away to make room for progress. That, perhaps, is one reason why we have so much more Americanism than love of America. It takes time to learn to love the new gas station which stands where the wild honeysuckle grew. Moreover, the great majority of Americans have risen in the world. They have moved out of their class, lifting the old folks along with them perhaps, so that together they may sit by the steam pipes, and listen to the crooning of the radio. But more and more of them have moved not only out of their class, but out of their culture; and then they leave the old folks behind, and the continuity of life is broken. For faith grows well only as it is passed on from parents to their children amidst surroundings that bear witness, because nothing changes radically, to a deep permanence in the order of the world. It is true, no doubt, that in this great physical and psychic migration some of the old household gods are carefully packed up and put with the rest of the luggage, and then unpacked and set up on new altars in new places. But what can be taken along is at best no more than the tree which is above the ground. The

Unity, coherence, and emphasis

roots remain in the soil where first they grew. — WALTER LIPPMANN.

2. Punishment is a blessed thing. I pity the young who have grown up without it. I pity the old, the masters and the mistresses of households, whom nobody dares to contradict, who are never, never put into the corner or whipped as they deserve. I pity the kings and emperors who have gone murderous-mad because no one stood up to them or made them behave themselves. But punishment is of no positive value; only negative. For any positive help towards living a nobler life, apart from the influence of friendship and of education, I can only fall back on that real and widespread possession of the human race of which we have already spoken: that instinct which shows itself in the existence of the Internal Censor. It is an instinct both moral and aesthetic, which rejects things both because they are bad and because they are ugly, and pursues things both because they are good and because they are beautiful. Philosophers insist on drawing a distinction between these two, but I confess that I never can feel it very real. As far as I can analyze my own feelings, I should say that the motive which keeps me from a bad action is a feeling that as I contemplate it I do not like the look of it or the smell of it. I feel it to be ugly or foul or not decent — not the sort of thing with which I want to be associated. And, similarly, the thing that nerves me towards a good but difficult action is a feeling that it seems beautiful or fine, the sort of thing that I love as I look at it and would like to have for my own. Though not infallible, this moral or aesthetic instinct is a true fact. I believe it to be generally very strong in young people, at any rate in those who have real life in them, and, though often misdirected while they make their usual experiments, it has a way of correcting its own errors and ultimately finding its right course. It, and perhaps it alone, answers the most troublesome of all questions which the cynic can put to the moralist: "Granted that it is useful to society that I should be honest, why should I mind about society if I can find my own profit in stealing?" — GILBERT MURRAY.

THE COMPOSITION AS A WHOLE

UNITY

168. A composition should treat a single subject, should have one definite purpose. If the composition can be summarized fully in one unified sentence or paragraph, it is a unified composition. (On the making of a plan, see Rule 186.) The general principle

The following composition is an example of the violation of unity by failure to hold to one subject:

Our Trip up Spruce Creek

While I was in Port Orange, Mr. Doty, the proprietor of the hotel there, took some of his guests five miles up Spruce Creek on a launch. It was the third of February. As the boat steamed up the creek, we stood on the deck, some of us taking pictures and others shooting at alligators with revolvers. The alligators are of all sizes. Sometimes you will see one seven or eight feet long, lying on the bank in the sunshine. As the boat goes past, he slides into the water and swims away with only his head above the water. When we have gone a little farther, we see another alligator about four feet long, with ten or twelve little ones crawling over her back.

When the launch has gone about five miles, it usually stops at the wharf of an orange grove. Here the passengers are allowed to take all the oranges they want. After they have walked about the grove for a while, they have a picnic dinner, and then start back.

The writer of this meandering composition keeps to his subject — a trip which he took up Spruce Creek on February 3 — for only three sentences. He shifts to a different subject after the third sentence — the Spruce Creek trips in general — and throughout the rest of the composition forgets all about "our trip." Unity may be given to this composition (*a*) by making it entirely a narrative, dealing with the trip of February 3; or (*b*) by making it, throughout, a general discussion of the Spruce Creek picnics provided by Mr. Doty.

Material loosely connected with the main idea

169. Use with caution, if at all, material loosely connected with the main idea of a composition. The relationship of this material to the composition may not be immediately clear to the reader. Either it should be omitted, or it should be so fully developed that its relationship to the main idea is clear, or it should be so placed that it will not divert the reader's attention from the main idea. The placing of this material at the beginning of the composition is especially unfortunate, for it may mislead the reader into thinking that it is the main idea.

Misleading: A composition on the Non-Partisan League begins with this sentence: *Mr. A. C. Townley, the founder of the Non-Partisan League, was thrown into prison for ninety days for criticizing the conduct of the war.* The incident is dropped here and the composition then discusses the history and organization of the Non-Partisan League. From the first sentence, however, the reader might conclude that the main idea of the composition is the attitude of the League toward the war, or the pacifism of the members of the League, or their defiance of the law.

Irrelevant introductions

170. Avoid introductions containing material not closely related to the main idea of the composition. Begin as near the main idea as possible. In a four-hundred-word composition that discusses the advisability of the government's owning its air fleet for transporting mail, the writer begins with this irrelevant paragraph:

Irrelevant introduction: Ever since the beginning of time, man has tried to find a faster means of transporting mail. The Romans sent their important messages by fast runners. Ships crossing the English Channel proved too slow: so the enterprising English sent their messages to Paris by carrier pigeon. In our country the pony express was established in an effort to shorten the time taken by mail going from coast to coast. Ever since men began sending letters, the cry has been for more speed, more speed, more speed. It was to supply this demand that the air mail was organized.

171. A very small composition on a very large subject — such as Character, Patriotism, Selfishness, Advertising, The Waste of Energy — often violates the principle of unity. It usually consists of a number of brief scraps of discussion, each dealing with a different division of the subject. The divisions of so large a subject are themselves large; the composition therefore reads like a fragmentary and disconnected treatment of a number of distinct subjects, not like a connected treatment of one.

Too large a subject

When a short composition is to be written on a large subject, it is best to choose some single, well-defined phase of the subject. For example, choose the subjects in the left column rather than those in the right.

Limited	*General*
The Difference between Character and Reputation	Character
The Work of Patriotic Women during the World War	Patriotism
Selfishness in the Conduct of Students toward Their Parents	Selfishness
Advertising as a Necessary Measure of Self-Defense	Advertising
The Value of a Daily Schedule	The Waste of Time
How Students' Adversities Aid Them toward Success	Success

COHERENCE

172. The material in a composition must cohere, must stick together, if it is to be clear to the reader.

General principle

Passages misplaced

173. Material belonging to one part of a composition should not be placed in another part.

In the following paragraph, the italicized sentence is evidently misplaced:

> The physical training department is very good and is constantly improving. *A good gymnasium for the women is greatly needed, to replace the present unsatisfactory makeshift.* As I am more acquainted with the work of the girls, I shall confine myself to the physical training provided for them.

The italicized sentence does not belong in this introductory part, but in a subsequent part; *viz.*, that which discusses the equipment for the girls' exercise.

Coherent beginning

174. The opening sentences of a formal composition should be self-explanatory; they should be clear to the reader without reference to the title of the composition.

Bad:

LAMPS

They are contrivances for furnishing artificial light. . . .

Improved:

LAMPS

Lamps are contrivances for furnishing artificial light. . . .

Bad:

MY WORK DURING THE PAST TERM

Latin and German were more difficult than any other studies. . . .

Improved:

MY WORK DURING THE PAST TERM

In my work during the past term, I had more difficulty with Latin and German than with any other studies.

Distinct introduction of a new part

175. The beginning of a new division should be clearly marked. Otherwise the reader may suppose that the preceding division still continues. For marking the beginning of a new part, the following devices are suggested:

a. Using a transitional sentence or group of sentences, such as the following:

Transition sentence or paragraph

So much for the amount of free time which the student has. It remains to discuss the use he makes of it.

The willingness of the faculty to allow student self-government is, then, unquestionable. But are the students equally willing to govern themselves?

Connective or transitional words and phrases

b. Using connective words, phrases, and other expressions. (See Appendix D for a list of these words.)

Placing key words at the beginning

c. Placing near the beginning of the first sentence of the new division the word or words that indicate the subject of the new division. For example, after a discussion of the abuses of college athletics, to begin a new division with the words *The remedy . . .* makes the change of topic immediately evident. After a discussion of a statesman's foreign policy, to begin a new division with the words *His internal administration . . .* makes the change of topic immediately evident.

Repetition of antecedent

d. Using a noun rather than its pronoun in the topic sentence of a paragraph.

For example, in a theme on the effect of the university upon the freshman, the third paragraph begins with this topic sentence: *This is broadened beyond its narrow sphere in high school. This* refers to a remote antecedent, *the student's point of view.* The whole paragraph would have been made more effective if the topic sentence had read: *The student's point of view is broadened beyond its narrow sphere in high school.*

Links

How the paragraphs of a composition may be joined in an unmistakably coherent sequence is shown by the following paragraph links found in Chapter 2 "What Is Liberty?" of George Soule's *The Future of Liberty:*

Links

What is liberty? The quick answer is that it is the *absence of restraint* upon the individual . . .

Suppose there were no society to impose *restraints* . . .

There is *also* a problem of liberty . . .

In saying *this*, we must avoid . . .

The first premise of any tenable conception of individual liberty, *therefore*, . . . Can we say that in this realm, liberty is *absence of restraint?*

A society in which there were *no restraints* by government would be . . . incompatible with another element of our basic faith — *equality*.

Men are, of course, *unequal* and different in native gifts . . .

If individuals were to have any kind of *equality* in status . . . *some restraints* must be imposed . . . either by government or by common consent and self-discipline.

Since liberty itself requires the imposition of *some restraint* . . .

So far, the doctrine . . .

Thus came John Locke's doctrine . . .

These mechanical and negative conceptions of liberty in society, however . . .

Let us be careful at this point, *however* . . .

Or consider John Stuart Mill's doctrine . . .

Such a distinction is impossible . . .

The difficulty with *this* principle . . .

Examples of *the latter* confusion . . .

The crude judgment of the workers in a *situation like this* . . . Thus the merely *negative concept of liberty* is not only useless, it is also actively dangerous.

Notice also, in addition to the paragraph links, how the final sentence is tied to the opening sentences of the chapter.

Coherence of a contradiction

176. Lack of connective words or sentences between a statement and a contradiction of it is especially apt to cause incoherence.

Incoherent: Some people think that clerking is an easy job and that a clerk ought never to be tired. Clerks stay closely housed day after day, working from six in the morning to ten at night. . . .

Coherent [the necessary connective is supplied]: Some people think that clerking is an easy job and that a clerk ought never to be tired. This is not the case. In the first place, clerks stay closely housed day after day, etc.

177. Avoid the shifting of tenses throughout a composition. In retelling a story or in composing a story, do not shift between the present and the past tenses. Decide at the beginning which tense to use, and use it consistently; ordinarily, prefer the past tense. (See Rules 35 and 121.) Shifting the tense

178. Avoid the shifting of point of view throughout a composition. Do not change from *I* to *one*, from *we* to *the observer*, from *you* to *a person*. If in a story the narrator tells in the first person what he saw or had a part in, the introduction of events or speeches or thoughts that he could not have seen or heard or known violates coherence. Shifting the point of view

Thus the italicized part of the following extract violates coherence:

I strolled down to the boathouse at six o'clock yesterday evening. As I got there a rowboat was approaching the wharf containing a man and a girl who I judged must have arrived from the country very recently. *They had started for Picnic Point at two o'clock. On the way the young man had had great difficulty at the unfamiliar work of rowing. Often his oars would slip and send a shower of water into the girl's lap, at which he would say, "Oh, I am so sorry!" and she would reply, "Oh, that's all right."* . . . *As they neared the wharf, he was anxiously wondering whether he could land without accident.* Jimmy, the keeper of the boathouse, stood ready to assist at the disembarkation. . . .

A story in which coherence is thus violated may be corrected (*a*) by omitting all events, speeches, and thoughts of which the narrator could not, according to his own account, have been aware at the time they took place (*e.g.*, omitting the italicized passage in the story quoted); (*b*) by introducing all such events, speeches, and thoughts as having been learned by the narrator after they took place (*e.g.*, making the oarsman in the story just quoted tell the narrator, in a subsequent conversation, what is illogically related in the italicized passage); or (*c*) by omitting all reference to the narrator — telling everything impersonally (*e.g.*, omitting from the story quoted all preceding the italicized part and continuing without any reference to the narrator).

EMPHASIS

General principle

179. If a composition is coherently arranged and clearly expressed, emphasis of the more important ideas or expressions will usually follow. But there are a number of special devices or ways by which emphasis is obtained.

Transitional phrases

180. Emphasis may be obtained by the use of phrases which directly state the importance of the material; as, for example, such phrases as: *The most important point of all is* . . .; and *Emphasis must be put upon this fact* . . .; etc.

Proportion

181. Emphasis may be obtained by giving greater space to more important material. This is a matter of proportion. For example, Huxley in his essay on "Science and Culture," in which he defends a scientific education against its two opponents, the practical man and the classical scholar, devotes approximately five and one-half pages to the practical man and twelve and one-half pages to the classical scholar.

Position

182. Emphasis may be obtained by putting important material at the beginning and at the end. Especially important is the end. In his essay on "The Three Hypotheses Respecting the History of Nature," Huxley discusses first and second the hypotheses that he shows later to be lacking in scientific proof, and last he discusses the hypothesis of evolution, which to him is the valid explanation of the universe.

NOTE. — Coherence must not be sacrificed to gain emphasis. If clearness demands that the material be presented in a certain order, that order must be followed regardless of whether important points come first or last.

183. Emphasis may be obtained by creating suspense; that is, withholding the important fact until the end. For example, J. B. S. Haldane, in his essay "On Being the Right Size" (Scott and Zeitlin, *College Readings in English Prose*, p. 175), presents many illustrations to prove that for every type of animal there is a most convenient size and that a large change in size inevitably carries with it a change in form. Not until the end of the essay does the important idea come; namely, that just as there is a best size for every animal, so there is a best size for human institutions and that a large nation cannot become a completely socialized state. Suspense

184. Emphasis may be obtained by arranging details in climactic order; that is, putting the more important and more forceful details after the less important details. Climax is closely allied to suspense. (See Rule 183.) Climax

EXERCISE

Cut down the following 1500-word theme to a theme of approximately 800 words. Be certain that the cut theme is clear. If necessary for clearness, supply short transitions to take the place of omitted matter. Show that the cut theme is unified and coherent. Unity and coherence in the composition

THE PASSING OF THE "BIG SWAMP"

A short time ago, I had the opportunity to make a motor trip through Florida. There are many interesting places in Florida — the old fort of St. Augustine, the orange groves, Palm Beach with its ten- and fifteen-million-dollar estates, Miami with its colorful resort hotels, Coral Gables — but

Reducing exercise

the part of Florida which I was most interested in seeing, even more than the bathing beauties, was the Everglades. The name has held a fascination for me ever since I first read it in my geography book in about the sixth grade. The information contained in our old geography, although quite complete on the city of Tampa, was indeed meager on the subject of the Everglades. I can remember vividly how sharply my teacher rebuked me — she was a sour old person anyway — for "taking up the class's time by asking so many questions about such an unimportant place." However, since that time I have come to the conclusion that the reason for my teacher's irritation was not that I was taking up the class time, but simply that she could not answer my questions. There is very little information published on the Everglades, and very few people indeed know any more about them than that "it's a big swamp in Florida." Although the entire area is termed a swamp, there were always extensive islands, many of them hundreds of acres in size, which were never under water.

Before I traveled through the Everglades, I did not have even the faintest idea that such a wild country still existed within the borders of our nation. Some sections of the swamp are as untamed as the African jungle; but the most amazing fact is that these sections are not remote, but rather only about an hour's drive from the modern city of Miami.

In some respects it might be said that Miami is the most modern city in the world. At least it has the most modern jail. During the big Florida boom, the city and county authorities decided to build a skyscraper to serve as a combined city hall and court house, and along with that they planned to rent out most of the upper floors of the building as office space, since desirable office space was at a premium at that time. But along came the Depression and away went the office renters. Not having any other use for this large amount of space, the authorities decided to use the upper floors of the skyscraper for a jail. Consequently the prisoners get the freshest air, plenty of sunlight, and a wonderful view. It must be a delightful place to live in.

The Everglades were discovered very early in the history of America by the Spanish explorers in their search for the "Fountain of Youth." The boundaries of the swamp were soon determined. It was found to extend from a narrow strip of high land along the east coast westward about forty-

Reducing exercise

five miles and northward over one hundred miles from the southern tip of the peninsula. But after the boundaries were marked out, little else could be discovered, and until the end of the nineteenth century the dense undergrowth successfully resisted the efforts of all explorers who tried to penetrate more than a few miles. Between 1850 and 1900 the United States government sent out several exploring expeditions, but all returned with the same report of failure to make any headway.

While white men could never manage to penetrate over a few miles, there are tribes of Indians who live in and who have roamed over the swamps for centuries. About the year 1900 a party of engineers succeeded in persuading some Indians to guide them and were able to make a survey. Out of this survey there has grown the greatest drainage project ever to be conceived anywhere in the world.

The total area of the Everglades is about four and one-half million acres. The initial drainage project consisted of about 200 miles of canals 60 feet wide by 5 feet deep. Crossing the canals and draining into them, there was to be a network of smaller ditches, about 1500 miles of them. The project was so vast that it was necessary to design and construct special machinery, far larger than any ever built for this purpose before, in order to make the project practical. When this first project was finally completed in 1916, about one million acres of land had been drained. Experiments showed that this land was capable of raising a wide variety of produce; in fact, it was found to be the most fertile land in the country. When it was seen that the drainage system was so successful, it was decided to extend it. At the present time about 1,500,000 acres have been reclaimed and are permanently dry. The total length of the canals in the system is over 600 miles, and there are almost 5000 miles of ditches. The figure "600 miles" looks large on paper, but it does not begin to convey a true idea of the actual length of the canals. It is only after one has driven on a road alongside one of them for almost an entire day, and sees the sun go down, and the canal still stretching on and on, that one can appreciate their extent.

For their entire length the canals are flanked by roads. The roads were easily constructed, for when the canals were built, instead of throwing half the dirt on each side of the cut, all of it was thrown on one side. After the elevated

Reducing exercise

ground which was thus created had settled, a layer of asphalt was put down, and the result was a fine road. Occasionally the road crosses the canal over a bridge and is built along the other side. I suppose that the reason that this happens is that the steam shovel operator's right arm would get tired, so that he would use his left, pulling the left lever and throwing the dirt on the opposite side of the ditch. Ten years later, when the road builders came along, they had to build a bridge everywhere the excavating machine operator had changed hands.

If you are traveling along a road in the northern part of the Everglades, where the land is well drained, you will see, on both sides, orderly and neatly arranged farms with all sorts of flourishing crops. Occasionally there will be a busy little village. Where the road runs along a beautiful lake on the northern edge of the swamps, there are some small towns. Each small town has its hotel strategically located to ensnare the tourist. Each hotel is dignified by a negro doorman in a general's gold braid, full-dress uniform. But much of the doorman's dignity is lost by reason of the fact that, when no one is going in the door, it is his business to get out in the road and shout and wave and try his best to direct the motorist with his call of "Hotel! Right this way! Drive right in!"

If you are traveling along the road running west from Miami, you will see no sign of human habitation except an occasional Seminole Indian village. The Indians live in huts made from cane poles and roofed with thatch. If the natives were a little blacker, and if they wore just a few less clothes, the village would resemble an African village. During the rainy season, the land on both sides of the road appears to be a great field of water, with thousands of islands, some small, some very large. But during the dry season much of the water dries up, and the islands are joined. The extensive territory thus formed, of which there is today about three million acres, then has the appearance of the African veldt. In places the trees and brush are so thick that it is a physical impossibility to force a way through. Great areas of this jungle have never even been seen by white men. Other parts of the area are great plains with only occasional clumps of trees. These plains are the best hunting grounds in the country. All sorts of animals are there, from the rabbit to the brown bear. There are hundreds of deer. A species of panther roams the plains, and this panther is the largest to be found in America, since he has plenty of deer and other game to feed upon.

This picturesque remnant of the Great American Wilderness cannot last for long. Each year the drainage system lowers the level of the water a fraction of an inch. As more canals and ditches are dug, the jungle-swamp will be slowly won from the forces of nature. Peaceful, prosperous farms will replace the jungle, domestic livestock will replace the deer, and the Indians will live in modern houses instead of in cane huts. Civilization will have scored against the forces of nature.

OUTLINING

Necessity of having a plan

185. To make a composition clear and effective, proceed by a definite plan. Even clear and interesting statements will not be clear and effective if the writer sets them down haphazard, just as they occur to him; they must be organized into a whole. As in warfare a band of men, though strong and brave individually, is collectively weak if it is not well organized, so a speech, a report, an editorial, an essay, any composition, though its parts may be clear or forcible or clever, is weak as a whole if it is not well organized.

For example, a composition on *Denver* consists of a short paragraph on each of the following topics:

1. Location.
2. History.
3. Local pride.
4. Water supply (derived from mountain snow).
5. Capitol and United States mint.
6. Museums.
7. Principal business.
8. Dwelling houses (none built of wood).
9. Schools.
10. Wealth of citizens.
11. The city as a health resort.
12. Churches.
13. Strange spectacle of men skating in winter in their shirt sleeves.

This production, however interesting its material, is a series of haphazard remarks not organized into a whole. There is no reason for placing most of the parts where they are — no reason, *e.g.*, for discussing public buildings after the water supply, or skaters' costumes after churches. The material may be organized into a whole by the method shown in the following outline. (The numbers within the brackets correspond to numbers in the preceding outline.)

I. History. [2]
II. Location and climate. [1 and 13 — 13 as an illustration of the statements about the climate.]
III. Especially striking peculiarities of the city.
  1. Evidences of its being a health resort. [11]
  2. Absence of wooden buildings. [8]
  3. Public buildings. [5]
  4. Water supply. [4]
  5. Most striking of all — local pride. [3]
IV. Conditions of the people's life.
  1. Economic: Principal occupations. General wealth. [7 and 10]
  2. Educational and moral: Schools, museums, churches. [9, 6, and 12]

Making an outline

186. An outline is an orderly plan of the material to be used in a composition. First look at the subject or the material of your composition as a whole, decide what your topic sentence is, then divide this central idea into its several main topics, coördinate in importance. If your material demands it, subdivide these main topics into their subtopics, etc. Do not, however, make too minute a subdivision. (See Rule 193.)

In outlining, the material may be condensed into topics, sentences, or paragraphs, so numbered and indented as to show their logical relationship. There are, therefore, three kinds of outlines: topic, sentence, and paragraph outlines. (Throughout an outline, the writer must adhere to one type consistently.) The topic and the sentence outlines are more commonly used. Of these two the sentence outline is to be preferred, for it states more explicitly the writer's thought. (Compare the two outlines given below.)

187. In a topic outline, give all the topics, as far as possible, the form of nouns, with or without modifiers. For example, write "Rapidity of Movement" rather than "Moves Rapidly." Also, as far as possible, make the topics parallel in form. The writer often forgets the form of his first topics by the time he has reached his third or fourth topics.

Nouns preferable to verbs in topic outline

Illogical:

I. Powers of the Senate as a separate house.
   A. To confirm appointments.
   B. To ratify treaties.
   C. Trial of impeachments.
   D. Adopting its own rules of procedure.
   E. Electing its own officers (except its presiding officer).

Logical:

I. Powers of the Senate as a separate house.
   A. To confirm appointments.
   B. To ratify treaties.
   C. To try impeachments.
   D. To adopt its own rules of procedure.
   E. To elect its own officers (except its presiding officer).

188. In a sentence outline, write each division in the form of a sentence which expresses the central idea of the division. Subheads may be expressed as subordinate members of this sentence, or as separate sentences.

Sentence outline

THE GOVERNMENT OF SWITZERLAND

Topic Outline

Specimen topic outline

I. Value to Americans of a knowledge of Swiss institutions.
II. The legislative department.

A. The National Council.
   1. Apportionment.
   2. Elections.
B. The Council of States.
   1. Apportionment.
   2. Elections.
C. Powers of the legislature.

III. The executive department.
   A. Organization.
   B. Executive powers. — Comparison of Swiss and American executives.

IV. The judicial department: the constitutional court.
   A. Organization.
   B. Judicial powers. — Comparison of Swiss and American judiciaries.

THE GOVERNMENT OF SWITZERLAND

Sentence Outline

Specimen sentence outline

I. Knowledge of Swiss institutions is of value to Americans.

II. The legislative department consists of a bicameral legislature, called the Federal Assembly, composed of the National Council and the Council of States.
   A. The National Council, the more numerous branch, represents the people.
      1. It consists of one member for each 20,000 persons, with at least one member from each canton or half-canton.
      2. Members are elected for three years, by popular vote.
   B. The Council of States, the less numerous branch, represents the cantons.
      1. It consists of two members from each canton, and one from each half-canton.
      2. The method of election, term, and qualification are prescribed by each canton itself.
   C. The legislature is the supreme authority in the state, and has all powers not reserved to the people or to the cantons, and not granted to any other body.

III. The executive department consists of a Federal Council of seven members, elected by the Federal Assembly for three years.
  A. One member of the Federal Council is designated by the Federal Assembly to act as Federal President for one year; each of the seven members acts as head of an executive department.
  B. The Federal Council is subordinate to the Federal Assembly, and its powers are not comparable to those of the American executive; the Federal President is merely a presiding officer with no independent powers of importance.

IV. The judicial department consists of a Federal Court of twenty-four judges, elected by the Federal Assembly for six years.
  A. For ordinary purposes the court sits in small divisions.
  B. Its jurisdiction is largely constitutional, though in this respect it is not so powerful as the American Supreme Court.

189. A system of numbering and lettering the topics and subtopics is commonly used, as follows: (See outline in Rule 188.) System of numbering and lettering

I.
  A.
  B.
    1.
    2.
      a.
      b.
      c.
        (1)
        (2)
          (*a*)
          (*b*)

II. etc.

There may be, of course, other methods; but whatever method is used, that one must be followed consistently throughout.

Proper alignment

190. Place all coördinate topics at the same distance from the left-hand margin. When there is not space enough on the line for the whole of the topic or sentence, that part left over should be indented two or three spaces to the right of the margin of its governing topic. The marginal line of a subtopic should never be the same as that of its governing topic. (See outline in Rules 188 and 189.)

Misuse of *Introduction* and *Conclusion*

191. Do not entitle the first division *Introduction* nor the last *Conclusion* unless their material is distinct from the body.

Misuse of *Introduction* and *Conclusion:*
I. Introduction: the start of the sleighride.
II. The journey out.
III. Conclusion: the return.

Correct use of *Introduction* and *Conclusion:*
I. Introduction: winter in North Dakota.
II. The start of the sleighride.
III. The journey out.
IV. The return.
V. Conclusion: comparison of sleighing and other sports.

Body or *Discussion* not to be used

192. Do not use the title *Body* or *Discussion;* place the topics belonging to the body, or discussion, of an essay flush with the left-hand margin, as in the topic outline under section 188.

Over-minuteness

193. Do not indicate minute and unimportant divisions.

Unimportant subdivisions:
I. Situation of building.
  A. In Ames County.
  B. On a hill.
  C. Facing east.

Sufficient:
I. Situation of building.

Certain Illogical Practices

194. As a rule, each topic that is subdivided should have at least two subheads; it is logically impossible to subdivide a thing into fewer than two parts. If the topic has only one subtopic, the subtopic should usually (*a*) be joined to the governing topic, (*b*) be omitted, or (*c*) be supplemented by other subtopics.

More than one subtopic necessary

Illogical:
I. Ancestors.
A. Scotch.
II. Birthplace.
A. Farm in Indiana.
Logical: (*a*)
I. Scotch ancestors.
II. Birthplace: description of the Indiana farm.
(See also topics III B, and IV in the topic outline in Rule 188.)

Illogical:
I. Founding of the city.
A. By Dionysius Jones.
II. Its principal industry.
A. Piano manufacturing.
Logical: (*b*) and (*a*)
I. Founding of the city.
II. Principal industry, piano manufacturing.

Illogical:
I. Situation.
A. Advantages.
Logical: (*a*)
I. Situation: its advantages.
Logical: (*c*)
I. Situation.
A. Geographical location.
B. Advantages.
II. Attempts to destroy it.
A. The first attempt.
B. The attempt of 1901.
C. Reason for the failure of all attempts.

NOTE. — A topic may have only one subhead if the subhead is an example, illustration, or reference, none of which is, strictly speaking, a subdivision.

Right:
I. Extension of Mohammedan power under the early caliphs.
  A. Eastward and northward.
    1. For example, Persian and Greek lands.
  B. Westward.
    1. For example, Syria, Egypt, and northern Africa.

Subheads to cover field of governing topic

195. Each group of subheads, taken together, should sufficiently cover the field stated in their governing topic. If they do not, the fault may be remedied either by (*a*) making the governing title narrower, or by (*b*) adding subheads.

Illogical:
I. Powers of the Senate as a separate house.
  A. To confirm appointments.
  B. To ratify treaties.
  C. To try impeachments.

Logical: (*a*)
I. Principal powers of the Senate as a separate house.
  A. To confirm appointments.
  B. To ratify treaties.
  C. To try impeachments.

Logical: (*b*)
I. Powers of the Senate as a separate house.
  A. To confirm appointments.
  B. To ratify treaties.
  C. To try impeachments.
  D. To adopt its own rules of procedure.
  E. To elect its own officers (except its presiding officer).

Overlapping topics

196. Topics must not overlap; they must be mutually exclusive. Overlapping, an error in logic, is often due to the fact that the basis of subdivision is changed. For example, in the following subtopics, the basis for subdivision is changed from a geographical to a chronological basis. As a result some material would have to be discussed twice.

Illogical:

I. Literature in the United States. [Both geographical and chronological basis of subdivision.]
  A. Literature of New England.
  B. Literature of the South.
  C. Colonial literature.
  D. Literature to 1860.

Logical:

I. Literature in the United States. [Geographical basis of subdivision.]
  A. Literature of New England.
  B. Literature of the South.
  C. Literature of the Middle West, etc.

Logical:

I. Literature in the United States. [Chronological basis of subdivision.]
  A. Colonial literature.
  B. Literature to 1860.
  C. Literature of the Civil War, etc.

197. Do not write as a subtopic a topic that is logically coördinate with the preceding topic.

Coördinate title written like a subtopic

Illogical:

I. The departure.
II. The arrival in the city.
  A. Journey to the store.
    1. Purchases.

[IIA and IIA1, coordinate with I and II, are written as subordinate.]

III. Return home.

Logical:

I. Departure.
II. Arrival in the city.
III. Journey to the store.
IV. Purchases.
V. Return.

Logical:

I. Departure.
II. Experiences in the city.
  A. Arrival.

B. Journey to the store.
C. Purchases.
III. Return.

Subtopic written like a coördinate title

198. Do not place a subtopic coördinate with its governing topic.

Illogical:
- I. Disadvantages of football.
  - A. Physical harm.
  - B. Distraction from studies.
- II. Encouragement of gambling. [II is a subtopic of I but is written as a coördinate topic.]

Logical:
- I. Disadvantages of football.
  - A. Physical harm.
  - B. Distraction from studies.
  - C. Encouragement of gambling.

Main title written like subtopic

199. Do not write the title of the composition like the topic of a division.

Bad:
- I. Shipbuilding in Maine.
  - A. Introduction.
  - B. Principal seats.
  - C. Methods.
  - etc.

Right:

Shipbuilding in Maine

- I. Introduction.
- II. Principal seats.
- III. Methods.
- etc.

EXERCISES ON THE COMPOSITION AS A WHOLE

Exercise 1

Outlining

Make brief outlines for 400- to 500-word compositions on the following subjects:

1. College Slang
2. How I Use My Leisure
3. My Methods of Memorizing

4. The Sophisticated Student
5. How to Serve a Tennis Ball
6. On Getting on in a Fraternity
7. Saturday Night in a Small Town
8. Training Household Pets
9. My Favorite Building
10. Why People Collect Stamps

Exercise 2

Discuss the suitability of the following subjects for 500-word expositions. If you find the subjects too large, suggest subdivisions that might be treated in 500-word themes. **Unity**

1. The limitation of armaments
2. Representative government
3. The Federal Reserve Banking system
4. Relieving unemployment
5. Earning one's way through college
6. Modern poetry
7. How a large business enterprise is managed
8. Road building
9. Religion
10. Training for the track team
11. The French Revolution
12. Early American magazines
13. Culture
14. Managing a summer camp
15. American newspapers
16. The commercializing of football
17. The place of jazz in American music

Exercise 3

Suppose that you are an instructor to whom this theme had been handed in. Write a commentary upon it, considering its unity and coherence. Also make specific suggestions for the revision of its diction and its sentence construction. **Theme revision**

As Life Changes

Every person is an individual made up of a very complex combination of hereditary characteristics. As each century comes and goes, each individual either unites his characteristics for a useful or worth-while purpose, or finds them worth-

Theme revision

less and throws all possibilities away in order to live a life of personal self-indulgence. Thus it has been since the time of man's beginnings.

When knighthood was in flower, the honorable members of King Arthur's Round Table were those who bravely fought for the honor of beautiful ladies or valiantly went to battle for their king. As time passed on, life changed and found new organizations of society. People began to live on farms and work diligently for their families. They made their own clothes, cultivated their own fields, and lived very simple lives of earnest endeavor to secure an existence. They were ignorant and clung to ancient superstitions. Their only duty was to survive and to help their families to do so. There were lords and aristocrats who needed only to be cultivated gentlemen with wealth to secure their position among men. The rulers looked upon them as the ideal leaders of society whether they had the moral or intellectual demands or not. If they were studied and elegant personalities, that was all that mattered.

The great Industrial Revolution swept over Europe. The intellectual, economic, and religious revolutions as well changed life remarkably. Machines caused peasants to move from the farms to the city. People were united and not separated as before. Ancient superstitions were done away with, and science took its stand as an explanation of the nature of things existing in life. The Catholic Church no longer predominated, but religious freedom conquered. Intellectual freedom of press and speech and individual class distinctions were abandoned to a large extent. The simple life of the preceding centuries was to no longer exist, but instead a united and complex machine age in which life needed to work together in common production for the welfare of others. Now, the individual is of value to more than his own family. He is of value to all of society and his own country.

Today life is not simple but complex. People must work together. If this is true, then we have need of men and women who are capable of playing their parts most efficiently. When the intellectual revolution turned the wheels in Europe, it brought education and intellectual development to a greater part of society so that now an ideal citizen needs the advancement an education can give. He needs to be a part of society working for its betterment, cultivating an ideal home for the development of valuable future citizens, and as well he needs a cultivated appreciation of life intellectually and physically.

Exercise 4

Revise the following outlines, giving reasons for your changes. Outlining

A. The Sequoia Washingtoniana

Thesis: The Sequoia Washingtoniana grows to a huge size.

I. Everyone has heard of the vast size of this tree.
   A. The trunk of a well-grown specimen has a diameter of 20 or 30 feet.
      1. This is equal to the width of an ordinary house.
      2. Such a tree often towers 250 or 350 feet.
      3. This size tree would be six times as high as a large elm.
   B. There is a large amount of lumber from a tree this size.
      1. First there is enough lumber for 3000 fence posts.
      2. Second there is enough lumber to shingle the roofs of 70 or 80 houses.
      3. Last there still remain hundreds of cords of firewood.

B. My Scrapbook

Thesis: My scrapbook is the record of some of the things that happened to me, to my classmates, and to my school.

I. My scrapbook is like many other scrapbooks in outside appearance.
   A. It is of a certain size.
   B. It has color.
   C. It is well constructed.
II. My scrapbook contains various things.
   A. It contains clippings.
      1. Concerning sporting events.
      2. Scholastic records.

Outlining

B. Souvenirs.
1. From dances, parties, etc.
2. Sporting events.

III. I have reasons for keeping a scrapbook.
A. I want an account of the things in which I or my school participated.
B. I want to save certain souvenirs.
C. I want to keep a scrapbook.

C. Radio as a Hobby

Thesis: Radio is not only an exceptionally fine hobby, but it is a very easy hobby to acquire and offers much to the person who is willing to apply himself.

I. Radio is one of the best of hobbies and is accessible to everyone.
A. Radio is an instructive and practical hobby.
1. It will open a field of which the average person knows little.
2. If you intend to become an engineer, it will make you more valuable in your profession.
3. A knowledge of radio will enable you to obtain a position in an enlarging field.
4. One may make many social contacts through a knowledge of the radio.

B. Radio is an interesting hobby.
1. Radio is entirely different from the work of most men and affords a pleasant relaxation.
2. There are many fascinating angles of the radio which are easy to experiment with.

C. Radio is a cheap hobby.
1. It is very easy to obtain old secondhand parts from various sources.
2. Radio parts may be sold for practically the same price as was originally paid for them.

D. One's experience in the field of radio will be very valuable to one's country in case of national emergency. Outlining

II. Radio is a very easy hobby to acquire.

A. There are several ways to start this hobby.
1. If you have friends who are amateurs, go to them for advice.
2. If you have access to a library, there is a wealth of information to be gained by a little research.

B. One of the first things a beginner should do is to build a simple set.
1. Look up diagrams in various radio manuals and magazines and decide which you would like to build.
2. Before you begin to assemble the set, bring together everything needed.
3. In case you experience troubles, go to a friend or repair man and have him diagnose the difficulty.

C. Next get a group together, practice code, and talk over your problems.

D. When you are ready, take your examination.

III. If you wish to obtain the maximum value from your license, use it.

A. When you receive your license, get out on the air and practice.
1. The more you practice the better you will become.
2. If you don't practice, you will lose your knack and your work will be for nothing.
3. It is well worth while to take pride in your set and keep it up-to-date.

B. Your radio can be a very good medium through which to make friends.
1. When you go on the air, try to make as varied contacts as possible.
2. Another method to gain friends is to organize a club to talk over recent radio improvements and inventions.

Outlining

D. The Rayon Industry

Thesis: Is the rayon industry supplanting the silk industry? What are the characteristics of rayon that qualify it to compete with silk?

I. It has always been a desire among men to reproduce by artificial means natural substances that, because of their scarcity or beauty, are estimated at a high value.

- A. A French naturalist, in his effort to produce artificial silk, went so far as to produce a twisted ply yarn from spider thread, which was knit into stockings weighing only two and one-fourth ounces.
- B. Later another Frenchman succeeded in his chemical experiment on the same subject.

II. Many improvements have been made since the time of Chardonnet's successful experiment.

- A. One process is called the Cuprammonium and Viscose process.
- B. There is also the Acetate process.
- C. I shall not discuss either of these methods, for they will probably be tiresome and uninteresting.

III. Rayon has many characteristic properties, which I shall just mention.

- A. There has been some discussion as to whether or not rayon is perishable.
- B. Will it stand washing and ironing?
- C. Varieties of rayon differ in their ability to turn water.
- D. It is claimed that the rayon made by a certain process conducts the beneficial ultra-violet rays of the sunlight and excludes the harmful rays.
- E. Celulose acetate rayon is very resistant to dyes, and it has been necessary to develop special dyes to be used on it.

IV. The world needs new textile fibers.
   A. With the increase in population and the rapid spread of civilization, there has been an expansion of the world's textile requirements.
   B. This need will be more noticeable in a few years hence, for the European countries are rapidly recovering from the prostration caused by the war.
   C. Rayon, an inexpensive substitute for silk, can fill the demand of many women who desire to wear silk but who cannot afford it.

V. The consumption of rayon is very extensive.
   A. Tables to show the increasing consumption of rayon.
   B. There is also much discussion as to whether or not rayon will supplant the cotton industry.

VI. Rayon may be compared with natural silk in many ways.
   A. The two may be compared as to color and beauty.
   B. There is considerable difference in the strength of the two textiles.

Exercise 5

Outlining

The following topics were jotted down to be developed into an autobiography. From them make a topical outline for your own biography, first formulating a central idea, such as "my chief aim in life," "my ambition," or "my great interest." With this unifying thesis in mind, make the necessary rearrangements and subordinations, and add a sufficient number of subtopics to make your meaning clear. Indicate how you would apportion the space in a theme of 1500–2000 words.

I. My ancestors
II. My parents
III. My schooling
IV. My hobbies

V. Childhood experiences
VI. My companions
VII. My reading
VIII. The traveling I have done
IX. My ambitions
X. Teachers who have influenced me
XI. Tragedies in my life
XII. Good fortunes that have come to me
XIII. My home surroundings
XIV. Life in a small town (or country, or city)
XV. My character as I see it

Exercise 6

Outlining

Turn the topic outline that you made for the preceding exercise into a sentence outline.

GRAMMAR

MATTERS OF NUMBER[1]

200. A verb should agree in number with its subject.

Agreement of subject and verb

a. **Be careful not to make a verb agree with a word between it and the subject, instead of with the subject.**

Intervening words

Wrong: A new order of ideas and principles have been instituted.

Right: A new order of ideas and principles has been instituted.

b. **Words joined to a subject by *with*, *together with*, *including*, *as well as*, or *no less than*, do not affect the number of the subject.**

Number of the subject not affected by *with*, etc.

Wrong: The captain, as well as the mate and the pilot, were frightened.

Right: The captain, as well as the mate and the pilot, was frightened.

c. **A verb agrees with its subject, not with its predicate noun.**

Incorrect agreement with a predicate noun

Wrong: The main part of this machine are the large rollers.

Right: The main part of this machine is the large rollers.

Wrong: Oak, brass, and steel is the material of the structure.

Right: Oak, brass, and steel are the material of the structure.

Wrong: You, the chairman, is the one to present the case.

Right: You, the chairman, are the one to present the case.

[1] For definitions of grammatical terms, see Appendix B.

Subjects joined by *and*

d. **Two or more subjects joined by *and* require a plural verb.** Note, however, that a compound subject designating the same person or thing takes a singular verb; and that a compound subject designating closely related ideas may take a singular verb.

Right: His patience and perseverance {was / were} never failing.

Right: The captain and the mate were frightened.
Right: My teacher and friend [the same person] was ready to help me.

Subjects joined by *or* or *nor*

e. **Two or more singular subjects joined by *or* or *nor* require a singular verb, unless there is a strong plural feeling.**

Wrong: Neither he nor she are here.
Right: Neither he nor she is here.

Less desirable: One or the other of those fellows have stolen it.

Preferred: One or the other of those fellows has stolen it.

Singular and plural substantives

f. **When a subject is composed of both plural and singular substantives, joined by *or* or *nor*, the verb agrees with the nearer.**

Wrong: Neither Jack nor the Smiths plays well.
Right: Neither Jack nor the Smiths play well.

There is and *there are*

g. ***There is* should be followed by a singular noun; *there are*, by a plural noun or nouns.**

Wrong: There is too many people in this room.
Right: There are too many people in this room.

Collective nouns

h. **A collective noun takes a singular verb when the group is thought of as a unit and a plural verb when the individuals are thought of separately.**

Right: The audience was gathering slowly.
Right: The audience were of different opinions about the play.

Right: The class has voted to increase its dues.

Right: The class have been consulted by letter regarding the proposed increase of dues.

NOTE. — This rule applies to such nouns as *number*, *remainder*, *rest*, etc.

Right: A number of boys have joined the various organizations in the school.

Right: The number of pages in the book is enough to discourage a reader.

i. **Quantities and sums or multiples of numbers when expressing a single idea may take a singular verb.** The use of a plural verb may often be justified. Quantities, sums, multiples

Right: Nine inches is one-fourth of a yard.
Right: Eight and three makes eleven.
Right: Eight times three is twenty-four.
Right: Ten dollars is too much to pay for that hat.
Right: There were ten one-dollar bills in the purse.

j. **Fractions take a singular verb if the object of the following *of*-phrase is singular; they take a plural verb if the object of the following *of*-phrase is plural.**

Right: Two-thirds of the text has been covered.

Right: One-third of the students have already gone home for vacation.

k. **The relative pronoun following *one of* expressions refers not to *one* but to the plural object of *of*. The relative pronoun is therefore plural.** Number of a verb in a relative clause

Wrong: He is one of those men who talks much and thinks little.

Right: He is one of those men who talk much and think little.

l. ***Each*, *every*, *either*, *neither*, *someone*, *somebody*, *anyone*, *anybody*, *everyone*, *everybody*, *no one*, *nobody*, etc. are regularly followed by a singular verb. *None* usually takes a plural verb, unless a singular idea is clearly intended; often in that case *no one* or *nobody* is substituted for *none*.** Number of verb with *each*, *every*, etc.

Right: Each of the suspected men was held.
Right: Every one of us was glad to see her go.
Right: Neither of the answers is correct.
Right: Each branch and twig was still. [Note the compound subject.]

Number of pronouns referring to *each, every,* etc.

201. A pronoun agrees with its antecedent in number. *Each, every, either, neither, someone, somebody, anyone, anybody, everyone, everybody, no one, nobody,* etc. should be referred to by singular pronouns. Since there is in English no singular pronoun of common gender, the pronoun *he* (or *his*) is used for both masculine and feminine. However, in colloquial and popular speech and in informal writing, the plural pronoun *they* (or *them*) is often used when there is a distinct plural implication or when the singular pronoun produces an awkward or artificial effect.

Right: Every one opened his window.
Right: Each one of them is willing to do his share.
Colloquial: Every young man or woman is taken for what they really are.
Correct but clumsy: Every young man or woman is taken for what he or she really is.
Acceptable: Everybody there objected and declared they thought it barbarous.
Right but artificial: Everybody there objected and declared he thought it barbarous.
Possible: All the people there objected and declared they thought it barbarous.

Agreement of *these* or *those* with its substantive

202. The demonstrative adjectives *these* and *those* agree in number with the substantives that they modify. Note that *kind, type, sort,* are singular and cannot therefore be modified by ***these*** and ***those*,** which are plural.

Wrong: I like these kind of notebooks better than those old-fashioned type.
Right: I like this kind of notebook better than that old-fashioned type; [or] I like these kinds of notebooks better than those old-fashioned types.

Exercise A

Give your reason for using the singular or plural verb.

Agreement of subject and predicate

1. The size of the bathing suits [varies *or* vary].
2. Bread and butter [is *or* are] served with the meal.
3. The thing that kept me awake [was *or* were] the children shouting in the streets.
4. There [is *or* are] pity and sternness and indignation in her book, and always, understanding and sympathy.
5. One of the most interesting athletic phenomena of our time [is *or* are] the emergence of American Negroes as the best sprinters and jumpers in the world.
6. All that we can offer [is *or* are] your expenses.
7. Neither the players nor the audience [was *or* were] satisfied with the decision.
8. There [is *or* are] heaps of fun in guessing the answer.
9. A lot of people [thinks *or* think] so.
10. Half of it [is *or* are] finished.
11. Half of them [is *or* are] done.
12. There [is *or* are] lots of mistakes in her work.
13. There [is *or* are] lots of skating on this river.
14. The cost of these cars [ranges *or* range] from four hundred dollars to one thousand.
15. Neither the salary nor the work itself [offers *or* offer] any inducement to him.
16. A large percentage of absences [is *or* are] due to the common cold.
17. Four years [is *or* are] too long for us to be separated.
18. None of the dresses [suits *or* suit] her.
19. Every boy and girl [is *or* are] taught to read and write.
20. The sum and substance of it [is *or* are] that most of the ills of society spring from economic causes.
21. The registration place and the polling place [is *or* are] the same.
22. Here is a message of importance to every man and woman who [votes *or* vote].
23. A number of us [has *or* have] asked for an extension of time.
24. She is one of those particular housekeepers who [makes *or* make] everyone uncomfortable.
25. Either you *or* I [am *or* are] making a mistake.

Exercise B

Agreement of subject and predicate

What number of verb is used with each of the following words? If necessary consult an unabridged dictionary. Write sentences using each word as a subject with the proper number of verb.

gallows, news, measles, few, many, all, some, mumps, mathematics, physics, athletics, gymnastics, scissors, class, alms, riches, politics, tactics, data

Exercise C

Agreement

Supply the proper pronoun (*he, his, him, she, her, hers, they, their, theirs, them, himself, herself, themselves*).

1. Everybody wants —— vacation at the same time.
2. None of the girls will take —— share of the responsibility.
3. Everyone liked your speech, and —— are coming to hear you tonight.
4. Nobody knows what war really is until —— have experienced it.
5. Everyone expects us and we must not disappoint ——.
6. Neither of them could speak French; so —— were in a predicament.
7. Every boy and girl must be given a chance to develop —— special aptitudes.
8. Everybody should learn to take care of ——.
9. Someone has left —— books in my room.
10. Everyone agreed that if —— were given a chance to live —— life (*or* lives) over again, —— would live it (*or* them) differently.

MATTERS OF CASE

Nominative case for subject

203. The subject of a verb (except of an infinitive; see Rule 205) should be in the nominative case.

Who not affected by *he says*, etc.

a. **A parenthetic expression like *I think* or *he says* intervening between the pronoun *who* and its verb does not change the case of the pronoun.**

Wrong: The man whom I thought was my friend deceived me.

Right: The man who I thought was my friend deceived

me. [*Who* is the subject of *was; I thought* is a mere parenthesis.]

Wrong: Whom did they say won?
Right: Who did they say won?

Right: The chairman whom they elected has resigned.

b. **The pronoun *who* or *whoever*, when it is the subject of a finite verb, is sometimes wrongly put into the objective case, because it appears to be the object of a preceding verb or preposition.**

Subject *who* or *whoever* not affected by preceding words

Wrong: Send whomever will do the work.
Right: Send whoever will do the work. [*Whoever* is the subject of *will do,* not the object of *send.* The object of *send* is the clause *whoever will do the work.*]

Wrong: The question of whom should be leader arose.
Right: The question of who should be leader arose. [*Who* is the subject of *should be,* not the object of *of.* The object of *of* is the substantive clause *who should be leader.*]

204. A predicate substantive completing a finite verb should be in the nominative case.

Predicate substantive with finite verb

Right: It is I. The beneficiaries are she, they, and we. It is we that you accuse? [*It is me* is an accepted colloquialism.]

205. The subject of an infinitive and the predicate substantive completing an infinitive should be in the objective case.

Subject and predicate complement of an infinitive

Right: The gazette reported him to be dead. [*Him* is the subject of the infinitive *to be.*]

Right: She imagined the burglar to be me. [*Me* is the predicate substantive completing *to be.*]

Right: The man whom I thought to be my friend deceived me. [*Whom* is the subject of *to be.* See the first two examples under Rule 203 *a.*]

206. The object of a verb or of a preposition should be in the objective case.

Object of verb or preposition

Right: He often told us children of his adventures. [Not *we* children.]

Right: Does that rule apply to us upperclassmen? [Not *we* upperclassmen.]

If the interrogative pronoun *who* begins a sentence and is the object of a preposition or a verb at the end of the sentence, the tendency in speech and in informal writing is to use the nominative case.

Acceptable: Who did you mean?
Acceptable: Who are you speaking of?

Case after pure conjunctions

207. The pure conjunctions *and*, *but*, *or*, *either . . . or*, *neither . . . nor* connect nouns and pronouns in the same case. If the substantive preceding the conjunction is in the nominative case, then the substantive following it is in the nominative case, etc. (See Rule 108.)

Wrong: When she said that to Sister and I, we couldn't help laughing.

Right: When she said that to Sister and me, we couldn't help laughing.

Wrong: Between you and I, I think that she is mistaken.

Right: Between you and me, I think that she is mistaken.

Appositives

208. An appositive should be in the same case as the noun with which it is in apposition.

Right: All are going — he, she, and we two.
Right: He spoke to some of us — namely, her and me.
Right: We all met — she, the officer, they you mentioned, and I.

Substantive after *than* and *as*

209. *Than* and *as* do not affect the case of a following substantive. They are not prepositions, but conjunctions introducing subordinate clauses.

Right: He is happier than I. [*Than I = than I am.*]

Right: I can do it as well as they. [*As they = as they can do it.*]

Right: I should help him more willingly than her. [*Than her* = *than I should help her*.]

NOTE. — The expression *than whom* is ungrammatical, but well established as an idiom. *Than whom*

Right: Through all my troubles, I depended upon my roommate, than whom no stancher friend exists.

210. Avoid the use of the possessive case for inanimate objects; use an *of*-phrase. Possessive case: Nouns not designating persons

Awkward: The porch's roof.
Improved: The roof of the porch.

Awkward: The store's management.
Improved: The management of the store.

NOTE. — Good usage justifies many exceptions, including expressions designating time or measure, as *a day's journey, a stone's throw, five minutes' walk, a month's wages;* and expressions implying personification, as *for pity's sake, duty's pleadings, the law's delay.* Permissible exceptions

211. The substantive preceding the gerund is usually in the possessive case. (A gerund is a verbal ending in *ing*, and is used as a noun.) Possessive with a gerund

My stumbling over the rock proved to be a lucky accident.
It was our leaving during the lecture that annoyed him.

The substantive with a present participle is in the nominative or the objective case according to the use of the substantive in the sentence. (A present participle is a verbal ending in *ing*, and is used as an adjective.)

I, believing he was honest, trusted him with my money. [*I* is in the nominative case, the subject of the sentence, and is modified by *believing*.]
I found him writing a letter. [*Him* is in the objective case, the object of the verb, and is modified by *writing*.]

It is often difficult to distinguish between gerunds and participles when they are used after verbs or prepositions, and therefore impossible to be dogmatic re-

Possessive with a gerund

garding the case of the substantive. It is much a matter of emphasis. That which is uppermost in the speaker's or writer's mind determines the verbal. If the act is uppermost, the writer will no doubt use the gerund, reducing the person (or thing) acting to a possessive adjective. If, however, the person (or thing) acting is uppermost, the writer will probably use the objective case for the person (or thing) and reduce the verbal to a participial adjective.

> Gerund: I have often thought of his sitting up half the night over his calculations. [The act of *sitting up* is more prominent than the person.]
>
> Participle: I have often thought of him sitting up half the night over his calculations. [The person is more prominent than the act of *sitting up*.]
>
> Gerund: Can you imagine my talking to a duchess? [The act of *talking* is more prominent than the person.]
>
> Participle: Can you imagine me talking to a duchess? [The person is more prominent than the act of *talking*.]

There are, instances, however, such as the following, in which the possessive is not used before the gerund.

a. When the substantive has no possessive form.

> Some students may vote dishonestly, but I do not know of any having done so. [*Any* has no possessive case.]

b. When the substantive is separated from the gerund by a modifier or an appositive.

> Who ever heard of anyone in his right mind making such a request?

Exercise

Case

Supply the proper case. Give the reason for your choice.

1. I will tell you [who *or* whom] I think is responsible.
2. We will send [whoever *or* whomever] is willing to take the risk.
3. [Who *or* whom] are you waiting for?
4. We are certain as to [who *or* whom] did it.
5. [Who *or* whom] do you think will be elected?

Case

6. [Who *or* whom] do you think is capable of carrying on this work?
7. [Who *or* whom] did you say you saw?
8. We did not decide the question of [who *or* whom] was to be appointed guardian.
9. The man [who *or* whom] I thought to be his brother is his son.
10. I convinced her that it was [I *or* me].
11. She has offered to send all of us to college, even James and [I *or* me].
12. She is younger by many years than [I *or* me].
13. You have counted everyone but [I *or* me].
14. It is a challenge for you and [I *or* me] to be the best kind of citizen possible.
15. They were all there except you and [I *or* me].
16. It appears like discrimination against [we *or* us] girls.
17. She repeated what she had heard about Gerald and [I *or* me].
18. I am taller than [she *or* her] by several inches.
19. He has gone far beyond you and [I *or* me].
20. He sat down beside Mary and [she *or* her].
21. A new group is to be formed including you and [he *or* him].
22. They are never so accurate in their calculations as [he *or* him].
23. I am certain of [it *or* its] being [he *or* him].
24. I heard [his *or* him] talking to his brother.
25. He talked about [Society *or* Society's] being to blame, not [he *or* him].
26. We found [his *or* him] searching through the records.
27. Can you picture [my *or* me] teaching school?
28. What could you expect, [he, his, *or* him] being what he is?
29. You can depend upon [his *or* him] answering promptly.
30. There is danger of the [enemy *or* enemy's] attacking from the rear.
31. He told us of the [business *or* business's] going into bankruptcy.
32. There were rumors of the [foreman *or* foreman's] demanding higher pay.
33. There is an item in the paper about [John Swift *or* Swift's], the captain of the team, injuring his knee.
34. She objected to [my *or* me] reading novels.

35. I shall always remember [his *or* him] standing at the gangplank waving good-by.
36. As one stands by the graves of these soldiers, one cannot help thinking of [their *or* them] all dying in their youth.

ADJECTIVES AND ADVERBS

Adverb or predicate adjective

212. The word following the verb should be an adjective if it describes the subject; if it modifies the action of the verb, it should be an adverb.

a. **Such verbs as *appear*, *be*, *become*, *seem*, *smell*, *sound*, *taste*, *feel*, *look*, etc., commonly require an adjective.**

ADJECTIVES

Right: I feel bad [*i.e.*, *sorry* or *in low spirits* or *in bad health*].
Right: I feel well [*i.e.*, *in good health*].
Right: I feel good [*i.e.*, *in good spirits* or *in a virtuous mood;* should not be used to mean *in good health*].
Right: I am well [*i.e.*, *in good health*, an adjective use of *well*].
Right: I am ill [*i.e.*, *in bad health*, an adjective use of *ill*].
Dialect: I feel badly.
Dialect: I feel poorly, *or* I am poorly.
Right: He appears good [*i.e.*, appears to be a *good man*].
Right: He appears well in public [*i.e.*, makes his appearance in a creditable manner].
Right: It stands immovable. It smells sweet. It tastes sour. Your hand feels cold. She looks dainty. That statement sounds queer.

ADVERBS

Right: She smelled of the food cautiously.
Right: He looked longingly at the doughnuts.
Right: He sounded the gong slowly.
Right: She tasted of the cake critically.
Right: She felt of his hair suspiciously.

Adjective or adverb after verb and its object

b. **The modifying word after a verb and its direct object may be either an adjective or an adverb according to whether the object or the verb is modified.**

Right: He holds it steady *or* steadily.
Right: He filled it full *or* fully.
Right: He kept it safe *or* safely.
Right: He wrapped it tight *or* tightly.

Adverbs *fast, slow, loud, soft,* etc.

213. Some adverbs have two forms, one form like the adjective and another form with *ly* added; for instance, *slow, slowly*; *loud, loudly*; *soft, softly*; *cheap, cheaply*; *sharp, sharply*; *quick, quickly*; etc. The current tendency favors the usage of the form without *ly* in informal speaking and writing, especially in short quick sentences, in imperative sentences in particular; and the *ly* form in more formal speaking and writing, especially in long declarative sentences.

Common usage; acceptable: Drive slow. Speak loud and clear. Look sharp.
Correct: You should drive slowly on wet pavements. On the platform you should speak loudly and clearly. You must look sharply for the last turn in the road.

Adjectives and adverbs in *ly*

214. Some words ending in *ly* are both adjectives and adverbs, such as *early, only, cowardly, likely, unlikely, friendly, lordly, kindly, stately, lively, hourly, daily, weekly,* etc. Persons who feel that some of these words cannot correctly be used as adverbs, either avoid using them or attempt to add *ily* as in *unfriendlily*, forming words that are not recognized in present usage.

Correct: He was a kindly man. [Adjective]
Correct: He treated us very kindly. [Adverb]
Correct: He is a likely candidate. [Adjective]
Correct: We shall very likely go. [Adverb]

Confusion of adjectives and adverbs

215. Do not confuse these adjectives and adverbs:

Adjectives	*Adverbs*
sure	surely
some	somewhat
real	really
good	

Adjectives	*Adverbs*
well (in good health; *used in the predicate to mean* fortunate, proper, etc.)	well (satisfactorily, favorably)
most (nearly all, greatest in number, etc.)	almost (nearly) most (to the greatest extent)

Wrong: I sure am glad that you came.
Right: I am surely glad that you came.

Wrong: She is some better today.
Right: She is somewhat better today.
Right: There were some twenty people there. [*Some* now used adverbially only before a numeral.]

Wrong: I am real glad that you like it.
Right: I am really (*or* very) glad that you like it.

Wrong: She is doing good in her work.
Right: She is doing well in her work.
Right: She is feeling well.
Right: It is well that you came.

Wrong: We are most finished.
Right: We are almost finished.
Right: Most people like him.
Right: We are most pleased.

Comparative and superlative degrees

216. In formal writing the comparative degree of an adjective or an adverb is used in speaking of two persons or things and the superlative degree in speaking of three or more persons or things. In popular and colloquial speech, however, the superlative degree is frequently used of two persons or things.

Colloquial: She was the most popular of the two sisters.
Right: She was the more popular of the two sisters.
Right: She was the most popular of the three sisters.

Comparison of incomparable words

217. Certain adjectives and adverbs are logically incapable of comparison; as, for example, *circular, round, perfect, absolute, immortal, faultless, unique, equal, entire, whole, conclusive, unanimous.* Words of this type, however, tend to lose their superlative force.

Many good writers and speakers use a perfective adverb with these absolute words to restore their finality.

Illogical: I feel more equal to the task now than I have ever felt before.

Logical: I feel more able to do the task now than I have ever felt before; [or] I feel more nearly equal to the task now, etc.

Common usage: His satire on the corrupt society of the 17th century is quite perfect.

Exercise

Give the reason for your choice of words within the brackets. If more than one word can be used, state any difference in meaning. Adjectives and adverbs

1. The fish tasted [bad *or* badly].
2. I feel so [good *or* well] that I could walk ten miles.
3. Did you sleep [good *or* well]?
4. The flowers smell [sweet *or* sweetly].
5. That dinner looks [good *or* well] to me.
6. It tastes [sour *or* sourly].
7. I feel [bad *or* badly] that you are taking so much trouble.
8. That sentence sounds [correct *or* correctly] to me.
9. You are looking very [bad *or* badly].
10. We feel [kind *or* kindly] toward her.
11. The bell rang out [clear *or* clearly].
12. She is doing [good, well, fine, finely] after her operation.
13. She is doing [good, well, fine, finely] in her schoolwork.
14. I [sure *or* surely] dread going.
15. Go [slow *or* slowly] around the curves.
16. She is [real *or* really] pleased with the results.
17. She clutched it [tight *or* tightly] in her arms.
18. Listen [close *or* closely] and you will hear it.
19. We are [most *or* almost] there.
20. We are [some *or* somewhat] nearer than we were yesterday.

MATTERS OF MODE

218. Although the subjunctive mode is used less than formerly, yet it appears in some instances in informal as well as formal writing and speaking. Subjunctive mode

Subjunctive mode

a. **Wish**

I wish that I *were* going. [Colloquial: I wish that I *was* going.]

b. **Condition, contrary to fact**

If this *were* Wednesday, I would go with you. [Colloquial: If this *was* Wednesday, etc.]

If she *were* thinner, she would be better looking. [Colloquial: If she *was* thinner, etc.]

NOTE. — An *if*-clause expressing an improbability is sometimes in the subjunctive mode, although the present tendency is toward the use of the indicative mode.

If he *be* guilty, let him suffer the consequences. [*If he is guilty* would be the more usual form. It also implies less doubt.]

c. **Concession, contrary to fact**

Even though she *were* to pay me, I would not tell her. [Colloquial: Even though she *was* to pay me, etc.]

d. **After *as if* or *as though***

She looks as if she *were* frightened. [Colloquial: She looks as if she *was* frightened.]

He acts as though he *were* drunk. [Colloquial: He acts as though he *was* drunk.]

e. **Indirect imperative**

The terms of the agreement demand that the dispute *be* settled out of court.

I insist that he *attend* to the matter today.

f. **Motions and resolutions**

I move that the minutes *be* approved.

Resolved, that this question *be* submitted to a committee.

EXERCISE

Subjunctive mode

Give the reason for your choice of words within the brackets. If more than one word can be used, state any difference in meaning.

1. If I [was *or* were] you, I should wait until next year.
2. He acts as if he [was *or* were] unwilling to sign the paper.

3. She is always wishing that she [was *or* were] somewhere else.
4. He demands that she [moves *or* move] her furniture out before the first of the month.
5. The United States demands that the war debts [are *or* be] paid.
6. If he [is *or* be] dead, then we can get no evidence.
7. Even though I [was *or* were] to give her all that she asks for, she would not be satisfied.
8. God [blesses *or* bless] you.
9. The law requires that he [is *or* be] a citizen of the United States.
10. If he [goes *or* go], he will let you know.
11. Even though he [apologizes *or* apologize], she will never forgive him.
12. I suggested that he [follows *or* follow] directions carefully.
13. It was his mother's wish that he [goes *or* go] to Harvard.
14. It is not necessary that the bread [is *or* be] fresh.
15. He asks that she [has *or* have] faith in him until he can prove his innocence.

MATTERS OF TENSE

Present tense for statements permanently true

219. Statements permanently true should be put in the present tense. When they occur in a subordinate clause in indirect discourse, following a verb in past time, guard against their being attracted into the past.

Illogical: He said that oak was the best wood for floors.
Logical: He said that oak is the best wood for floors.

Illogical: I have always heard that the four years of college were the happiest in a man's life.
Logical: I have always heard that the four years of college are the happiest in a man's life.

The present tense is preferred, as a rule, in book reviews, criticisms, etc., for statements of permanent truth regarding a work of art. In statements relating the events of the author's life, etc., the past tense would, of course, be used.

Right: In *Old China*, Charles Lamb *pictures* most charmingly his home life with his sister Mary, to whom he *was* very devoted.

Right: Jane Austen's settings *are* of the English village life that she *knew* so well.

NOTE. — For the use of the historical present, see Rule 35.

The undated past tense

220. Obscurity, or an effect of incompleteness, arises from the use of a verb in the past tense when it is unaccompanied by a time modifier, and when there is in the context no indication of the time of the action.

Obscure and incomplete: In accounting for the origin of Lake Wingra, geologists say that a small stream ran through the territory where the lake now lies.

Clear [The necessary time modifier of *ran* is supplied]: In accounting for the origin of Lake Wingra, geologists say that at some remote period a small stream ran through the territory where the lake now lies.

NOTE. — When a sentence introduces a new or additional idea, obscurity is often avoided by the addition of a time modifier, no matter what the tense of the verb may be. Words expressing indefinite time, such as *now and then*, *always*, *frequently*, etc., are at times indispensable. Similarly adverbs and adverbial phrases or clauses expressing place or attendant circumstances should not be omitted when they make the meaning clearer. An example of the first part of this suggestion is found in the use of *at times* in the second sentence of the text of this paragraph.

Confusion of past and present tenses

221. The past tense and the present perfect tense should not be confused. The past tense represents action completed in the past. The present perfect represents action going on at any time up to the present.

Illogical: I have asked her yesterday to give me her address.

Logical: I asked her yesterday to give me her address.

Logical: I have asked her many times to give me her address.

Illogical: At present we did not have a reply from them.

Logical: At present we have not had a reply from them.

222. Maintain proper sequence of tenses. The tense of a verb in a subordinate clause should conform logically with the tense of the verb in the principal clause. The past is not all one, but may be said to consist of the particular time of the main narrative, previous time, and subsequent time down to the present, each time having its appropriate tense. Sequence of tenses

Illogical: They informed us that they wrote to Paris for instructions, but since then we did not hear the outcome of their inquiry.

Logical: They informed us [past time, past tense] that they had written [previous time, past perfect tense] to Paris for instructions, but since then we have not heard [subsequent time, perfect tense] the outcome of their inquiry.

Obscure: Mitchell hired a jockey named Brunt to ride Shackles in the approaching race. *Brunt was injured in a jump-race and gave up racing for a time.* But Mitchell persuaded him to begin again. [The reader supposes that the events stated in the italicized sentence followed the employment of Brunt by Mitchell; whereas the writer intends to say that those events preceded the employment. The use of the past tense in the italicized sentence is thus entirely misleading.]

Clear: Mitchell hired a jockey named Brunt to ride Shackles in the approaching race. Brunt *had been injured* in a jump-race and *had given up* racing for a time. But Mitchell persuaded him to begin again.

223. A conditional verb-phrase in a dependent clause should be in the present tense unless it represents action prior to that of the governing verb. Guard against its being attracted into the perfect. Sequence of tenses in conditional clauses

Illogical: I should not have said it if I had thought it would have shocked her.

Logical: I should not have said it if I had thought it would shock her.

224. An infinitive should be in the present tense unless it represents action prior to that of the govern- Tense of infinitive

ing verb. Guard against its being attracted into the perfect.

Illogical: It was not necessary for you to have gone.
Logical: It was not necessary for you to go.

Illogical: I intended to have answered.
Logical: I intended to answer.

NOTE. — After past tenses of *hope, fear, expect* and the like, the perfect infinitive is used, incorrectly indeed and unnecessarily, but so often and with so useful an implication that it may well be counted idiomatic. That implication is that the thing hoped . . . did not come to pass . . . — H. W. FOWLER.

Tense of participle

225. The past participle represents action prior to that of the governing verb; the present participle, action at the time expressed by the verb.

Wrong: It is old, being founded in 1809.
Right: It is old, having been founded in 1809.

Wrong: Starting for London, he arrived there two weeks later.
Right: He started for London and arrived there two weeks later.

EXERCISE

Tense

Correct any errors in tense in the following sentences. Give your reasons for changes.

1. He stopped the car to see whether his tire blew out.
2. Did the bell ring yet?
3. Did you ever wonder whose machine-gun voice utters the words, "Time marches on"?
4. I was ready since Saturday.
5. I saw him only once since we were in college.
6. I heard nothing but "Henry, Henry, Henry" from you all week.
7. This was the first and last time that Stalin let himself be photographed by a newspaperman.
8. I should have liked to have told her what I thought about her.
9. I hoped to have seen you before this.
10. I had expected to have gone by this time.

11. Thinking they were the right persons, I gave them the money.
12. Coming across the field toward us, he laid his pipe on the stump.
13. Have statistics proved that cigarette smoking was harmful?
14. It is a long time since I have seen you.
15. It is ten years since Henry has been home.
16. She was the ugliest woman I ever saw.
17. Raising the huge brass knocker and letting it fall, we heard a shuffling in the entry.
18. After being separated for fifteen years, they were married in Rome. They met as undergraduates and become engaged. After his graduation, he went into the diplomatic service and was sent to the Far East. They drifted apart, each marrying someone else. By a strange coincidence they, both widowed, ran across one another in Rome and became acquainted again.
19. It was a perfect afternoon, and Mack and I had splendid luck in the morning, each catching four fine bass. The sun was just touching the top of the east wall of Apple River Canyon, which was not really a canyon although the natives called it that.
20. I thought that you would have understood.

SHALL AND *WILL*

Shall and *will.* Expectation

226. To represent simple future use *shall* (or *should*) in the first person, and *will* (or *would*) in the second and third persons. Most of the errors in the use of *shall* and *will* consist in the use of *will* for *shall* in the first person, future. *I will miss her very much* means, in the idiomatic sense, *I am willing* or *I am determined to miss her*. The intended meaning is, of course, the simple future, *I am going to miss her*.

Memorize the following formula:

I shall (should)	we shall (should)
you will (would)	you will (would)
he will (would)	they will (would)

Right: I think I shall be able to go.
Right: I think he will be able to go.

Right: I feared I should fail.
Right: I feared you would fail.

Determination, etc. of the speaker

227. To represent determination, desire, intention, willingness, promise, prophecy, or threat on the part of the speaker, use *will* (or *would*) in the first person, and *shall* (or *should*) in the second and third persons. The following is the formula for such expressions:

I will (would)	we will (would)
you shall (should)	you shall (should)
he shall (should)	they shall (should)

Right: I will help you; I promise it. You shall not stir; I forbid it. They shall be hanged at sunrise; we, the court, decree it.

NOTE. — In the first person, the subject of the sentence and the speaker are the same; therefore it is the subject who is determined, willing, etc.: *I will go* means *I am determined to go.* In the second and third persons, however, the subject is not the speaker but a person under the control of the speaker: *he shall go* means *I am determined that he will go.*

Determination, etc. of the subject of the sentence

228. To represent determination, desire, etc. on the part of the subject of the sentence rather than on the part of the speaker or writer, *will* is used with all persons. (In the first person, the subject and speaker are the same person.) In speaking, *will* is stressed.

You wíll go, I see, in spite of all we say.

He wíll speed, no matter how many times he is fined.

Shall and *will* with *like*, etc.

229. The verbs *like*, *prefer*, *care*, *be glad*, *be inclined*, etc. use the auxiliary for the future: *shall* for the first person and *will* for the second and third. *I will be glad to go* means, in the idiomatic sense, *I am determined to be glad*, or *I am willing to be glad.* The determination, etc. is expressed in the *like, prefer,* etc. and should not be repeated in the auxiliary.

Right: I should like to see her when she returns.
Right: He would like to see her when she returns.

230. ***Should*** **is used for all persons and both numbers in the following instances:** *Should* for all persons

a. **To express obligation or duty**

I should not have said that.
You should mind your own business.
They should know better.

b. **To express a condition in an *if*-clause**

If I *should* leave, he would not care.
If you *should* leave, he would not care.
If he *should* leave, I should not care.

231. ***Would*** **is used for all persons and both numbers to express an habitual action or a tendency.** *Would* for all persons

I would sit by the hour waiting for her to come.
When you were little, you would always ask for the neck of the chicken.
He would always whistle when he went by the graveyard.

232. In questions: In questions

a. **Use *shall* with the first person and *will* with the third person to express simple future.** Almost always the question is one of simple future.

Right: Shall I go now? [Future]
Right: What shall we do? [Future]
Right: Shall I see you tomorrow? [Future]
Right: Shall we be in time for the concert? [Future]
Right: Will I help you? Why certainly. [Speaker repeats the question addressed to him.]
Right: Will he answer my letter? [Future]
Right: Will he be there to meet us? [Future]
Right: What shall he do next? [What does the person addressed wish him to do next?]

b. **With the second person, use the auxiliary that will be used in the answer.**

Future: Shall you be recognized, do you think? [The answer, according to Rule 226 would be either, *I shall be* or *I shall not be;* therefore *shall* should be used in the question.]

Willingness: Will you do it? [The answer, according to Rule 227, would be either *I will* or *I will not;* therefore *will* should be used in the question.]

Shall and *will* in subordinate clauses

233. In indirect quotations and questions:

a. **To express the simple future, the auxiliaries are used according to the general rule: *shall* (or *should*) with the first person, and *will* (or *would*) with the second and third persons.**

Future: I think that I shall wait for you.
Future: He said that I should wait for you.
Future: I know that you will be invited.
Future: She asked him whether he would be late for dinner.

b. **To express determination, desire, etc., the auxiliaries used are those that would be used in the direct form.**

Willingness: He says that he will help. [Direct: I will help.]
Promise: She asked him whether he would give her the money. [Direct: Will you give me the money?]

Tendency toward simplification

234. Some of the rules for *shall*, *will*, *should*, and *would* are disregarded by many intelligent and educated persons especially in informal speech and writing.

If the present widespread use of *will* in all three persons as a sign of the pure future should become finally established in the literary language, it would be a distinct gain to English expression in the direction of greater simplicity. We should, however, in this event lose some useful distinctions in the first person. These distinctions are not so intricate that they could not be grasped by most people, for in England the uneducated, in general, observe them. But the great mass of English-speaking people are today at this point borne along unconsciously by the strong drift toward a greater simplicity of expression. — G. O. Curme, *Syntax*, p. 371.

Exercise

Shall and *will*, etc.

Fill in the blanks with *shall*, *will*, *should*, or *would*. State your reasons for your choice. If more than one could be used, explain the difference in meaning.

1. —— you be ready to give your report tomorrow?
2. She —— have had more sense.
3. If they —— pay in advance, we could reimburse you.
4. If he —— only listen.
5. What —— I do if he comes?
6. —— I answer the telephone?
7. I —— not do that if I were you.
8. She —— bite her fingernails despite all our efforts.
9. I —— like to apply for a position.
10. He —— do as he is told.
11. He says that he —— go when his turn comes.
12. I —— be glad to give you a recommendation.
13. If you —— follow the directions carefully, you —— have no trouble.
14. I —— do as I please, no matter what she says.
15. He asked us whether we —— wait for him.
16. —— you go to Paris when you are abroad this summer?
17. We —— hear from him again; he —— never forgive us.
18. I —— be foolish to miss this opportunity, ——n't you think so?
19. —— we meet downtown?
20. How much —— you give to know the answer?

EXERCISE ON GRAMMAR

Grammar

Correct any errors in grammar that you may find in the following sentences. Give your reasons for making the changes.

1. Diamonds is trump.
2. Are you sure that it is I who is wanted?
3. Half of the city's fire-fighting engines were called out.
4. Most of the corn and wheat have been damaged by the drought.
5. Our complete stock of diamonds, jewelry, standard-make watches, and silverware are going on the auction block.

Correcting errors in grammar

6. It is the few finishing touches that postpone the opening of the new bridge.
7. Neither of the boys were sick a day while they were gone.
8. Each of us try to help the other.
9. Differential and integral calculus was difficult for me.
10. After the preliminary plans and the necessary legislation was completed, the actual operations were started.
11. In so dense a forest, there was no chance of him escaping without some injury.
12. As a small boy, my ambition was to be a jockey, and when I was eighteen, the opportunity presented itself.
13. These people are just a background that help in forming us.
14. He was pitcher on the side opposite my friend and I.
15. The machine is driven by the power from the boat's engine, and so rapid does it work, that three men are required to remove the fish from the net.
16. I will gladly answer any questions that I can.
17. Colleges are filled with students who are hoping to be educated so that they might do business better than the uneducated.
18. I was so much excited that I did not even ask Ned who he was trying to get to help.
19. It was the fate of my cousin and I to have to play a cornet duet.
20. I know now that death comes unexpected under all circumstances.
21. Economists predict that, according to statistics, the earth, two centuries hence, would be overflooded with population.
22. There has been many attacks upon present-day college education.
23. My lamb had grown to a great size, and his nimble black legs grew sleek and strong, his large brown eyes became almost human in understanding, and his wool had become bountiful and fine in texture.
24. We crept up slower and slower, finally reaching the house.
25. When I asked to sleep in the "best room," my request had met with surprisingly little objection.

Correcting errors in grammar

26. Sleeping cars are built of steel, which make them safe in case of a wreck.
27. Sometimes I wonder whether I will ever be of as much use as my grandmother was when she was young.
28. Age has added its mellowing touch to the older buildings — the original fortress, the blockhouses, the sturdy remains of what in that time were the acme of perfection in defensive structures.
29. Although we are all created equally, some of us still feel a little better than others.
30. The old hen with her large brood of little chicks were all trying to crowd into the tiny playhouse.
31. Two-thirds of my time is spent on my mathematics.
32. None of us is going to the concert.
33. He gave the most complete explanation of all.
34. She is one of those comfortable kind of persons who always makes you feel at ease.
35. I am more worried than her about the news.
36. He cut her off short in the middle of her story.
37. Would you care to come with us?
38. I would like to apply for a position in your high school.
39. The whole family were there: her, her mother, and her four sisters.
40. Drive slow. Dangerous hill ahead.
41. She would not dare say that to either you or I.
42. Whom do you think would be able to fill such a position?
43. I feel good this morning for the first time since I took cold.
44. His father is determined that he goes to college.
45. What will we do if the doors are locked?
46. Who should he choose for his partner but I!
47. They were to have gone yesterday.
48. I had enough money left to buy some lunch for my friend and I.
49. As the car's headlights blazed into my eyes, I was blinded.
50. He consulted all people who he considered wiser than himself.
51. For pledging dinner, you will wear a formal, but you will not need them again until October or November.
52. The few ashes resulting from the burning of hard coal means less disagreeable work.

Correcting errors in grammar

53. The storm of questions and suspicions and rumors, some confirmed, others unconfirmed, have been so violent as to raise in any reasonable person's mind a further question.
54. We left for Paris the next day, arriving there on Sunday.
55. If that was true, then I did right.
56. Which is the man who they thought him to be?
57. There is to be a dance and a bridge party there tonight.
58. They were all there, each one of them dressed up in their best.

PUNCTUATION

SUMMARY OF THE MOST SERIOUS ERRORS IN PUNCTUATION

Principal clause, subordinate clause, phrase to be distinguished

235. The most serious errors in punctuation are due to the confusion between the comma and the period; and between the comma and the semicolon, a weak period. The difference between these marks is one of degree: the comma is the weakest mark, the semicolon the next in strength, the colon still stronger, and the period the strongest. Their use depends upon the closeness or the remoteness of the relationship between the parts of the sentence. A writer will not always be certain of this relationship and therefore will not use these marks correctly unless he knows the difference between independent and dependent ideas; that is, the difference between a principal clause, a subordinate clause, and a phrase. He must also know what constitutes a complete sentence. (For grammatical definitions see Appendix B.)

A principal clause can be distinguished from a subordinate clause by the fact that the subordinate clause is introduced by (and usually begins with) a relative pronoun or a subordinating conjunction. The relative pronouns are *that, who, what, which, whoever, whatever,* and *whichever.* The principal subordinating conjunctions are *if, as if, even if, though, although, whether, lest, unless, than, as, that, in order that, so that, because, since, when, whenever, while, after, where, whereas, wherever, provided, provided that, before, how, however, until.* Simple conjunctions and conjunctive adverbs, which do not subordinate the subjects and predicates following them, should be carefully distinguished from relative pronouns and subordinating conjunctions. (See Appendix D.)

A phrase can be distinguished from a clause by the fact that it does not contain a finite verb. A phrase and a subordinate clause cannot alone compose a sentence; they depend for complete meaning upon a principal clause. Therefore every sentence must contain a principal clause.

Principal clause (complete sentence): The hours passed slowly.
Subordinate clause (incomplete sentence): Although the hours passed slowly . . .
Participial phrase (incomplete sentence): The hours passing slowly . . .
Prepositional phrase (incomplete sentence): With the slow passing of the hours . . .

COMMA AND PERIOD

Period fault **236. Do not use a period instead of a comma after a fragment of a sentence.** This error, the "period fault," is one of the most serious, for it breaks up a complete thought into incomplete fragments. It shows that the writer either is careless or is ignorant of what constitutes a complete sentence.

Incomplete sentence: After we had rested. [Subordinate clause; no principal clause]
Complete sentence: After we had rested, we started digging our way out. [Subordinate clause; principal clause]
Incomplete sentence: The weather being pleasant today. [Participial phrase]
Complete sentence: The weather is pleasant today. [Participle changed to a finite verb]
Incomplete sentence: We settled down to the long grind. The roar of the engine filling the cab. [The first sentence is complete; the second is incomplete because there is no finite verb.]
Complete sentence: We settled . . . The roar of the

engine filled the cab; [or] We settled down to the long grind, the roar of the engine filling the cab.

Incomplete sentence: Head high, I marched to my seat. Amidst a dead silence. [The first sentence is complete; the second is incomplete — it is only a prepositional phrase.]

Complete sentence: Head high, I marched to my seat amidst a dead silence. [Not even a comma is necessary after *seat.*]

Permissible sentence fragments

An incomplete sentence is to be distinguished from the correct abbreviated forms of complete ideas such as are illustrated in the following cases:

1. Questions and answers to questions, especially in conversation.

Why not?
Because it is too late.

2. Exclamations.

A pretty situation!
At last!

3. Transitions.

Now for the next objection.
To consider the next point.

Incomplete sentences may properly be used to gain emphasis or realism in efforts to reproduce the style of speech. There is a great difference between the incomplete sentence designedly used by the skilled writer and that of the illiterate who places a period in his sentence before he has completed it. Contrast these examples:

He began to plan what he would do with his Saturday afternoons and his Sundays. He would not go to the club for lunch on Saturday. No, cut away from the office as soon as possible and get them to give him a couple of slices of cold meat and half a lettuce when he got home.

— Katherine Mansfield.

Fishing attracts men of all professions. Whether they are farmers, lawyers, merchants, or doctors.

A writer should not use incomplete sentences until he is absolutely certain that he knows the difference between a complete and an incomplete thought. Even then incomplete sentences should be used with caution; they are likely to produce a jerking, exclamatory, and artificial style that soon becomes tiresome.

Exercise

Sentence fragments

(*a*) Point out the sentence fragments, and show why they are fragments. (*b*) Are any of them permissible? Why are they excusable? (*c*) Revise those fragments that need revision. Add words if necessary.

1. The courtyard was damp with the early morning dew. Except in those spots where the sun shone directly down.
2. The bougainvillea and wisteria, which followed the graceful curves of the fan-shaped windows of the old house, swayed back and forth in the morning breeze. And from time to time let fall a few purple petals.
3. At last we were lined up for the spelling match. The boys shaking their fists at one another across the room, the girls shifting nervously from one foot to the other.
4. The master builder of Beauvais must have been an inspired man. What youthful spirit! What restless vigor!
5. He moved onto the poorest farm in the neighborhood. His sorry horses breasting the keen March wind with stolid pertinacity.
6. Although traveling first-class in Europe is much more comfortable. I find third-class much more interesting.
7. Wacker Drive, Chicago. A boulevard of rare beauty, with impressive structures of stone and steel towering into the air. Business and tumult, with the roar of trains buzzing in one's ears; while above, in magnificent offices resplendent with fine furniture and tapestry, ticker tape flows in never-ending coils.

8. Hayseeds, grain dust, and butchering grease — undesirable things, yet the spice of farm life.
9. Just try serving a threshing dinner in grand style! All that the men want is good food and plenty of it. Bread, meat, potatoes, gravy, pie, and coffee. Salads and fancy desserts not necessary.
10. But returning to the subject of Mrs. Mincer's funeral. I am sure that if she had been there, it would have been much more efficiently managed. Perhaps a good thing that she did not know what happened.
11. While the western nations have been alleviating famine and removing pestilence. At the same time by every conceivable device of science, they have been increasing the destructiveness of war.
12. War gives men the intensest excitement that they can experience. That of killing men.
13. Dip, pull, rest. Dip, pull, rest. On and on, mile after mile, while the trees on shore swing to the rhythm of the paddle.
14. She would not answer his letter immediately. Probably not for some time. A long puzzling silence, during which he would wonder, then grow anxious, and probably even frantic because she did not care any more.
15. Those favoring old-age pensions believe that a greater national efficiency can be attained by its adoption. Since each rising generation would be freed of the burden of supporting its parents.

COMMA AND SEMICOLON

237. Distinguish between a comma and a semicolon. Comma and semicolon

a. **Between principal clauses connected by the pure conjunctions *and*, *or*, *but*, *for*, a comma is sufficient.** Sometimes if the clauses are very short, not even a comma is needed. (See Rule 246.)

Right: I spent the whole evening on my mathematics lesson, but I could not solve more than two problems out of ten.

Right: The winters are cold and the summers are hot.

b. **Between a preceding subordinate clause and its principal clause, a comma is sufficient.** Since a sub-

Comma and semicolon

ordinate clause is incomplete in meaning without its principal clause, a semicolon must not be placed between them. (See Rule 261.)

Right: If I do not go tomorrow, she will be angry.

c. **Between two principal clauses not joined by a pure conjunction, a semicolon is necessary.** The gap in thought is too great for a comma unless the clauses are short and parallel in form. Placing a comma between two unconnected principal clauses is called a comma fault, and like the period fault, it is a serious error. It indicates that the writer is not aware of the difference between independent and dependent ideas. (See Rule 247.)

Wrong: He did not wait for an answer, he grabbed his hat and ran.

Right: He did not wait for an answer; he grabbed his hat and ran.

d. **Between principal clauses joined by a pure conjunction when there are commas within the clauses, a semicolon is the logical mark.** (See Rule 269.)

Bedlam would be comic, perhaps, if there were only one madman in it; and your Christmas pantomime is comic, when there is only one clown in it; but when the whole world turns clown, and paints itself red with its own heart's blood instead of vermilion, it is something else than comic, I think. — Ruskin.

e. **Between principal clauses joined by one of the conjunctive adverbs *however*, *therefore*, *moreover*, etc., a semicolon is necessary.** (See Rule 268.)

Right: The ferry could not break through the ice; therefore we had to walk to shore on the ice.

Summary of rules for comma, semicolon, period

238. The following chart summarizes the principal rules regarding the use of commas, semicolons, and periods with simple, compound, and complex sentences.

Summary of rules for comma, semicolon, period

Clause	Punctuation	Conjunction	Clause	Rule	Comment
Principal (Simple sentence)	.			239	
Principal	,	*and* *or* *but* *for*	principal	246	Not necessary if clauses are short and closely connected.
Subordinate	,		principal	261	Usual
Principal			subordinate	261	Exception: 259 *a*
Principal	; or .		principal	247	A period should be used if the clauses are not closely enough related to form a unified sentence.
Principal containing commas	;	*and* *or* *but* *for*	principal containing commas	269	The semicolon is the logical mark to indicate the strongest break in the sentence.
Principal	;	*therefore* *however* *moreover* *nevertheless* etc.	principal	268	

Exercise

Comma fault

(*a*) Point out the comma faults. Show why they are comma faults. Correct them. (*b*) Are there instances in these sentences where commas could be used between the coördinate principal clauses? Give your reasons.

1. My education, especially in high school, had been almost wholly technical, I had spent much of my

Comma fault

time in drafting rooms and in the various departments of shop-practice training.

2. After several years of this sort of education, my love for mechanical things still remained, in fact, it was stronger than ever.
3. The town is not progressive, all the ambitious young people leave as soon as they graduate from high school.
4. For night hitchhiking, gas stations are the ideal take-off points, your chances of being picked up on the open road are very slim.
5. He was always short of funds, he was always behind in his studies, and of course he was always involved in a torrid romance.
6. My hands shook, my lips were dry, my heart pounded.
7. He put on weight, his sallow face became ruddy, the restless look in his eyes disappeared.
8. Here there are no flowers, they have been snuffed out by the huge trees whose far-reaching roots have found and have consumed all the fertility from the soil.
9. There are great numbers of fish, snakes, and lizards, and there are many whirring flocks of quail, ducks, and geese.
10. Great gray cranes soar up from their haunts, a horny fish leaps and quivers in the dark water, a burly ground hog pops his head out of a hole and basks in the sunlight.

END PUNCTUATION

THE PERIOD (.)

Close of a sentence

239. A period is used after a complete declarative or imperative sentence.

Abbreviations

240. A period is used after an abbreviated word or a single or double initial letter representing a word; as *etc.*, *viz.*, *Mrs.*, *i.e.*, *e.g.*, *LL.D.*, *pp.*

NOTE. — It is scarcely practicable to make a distinction here between abbreviations and contractions. *Dr.* for *Doctor*, *Mr.* for *Mister*, *Mrs.* for *Mistress* are usually called abbreviations although they are shortened by the omission of letters within the word. There is variation in the use of the period after them. Note that a period is not used after *Miss*, a contraction of *Mistress*.

241. Periods or dots, usually three, are used to indicate the omission of words from a quoted passage. Omissions

A score of people all doing apparently the same quality of work in the professional world, all enjoying a popular reputation, all backed by a college education, . . . will often be found to show a lack of mental sympathy so profound that one wonders how such people can smilingly continue to seem to be living in the same world. — R. BOURNE.

242. Periods or dots, usually three (four at the end of a sentence closed by a period), are often used in dialogue and interrupted narrative to indicate hesitations, pauses, emotional stress, etc. They should be used with caution. In dialogue, etc.

I talk about being done with it — with the bally thing at the back of my head. . . . Forgetting . . . hang me if I know! I can think it quietly. After all, what has it proved? Nothing. I suppose you don't think so. . . . — J. CONRAD.

THE QUESTION MARK (?)

243. A question mark is used after a direct question, but not after an indirect question. Direct, not indirect questions

Bad: He asked what caused the accident?
Right: He asked what caused the accident.
Right: He asked, "What caused the accident?"
Right: Will he come? and how long will he stay?

244. A question mark between parentheses is used to indicate that a statement is conjectural. It should not be used to indicate humor or irony. (See Rules 295 *h* and 420.) Use for conjectural statement

Right: This event occurred in 411 B.C.(?)
Objectionable: After his polite (?) remarks, we have nothing to say.
Right: After his polite remarks, we have nothing to say.

THE EXCLAMATION MARK (!)

Use of exclamation mark

245. An exclamation mark is used after a sentence, a virtual sentence, an exclamation in question form, or an interjection, to indicate strong emotion.

Right: I cannot and will not believe it!
Right: A pretty situation! What! How dare you say so!

PUNCTUATION WITHIN THE SENTENCE

THE COMMA (,)

Coördinate clauses joined by a conjunction

246. A comma is used to separate coördinate clauses joined by one of the pure conjunctions, *and*, *but*, *for*, *or*, *neither*, *nor*, unless the clauses are short and closely connected.

Right: The telephone rang violently, but no one answered.
Right: The question was laid before them, and after weeks of arguments it was still unsettled.
Right: I called but she was away.

Comma before *for*

NOTE 1. — The observance of the foregoing rule is especially important in the case of clauses connected by the coördinating conjunction *for*. Unless a comma is placed between such clauses, the *for* may be mistaken momentarily for a preposition.

Misleading: She was obliged to give up the dinner for her cook was leaving.
Clear: She was obliged to give up the dinner, for her cook was leaving.

NOTE 2. — This rule concerns only coördinate *clauses* joined by conjunctions; it does not refer to a clause containing a compound predicate of two verbs.

Comma unnecessary: He seized the rope, and hauled the boat alongside.
Right: He seized the rope and hauled the boat alongside.

NOTE 3. — Do not put the comma after the conjunction.

Wrong: The telephone rang violently but, no one answered.

Right: The telephone rang violently, but no one answered.

247. Do not use a comma between coördinate principal clauses that are not joined by one of the pure conjunctions, *and*, *or*, *but*, *for*, etc., unless the clauses are short, have no commas within themselves, and are closely parallel in form and substance. Use a semicolon if the clauses can be put into one unified sentence; otherwise use a period between them. Comma fault

Wrong: He could not concentrate, this was the cause of his failure.

Right: He could not concentrate; this was the cause of his failure.

Wrong: He threw the weapon from him, it clattered noisily on the floor.

Right: He threw the weapon from him; it clattered noisily on the floor.

Wrong: We have won for two years, if we win today, we retain the trophy.

Right: We have won for two years; if we win today, we retain the trophy. [Note that the semicolon break comes between the first principal clause and the subordinate clause depending upon the second principal clause.]

Undesirable: Oh, come, you'd better.

Right: Oh, come; you'd better.

Right: The curtains fluttered, the windows rattled, the doors slammed.

Right: Nothing future is quite secure; states enough have inwardly rotted; and democracy as a whole may undergo self-poisoning. — WILLIAM JAMES. [Although the clauses are closely parallel in form, yet commas would be too light.]

Bad: Student organizations give one a training for leadership in business organizations, for they duplicate, to a large extent, conditions of a business or-

Comma fault

ganization; work with a student organization teaches one to coöperate with others, to take responsibility, and to direct others.

Improved: Student organizations give one a training for leadership in business organizations, for they duplicate, to a large extent, conditions of a business organization. Work with a student organization teaches one to coöperate with others, to take responsibility, and to direct others.

NOTE 1. — A worse fault than the "comma fault" is that of putting together two principal clauses without any mark of punctuation.

Wrong: I enjoyed my week in Chicago it was my first visit there.

Right: I enjoyed my week in Chicago. It was my first visit there.

NOTE 2. — A comma is sufficient between a statement and a question depending upon that statement.

Right: You are leaving today, aren't you?

Wrong: I liked the play very much, did you?

Right: I liked the play very much. Did you? [or] I liked the play very much; did you?

NOTE 3. — In a sentence beginning with a *that*-clause from which the *that* is omitted, a comma is sufficient between the *that*-clause and the principal clause. In such cases the comma is not being used between principal clauses.

Right: Our vacation is over, I am sorry to say. [I am sorry to say that our vacation is over.]

Right: He will stay longer, he tells me. [He tells me that he will stay longer.]

Right: She did not understand a word of his talk, it could clearly be seen. [It could clearly be seen that she did not understand a word of his talk.]

Right: You can hardly walk, the chickens gather so closely about your feet. [The chickens gather so closely about your feet that you can hardly walk.]

Weight of clauses

248. The importance or weight of clauses may suggest whether a comma, a semicolon, a colon, or a

period is to be used. A semicolon or a period may be used between clauses connected by a pure conjunction, if the second clause is important even though it is short. It is given emphasis by the semicolon or period that it would not receive from the comma.

There were four beds in the little upstairs room; and we slept six. — STEVENSON.

I took the story home to my father and mother and they were moved by it. For in their starved and lonely lives they had set all their hopes on me. And these hopes were liberal and fine. — L. LEWISOHN.

EXERCISE

Commas between principal clauses

Should commas be used in these sentences? Give your reasons.

1. He took the letter and ran down the street.
2. The optimist is often disappointed but the pessimist rarely is.
3. We had just moved to Arkansas and were looking for a place to live.
4. My illusions were shattered my dreams were destroyed.
5. My heart jumped to my mouth and a heavy lump settled in the pit of my stomach.
6. Two combines are used Bud works on one and I work on the other.
7. The morning dew has disappeared and we are ready to begin threshing.
8. The owners are respectable they belong to culture clubs they collect antiques they are the progeny of the restless men who came in the great westward migrations.

Terms in a Series

Words etc. in a series

249. Words, phrases, and clauses used in a series should be separated by commas.

Right: He rose, braced himself against the desk, and waited for the verdict.

Right: It should be of medium weight, of fine texture, and of a practical color.

Right: We packed her trunk, we bought her ticket, we put her on the train.

Note 1. — A comma should not be used before the first member of the series.

Wrong: During my senior year I studied, Latin, Greek, and chemistry.

Right: During my senior year I studied Latin, Greek, and chemistry.

Wrong: It is valuable, (1) to the student, (2) to the statesman, and (3) to the merchant.

Right: It is valuable (1) to the student, (2) to the statesman, and (3) to the merchant.

Note 2. — A comma should not be used after the last member of the series.

Wrong: Latin, French, and history, were my favorite subjects in high school.

Right: Latin, French, and history were my favorite subjects in high school.

Wrong: She planned, prepared, and served, all the meals without any help.

Right: She planned, prepared, and served all the meals without any help.

Wrong: The heroine was a beautiful, young, and gay, lady.

Right: The heroine was a beautiful, young, and gay lady.

Coördinate adjectives

250. Two adjectives modifying the same noun should be separated by a comma if they are coördinate; that is, equal in rank. They are equal if they can be joined by *and*. In many instances the second adjective is so closely linked with the noun that together they practically form a compound noun. The two adjectives are, in such instances, not coördinate, and are therefore not separated by a comma.

Right: A faithful, sincere friend. [The adjectives are coördinate in thought: *faithful* and *sincere;* they both modify *friend.*]

Right: A big gray cat. [The adjectives are not coördinate: *gray cat* is practically a compound noun; *big* modifies both words.]

Right: A new spring coat. A heavy winter coat. A long, hard winter.

Series of the form a, b, and c

251. In a series of the form *a*, *b*, and *c*, a comma should precede the conjunction. The practice of omitting the comma before the conjunction is not favored by the best modern usage.

Objectionable: There were blue, green and red flags. [The punctuation here couples *green* and *red* and makes them appear to be set apart, as a pair, from *blue;* whereas the intention is to make all three adjectives equally distinct.]

Right: There were blue, green, and red flags.

NOTE. — This rule applies to a series with *or* or *nor* the same as to one with *and.*

Right: Is the man white, black, or yellow?

Words in pairs

252. A comma is used to separate words or phrases that are contrasted, or arranged in pairs.

Liberty and Union, now and forever, one and inseparable.

Geographical names, addresses, dates, references

253. A comma is used to separate the parts of addresses, dates, references, and geographical names.

Right: Her address is 233 West 118th Street, Detroit, Michigan.

Right: I returned on Friday, February 4, 1937.

Right: The quotation is from *King Lear*, II, 1.

Right: He lived in Summit, New Jersey.

EXERCISE

Terms in a series

Use commas where necessary in the following sentences. Give your reasons.

1. For a carpet of crackling leaves and soft grass, they gave me a hard dark floor. For hills and mountains blue sky and bright sun, they gave me dull walls and an unchanging ceiling. For the companionship

of brothers and sisters, they gave me books pencils and papers.

2. I was with him on Friday May 5 at his home in Lansing Michigan.
3. They asked me to read Act I Scene 1 Act II Scene 2 and Act IV Scene 3.
4. Dissatisfied farmers slovenly vagabonds and ignorant foreigners made up the incoming troop.
5. She is a rich arrogant old woman.
6. He remarked that seven hours spent in school ten in study and two at meals totaled nineteen leaving five hours a day for sleep diversion exercise and letter-writing.
7. He worked on the farm he joined the militia he taught school he studied law he entered politics and spent a term in the state legislature he won and lost a fortune in land speculation.
8. Religion should be as honest as science as beautiful as the arts and as vital as life.

Expressions Inserted into the Sentence

Commas before and after

254. An expression that is inserted into the sentence is set off by commas; that is, commas are placed before and after the expression.

Direct address

255. A substantive used in direct address is set off by commas.

Right: For once, Tom, you are correct.
Right: Our conclusions, my friends, were not far from wrong.

NOTE. — If the substantive in direct address comes at the first of the sentence, it is followed by a comma; if at the end, it is preceded by a comma.

Right: James, listen to me.
Right: Come here, my boys.

Appositives

256. An appositive is set off by commas.

Right: We motored over to Greenfield, the county seat, to see the annual fair.
Right: Anne Dunham, my roommate, is coming.

NOTE 1. — If the appositive comes at the end of the sentence, it is preceded by a comma.

Right: He introduced his uncle, Mr. Harris.

NOTE 2. — A restrictive appositive, one that distinguishes its principal from others of the same class, is not usually set off by commas.

Right: The poet Masefield. Charles the Bold. My son Robert. The word *maelstrom.*

257. Absolute phrases are set off by commas. Absolute phrases

Right: It seems queer, the affair being as you say, that he should be angry.

NOTE. — If the absolute phrase comes at the beginning of the sentence, it is followed by a comma; if at the end, it is preceded by a comma.

Right: The brakes being worn, we stopped barely in time.
Right: I doubt whether they will come, the roads being so bad.

258. Parenthetic words, phrases, or clauses for which parentheses or double dashes are not suitable are set off by commas. (See Rule 282.) Note particularly such expressions as the following: *for example, in the first place, of course, to tell the truth, that is, in fact, I think, I believe, he says, I repeat.* Parenthetic members

Right: The house stood, I believe, on this very spot.
Right: This morning, for example, the toast was burned.
Right: The trip was, to tell the truth, rather a failure.

NOTE 1. — For setting off a parenthetic expression, prefer commas to parentheses or dashes where commas will make the sentence clear; but notice that the use of commas for this purpose may cause obscurity in some cases — particularly when the parenthetic expression is a complete sentence.

Obscure: By all appearances, of course this is a secret, he is likely to win.
Clear: By all appearances (of course this is a secret)

he is likely to win; [or] By all appearances — of course this is a secret — he is likely to win.

NOTE 2. — Commas as a rule are not used to set off *also*, *perhaps*, *indeed*, *therefore*, *of course*, *at least*, *in fact*, *nevertheless*, *likewise*, and other parenthetic expressions that do not require a pause in reading.

Right: I am indeed glad that you are coming.

NOTE 3. — This rule does not apply to *however*, *moreover*, and the other conjunctive adverbs when they are used to join principal clauses; a semicolon is necessary in such cases. (See Rule 268.)

Right: He will, however, understand why I did it. [Parenthetic.]
Right: He will understand why I did it; however he will not approve of my doing it. [Conjunctive adverb joining the clauses.]

Restrictive and non-restrictive modifiers: Clauses

259 a. A non-restrictive clause should be set off by commas; a restrictive clause should not be set off by commas. A non-restrictive clause is a clause the omission of which would not change the meaning of the principal clause. (If it can be *omitted*, it should be *set off by commas*.) It is explanatory or parenthetic, giving additional information about a word that has already been limited or that needs no limitation. A restrictive clause is a clause the omission of which would change the meaning of the principal clause. It limits a word that has not already been limited or defined.

Right: My old fountain pen, *which never leaked or clogged*, is broken. [Non-restrictive clause; can be omitted: *My old fountain pen is broken.* The pen is already limited to one particular pen by the words *my old fountain.*]
Right: A fountain pen *that leaks* is worse than none. [Restrictive clause; cannot be omitted: *A fountain pen is worse than none.* The pen is not already limited to one particular pen by the words *a fountain.*]

Right: Foch, whose genius won the war, was a theorist and a schoolteacher. [Non-restrictive.]
Right: The general whose genius won the war was a theorist and a schoolteacher. [Restrictive.]

NOTE. — The meaning of the sentence may be altered by the addition or omission of commas.

Right: She has made a special study of the native women, who are monogamous. [Non-restrictive.]
Right: She has made a special study of the native women who are monogamous. [Restrictive. The study deals with only those women who are monogamous.]

259 b. A non-restrictive phrase following its principal should be set off by commas; a restrictive phrase following its principal should not be set off by commas. **Phrases**

Right: The ruined spire, *rising above the deserted village,* marked the end of our journey. [Non-restrictive.]
Right: The tree standing in the corner of the garden was the favorite haunt of the children. [Restrictive.]

EXERCISE

Point out the restrictive and non-restrictive modifiers in the following sentences and punctuate them accordingly. **Restrictive and non-restrictive modifiers**

1. Henry who ran the country store was a famous hunter.
2. Many are the poor fools who have gambled away their fortunes here.
3. The proprietor was a good-natured German whom I called "Saucer."
4. All those who were to receive pay checks were at the cashier's window.
5. There is the house that has been the scene of many famous conferences.
6. I was the guest of two British officials who were stationed at Jakedaw which is about forty miles into the jungle.
7. In the rear of the hut was the cook house where our native servant cooked some vile-tasting messes on three stones which served as a stove over a charcoal fire.

8. We drove on to the next town where we found a comfortable hotel.
9. His shoes which were larger than any I have ever seen were bright orange and highly polished.
10. Henry who is distantly related to me is always turning up at the wrong time.

He said, etc.

260. Quotation expressions such as *he said* etc. are set off by commas. (For other rules regarding the punctuation of direct quotations, see Rules 286–289.)

Right: "When I was a child," he said, "I had to walk two miles to school."

NOTE 1. — When the quotation expression comes at the first of the sentence, it is followed by a comma; when it comes at the end, it is preceded by a comma, unless the quotation is a question or an exclamation. (See Rule 288 *c*.)

Right: He said with a frown, "They are acting suspiciously."
Right: "You are entirely mistaken," she retorted.

NOTE 2. — Do not put a comma after *he said* etc. when the quotation following is indirect.

Wrong: The boatswain said, that the wheel was damaged.
Right: The boatswain said that the wheel was damaged.
Wrong: I always supposed, that the foreman was to blame.
Right: I always supposed that the foreman was to blame.
Wrong: They told us, how they had escaped.
Right: They told us how they had escaped.

Introductory Sentence-Elements

Subordinate clauses

261. A subordinate clause that precedes its principal clause is usually followed by a comma. When the subordinate clause follows the principal clause, a comma is not necessary if the clause is restrictive (see Rule 259 **a**), but a comma is usually required if the clause is non-restrictive.

Right: When the ship is in, the lock is closed.
Right: If you have time, telephone me from the station.
Right: Telephone me from the station if you have time.
Right: He was not in his room, though his light was burning.
Right: I am very glad to subscribe, especially since Pryor is to contribute.
Right: He told us that the boat was ready.
Right: I do not know how it occurred, and I have no idea whether Harris was mixed up in it.

262. An introductory phrase containing a verb is usually followed by a comma. One not containing a verb should usually not be followed by any mark of punctuation. Phrases

Right: In order to live, we must eat. [Phrase containing an infinitive.]
Right: Despite his efforts to escape, he remained a prisoner. [Phrase containing an infinitive.]
Right: Upon opening the door, she smelled escaping gas. [Gerund phrase.]
Right: To succeed in your undertaking, you must follow your lawyer's advice. [Infinitive phrase.]
Right: After all the hardships he has suffered, he deserves some rest. [Phrase containing a clause.]
Right: In about an hour our friends arrived.

263. Such words as *yes*, *no*, *surely*, *certainly*, *indeed* may be used as introductory words or as elliptical sentences. They should be punctuated according to their use. *Yes, no, surely*, etc.

"Yes, it was bad," said Austin. — MEREDITH

"Me, Mr. Copperfield?" said Uriah. "Oh, no! I'm a very 'umble person." — DICKENS.

"Indeed, he is almost as good as the puppets, only of course not quite so natural." — OSCAR WILDE.

"Indeed! But we thought you were going home?"
— KIPLING.

With interjections

264. After an interjection which is intended to be only mildly exclamatory, use a comma rather than an exclamation point.

Right: Oh, come when you are ready.
Right: But alas, this was not the case.
Right: Well, I am not going.

Unnecessary commas

265. Guard against the use of commas where they are not necessary, but use them where they may be necessary for clearness.

a. **Especially, do not put a comma between a verb and its subject.** As a rule, do not put a comma where no pause is made in reading.

Unnecessary commas: As I neared the group, I saw three lifeguards, working madly, and furiously with ropes.

Improved: As I neared the group, I saw three lifeguards working madly and furiously with ropes.

b. **Use a comma to separate any sentence-elements that might be improperly joined in reading.**

Misleading: Ever since he has devoted himself to athletics.

Clear: Ever since, he has devoted himself to athletics.

Misleading: Inside the fire shone brightly.

Clear: Inside, the fire shone brightly.

Misleading: While we were washing the lieutenant a man for whom we had no affection, suddenly appeared.

Clear: While we were washing, the lieutenant, a man for whom we had no affection, suddenly appeared.

Ambiguous: He stepped up to his opponent shaking his fist under his nose.

Clear: He stepped up to his opponent, shaking his fist under his nose.
[Here the comma is used before the participle phrase to indicate that the phrase does not modify the nearest noun.]

266. Punctuation should be consistent throughout a sentence. Coördinate elements should be punctuated alike. Punctuation consistent

Wrong: We liked the house very much because it was on a quiet side street; because it had a large yard, and because it was spacious enough for our family.
Right: We liked the house very much because it was on a quiet side street, because it had a large yard, and because it was spacious enough for our family.

Wrong: A salesman should have a pleasing appearance; a courteous, and agreeable manner, and a persuasive tongue.
Right: A salesman should have a pleasing appearance, a courteous and agreeable manner, and a persuasive tongue.

Wrong: In the yard the pig iron is weighed; the grade of iron is marked on it, and it is then loaded upon cars.
Right: In the yard the pig iron is weighed, the grade of iron is marked on it, and it is then loaded upon cars.

Wrong: She had every kind of misfortune, her father's death, her mother's illness the loss of their property, but she continued her college work and graduated with high honors.
Right: She had every kind of misfortune: her father's death, her mother's illness, the loss of their property; but she continued her college work and graduated with high honors.

Exercise

Punctuate the following sentences. State the reasons for your punctuation. Comma

1. Whenever I was late for school and this was more than a few times I always had the one valid excuse I had to wait for the ferry.
2. When snow covered the landscape it was as if purity had been added to the serenity of the river and woods for it was like a great avenue leading nowhere it was an end in itself.
3. Heavens Mary you have misspelled another word.

4. He was much better looking than any of the other boys his clothes were always new and he wore them with a dash.
5. Robert E Lee was born at Stratford Westmoreland County Virginia on January 19 1807.
6. My aunt who is eighty and wealthy spends Christmas with us each year.
7. The pledge must learn to take it learn to become accustomed to being hectored and stepped on by the actives looked upon by all as the lowest form of animal life he must realize his own comparative insignificance and his ignorance of everything.
8. If during the course of a dinner the pledge be asked for the benefit of the actives and the fellow-pledges to eat his blueberry pie without the use of his hands or proper utensils he must respond with alacrity put his face into the pie and eat.
9. He was a queer hunched gray old man of seventy with small twinkling eyes heavy bushy brows hooked nose and pointed chin.
10. Since I wished to enter college as soon as possible I gulped down the required elementary and high-school work in one year working harder than I had ever worked before. My efforts were well rewarded however when I succeeded in gaining admission to the university this fall.

THE SEMICOLON (;)

Between clauses of a compound sentence

267. A semicolon is used between clauses of a compound sentence that are not joined by a conjunction.

Right: He did not go to Canada; he went to Mexico.

Caution

NOTE. — As a means of combining sentences into compound sentences, the semicolon may easily be abused. A series of sentences should not be grouped together in this way unless the compound sentence so formed has a distinct and readily felt unity.

Before *so*, *therefore*, etc.

268. A semicolon is used between clauses of a compound sentence that are joined by one of the conjunc-

tive adverbs, *so*, *therefore*, *hence*, *however*, *nevertheless*, *moreover*, *accordingly*, *besides*, *also*, *thus*, *then*, *still*, *otherwise*, *in fact*, etc. Before *so*, *therefore*, etc.

Wrong: I saw no reason for moving, therefore I stayed still.
Right: I saw no reason for moving; therefore I stayed still.

Wrong: He went below and lit the fuse, then he returned to the deck.
Right: He went below and lit the fuse; then he returned to the deck.

The difference between the pure conjunctions as connectives between principal clauses and the conjunctive adverbs as similar connectives can readily be seen. A comma is sufficient before a pure conjunction because the conjunction makes a very close joining; it does nothing else but connect; it cannot be moved to another place in the sentence. A semicolon is usually necessary before the conjunctive adverb because it does not link the clauses so closely; it is also an adverb and can usually be moved nearer its verb.

Right: I read constantly, but I cannot keep up with the best of the new books.
Right: We were delayed by the heavy rains; therefore we did not arrive in time for the meeting.
Right: We were delayed by the heavy rains; we did not therefore arrive in time for the meeting.

NOTE. — If a semicolon is used, be certain (*a*) that *however*, etc. is used between *principal* clauses and (*b*) that *however*, etc. is used as a *conjunctive* adverb and not as an adverb.

Wrong: If he is right; then we must correct our mistake.
Right: If he is right, then we must correct our mistake.

Wrong: He may; however, be right.
Right: He may, however, be right; [or] He may however be right.

Semicolon between sentence-elements containing commas

269. A semicolon is usually needed between coördinate principal clauses that are joined by a pure conjunction, when these clauses are somewhat long, or are subdivided by commas, and between coördinate subordinate clauses that are subdivided by commas. Note that the break between the clauses is greater than the breaks within the clauses. To punctuate these breaks alike may mislead the reader.

Right: The care of his own health and morals is the greatest trust which is committed to a young man; and often the loss of ability, the degeneracy of character, the want of self-control are due to his neglect of them. — Benjamin Jowett.

Misleading: If I were a millionaire, I would have horses, and motors, and yachts, and the whole world should minister to my pleasure.

Clear: If I were a millionaire, I would have horses, and motors, and yachts; and the whole world should minister to my pleasure.

Right: He said that he had lent his neighbor an ax; that on the next day, needing the ax, he had gone to get it; and that his neighbor had denied borrowing it. [The three objects of *said* are separated not by commas, as ordinarily three objects of a verb would be, but by semicolons, because one of the objects has commas within itself.]

Semicolon with coördinate sentence-elements

270. Be certain that semicolons are placed between coördinate sentence-elements; that is, between elements that are equal. A semicolon is used between principal clauses or between subordinate clauses, but not between a subordinate clause and its principal clause.

Wrong: If you get no thanks from a person you have favored; you have no respect for him.

Right: If you get no thanks from a person you have favored, you have no respect for him.

Right: Well, there I might live, I said; and there I did live, for an hour, a summer and a winter life; saw

how I could let the years run off, buffet the winter through, and see the spring come in. — THOREAU. [Note that the semicolons are used between principal clauses, the second semicolon being followed by an elliptical clause.]

271. Avoid using semicolons for commas unless special emphasis is desired. Either a semicolon or a dash may then be used. (See Rule 248.)

Semicolons for commas

Over-emphatic: He was black-eyed; dark-complexioned; and altogether very handsome.

Preferred: He was black-eyed, dark-complexioned, and altogether very handsome.

Acceptable: Above the incessant din of the jungle insects, I heard the monotonous beating of the Burmese drums; and then near by the scream of a tiger. [Or] . . . I heard the monotonous beating of the Burmese drums — and then near by the scream of a tiger.

EXERCISE

Explain the punctuation in the following sentences. In order to do so, it will be necessary to distinguish between principal clauses, subordinate clauses, and phrases.

Commas, semicolons

1. Adam called his house heaven and earth; Caesar called his house Rome; you perhaps call yours a cobbler's trade, a hundred acres of land, or a scholar's garret. — EMERSON.
2. Splendid as our literature is, it has not voiced all the aspirations of humanity, nor could it be expected to voice an aspiration that has not characteristically belonged to the English race; the praise of intelligence; that stupidity is first cousin to moral conduct, and cleverness the first step into mischief; that Reason and God are not on good terms with each other; that the mind and the heart are rival buckets in the well of truth . . . — JOHN ERSKINE.
3. If an international court of justice, backed by international force makes good in the settlement of two or three national disputes, allays two or three crises, it will with each success be the firmer and the more difficult to uproot; it may very well become as much

a matter of course in the eyes of the nations as our national courts of justice are in the eyes of individual citizens. — JOHN GALSWORTHY.

4. The State universities in the Middle West have gone the whole hog; they frankly put the professor of swine husbandry and his colleague of ice-cream making above the forlorn fellows who presume to inquire into such useless subjects as philology and archæology. — H. L. MENCKEN.
5. But now the world, except for a few troubled spots, is at peace; and yet we stand aghast before the future . . . Without any attempt to be exact, it might perhaps be estimated that not more than one war in a hundred has brought any advantage to anybody; and that not more than one action in a thousand in connection with these wars has, judged by any standard, been a good action. — E. P. CHEYNEY.

THE COLON (:)

A sign of introduction

272. A colon is used after an introductory expression to indicate that something follows, usually of a formal nature. It may introduce a list, an enumeration, a long quotation, an explanation, etc.

Right: There are three causes: poverty, injustice, and indolence.

Right: In 1803, Thomas Jefferson said: "We have seen with sincere concern the flames of war lighted up again in Europe . . ." [A long quotation follows.]

Right: He did it in the following way: First, he cut an ash bough, which he bent into a hoop. Then . . .

Right: The case was this: I would not and he could not.

NOTE 1. — The lists, enumerations, explanations, etc. that follow a colon should be appositives.

Undesirable: We furnish: towels, sheets, pillow slips, dishes, cooking utensils, silverware.

Right: We furnish these articles: towels, etc. [Or] We furnish towels, etc.

Undesirable: There were: Boston bulls, Scotch terriers, chows, German police dogs, collies, and shepherd dogs.

Right: There were many kinds of dogs: Boston bulls, etc. [Or] There were Boston bulls, etc.

Right: He regarded the demand for popular rights as a king might regard it: that is, as a mode of usurpation.

NOTE 2. — A colon is not used before an indirect quotation.

Wrong: She said: that she could not come.
Right: She said that she could not come.

273. A colon may be used after the salutation of a business letter. Use after a salutation

Right: Dear Sir: Gentlemen: My dear Mr. Harris:

274. A colon is used between the parts of titles, references, and numerals. Use in titles, references, numerals

Right: *The Ordeal of Richard Feverel:* a History of a Father and Son.
Right: *Proverbs* 28:20.
Right: 6:15 P.M.

275. A colon may be used instead of a period between clauses which themselves contain commas or semicolons, but which the writer does not wish to set out as sentences; or between short clauses, which are thus tersely and bluntly emphasized.

Right: Men employed in any kind of manual labor, by which they must live, are not likely to take up the notion that they can learn any other art for amusement only; but amateurs are: and it is of the highest importance, nay, it is just the one thing of all importance, to show them what drawing really means; and not so much to teach them to produce a good work themselves, as to know it when they see it done by others. — J. RUSKIN.

Right: The system deserves a short description. It is novel: it is effective: its example may probably be followed elsewhere. — J. BRYCE.

Exercise

Colon

Discuss the use of the colon in the following sentences:

1. For definitions are very dreadful things: they do the two things that most men, especially comfortable men, cannot endure. They fight; and they fight fair. — G. K. Chesterton.
2. There is nothing that you can point to in this country and say: This is the National Government. — Frank Aydelotte.
3. Rousseau said, "I hate books, for they enable people to talk about things that they don't know anything about."
4. And then comes the peculiarly Wordsworthian application of this truth to conduct: a man makes shipwreck of his life unless he carries into his maturity and old age the intuitions of his childhood, so that there shall be no tragic disruption, no break with his past, no revolution, but evolution. — J. D. Spaeth.
5. And so far as they [those who go to college for social reasons] are concerned, the remedy is plain: a stern insistence on the part of the college authorities that they demonstrate a right to be there, and understand that the college idler is no longer welcome; and that no social consideration shall be an excuse for him to occupy a place better filled by someone who means business. — Richard Burton.

THE DASH (—)

Interruptions

276. Use a dash to indicate that a sentence is abruptly changed or interrupted or broken off. If the parenthetic matter comes within the sentence, use a pair of dashes. (See Rule 242.)

Right: If the scythe is rusty — by the way, did you get that scythe at Pumphrey's?

Right: I dressed — you may not believe this, but it is true — in ten minutes.

(For the use of parentheses, dashes, commas with parenthetic matter, see Rule 282.)

277. Use a dash before a sentence-element summarizing the preceding part of a sentence. With summarizing words

Right: If you go to bed early, get up early, never loiter or trifle, always employ periods of enforced idleness in serious thought or instructive reading — if you do all this, you will be derided by the Omicron Pi Chi fraternity.

278. Use a dash before a repetition or modification or intensification having the effect of an afterthought. Before an expression having the effect of an afterthought

Right: Oh, yes, he was polite — polite as a Chesterfield — obsequious in fact.

279. A dash may be used before an appositive, or before an appositive that is separated by several words from its principal substantive. Note that commas could be used in these instances. Dashes, however, are much more emphatic. Before appositives

Right: I wish to ask regarding one particular law — the pension law.

Right: One of my old classmates hailed me on the street — a man named Roberts.

280. Commas may precede both dashes if a comma would be required were the material within the dashes to be omitted. However, usage permits the omission of commas with dashes even when the commas would be required if the dashes and the matter between them were omitted. Comma and dash

Right: If you should see him, — you might meet him on the train, — give him my message.

Right: If you should see him — you might meet him on the train — give him my message. [If you should see him give him my message.]

Right: The ruined spire, rising above the deserted village, — it had not been rebuilt since the war, — marked the end of our journey. [The ruined spire, rising above the deserted village, marked the end of our journey.]

Right: The ruined spire, rising above the deserted village — it had not been rebuilt since the war — marked the end of our journey.

NOTE. — The comma and the dash together are more emphatic than the dash alone. For this reason, a comma is sometimes used before a dash preceding a repeated word.

Right: Differences of course there are between the human type as developed in different regions of the country, — differences moral and intellectual as well as physical. — J. BRYCE.

Indiscriminate use of dashes

281. Do not use dashes indiscriminately in place of commas, semicolons, or periods. The overuse of dashes may indicate that the writer is careless or that he does not know how to use the other marks of punctuation, or that he is striving to gain emphasis by the easy device of punctuation rather than by exact and vivid diction or effective structure.

EXERCISE

Dashes

Why are dashes used in the following sentences?

1. But the fact remains that some nations are stronger than others, that some have bigger armed forces than others — forces better provided with rapidly available reserves, well-trained and ready to march to the sound of the drums. — E. COLBY.
2. A sense of the value of time — that is, of the best way to divide one's time into one's various activities — is an essential preliminary to efficient work; it is also the only method of avoiding hurry. — A. BENNETT.
3. We admit that we are hard, keen, practical — the adjectives that every casual European applies to us — and yet any bookstore window or railway newsstand will show that we prefer sentimental magazines and books. — H. S. CANBY.
4. The chance to sit on a committee with no big issues to debate, the prospect of introducing bills which will never be reported, the opportunity to write speeches that will rarely be delivered — these are not horizons toward which an able man will strain. — H. LASKI.

5. Engineers have assured us that technical knowledge is now available, which — if it could be put to work — would banish poverty, double or treble the standard of living, turn ugly cities into noble cities, and by means of giant power and decentralization bring the culture of the town to the countryside. — S. CHASE.
6. Anything else — be it anthropology or zoölogy or any elective in between — he [the modern college student] will resent and actively condemn. He'll be damned if he's got time to waste on wisdom — or knowledge — or truth and beauty — or cultural development — or individuality — or any of the other matters with which the colleges used to be concerned. — B. DE VOTO.

PARENTHESES ( )

282. Parenthetic material may be put into parentheses. Parentheses, dashes, and commas are all used to set off parenthetic material. (See Rule 258.) Arbitrary rules for their use cannot be laid down. Commas are the most frequently used for this purpose, with dashes second, and parentheses third. For short material very closely related in thought to the rest of the sentence, commas are the most usual marks. If the parenthetic material is long and if it contains commas, dashes are customarily used, but sometimes parentheses. The most emphatic of these marks are dashes.

Parenthetic material

Right: She had, as strong natures always have, an unbounded confidence in her luck. — J. R. GREEN.

Right: And meantime there goes the idler, who began life along with them — by your leave — a different picture. — STEVENSON.

Right: The interpretation of "nature" for its own sake (in the narrower sense in which "nature" is opposed to man) is a modern and romantic development that would have been unintelligible to a Greek. — G. L. DICKINSON.

NOTE 1. — Use parentheses to enclose a letter, number, or symbol only when it is used appositively. Usually the repetition of the letter, number, or symbol is not necessary, but is often employed in legal papers and other documents requiring particular accuracy.

Bad: A (v) shaped plate of steel.
Improved: A v-shaped plate of steel.

Bad: It was marked with the figure (2).
Improved: It was marked with the figure 2.

Possible: He must add twenty-one (21) inches.

NOTE 2. — Do not use parentheses to cancel a word or passage. Draw a line through it to indicate omission.

NOTE 3. — A complete sentence enclosed in parentheses and standing between two sentences begins with a capital letter. A complete sentence enclosed in parentheses and standing within a sentence usually begins with a small letter.

Relative position of other marks

283. When the parentheses and another mark of punctuation occur together —

a. **The mark of punctuation follows the second parenthesis of the pair when this mark applies to the sentence as a whole and not to the passage in parentheses.** Note that the mark of punctuation should not precede the first parenthesis.

Right: I will ask him by telephone (assuming he has a telephone), and I think he will agree (though I may be mistaken).

Right: The general law, then, respecting just or economical exchange, is simply this: There must be advantage on both sides (or if only advantage on one, at least no disadvantage on the other) to the persons exchanging; and just payment for his time, intelligence, and labor, to any intermediate person effecting the transaction (commonly called a merchant); and whatever advantage there is on either side, and whatever pay is given to the intermediate person, should be thoroughly known to all concerned. — RUSKIN.

b. **The mark of punctuation precedes the second parenthesis of the pair when this mark applies to the passage in parentheses.**

Right: This essay ("Literature and Science") was first published in 1882.

Right: In general, the war powers of the President cannot be precisely defined, but must remain somewhat vague and uncertain. (See Wilson's *Constitutional Government in the United States.*)

Right: I will ask him by telephone (I do not wish to see him!) and I think he will agree (though I may be mistaken).

284. A comma should not be used with parentheses unless it would be required were there no parenthetic matter. **Incorrect use of commas with parentheses**

Wrong: The sheriff gave him (as his oath required), the most effective help. [The sentence *The sheriff gave him the most effective help* requires no comma after *him.*]

Right: The sheriff gave him (as his oath required) the most effective help.

BRACKETS [ ]

285. Square brackets, [ ], are used to enclose a word or words interpolated in a quotation by the person quoting. Words enclosed in parentheses, ( ), occurring in a quotation, are understood to belong to the quotation; words enclosed in brackets, [ ], are understood to be interpolated by the person quoting. **Words interpolated in a quotation**

Right: "I would gladly," writes Landor, "see our language enriched . . . At present [in the nineteenth century] we recur to the Latin and reject the Saxon . . ."

NOTE. — The word *sic* (meaning *thus*) enclosed in brackets is sometimes inserted in a quotation after a misspelling etc. to indicate that the misspelling etc. occurs in the original.

He sent this written confession: "She followed us into the kitchen, snatched a craving [*sic*] knife from the kitchen cabinet, and came toward me with it."

Exercise A

Parentheses

Why are parentheses used in the following sentences? Could commas or dashes be used in their place? If so, with what effect?

1. He had already joined the Quakers, and was an occasional speaker in their meeting-house. (They have no ordained ministers.) He went with his wife, who shares his religion, to a workman's flat in East London . . . — G. Murray.
2. And alas, much as we like listening to French or Italian, for example, Italians and Frenchmen (if we insist on having their opinion) will confess that English has for them a rather harsh sound. — M. Beerbohm.
3. The pure-bred American once cared for culture, and no longer — to the same extent, at least — does. If any one asks why America (I use the word loosely, as meaning our United States), having always, since the Revolution, been a democracy, can have cared for so undemocratic a thing, the answer is simple. — K. F. Gerould.
4. Men used to make things as well as they could for the pride they took in making them (and because they sometimes used the thing themselves). — J. Galsworthy.
5. It becomes necessary — let us say — to provide a million dollars worth of furniture for a ten million dollar hotel (itself to be superseded and scrapped in perhaps ten years) and naturally only the most intensive and efficient factory system can meet this demand. — R. A. Cram.

Exercise B

Punctuating parenthetic passages

Punctuate the italicized parenthetic passages in the following sentences with commas, semicolons, dashes, parentheses, or brackets. State your reasons for punctuating as you do.

1. I would lead a band of desperadoes *in fancy of course* through a jungle of grass to the impenetrable thicket of blackberry bushes.

2. Anything might come out of those grapevines, perhaps *as I thought* even the fairies themselves to dance in a ring under the moon. Punctuating parenthetic passages
3. As the moments passed *moments that seemed hours* I began to realize that I was standing on a snake.
4. Not long before my grandmother's marriage to my grandfather, the two of them went to a small town *the largest in the region* to select necessities for the home they planned to establish.
5. His favorite story had to do with real treasure, which had been buried somewhere *he didn't know the exact spot* within a few hundred yards of the very pier from which he fished.
6. For the large sum of three dollars a month, I milked cows *three of them, Daisy, Dinah, and Nellie,* chopped wood, carried water, washed dishes, and swept floors.
7. My mother was *and is* overindulgent with me.
8. Inspector Gray *nice solid English name* questioned the guests separately and collectively.
9. This is what my English teacher said, "Between you and I," *yes, she did say it. I have witnesses.* "I think you should major in journalism."
10. How the neighbors had found out her story, Fannie did not know *Fannie never talked about her affairs to anyone.* Neighbors, however, have a way of putting two and two together and getting more than four out of them.

MISCELLANEOUS MARKS OF PUNCTUATION

QUOTATION MARKS (" ")

NOTE. — See Rules 148–150 for the paragraphing of direct quotations and of dialogues, and Rule 404 for the capitalization of direct quotations and of dialogues.

286. Use quotation marks to enclose a direct quotation, but not to enclose an indirect quotation. For direct, not indirect quotations

Wrong: He said "that he was grieved."
Right: He said that he was grieved.
Right: He said, "I am grieved."

Misuse within a quotation

287. Do not punctuate sentences of a single speech as if they were separate speeches.

Bad: She said, "Is this the truth?" "Then I must tell my husband." "He ought to know."
Right: She said, "Is this the truth? Then I must tell my husband. He ought to know."

Note, however, that sentences that are not parts of a single speech should be punctuated as separate quotations.

Right: He antagonized nearly everyone there by such sweeping statements as: "All of the officers were crooks; they got as much as they could by graft"; and "Ireland deserves all that she gets from England."
Right: We heard such questions as these: "Can I get a taxi?" "Oh! do you think I have missed the train?" "When does the next train go south?"

Quotations with *he said*

288. When the expression *he said* etc. occurs with a quotation, the following rules apply:

He said excluded

a. ***He said* should not be included within the quotation marks.**

Wrong: "If that is true, he said, I am lost."
Right: "If that is true," he said, "I am lost."

He said preceding

b. **When *he said* precedes the quotation, it is separated from the quotation by a comma if the quotation is short and informal, or by a colon if the quotation is long and formal.** (See Rules 260 and 272.)

He said interpolated or at the end

c. **When the quotation precedes *he said*, it should not be separated by a semicolon or a period from *he said*, but only by a comma unless the quotation is a question or an exclamation, in which instance the question mark or exclamation mark is placed within the quotation marks.** (See Rules 289 *c* and 260, Note 1.)

Right: "I will help," he said.
Right: "Will you help?" he asked.
Right: "What a help you have been!" he cried.

Note that if the question or exclamation is interrupted by *he said,* the question mark or the exclamation mark is placed at the end of the quotation.

Right: "Are you planning to teach," he asked, "after you have taken your degree?"

Note that no comma or period should be used in addition to the quotation mark and the question or exclamation mark.

Wrong: He cried "Fire!", and began to run.
Right: He cried "Fire!" and began to run.

Wrong: Did he say, "I object."?
Right: Did he say, "I object"?

d. **If the quotation preceding *he said* forms a complete sentence, a period should follow *he said.* Remember that a question and an exclamation may be complete sentences.** Marks after *he said:* Period

Wrong: "Won't you come?" she said, "we need you."
Right: "Won't you come?" she said. "We need you."

e. **If *he said* is placed between parts of a quotation separated by a semicolon, the semicolon is placed after *he said.*** Semicolon

Right: "He didn't go to Canada," the teller informed me; "he went to Mexico." ["He didn't go to Canada; he went to Mexico."]

f. **If no other mark of punctuation is required after *he said*, a comma should follow.** Comma

Right: "I am sure," he said, "that we can find a substitute."

289. When a quotation mark and another mark of punctuation both follow the same word — Relative position of marks:

a. **A dash, a question mark, or an exclamation mark should stand within the quotation mark if it applies to the quotation only and not to the sentence containing the quotation.** (See Rules 288 *c* and 289 *d.*) Dash, question mark, exclamation mark within quotation mark

Wrong: He said, "Are you hurt"?
Right: He said, "Are you hurt?"

Right: "I am in such a hurry that —" she began, but she was gone before she had finished.

Right: "God knows!" said I, at my wit's end; "it may be one of the royal family, for aught I know, for they are all stout gentlemen!" — IRVING.

Dash, question mark, exclamation mark outside quotation mark

b. **A dash, question mark, or exclamation mark should stand outside the quotation mark if it applies not to the quotation, but to the sentence containing the quotation.**

Right: "I do not mean that I want to be poor; but there was a middle state" — so she was pleased to ramble on — "in which I am sure we were a great deal happier." — LAMB.

Right: Did the letter say, "Come tonight at ten"?

Right: It was the last word of the whole record. It ended with "dust"! and that is exactly what happens in life. — STRINDBERG.

Right: Yes, he said "Please come if you can"; but what he meant was, "Stay where you are"!

Period or comma always inside

c. **A period or a comma should always precede, not follow, the quotation mark.**

Right: "If you have a light," said John, "give it to me."

Right: He asked if I carried what he called "the makings," but I could not satisfy him.

Colon or semicolon always outside

d. **A semicolon or a colon should always follow, not precede, the quotation mark.**

Right: I have seen that "abode of poverty"; and the "poverty" is truly marvelous.

Right: I have this to say regarding the man's "abject poverty": that it is fictitious.

e. **Ellipsis marks (. . .) or the phrase *etc.* should be included within the quotation marks if the material omitted is a part of the quotation; but they come outside the quotation marks if the material omitted is not a part of the quotation.**

Right: Emerson said, "In this country, we are very vain of our political institutions . . . " [Part of Emerson's sentence is omitted.]

Right: The book has such title headings as these: "Learning to Know Yourself," "Making Your Personality Bloom," "Convincing Others of Your Worth," etc. [Additional chapter headings, which are not a part of the last quotation, are omitted.]

290. Titles of literary, musical, and artistic works and of periodicals may be enclosed in quotation marks, but the preferred practice is to italicize titles of whole publications or works and to use quotation marks for the titles of chapters, articles, etc. (See Rule 412.) Titles

Right: The second chapter of Meredith's *Evan Harrington* is entitled "The Heritage of the Son."

291. A quotation within a quotation is marked by single quotation marks; one within that, by double marks. Quotation within a quotation

Right: I repeated those lines of Tennyson,
"Thou shalt hear the 'Never, never,' whispered by the phantom years,
And a song from out the distance in the ringing of thine ears,"
until I knew them by heart.

292. When a quotation consists of several paragraphs (see Rule 362), **quotation marks should be placed at the beginning of each paragraph, and at the end of the quotation.** For illustration, see the example under Rule 362. Quotations of several paragraphs

293. Quotation marks are used for direct borrowings and not for the ideas of an author put into other words. (Credit in the latter instance is of course given in the text. See pp. 24–25.) If the author's phrases appear in the indirect quotation, the use of quotation marks varies. It is advisable to use them if there is a chance Quotation marks with borrowed material that the author might not receive full credit for his words or if it is necessary to point out the limits of the direct quotation or if special emphasis is to be placed upon the quoted words.

Right: Newman's great writer is not one who can merely turn out swelling sentences, but one who has something to say and knows how to say it.

Right: Like Hamlet, our fiction has become "fat and scant of breath." — F. L. PATTEE. [The quotation marks could be omitted; special emphasis, however, is gained by their use.]

Quoted sentences in a context

294. Quoted sentences may be embedded in a context without capitals or periods. (A period would, of course, be required if the quoted sentence came at the end of the context.)

Right: Bacon's aphoristic style can be illustrated by such sentences as these: "studies serve for delight, for ornament, and for ability"; "reading maketh a full man; conference a ready man; and writing an exact man"; and "revenge is a kind of wild justice; which the more man's nature runs to, the more ought law to weed it out."

Unnecessary quotation marks: Titles

295. Do not use quotation marks unnecessarily.

a. **Do not enclose the title at the head of a composition unless the title is a quotation.**

Proper names

b. **Do not enclose proper names, including names of animals.**

Wrong: I expect to go to "Oberammergau."
Right: I expect to go to Oberammergau.

Wrong: "Thomas" and "Rover" were good friends.
Right: Thomas and Rover were good friends.

Commonly used nicknames

c. **Do not enclose commonly used nicknames such as *Al Smith*, *Babe Ruth*, *Stonewall Jackson*.**

Slang in informal writing

d. **In informal writing do not enclose slang that would obviously be recognized as such.**

Unnecessary: When radicalism "threw up its hat" for "Rob" Rowland, "roughhouse," and reform, conservatism "took to the tall timbers." "Rob," though "cock of the walk" in the capital, has been "sassed" by his home paper, which attributes his influence to hypnotism and "hot air."

Improved in effectiveness: When radicalism threw up its hat for Rob Rowland, roughhouse, and reform, conservatism took to the tall timbers. Rob, though cock of the walk in the capital, has been sassed by his home paper, which attributes his influence to hypnotism and hot air.

In formal writing, slang may be apologized for by quotation marks. Do not, however, apologize for good English expressions such as: *hard hit, brace up, rough it, to duck, to oust, to loaf, to cut a figure, the whys and wherefores, the forties, willy-nilly, day dreams, proxy, bugbear, humbug, hoax, tomfoolery, bamboozle, whoop, ninny, milksop, skinflint.*

e. **Do not enclose familiar technical terms such as the following: *off year*, *touchdown*, *kickoff*, *corner the market*, *hookup*, *static*, etc.** Less familiar terms are sometimes enclosed in quotation marks or are italicized.

Familiar technical terms

Right: In this paper I shall endeavor to make clear the meaning of the term "phoneme." [Or] . . . the meaning of the term *phoneme.*

f. **Do not enclose fragments of familiar sayings such as *nipped in the bud*, *mad as a March hare*, *sadder but wiser*.**

Fragments of familiar sayings

g. **Avoid enclosing words coined extempore.**

Extempore coinings

Right: It is not bronchitis or peritonitis or any of the itises.

h. **Do not label humor and irony with quotation marks when their intent would be obvious to the reader.**

Humor and irony

Unnecessary: Such is the ardor of this "pious" Hotspur.

Right: Such is the ardor of this pious Hotspur.

Unnecessary: Senator Platt's speech on the bill was a sort of "funeral oration."
Right: Senator Platt's speech on the bill was a sort of funeral oration.

For emphasis

i. **Do not use quotation marks to call attention to words unless they are quoted words. Use italics if necessary.**

Bad: If the Creator in his "power and munificence" is good to me, I shall gain "distinguished success."
Right: If the Creator in his power and munificence is good to me, I shall gain distinguished success.

Quotations in form only

296. Quotation marks are used for implied speech, but are not customarily used for unspoken thoughts.

He ceased abruptly; his eyes fell into their dream. Very like the girl Charcot showed me in my younger days, thought Professor Malzius. — S. V. BENÉT.

He was thinking of certain cells of the body that rebel against the intricate processes of Nature and set up their own bellicose state. Doubtless they too have a destiny, he thought, but in medicine it is called cancer. — S. V. BENÉT.

She thought, suddenly, I have not really been alive or had any consciousness of reality in the whole time that he was away. — N. HALE.

What do you find in him to hold against him? he could hear Mr. Virgil's voice complaining. — K. BOYLE. [The character imagines Mr. Virgil's speaking.]

And in her expressionless tone which conveyed "So that was that," Mrs. Burns was horrified to recognize that impulse that sometimes occurs like a chip of flint in the normal mind — that from the normal mind is instantly extracted — that flash of feeling, "I injured him; the thought of him insults me in my own thoughts; I can't bear that he should be alive." — S. BENSON.

The general did not laugh. He made half a turn instead, toward the man at the desk. The gesture said, "You see, he is well trained." — S. V. BENÉT.

EXERCISE

Quotation marks

Where necessary, use quotation marks in the following sentences:

Quotation marks

1. Once when old Henry thought that his boy was unusually silent in the store, he called out from the desk at the rear, Jim! And Jim quickly absolved himself by shouting back, It's a darned lie! I'm not in the tobacco.
2. Archie kept on polishing a glass. He did not bother to turn around or even turn his head; he merely glanced my way and said, So you're the new fountain boy, are ya? Thus he acknowledged our introduction and indicated that no more need be said. . . . This tap is Griesedieck, Archie said, this one Light Lager; bottled beer here; the pumps are coke. Don't pay any 'tention to the labels — all wrong. Anything ya don't know, as' me. That was all. . . . Although apparently unconscious of my presence, he would seem to sense my indecision and at just the right moment would softly suggest, Use number twelve dipper, or Top with whip' cream an' cherry. . . . Once Archie suddenly turned and said, Thirsty, Bud? (Every boy was Bud to Archie.) Here's a mistake. He did not know that I had watched him mix the mistake, and that I knew it was never meant for a customer. . . . In answer to Mr. Paine's question about my catching on, Archie's expressive Uh huh seemed to me to be perfect. Archie never said yes, sir or no, sir to Mr. Paine — or to anybody. He always talked in a well modulated voice and with an intimate manner. Everything he said was confidential and inside dope and his audience always listened with respect.
3. The mate dashed to the captain's cabin and yelled, Sir, the ship's on fire. It's in hold three!

   The captain, followed by the mate, dashed onto the deck where all was confusion. His quick orders, Batten down all holds. Rig up the pumps. Flood the forward holds, quickly restored order from out of the chaos.
4. The customary red cap took our bags and said, Right this way, sir. The plane leaves in five minutes.
5. It flattered me to be asked to sing at a Children's Day program, or at the Friday afternoon program in the primary school. (I was especially adept at Teddy Bear Has His Lair under Johnnie's Rocking Chair.)

6. I walk about the campus and say to myself, Well, I am here at last. And although I know that I shall never be quite one of the student body, I am rejuvenated by associating with the younger students. . . . I shall laugh, play, dance. Life is wonderful. I have gone collegiate. Whoops, my dear.
7. Her conversation runs like this: George Jean Nathan? Oh yes, I read his book on the drama last night. And upon a little more questioning, You know, my dear, I can't remember the names of the books I read. What was this about? Oh, I don't remember exactly — rather psychic, I thought.
8. We're in this mine sixty feet now, I said, and that's way past state regulations.
9. He is the type of man who thinks that Society has it in for him and that he will never get a break.
10. The saying where there is smoke there must be fire, is very true in this case.

THE APOSTROPHE (')

Possessive case

297. Use the apostrophe to indicate the possessive case.

Right: Milton's poems; the girl's hat; the lady's dress; the ladies' dresses.

Never use the apostrophe to form the nominative plural.

Wrong: The Powers's and the Jones's sold piano's.
Right: The Powerses and the Joneses sold pianos.

's for the singular possessive

298. To form the possessive singular, add *'s* to the nominative.

SINGULAR

Nom.	boy	fox	man	hostess
Poss.	boy's cap	fox's tail	man's hat	hostess's dress

NOTE. — Observe the exception in these idiomatic phrases in which the word following the possessive begins with an *s*-sound:

Right: For conscience' sake; for old acquaintance' sake; for goodness' sake; for righteousness' sake.

299. To form the possessive plural:

's or ' for the plural possessive

a. **If the nominative plural does not end in an *s*-sound, add '*s* to the nominative plural.**

PLURAL

Nom.	men	women	children
Poss.	men's hats	women's hats	children's toys

b. **If the nominative plural ends in an *s*-sound, add ' to the nominative plural.**

PLURAL

Nom.	boys	foxes	hostesses
Poss.	boys' caps	foxes' tails	hostesses' dresses

300 a. Proper names ending in an *s*-sound form the possessive singular by adding '*s* to the nominative.

Proper names

Right: Jones's house; Burns's poems; Davis's automobile; Dickens's novels.

Never thrust the apostrophe before the *s* that belongs to the name.

Wrong: Jone's house; Dicken's novels.
Right: Jones's house; Dickens's novels.

300 b. For the possessive plural of proper names ending in *s*, add only ' to the nominative plural.

Right: The Davises' automobile is parked in front of the Joneses' house.

301. In joint possession the last noun takes the possessive form. In individual possession each name should take the possessive form.

Joint possession or individual possession

Joint possession: Marshall and Ward's St. Paul branch.
Individual possession: John's, George's, and Harold's separate claims.

302. In compound words the possessive form is usually added to the last word.

Compound words

Right: my mother-in-law's visit.

Note also these preferred forms: *someone else's book; somebody else's opinion.*

Indefinite or impersonal pronouns

303. The possessive case of indefinite or impersonal pronouns requires the apostrophe.

Right: one's rights; someone's glove; each other's books; neither's answer.

No apostrophe with personal pronouns

304. Never use an apostrophe with the possessive adjectives *his*, *hers*, *its*, *ours*, *yours*, *theirs*. The form *it's* is a contraction for *it is*.

NOTE. — Do not use the possessive with the intensives and reflexives.

Wrong: one'self
Right: oneself

With inanimate objects

305. If the possessive case is used for inanimate objects, the apostrophe should not be omitted. (See Rule 210.)

Right: an hour's delay; a day's work; two weeks' vacation, a hair's breadth.

With contractions, etc.

306. In a contracted word an apostrophe should stand in the place of the omitted letter or letters, not elsewhere.

Wrong: Hav'nt, do'nt, does'nt, ca'nt, is'nt, oclock.
Right: Haven't, don't, doesn't, can't, isn't, o'clock.

Note that the apostrophe is used to indicate the omission of a part of a date.

Right: class of '36.
Right: the blizzard of '88.

In forming plurals

307. The plural of letters and of numbers is formed by adding '*s*. The plural of a word considered *as a word* may also be formed in the same way. The apostrophe is commonly omitted from the plural of figures referring to interest-bearing bonds.

Right: His *U's* were like *V's* and his *2's* like *Z's*.
Right: In your letter there are too many *I's* and also too many *and's*.
Right: Rock Island 4s.
Right: Georgia Power 5s, 1967.

Exercise

Where necessary, use apostrophes in the following sentences. **Apostrophe**

1. Its too expensive.
2. You use too many sos and ands.
3. Doesnt your mother like it?
4. He gave me a volume of Keats poems.
5. Whose turn is it?
6. Whos able to go?
7. Whats the matter?
8. We followed the princesses automobile. [Write the singular possessive form also.]
9. Someone elses car is in Charless garage.
10. He owes me three days pay.
11. For pitys sake, let me alone.
12. She designed the actresses gowns. [Write the singular possessive form also.]
13. He bought a quarters worth of sugar.
14. Ladies hats are sometimes very strange.
15. This book is yours.
16. You can whisper to your hearts content.
17. Are you invited to the Joneses and the Davises parties?
18. For heavens sake, dont listen to him.
19. Hers is larger than theirs.
20. The mens club has just been finished after a years delay.
21. Whose else [or who elses] name have you?

THE HYPHEN (-)

The only use of the hyphen that is strictly a matter of punctuation is in dividing a word between syllables at the end of a line; all other uses, both for combining and for separating, are perhaps matters of spelling. For convenience, rules for hyphenation are placed in this section.

No arbitrary rules with compounds

308. Compounds may be written solid as one word or as two words joined by a hyphen or as two separate

words. In general the hyphen is used in recently made compounds and compounds still in the process of becoming one word. Usage varies considerably, and for that reason no arbitrary rules can be laid down. When in doubt consult the latest edition of an unabridged dictionary. The following "rules" represent the usual current practice, but writers are likely to connect with hyphens any words which are to be read as distinctly single units.

One idea or two ideas

309. When two words are joined to express a single idea, they are usually written as one word, but when the words express separate ideas, they are usually written with a hyphen.

Right: railroad, taxpayer.
Right: actor-manager, soldier-king.

Compound adjective before a noun and after

310. Words used as a single adjective *before* a noun are usually hyphenated.

Examples:

coal-black hair
bright-eyed child
strong-minded woman
silver-tongued orator
bull-necked fighter
far-reaching results
well-meaning blunderer
well-educated teachers
worn-out clothing
three-inch board
self-possessed child
matter-of-fact statement
right-hand man
month-old baby
all-around man
hit-and-miss driver

When these compound adjectives *follow* the noun, they often lose their compound character and usually do not require the hyphen.

Right: The snow-covered mountains lay ahead.
Right: The mountains are snow covered.

When an adverb ending in *ly* is used with an adjective or a participle, the compound is not usually hyphenated; but it may be.

Right: Our carefully laid plans were not carried out.
Right: Our carefully-laid plans were not carried out.

Compound with a preposition or adverb

311. A hyphen is often used in compound words when the last member is a preposition or an adverb: make-up, tie-up, hang-over, passers-by, etc. But: kick-off, knockout, blowout, roundup, holdup. (See Rule 318.)

Distinct prefix

312. When a prefix still retains its original strength in the compound, a hyphen is used. In most instances, however, the prefix has been absorbed into the word and should not be separated by a hyphen. Contrast the following pairs of words:

ex-president, excommunicate	ultra-violet, ultramarine
vice-president, viceroy	pan-hellenic, pantheist
pre-Christian, preconception	un-American, unbiased
pro-British, procreation	by-laws, bystander

Note that in some words a difference of meaning is indicated by the hyphen:

She recovered her strength.
She re-covered her quilt.

There is a re-creation of energy.
New recreation fields are being set aside.

Fractions

313. Use a hyphen between the numerator and the denominator of a fraction unless either part is written with a hyphen; *three-fourths*, *three twenty-fourths*, *nineteenths*, *thirty-one fortieths*. It is not necessary to hyphenate if the numerator is felt to be an adjective and is emphasized.

Right: He gave me one half and kept the other half.
Right: I have read only one third of the book.

Numerals

314. Use a hyphen in compound numbers from twenty-one to ninety-nine.

Right: twenty-six; sixty-three; but one hundred thirty.

Any, etc. with *body*, etc. written solid

315. Write as one word *any*, *every*, *no*, *some* combined with *body*, *one*, *thing*, *where*, as in *anybody*, *anyone*, *anything*, *anywhere*, *everybody*, *everyone*, *everything*, *everywhere*, etc. Note however that *any one*, *every one*, *some one* may also be written separately and that *no one* is always written separately. (See Rules 318 and 319.)

Self, *ever*, etc. written solid

316. Write as one word compounds ending with *self*, *ever*, *hood*, *ship*: *himself*, *herself*, *themselves*, etc., *whoever*, *whichever*, *whatever*, *childhood*, *falsehood*, *friendship*, *hardship*. Note that *self* as a prefix is usually followed by a hyphen: *self-made*, *self-help*, *self-satisfied*. But: *selfsame*. (See Rules 318 and 319.)

Hyphen to avoid ambiguity

317. To avoid ambiguity, a hyphen may be necessary.

Ambiguous: A detail of fifty foot patrolmen was on duty.
Clear: A detail of fifty foot-patrolmen was on duty.

Ambiguous: She is a normal school student.
Clear: She is a normal-school student.

Words written solid

318. The following words are written solid: (See Rules 315 and 316.)

almighty
almost
already (See Appendix A)
although
altogether (See Appendix A)
bankbook
baseball
bedroom
beforehand
blowout
cannot
downright
downstairs
downward
everybody
extraordinary
farewell
folklore
football
foothold
forehead
furthermore
herself
himself
inasmuch
indoors
insofar (*but* in so far as)
itself
kickoff
knockout

Words written solid

letterhead
lifetime
lightweight
likewise
livestock
misspell
moreover
mudguard
myself
necktie
nevertheless
nobody
northeast
northwest
notebook
notwithstanding
nowadays
oneself
ourselves
outdoor
outstanding
overcharge
overcome
overhead
percent or per cent
postmaster
roommate
roundup
schoolroom
semicolon
somehow
something
sometimes
somewhat
southeast
southwest
steadfast
stepmother
teaspoonful
textbook
themselves
thereupon
throughout
together
touchdown
toward
twofold
upright
upstairs
upward
whatever
whenever
whereas
whichever
whoever
without
withstand
workman
yourself
yourselves

Also, when used as adverbs:

someday
someway

319. The following words are written separately:

Words written separately

all ready (*already* means previously)
all right
any day
any time
by the bye
each other
en route
every time
ex officio
good night
high school
in order
in spite of
near by
night letter

no one
(on the) other hand
parcel post
per cent (or percent)
post office
pro tempore
real estate
side line
some place
up to date

Also, when emphasis is on the noun:

any one
some day
some way
every day
by the way (or by-the-way)
every one
any place
some one

320. In dividing a word at the end of a line, place a hyphen after the first part of the divided word and there only; never put a hyphen at the beginning of a line. (See Rules 365–372.)

EXERCISE

Hyphen Should the compounds in the following sentences be written solid, with a hyphen, or separately? Consult a recent edition of a good dictionary.

1. We need an eight foot rod.
2. All the creeks are bone dry.
3. He gave away one fourth of his income.
4. The United States is a world power.
5. He was our go between.
6. She is very good looking.
7. The younger son was a ne'er do well.
8. Let us sing the chorus all together.
9. They are building on a T shaped wing.
10. The street was filled with on lookers.
11. She is getting a badly needed rest.
12. You are all together mistaken.
13. Are you all ready?
14. We were all ready there when he came.
15. The leak was in the sub basement.
16. He was anti British.
17. She does her work in a half hearted manner.
18. I don't like your chip on the shoulder manner.
19. She always was old fashioned.
20. A high school course is required for admission.

21. He gave us first hand information.
22. I do not trust second hand information.
23. Below us lay the deep blue sea.
24. He is as pig headed a man as I ever knew.
25. He will not accept any thing second rate.

PUNCTUATION WITH *SUCH AS, NAMELY, VIZ.,* ETC.

321. When *such as* introduces short illustrations, it is usually preceded by a comma. When it introduces long illustrations, it may be preceded by a dash or a colon. It is usually followed by no mark of punctuation.

Punctuation with *such as*

Right: I read many historical novels, such as *Romola, Rienzi,* and *Quo Vadis.*

Right: He asked us about a number of rules of punctuation: such as the use of the comma with non-restrictive relative clauses; the use of the semicolon between clauses of a compound sentence, etc.

322. The punctuation with *namely, viz., e.g., that is, i.e.* varies.

Punctuation with *namely, viz.,* etc.

a. **They may be preceded by a comma, semicolon, colon, dash, or period,** according to the length and the grammatical dependence or independence of the following material. For short, grammatically dependent material, the comma is sufficient. The colon, dash, and period may be used for long, grammatically independent material, the colon being more formal than the dash. The semicolon is not so frequently used as these other marks.

b. **They may be followed by a comma or a colon according to the length and grammatical dependence or independence of the following material.**

These combinations of punctuation are used:

Frequent:	, namely
Not preferred:	, namely,
Frequent:	— namely,

More formal: — namely:
More formal: : namely,
More formal: . Namely:

Illustrations:

I am a citizen of the United States, but there is another country that will have my love and my allegiance throughout my life, namely England.

That a majority is always right, *i.e.*, that every decision it arrives at by voting is wise, not even the most fervent democrat has ever maintained.

I selected it for two reasons — namely, because it was well made and because it was inexpensive.

All sorts of animals inhabit these plains — for example: there are brown bears and hundreds of deer; the species of panther found here is the largest in America, since it has plenty of deer and other game to feed upon.

There is a vital difference between them: *i.e.*, the Greek is an artist, and the Roman is a statesman.

Dickens's novels were influential in bringing about social reform in England. For example: the measures for the treatment of the poor were greatly improved through *Oliver Twist* and *Our Mutual Friend;* the debtors' laws were amended through *Little Dorrit;* the procedure in the court of Chancery was remedied through *Bleak House;* and the conditions in boys' schools were changed through *Nicholas Nickleby.*

Exercise

Such as, namely, etc

Punctuate *such as, namely, viz.*, etc. in the following sentences. Give your reasons for punctuating as you do.

1. They arrested the man who was really responsible namely the cashier.
2. My jobs have been many for instance I have sorted candy, knitted stockings, and worked in a tailor shop. One thing I do know that is that each successive place was less noisy than the preceding.
3. Our circus boasts of its aristocracy for example some of the trapeze performers are university graduates; our tightwire artists are descendants of royalty; the young Japanese tumbler is heir to half a million dollars.

4. In our circus there is a panorama of nations *i.e.* there are pink-cheeked German athletes, Japanese tumblers, duck-billed women from Africa, Cossack riders from the steppes of Russia, handsome Spaniards and beautiful señoritas.
5. Feeding the circus was no small feat for instance I had to see that 1600 people, 1000 wild animals, and 700 horses got daily their proper number of calories.
6. We picked up several bargains such as a tent in good condition, a new cooking outfit, and a camp stove.

Marks of punctuation at the beginning of lines

323. Never put a period, a comma, a semicolon, a colon, an exclamation point, or a question mark at the beginning of a line; put it instead at the end of the preceding line. A dash, however, may be placed either at the end of a line or at the beginning of the following line.

EXERCISES ON PUNCTUATION

Exercise 1

General exercise in punctuation

Punctuate the following sentences, or correct any errors in the punctuation already there. State the reason for the use of each mark of punctuation.

1. [Newspaper headline] No jury trial bill is passed by lower house.
2. He was angry at what he called my high pressure salesmanship so I told him what he could do about it.
3. It is true that a few freshmen who have not yet been instructed in the rudiments of college life have broken this ruling but once they are enlightened they too refrain from smoking on the campus.
4. I cannot agree with the author in this statement That government is best which governs not at all.
5. Jim ran up the stairs as fast as he could go his only hope was to reach his mothers room before his sister could overtake him.
6. Well I must be going he said after a long pause.
7. If every one thought as he thought the world would be two hundred years behind.
8. For four years we struggled with mathematics languages and many other subjects.

Punctuation

9. After two wagons have been loaded the machine has been set and the belts have all been put on their pulleys then the threshing begins.
10. At Commencement time a meeting place for the alumni is needed also a place for visitors to gather in a good Union Building would be most useful for these purposes.
11. Those who wish to play golf on Sunday must go to the country club golf course which is the only one open on Sunday.
12. Having only a small business this merchant had no moving van so the members of the play cast had to hire a truck to haul the furniture.
13. My opinions what is the use of my having any opinions my parents only laugh at my opinions.
14. By this new process more knives could be produced in the same amount of time. Thus increasing the output and the quality of our product.
15. You believe that college has changed since you went to school well so it has but not as you think.
16. By the way do you remember Walter Edmonds he sails on June the sixth on the Ile de France.
17. Freshmen who like to play usually go home to stay at the end of the first semester.
18. Even a gentleman however does not always have a good disposition but when he is not feeling well or when luck seems to be against him he does not allow his feelings to control his actions that is he is master of his emotions he does not allow his mood to become apparent.
19. I want you Mother to realize that I do not consider college a place for a good time only.
20. Our course in rhetoric included many things besides rhetoric for example we often discussed politics or religion or philosophy.
21. An education used to be a luxury now it is a necessity.
22. The meadows were an early green the trees were in half leaf a few birds were back from their southern winter and we were planning our summer vacation.
23. The Dean looked up; a half-smile on his face.
24. There has been some mistake, Mr. Smith, I did not cut class yesterday.

25. I am planning to take the examinations in the fall, therefore I shall spend most of the summer studying. Punctuation
26. Then I saw the dark side of this picture, called Life.
27. I think that it is advisable to bring one or two semi formal dresses because you never can tell you might need them in September.
28. There was no school the next day and it was only eightthirty too early to go home consequently we took plenty of time to decide what to do.
29. Friendship is I think contrary to popular opinion more rare than anything else in the world.
30. When the temple was first completed many residents of Salt Lake City not members of the Mormon Church were shown through it but since it's dedication no visitors have been admitted.
31. I shall be glad to leave still I shall miss my friends.
32. This ruling would affect two kinds of people those who would be able to get a college education in spite of cuts and those whose college course would be shortened to one semester on account of cuts.
33. I had always liked oh more than liked her.
34. His text was 1 Corinthians 16 1 to 9.
35. Thomas Hardys first popular success Far from the Madding Crowd appeared anonymously in the *Cornhill Magazine*.
36. Its I come on lets go.
37. Faces in the fire will smile at him mock him frown at him call and repulse or if there be no faces the smoke will take a thousand shapes and lead his thoughts by delightful paths to the land of reverie or he may watch the innermost heart of the fire burn blue especially if there is frost in the air or poker in hand he may coax a coal into increased vivacity this is an agreeable diversion suggesting the mediaeval idea of the Devil in his domain. — E. V. LUCAS.
38. She wrote the letter for her mother was ill.
39. A strong west wind filled the sails.
40. It shivered from head to foot and its teeth chattered and as it stared at me persecutor devil ghost whatever it thought me it made with its whining mouth as if it were snapping at me like a worried dog. — DICKENS.
41. Shovel a man of seven had said None of your lip.

Punctuation

You weren't never at Thrums yourself. Tommy's reply was Ain't my mother a Thrums woman? Shovel who had but one eye and that bloodshot fixed it on him threateningly. The Thames is in London he said. Cos they wouldnt not have it in Thrums replied Tommy. 'Amstead 'Eaths in London, I tell yer Shovel said. The cemetery is in Thrums said Tommy. There aint no queens in Thrums anyhow. There is the Auld Licht minister. Well then if you jest seed Trafalgar Square. If you jest seed the Thrums town house. St. Pauls aint in Thrums. It would like to be. After reflecting Shovel said in desperation Well then my father were once at a hanging. Tommy replied instantly It were my father what was hanged. — J. M. Barrie.

42. They had much in common namely their devotion to their children their interest in public affairs and their love of art.
43. I had to answer a number of questions such as what my major and minor subjects were, what athletics I had taken part in, what my church affiliations were etc.
44. After two years delay our government sent a reply.
45. My career was decided upon, I was to be a great novelist.
46. Old Cato whose *De Re Rustica* is my Cultivator says and the only translation I have seen makes sheer nonsense of the passage, When you think of getting a farm turn it thus in your mind not to buy greedily nor spare your pains to look at it and do not think it enough to go around it once. The oftener you go there the more it will please you if it is good. I think I shall not buy greedily but go round and round it as long as I live and be buried in it first that it may please more at last. — H. D. Thoreau.
47. I told her what else could I say to her that she would be well enough to go home very soon.
48. Do you recall that Hazlitt said that the soul of a journey is liberty perfect liberty to think feel do just as one pleases.
49. When Patrick Henry said give me liberty or give me death what do you think did he mean by liberty.

EXERCISE 2

Punctuate the following passage, stating the reason for the use of each mark of punctuation. Punctuation

Call me Ishmael some years ago never mind how long precisely having little or no money in my purse and nothing particular to interest me on shore I thought I would sail about a little and see the watery part of the world it is a way I have of driving off the spleen and regulating the circulation whenever I find myself growing grim about the mouth whenever it is damp drizzly November in my soul whenever I find myself involuntarily pausing before coffin warehouses and bringing up the rear of every funeral I meet and especially whenever my hypos get such an upper hand of me that it requires a strong moral principle to prevent me from deliberately stepping into the street and methodically knocking peoples hats off then I account it high time to get to sea as soon as I can this is my substitute for pistol and ball with a philosophical flourish Cato throws himself upon his sword I quietly take to the ship there is nothing surprising in this if they but knew it almost all men in their degree some time or other cherish very nearly the same feelings toward the ocean with me. — HERMAN MELVILLE.

EXERCISE 3

Make a study of punctuation in good contemporary writing. Choose one mark of punctuation for special study. Collect and tabulate examples of its use. Take the colon, for instance. Is it used frequently in informal writing? Do you find it used in place of a semicolon to indicate a break between coördinate clauses? If you examine long enough and widely enough, you may be able to draw conclusions regarding the present popularity of certain marks of punctuation. Punctuation in contemporary writing

SPELLING

The way to reform

The way to reform bad spelling is to work at it determinedly, correcting a few faults at a time. In most cases, the bad speller does not *see* words correctly; his mental photograph of them is wrong, or blurred. In many cases he does not *hear* and *pronounce* the words correctly; he adds syllables, he transposes or omits letters, and he confuses one word with another. A misspelling should never be hastily corrected. The student should look up the correct spelling and fix it in memory by careful observation and by writing it out. He should keep a list of words he misspells, and should refer to it regularly.

Careful study of the following rules, and of the lists in Rule 338 and in Appendix C will aid the student to recognize his misspellings, and will provide him with principles by means of which he can remember more easily the correct spellings.

Accurate pronunciation

324. Careless pronunciation is often the cause of misspelling.

Mispronounced vowels

a. **Do not mispronounce vowels in unaccented syllables:**

acc*u*rate
advis*e*r
begg*a*r
doct*o*r
conquer*o*r
d*e*scription
d*e*spair
d*i*vide
hum*o*rous
int*ro*duce
partic*u*l*a*r
priv*i*l*e*ge

Omitted letters

b. **Do not omit letters:**

accident*al*ly
ar*c*tic
bound*a*ry
can*d*idate
Feb*r*uary
gener*al*ly

gover*n*ment	quan*t*ity
hist*o*ry	re*a*lly
int*e*resting	reco*g*nize
lab*o*ratory	soph*o*more
lib*r*ary	stric*t*ly
occasion*al*ly	su*r*prise
parl*ia*ment	temper*a*ment
proba*b*ly	us*u*ally

c. **Do not add letters:**

Added letters

athletics	hindrance
develop	lightning
disastrous	mischievous
elm	remembrance
entrance	umbrella

d. **Do not transpose letters:**

Transposed letters

Brit*ai*n	p*er*form
child*re*n	p*er*spiration
g*u*ard	p*re*fer
hund*re*d	pre*j*u*d*ice
irre*le*vant	p*re*scription
lon*el*y	p*re*sume
marr*ia*ge	tra*g*e*d*y

325. A monosyllable or a word accented on the last syllable, ending in one consonant preceded by one vowel, doubles the final consonant before a suffix beginning with a vowel: *bid, bidden; quiz, quizzes; drop, dropping, dropped; glad, gladder, gladdest; man, mannish; tin, tinny; prefer, preferred.* (Remember that the final consonant is doubled to keep the preceding vowel short. Compare *hopping* with *hoping.*) Exceptions: *chagrin, chagrined; transfer, transferable; infer, inferable; gas, gaseous, gases.*

Doubling final consonants

a. **The final consonant is not doubled in words in which the accent is shifted to a preceding syllable upon the addition of the suffix:** *refer, reference* (but *referred*); *confer, conference* (but *conferring*); *prefer, preference* (but *preferring*). Exception: *excel, excellence.*

Refer, reference, etc.

Benefit, etc.

b. **The final consonant in words not accented on the last syllable is not usually doubled before a suffix:** *benefit, benefited.* In *worship, kidnap, bevel, counsel, quarrel*, etc., the final consonant may be doubled, but not preferably: *worshiper, worshiping, worshiped; kidnaped; traveler, quarreling*, etc.

Suffix beginning with a consonant

c. **A final consonant is not doubled before a suffix beginning with a consonant:** *fit, fitting*, but *fitness.*

EXERCISE

Doubling final consonants

Make as many combinations as you can of the following words and suffixes. Give your reason for doubling or not doubling the final consonant. Suffixes: *able, ible, ary, ery, age, er, est, ance, ence, ess, ous, ed, ish, ing, ity, ly, ful, ment, ness, hood, es, s*, etc.

occur	scrap	ravel	man	libel
happen	red	kidnap	vassal	will
begin	equip	hazard	sum	skill
god	commit	read	stop	expel
shrub	equal	rid	clan	rival
glad	profit	level	avoid	jewel
fat	model	cancel	discern	marvel

Dropping final *e*

326. Words ending in silent *e* usually drop the *e* before a suffix beginning with a vowel. Thus: *love, lovable; stone, stony; blue, bluish; guide, guidance; plume, plumage; eye, eying; hie, hying; shine, shining.* Exceptions: *dye, dyeing; hoe, hoeing; shoe, shoeing; singe, singeing; tinge, tingeing.* Note further exceptions under the next rule.

Derivatives from words in *ce* and *ge*

327. Words ending in *ce* or *ge* do not drop the *e* when *ous* or *able* is added. Thus: *notice, noticeable; outrage, outrageous.*

NOTE. — *C* and *g* in words of French, Latin, and Greek derivation usually have the soft sound before *e, i*, and *y*, as *cede, genial, civil, giant, cyanide, gymnasium;* elsewhere they have the hard sound, as *calendar, Gallic, code, gorgon, acute, gusto.* (*Get, geese, gewgaw, geld, giddy, gift, gig, giggle, gild, begin, gird, girdle, girl,* and *give* are not of the above-mentioned derivation.) Notice how the principle applies to *accent, accident, flaccid, occiput, accept, accurate, desiccate, except, excuse.* On account of this principle, the *e* must be retained in such words as *noticeable* and *courageous,* in order to keep the soft sound of *c* and *g.*

Exercise

Final *e*

Add suffixes to the following words. (See list of suffixes in the exercise under Rule 325.) Give your reason for dropping or retaining the *e.*

interfere	judge	advantage	woe
use	true	membrane	nine
argue	manage	whole	come
force	acre	acknowledge	help
sense	mile	trouble	like
guide	sale	peace	obese
indulge	outrage	response	abridge

***Picnicked,* etc.**

328. Words ending in *c* add *k* before a suffix beginning with *e, i,* or *y.* Thus: *picnic, picnicked; traffic, trafficking; panic, panicky.*

Plural of nouns

329. Most nouns form the plural by adding *s* to the singular: *girl, girls.*

Nouns ending in *ch* and *s*-sounds

a. **Nouns ending in the *ch* sound, as in *touch,* or in an *s*-sound add *es.*** Note that the *es* in the plural forms an extra syllable. Thus: *church, churches; fox, foxes; glass, glasses.*

Nouns ending in *y*

b. **Nouns ending in *y* preceded by a consonant change the *y* to *i* and add *es:*** *library, libraries; lady, ladies.* When the *y* is preceded by a vowel, the *y* remains unchanged: *valley, valleys.*

***Leaf, thief,* etc.**

c. **Most nouns like *leaf, thief, self* form the plural in *ves.*** Thus: *leaves, thieves, ourselves.* **Some nouns ending in *f* form the plural in *fs.*** Thus: *beliefs, chiefs, griefs, hoofs* (rarely *hooves*), *scarfs* (sometimes *scarves*), *dwarfs.*

Nouns ending in *o*

d. **Some nouns ending in *o* add *es* to form the plural.** Thus: *buffaloes, calicoes, echoes, mosquitoes, Negroes, potatoes, volcanoes, dominoes, embargoes, heroes, jingoes, mulattoes, noes, tomatoes, tornadoes.* **Some add only *s*.** Thus: *banjos, dynamos, Eskimos, pianos, silos, solos, sopranos, zeros.* **A few plurals may be written either *os* or *oes*.**

Letters, symbols, etc.

e. **The plurals of letters of the alphabet, of numerical symbols, and of a word considered *as a word* are formed by adding *'s*.** (See Rule 307.) Thus: "Mind your *p's* and *q's*," "His *well's* and his *and's* made up half his story."

Foreign nouns

f. **Observe that certain nouns of foreign origin retain their foreign plurals.** Note especially *datum, data; phenomenon, phenomena; analysis, analyses; parenthesis, parentheses; thesis, theses.*

NOTE. — The plural of some words may have either the foreign or the anglicized form. Thus: *formula, formulae,* or *formulas; syllabus, syllabi,* or *syllabuses.*

Words ending in *y*

330. Words ending in *y* preceded by a consonant usually change the *y* to *i* before a suffix. Thus: *happy, happiness; beauty, beautiful.*

Verbs ending in *y*

331. A verb ending in *y* preceded by a consonant forms the third person singular of the present tense by changing the *y* to *i* and adding *es*, and forms the past tense by changing the *y* to *i* and adding *ed*. Thus: *rely, relies, relied; marry, marries, married.* When the *y* is preceded by a vowel, the *y* is not changed. Thus: *pray, prays, prayed; display, displays, displayed.* Exceptions: *laid, paid, said.*

Studying, etc.

Note that verbs ending in *y* do not drop or change the *y* before *ing: study, studying; hurry, hurrying.*

Verbs ending in *ie*

332. Verbs ending in *ie* change the *i* to *y* and drop the *e* before *ing*: *lie, lying; die, dying.*

Exercise

Add suffixes to the following words. (See list of suffixes in exercise following Rule 325.) State your reason for spelling the word as you do. **Change of *y* to *i***

mercy	relay	hardy	bounty	medley
duty	study	wordy	jockey	galley
pulley	essay	fancy	modify	body
tardy	ecstasy	defy	typify	anarchy

333. Adjectives ending in *n* do not drop the *n* before *ness*. Thus: *sudden, suddenness; green, greenness.* *Suddenness,* etc.

334. Words ending in *l* do not drop the *l* before *ly*. Thus: *final, finally; cool, coolly.* *Finally,* etc.

335. The following groupings may aid in the spelling of *ei* and *ie* *ei* and *ie*

a. When sounded as *ē:*

Put *i* before *e*
Except after *c*

			Exceptions
ach*ie*ve	p*ie*r	c*ei*ling	*ei*ther
bel*ie*f	p*ie*rce	conc*ei*t	l*ei*sure
bel*ie*ve	rel*ie*f	conc*ei*ve	n*ei*ther
br*ie*f	rel*ie*ve	dec*ei*t	ob*ei*sance
ch*ie*f	repr*ie*ve	dec*ei*ve	s*ei*ze
f*ie*ld	retr*ie*ve	perc*ei*ve	w*ei*rd
f*ie*rce	sh*ie*ld	rec*ei*pt	
fr*ie*ze	shr*ie*k	rec*ei*ve	
gr*ie*f	s*ie*ge		
gr*ie*ve	th*ie*f		
n*ie*ce	w*ie*ld		
p*ie*ce	y*ie*ld		

b. When not sounded as *ē*, the order is usually *ei*

(1) When sounded as *ā:*

feint	reign	veil
freight	rein	weigh
neighbor	skein	weight
obeisance		

(2) Miscellaneous

foreign	height	sovereign

(3) Exceptions

fiery	friend	handkerchief	
mischief	mischievous	sieve	view

c. Note the following *ier* group:

cashier	brigadier	glacier
clothier	financier	soldier

Principal and principle

336. In case of doubt whether to use *principal* or *principle*, remember that *principle* is always a noun and that the word which contains *a* (princip*a*l) is the adjective. *Principal* is occasionally a noun: *the principal of the school, both principal and interest.*

Oh and *O*

337. The common interjection is spelled *oh*. It is capitalized only at the beginning of a sentence, and is followed by an exclamation point, a comma, or no mark at all.

Examples: "Oh, no, it is no trouble." "Oh! you ought not to do that," "My child! oh, my child!" "I will do it — and oh, by the way, where's the key?"

The sign of direct address (poetic or archaic) is spelled *O*. It is always capitalized, and is not followed by punctuation.

Examples: "I am come, O Caesar," "O ye spirits of our fathers," "O God, we pray thee," "I fear for thee, O my country."

A list of words that are commonly misspelled

338. The following list is composed chiefly of ordinary words which are often misspelled. With many of these are grouped — for the sake of comparison and distinction — related words, words not often misspelled, and words of different derivation commonly confused with them. (Numbers refer to rules.)

absence
absorb
absorption
absurd
accept (*receive*)
  except (*exclude, aside from*)
access (*admittance*)
  excess (*greater amount*)
accessible
accident
accidentally
accommodate
accompanying 331 note
accumulate
accustom
acquainted
acquitted
across
additionally
address
advice (noun)
advise (verb)
adviser
Æneid
affect (verb, *to influence*)
  effect (verb, *to produce*)
  effect (noun, *result*)
    (There is no noun *affect*)
aggravate
aghast
airplane
aisle (*in church*)
  isle (*island*)
all right (There is no such word as "alright" or "all-right")
alley (*small street*)
alleys 329 *b*
allies 329 *b*
alliteration
allotted
allusion (*hint*)
  illusion (*false image*)
ally (*confederate*)
already
all ready
altar (*shrine*)
alter (*change*)
altogether
alumna (feminine singular)
alumnæ (feminine plural)
alumni (masculine plural)
alumnus (masculine singular)
always
amateur
among
analysis
analyze
angel (*celestial being*)
angelic
angle (*corner*)
annual
answer
anxiety
apart
apartment
apiece 335 *a*
apology
apparatus
apparent
appearance
appreciate
appropriate
arctic
arguing 326
argument
arise
arising 326
arithmetic
around
arouse
arrangement
arranging 326
arrival 326
arriving 326
article

ascend
ascends
ascent
  assent (*agreement*)
assassin
assassinate
association
athlete (two syllables)
athletic
athletics
attack (present)
attacked (past)
attendance
audience
auxiliary
awkward
bachelor
balance
banana
Baptist
baptize
barbarous
bare
barely
baring
barring
based
bearing
becoming
before
beggar 325
believe 335 *a*
benefit
benefited
berth (*bed*)
  birth (*beginning of life*)
boarder (*one who boards*)
border (*edge*)
born ("I was born in 1920.")
borne ("borne by the wind"; "She has borne a son.")
boundary
breath (noun)
breathe (verb)
bridal (*nuptial*)
bridle (*for a horse*)
brilliant
Britain (*the country*)
Britannia
Britannica
Briton (*a native*)
buoyant
bureaus
burglar
buries 331
bus (*omnibus*)
  buss means *kiss*
business 330
cafeteria
calendar
candidate
can't
canvas (*cloth*)
canvass (*review*)
capital (*city*)
capitol (*building*)
career
carriage 330
  (See *marry, marriage*)
carry
caucus
ceiling
cemetery
certain
change
changeable 327
changing 326
chaperon
characteristic
chauffeur
chautauqua
choose, choosing 326 } (present)
chose, chosen } (past)
chord (*of music*)

clothes (*garments*)
cloths (*kinds of cloth*)
coarse (*not fine*)
  course (*path, series*)
colonel
column
coming 326
commission
commit
committed 325
committee
committing 325
comparative
comparatively
compel
compelled
competent
complement (verb, *to complete*)
complement (noun, *completing part*)
compliment (verb, *to praise*)
compliment (noun, *pleasing speech*)
complimentary (*gracious*)
comrade
comradeship
concede
conceit 335 *a*
conceive 335 *a*
confidant (noun)
confidence
confident (adjective)
confidently
  confidentially (*secretly*)
connoisseur
conquer
conqueror
conscience (*inner guide*)
conscientious
conscientiousness
conscious (*aware*)
consciousness
considered
contemptible (*worthy of scorn*)
contemptuous (*scornful*)
continuous
control
controlled 325
cool
coolly 334
copy
copied 331
copies 329 *b*, as a verb, 331
cord (*string*)
corps (*squad*)
corpse (*dead body*)
costume (*dress*)
  custom (*manner*)
council (noun, *assembly*)
councilor (*member of a council*)
counsel (noun, *advice, legal adviser*)
counsel (verb, *to advise*)
counselor (*adviser*)
country
courteous
courtesy
creep
crept
criticism
criticize
cruelty
cylinder
dealt
debater
deceased (*dead*)
  diseased (*ill*)
deceit 335 *a*
deceive 335 *a*
decide
decision
deep
defendants

definite
dependant (noun)
dependent (adjective)
depth
descend
descends
descent (*slope*)
  decent (*proper*)
  dissent (*disagreement*)
describe
describing 326
description
desert (*waste place*)
  dessert (*food*)
desiccate
despair
desperate
destroys
develop (preferable to *develope*)
device (noun)
devise (verb)
diary (*daily record*)
  dairy (*milk room*)
dictionary
die
dying 332
difference
different
digging
dining room 326
dinning
diphtheria
dirigible
disappear (dis+appear)
disappoint (dis+appoint)
disaster
disastrous
discipline
disease
diseased. See *deceased*
dissatisfied
dissipate
distribute
divide
doctor
don't
dormitories 329 *b*
dual (*twofold*)
duel (*fight*)
ecstasy
effect. See *affect*
eight
eighth
elicit (*to draw out*)
  illicit (*unlawful*)
eligible
eliminate
embarrass
eminent
emphasize
encouraging
enemy
enemies 329 *b*
equipped
ere (*before*)
  e'er (*ever*)
especially
etc. (*et cetera*)
everybody
exaggerate
exceed
excellence
excellent
except
exceptionally
excess. See *access*
exercise
exhaust
exhilarate
existence
expense
experience
explanation
extraordinary
facilities

familiar
fascinate
February
fiery
finally 334
financier
forebode
foreboding 326
forehead
foreign
foremost
forfeit
formally (*ceremoniously*)
formerly (*at a former time*)
forth (*forward*)
  fourth (*4th*)
forty. But —
  four
  fourteen
frantically
fraternities 329 *b*
freshman (adjective)
freshman (noun, singular)
freshmen (noun, plural)
friend
fulfill *or* fulfil
furniture
gambling (*wagering*)
gamboling (*frisking*)
gauge *or* gage
ghost
government
grabbing 325
gammar
grandeur
grief 335 *a*
grievous
guard
guess
guidance
handkerchief
handsome
harass
having 326
hear (verb)
  here (adverb)
height
heinous
hinder
hindrance
hop
hopping 325
hope
hoping 326
human (*of mankind*)
humane (*merciful*)
humorous
hurried 331
hypnotize
hypocrisy
illiterate
imaginary
imagining 326
imitation
immediately
impetuosity
impromptu
incident (*occurrence*)
  incidence (*way a thing falls or strikes* — scientific term)
incidentally
incredible
incredibly
independence
independent
indictment
indispensable
infinite
ingenious (*clever*)
ingenuous (*frank*)
innocence
instance (*occasion*)
instant (*moment*)
intellectual
intelligence

intentionally
intercede
invitation
irrelevant
irresistible
itself
knowledge
laboratory
laid
later (*subsequent*)
latter ("the former, the latter")
lead (*metal*)
led (past tense of *lead*)
legitimate
lessen (*make less*)
lesson
liable
library
lightening (*making less heavy*)
lightning (noun)
likely
literature
livelihood 330
liveliness 330
loneliness 330
loose (adjective)
lose (verb)
lying
maintain
maintenance
maneuver
mantel (*chimney shelf*)
mantle (*cloak*)
manual
manufacture
manufacturer
marriage 330
marries
mathematics
mattress
meant
metal (*e.g., iron*)
mettle (*spirit*)
millionaire
miniature
minute
mischievous
misspelled
momentous
murmur
muscle
mysterious
mystery
naïve
naphtha
necessary
Negroes
neither
nine
nineteen
ninetieth. But *ninth*
ninety
noticeable 327
notoriety
nowadays
nucleus
oblige
obstacle
occasion
occasionally
occur
occurred 325
occurrence 325
occurring 325
officer
omit
omitted
omission
oneself
operate
opportunity
optimism
organization
origin

outrageous
overrun
pageant
paid
pamphlet
parallel
paralysis
parliament
parliamentary
particularly
partner
passed (verb, past tense of *pass*)
past (adjective, adverb, and preposition)
pastime
peace
perceive 335 *a*
perform
perhaps
permissible
perseverance
persistent
personal (*private*)
personnel (*persons collectively employed*)
persuade
Philippines. But *Filipino*
physical
physician
picnicking
plan
planned 325
plain (adjective, *clear, simple*)
plain (noun, *flat region*)
plane (adjective, *flat*)
plane (noun, geometric term; *carpenter's tool*)
pleasant
politics
pore (*read intently*)
pour
possess
possible
practically 334
practice (noun and verb)
prairie
precede
preced′ence
prec′edents
preference 325 *a*
prejudice
preparation
presence
presents (*gifts*)
principal 336
principle 336
privilege
probably
proceed
professor (pro+fessor)
promenade
pronunciation
prove
pumpkin
pursue
quiet (*still*)
quite (*entirely*)
quiz
quizzes 325
rarefy
really 334
recede
receipt
receive 335 *a*
recognize
recommend
reference 325 *a*
referred 325
reign (*rule*)
rein (*of a bridle*)
religion
religious
repetition
replies

representative
reservoir
respectfully (*with respect*)
respectively (*as relating to each*)
restaurant
rhetoric
rheumatism
rhyme
rhythm
ridiculous
right
rite (*ceremony*)
sacrificing 326
sacrilegious
safety
sandwich
scene
schedule
secretary
seize
separate
sergeant
severely
shining 326
shone (past tense of *shine*)
  shown (past participle of *show*)
shriek 335 *a*
siege 335 *a*
similar
simultaneous
sincerely
site (*place*)
  cite (*refer to*)
  sight (*view*)
soliloquy
sophisticated
sophomore (three syllables)
specifically
specimen
speech. But *speak*
statement
stationary (adjective)
stationery (noun)
statue (*monument*)
staturė (*height*)
statute (*law*)
stopping
stops
stretch
studying 331 note
succeed
suffrage
suit (*of clothes*)
suite (*of rooms*)
superintendent
supersede
suppress
sure
surprise
syllable
symmetrical
symmetry
temperament (four syllables)
temperature (four syllables)
tendency
their (possessive of *they*)
there ("here and there")
there (expletive; *e.g.*, "there is no use")
therefor (See *thereof*, *thereby*, *therein*)
therefore (*for that reason*)
thorough
thousandths
threw (past tense of *throw*)
through (preposition and adverb)
to ("go *to* bed")
too ("*too* bad!" "me *too!*")
two (2)
together
track (*mark*)
tract (*area*)
tragedy

tries
truly
Tuesday
typical
tyrannically
undoubtedly
unprecedented
until. But *till*
usage
use
using 326
usually
vengeance
vilify
village
villain
weather
whether (*which of two*)
weird 335 *a*
who's (*who is*)
whose
woman (singular)
women (plural)
writer
writing 326
written
yacht
you're (*you are*)

EXERCISES ON SPELLING

Exercise 1

Doubling final consonants

Write the infinitive, the present participle, and the past participle of each of the following verbs (*e.g.*, *stop*, *stopping*, *stopped*): *fib*, *dub*, *rub*, *gad*, *shred*, *wed*, *lag*, *nag*, *drag*, *brag*, *rebel*, *excel*, *dispel*, *fulfil*, *distil*, *instil*, *dam*, *slam*, *stem*, *gum*, *span*, *pen*, *begin*, *slap*, *snap*, *rap*, *trap*, *step*, *chip*, *clip*, *shot*, *hop*, *war*, *jar*, *transfer*, *inter*, *abhor*, *incur*, *recur*, *defer*, *fit*, *chap*, *mat*, *pat*, *emit*, *knit*, *acquit*, *outwit*.

Exercise 2

Dropping final *e*

Write the following words together with the adjectives ending in *able* derived from them (*e.g.*, *love*, *lovable*): *dispose*, *move*, *mistake*, *reconcile*, *prove*, *compare*, *console*, *blame*, *imagine*, *decline*, *cure*, *measure*.

Exercise 3

Final *e* retained

Write the following words together with their derivatives ending in *able* (*e.g.*, *notice*, *noticeable*): *trace*, *service*, *marriage*, *charge*, *damage*.

Exercise 4

Change of *y* to *i*: nouns

Write the singular and the plural of the following nouns (*e.g.*, *lady*, *ladies*): *baby*, *lullaby*, *hobby*, *democracy*, *policy*, *regency, tragedy, remedy, elegy, theology, academy, enemy, anatomy, destiny, poppy, diary, laundry, treaty, delay, spray, alley, attorney, journey, turkey, decoy, alloy, corduroy, convoy.*

Exercise 5

Change of *y* to *i*: verbs

Write the first and third persons present indicative, and the first person past, of the following verbs (*e.g.*, *I cry, he cries, I cried*): *fancy, pacify, terrify, qualify, accompany, spy, reply, occupy, vary, dry, ferry, worry, pity, envy, levy.*

Exercise 6

Change of *ie* to *y*

Write the infinitive and the present participle of the following verbs (*e.g.*, *lie, lying*): *belie, hie, tie, die, vie.*

Exercise 7

Plurals in *s* and *es*

Write the singular and the plural of the following nouns (*e.g.*, *bead, beads*): *limb, seed, sword, church, match, yacht, witch, varnish, bank, cannibal, scream, robin, stump, cedar, savior, bus, compass, class, abbess, princess, convict, socialist, blow, ax, axis, matrix, six, quiz, waltz.*

Exercise 8

Present third singular in *s* and *es*

Write the indicative present, first and third persons singular, of the following verbs (*e.g.*, *refer, refers*): *stab, need, dig, pinch, stitch, watch, wash, fish, drink, deal, dream, lean, grasp, fear, guess, amass, trust, bow, buzz.*

Exercise 9

The prefix *dis*

Study the following words, observing that in all the prefix is not *diss*, but *dis*: *dis+able, dis+advantage, dis+agree, dis+approve, dis+engage, dis+interested, dis+obedient, dis+orderly, dis+organize, dis+own.*

Exercise 10

The prefix *un*

Study the following words, observing that in all the prefix is not *u*, but *un*: *un+natural, un+nerve, un+necessary, un+noticed, un+numbered, un+named, un+neighborly, un+navigable.*

Exercise 11

Study the following words, distinguishing between the prefixes *per* and *pre*. Keep in mind that *per* means *through, throughout, by, for;* and that *pre* means *before.*

The prefixes *per* and *pre*

perceptible	precarious
perception	precaution
peremptory	precept
perforce	precipitate
perfunctory	precise
perhaps	precocious
perspective	prerogative
perspiration	prescription

Exercise 12

Study the following adjectives, observing that in all the suffix is not *full*, but *ful: peaceful, dreadful, handful, graceful, forceful, wakeful, shameful, grateful, faithful, healthful, pitiful, dutiful, thankful.*

The adjective suffix *ful*

Exercise 13

Study the following words, observing that in all the ending is not *us*, but *ous: bulbous, viscous, advantageous, gorgeous, membranous, extraneous, piteous, courteous, dubious, specious, precious, vicious, conscious, fastidious, odious, studious, religious, perilous.*

The adjective suffix *ous*

Exercise 14

Study the following words, observing that in all the suffix is not *y*, but *ly: final+ly, verbal+ly, radical+ly, logical+ly, ethical+ly, comical+ly, ironical+ly, typical+ly, physical+ly, political+ly, critical+ly, local+ly, real+ly, legal+ly.*

The suffix *ly*

Study the following words, observing that in all *al* precedes *ly: accidentally, apologetically, pathetically, terrifically, specifically, emphatically, exceptionally, elementally, professionally.*

Exercise 15

Study the following words, observing that the suffix is not *ess*, but *ness: clean+ness, drunken+ness, mean+ness,*

The suffix *ness*

plain+ness, stubborn+ness, sudden+ness, wanton+ness, stern+ness, forlorn+ness, lean+ness, keen+ness.

Exercise 16

The suffixes *able* and *ible*

Study the following words, observing which ones have the suffix *able*, and which ones the suffix *ible:*

abominable	desirable	inscrutable	serviceable
admirable	despicable	inseparable	sizable
advisable	detestable	intolerable	sociable
allowable	eatable	irreparable	suitable
applicable	excusable	justifiable	syllable
avoidable	explicable	laughable	teachable
believable	hospitable	movable	tolerable
changeable	imaginable	noticeable	traceable
charitable	improbable	peaceable	treasonable
comfortable	incurable	perishable	unbearable
commendable	indispensable	preferable	unmistakable
comparable	inestimable	presentable	unspeakable
conceivable	inevitable	profitable	unutterable

accessible	divisible	indelible	permissible
admissible	eligible	indestructible	plausible
audible	flexible	inexhaustible	possible
compatible	forcible	inexpressible	reducible
comprehensible	horrible	intelligible	reprehensible
contemptible	imperceptible	invincible	responsible
convertible	impossible	invisible	sensible
destructible	incompatible	irresistible	susceptible
digestible	incredible	legible	tangible
discernible	indefensible	perceptible	terrible

Exercise 17

The suffixes *ain* and *ian*

Study the following groups of words:

ain		*ian*	
Britain	curtain	Austrian	guardian
captain	fountain	barbarian	Italian
certain	mountain	Christian	musician
chieftain		civilian	physician
		collegian	politician
		electrician	ruffian

Exercise 18

Study the following groups of words: *ede* and *eed*

ede		*eed*
accede	precede	exceed
antecede	recede	proceed
concede	secede	succeed
intercede		

Exercise 19

Fill the blanks with *principal* or *principle:* *Principal, principle*

1. The —— will be due on the tenth of the month.
2. He will fight for his ——.
3. This is my —— reason for going.
4. The —— has asked that we hold our meeting tomorrow.
5. He did not even know the first —— of the game.
6. Can you give the —— parts of the verb?

Exercise 20

Fill the blanks with *affect* or *effect:* *Affect* and *effect*

1. I do not like her ——ed manner.
2. An entrance was ——ed by force.
3. The —— upon her is noticeable.
4. The law will take —— in July.
5. It was an ——ive remedy.
6. The hot weather will —— the crops.
7. There was no serious after——.
8. She ——ed ignorance of the whole matter.

Exercise 21

Fill the blanks with *consul, council, counsel:* *Consul, council,* and *counsel*

1. He was —— to Japan.
2. He keeps his own ——.
3. There is a meeting of the city ——.
4. He was —— for the defense.
5. They met in ——.
6. I always go to her for ——.
7. What would you —— me to do?

Exercise 22

Passed and *past*

Fill the blanks with *passed* or *past*. *Passed* is the past participle of the verb *pass*; *past* can be an adjective, noun, adverb, or preposition.

1. We —— your house.
2. She went —— me.
3. He whistled as he —— by.
4. He is a man with a ——.
5. He is —— master at the art of lying.
6. He is —— his prime.
7. Many years —— before he returned.
8. It is long —— bedtime.

Exercise 23

Speak and *speech*

Fill the blanks with *speak* or *speech*. *Speak* is a verb; *speech*, a noun.

1. "—— the ——, I pray you, as I pronounced it to you."
2. His —— is halting.
3. He will —— tonight.
4. Did you hear his —— on India?

Breathe and *breath*

Write the following sentences, filling the blanks with *breathe* or *breath*. *Breathe* is a verb; *breath*, a noun.

1. —— deeply, and hold your ——.
2. I caught a —— from the sea.
3. Do not —— this to anyone.
4. She said it under her ——.

Exercise 24

Its and *it's*

Fill the blanks with:

(*a*) *Its* (pronoun in the possessive case) or *it's* (contraction of *it is*).

1. —— raining.
2. The cat has had —— supper.
3. The clock is in —— old place again.
4. —— now six years since the accident.
5. I think that —— too late to go.

Your and *you're*

(*b*) *Your* (pronoun in the possessive case) or *you're* (contraction of *you are*).

1. —— mistaken; it is —— fault.
2. —— position is assured.
3. —— to go tomorrow.
4. I hope that —— taking —— vacation in July.

(*c*) *There* (adverb or interjection), *their* (pronoun in the possessive case), or *they're* (contraction of *they are*). **There, their, and they're**

1. It is —— turn.
2. —— ready to go.
3. ——, that is over with.
4. —— car was stolen.
5. —— back from —— trip.

(*d*) *Whose* (pronoun in the possessive case) or *who's* (contraction of *who is*). **Whose and who's**

1. —— turn is it?
2. There is the man —— running for mayor.
3. —— responsible for this?
4. —— book is this?

Exercise 25

Fill the blanks with *already* or *all ready*. After each sentence state in parentheses the construction of the expression supplied. **Already and all ready**

1. We were —— there.
2. We were —— to go.
3. How many are —— to give the answer?
4. He had —— answered the question.
5. They have —— gone.
6. He is —— for the examination.
7. He was —— with a retort.

Exercise 26

Fill the blanks with *altogether* or *all together*. After each sentence state in parentheses the construction of the expression supplied. **Altogether and all together**

1. Our family is —— again.
2. I am —— pleased with the results.
3. You are —— too young to go.
4. I have gathered my material ——.
5. Now, —— again, the first verse.

MECHANICS[1]

LEGIBILITY

Space between lines

339. In handwritten manuscript, leave enough space between consecutive lines to prevent any interlocking of letters. (Compare Plates I and II, pp. 316–317.) In typewritten manuscript, double space the lines except in footnotes or in quotations set apart on the page.

Space between words

340. In handwritten manuscript, do not crowd words close together. (Compare Plates I and II.) In typewritten manuscript, leave one space between words in the same sentence.

Spacing with punctuation

341. In a typewritten manuscript, space as follows (Equivalent spacing should be used for handwritten manuscript. See Plate II, lines 1, 2, 3, and 9; and compare with the corresponding lines in Plate I.):

a. One space after a comma or a semicolon.

b. One or two spaces after a colon.

c. Two or three spaces after a period, question mark, or exclamation mark.

d. No space between quotation marks and the material quoted. Two or three spaces after the second pair of quotation marks.

e. No space before and after a hyphen.

f. No space or only a thin space before and after a dash used within a sentence.

Crowding at bottom of page

342. Do not crowd the writing at the bottom of a page; start a new page.

[1] For full discussion of matters of mechanics, see *A Manual of Style,* University of Chicago Press. 1937.

Gaps between letters

343. Do not leave gaps between consecutive letters in a word. Especially avoid leaving a wide interval between an initial capital and the rest of the word.

Oblique *and* and &

344. Do not write *and* on an oblique line. Do not use & except for commercial purposes.

Dots and cross-strokes

345. Do not neglect to dot *i's* and *j's* and to cross *t's* and *x's*. Use dots, not circles, over *i's* and *j's* and place the dot immediately over the letter. Cross the stem of the *t* with a short straight horizontal stroke.

Shape of quotation marks and apostrophes

346. Form quotation marks and apostrophes as in this illustration:

Ann's motto is "What's the use?"

Shape of Roman numbers

347. Write Roman numbers in this manner:

II. III. IV. VIII. IX.

Conspicuous ornament

348. Do not decorate a letter with unnecessary flourishes or with shading. Avoid especially such forms as the following:

B. C. D. E. F. H. M. N. O. T

Prefer plain forms like the following:

B, C, D, E, F, H, M, N, O, T.

ARRANGEMENT OF MANUSCRIPT

THE MANUSCRIPT AS A WHOLE

Writing materials, etc.

349. Use unruled paper, unless ruled paper is required. If the manuscript is written by hand, use black or blue-black ink. Write on only one side of the sheet. If necessary, fold a manuscript; never roll it.

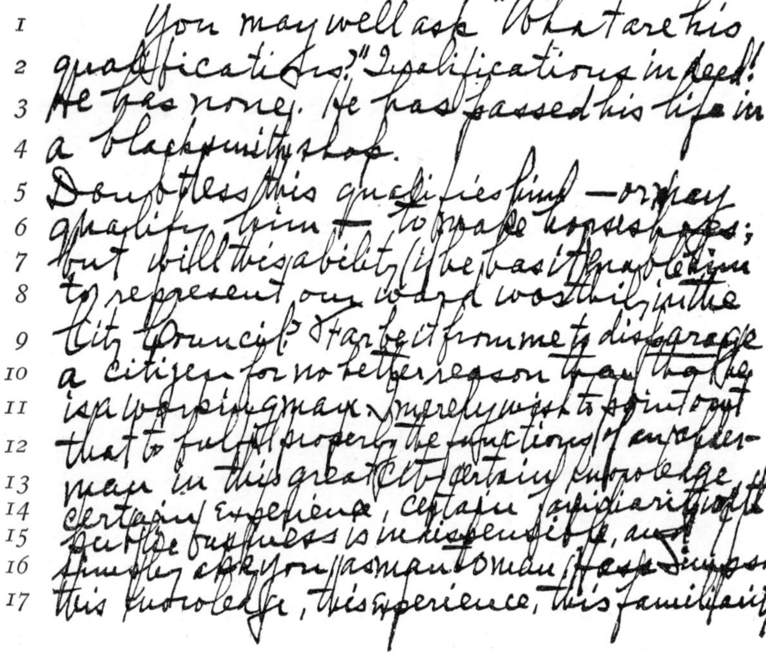

You may well ask "What are his qualifications?" Qualifications indeed! He has none. He has passed his life in a blacksmith shop.

Doubtless this qualifies him—or may qualify him—to make horseshoes; but will this ability (if he has it) enable him to represent our ward worthily in the City Council? Far be it from me to disparage a citizen for no better reason than that he is a workingman. I merely wish to point out that to fulfill properly the functions of an alderman in this great City certain knowledge, certain experience, certain familiarity with public business is indispensable, and I simply ask you as man to man, Has Simpson this knowledge, this experience, this familiarity?"

PLATE I

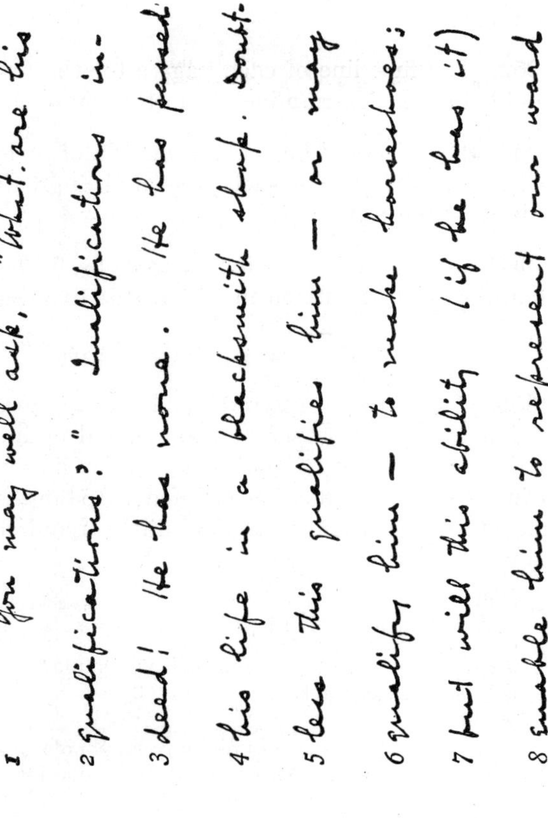

You may well ask, "What are his qualifications?" Qualifications indeed! He has none. He has passed his life in a blacksmith shop. Doubtless this qualifies him — or may qualify him — to make horseshoes; but will this ability (if he has it) enable him to represent our ward worthily in the City Council? Far

PLATE II

Page numbers

350. The pages of a manuscript should be numbered at the top in Arabic, not Roman, numbers.

Position of title

351. The title should be written at least two inches from the top of the page. Between the title and the first line of the composition, at least an inch should intervene.

Margin at the top

352. The first line of each page after the first page should stand at least an inch from the top of the page.

Margins at the sides

353. There should be a blank margin of at least an inch at the left side of each page and approximately an inch at the right side.

Uniform indention

354. Indent uniformly for paragraphs. The usual indention for typewritten manuscript is five spaces.

ALTERATIONS IN MANUSCRIPT

Insertion

355. Words to be inserted should be written above the line and their proper position should be indicated by the sign ∧ (not ∨) placed below the line. Words so inserted should not be enclosed in parentheses or brackets unless these marks would be required were the words written on the line.

Bad:
as an agreeable means of
Although tennis is at present very popular ∧ it prob-
exercising the muscles,
ably will never rank with football as a game for supremacy between colleges.

Right:
as an agreeable means of exercising the muscles,
Although tennis is at present very popular ∧ it probably will never rank with football as a game for supremacy between colleges.

Right:
as an agreeable means of
Although tennis is at present very popular ∧ ~~it~~
exercising the muscles, it probably
∧ ~~probably~~ will never rank with football as a game for supremacy between colleges.

356. Cancel words by drawing a line through them. Parentheses or brackets should not be used for this purpose. **Canceling words**

357. Words written in one place which are to be transposed to another should be canceled (see Rule 356) and inserted in the proper place by the method shown in Rule 355. **Transposition**

358. When it is desired that a word standing in the midst of a paragraph should begin a new paragraph, the sign ¶ should be placed immediately before that word. **Indicating a new paragraph**

359. A paragraph division should be canceled by writing "No ¶" in the margin. **Canceling a paragraph division**

VERSE AND PROSE QUOTATIONS

360. If an entire line of poetry cannot be written on one line of the page, the part left over should be indented. **Run-over lines**

Wrong:

Lombard and Venetian merchants with deep-laden
argosies;
Ministers from twenty nations; more than royal
pomp and ease.

Right:

Lombard and Venetian merchants with deep-laden
    argosies;
Ministers from twenty nations; more than royal
    pomp and ease.

361. A quotation of poetry should be grouped into lines exactly as the original is grouped. **Grouping of verse into lines**

Right:

Once to every man and nation comes the moment to
    decide
In the strife of truth with falsehood for the good or
    evil side.

Extended quotation of verse or prose

362. An extended quotation of verse or prose is usually set off from the body of the text by these methods:

a. It begins on a new line.

b. It is usually separated from the text by extra spacing.

c. It is usually given a wider margin than the text. In a quotation of poetry, the lines are usually centered on the page; they are aligned to the left, however, in proper relation to each other.

d. In typewritten manuscript, it is usually single-spaced.

The text following such a quotation should also begin on a new line, indented if it begins a new paragraph, or flush with the left-hand margin if it continues the paragraph containing the quotation.

> Right:
>
> While Tennyson admits that sorrow may be for our ultimate advantage and that, as his great memorial says,
>
> "Men may rise on stepping stones
> Of their dead selves to higher things,"
>
> yet he finds it impossible to get any present consolation from the thought.
>
> Right:
>
> In his essay called "Drift," Walter Lippmann writes of those who dream of the past:
>
> "The weary man sinks back into the past, like a frightened child into its mother's arms. He glorifies what is gone when he fears what is to come. That is why discontented husbands have a way of admiring the cakes that mother used to bake."
>
> It is only those, Mr. Lippmann says, who are at home in the world who find life more interesting as they mature.

A quotation of only a few words may be incorporated into the text.

Right: The battlefield stretched far and white under the "glimpses of the moon."

TABULATED LISTS

363. If an item in a tabulated list is so long as to require a second line, hanging indention should be used. (See Rule 190.) **Indention**

Right:

The principal powers of the President are —

a. The power to conduct foreign affairs.
b. The power to command the army and navy in time of war. [hanging indention]
c. The power to veto bills.
d. The power to appoint officers (subject to the approval of the Senate). [hanging indention]

364. A list of items in tabular form should be set apart from the matter preceding and following it, in the same manner as a quotation of verse or prose (see Rule 362). **Tabulated matter set apart on the page**

Bad:

Under this subject there are three important headings:
a. Position of pronouns
b. Use of connectives
c. Position of phrases
all of which are to be carefully studied.

Right:

Under this subject there are three important headings:

a. Position of pronouns
b. Use of connectives
c. Position of phrases

all of which are to be carefully studied.

Note. — The passage above could also be written without tabulating the items; thus:

Right:

Under this subject there are three important headings: (*a*) Position of pronouns; (*b*) Use of connectives; and (*c*) Position of subordinate expressions — all of which are to be carefully studied.

SYLLABICATION

Division between syllables

365. In dividing a word at the end of a line, make the division between syllables only. Parts of divided words must be pronounceable. (When in doubt as to where the division between syllables comes, consult a good dictionary. For a comprehensive treatment of syllabication, consult the introduction of a good dictionary.)

Right: maca-roni, gravi-tation, ele-ment, contro-versy, ca-tholi-cism.

Mono-syllables

366. Never divide a monosyllable.

Never: thr-ough, str-ength.

Syllable of one letter

367. Do not divide a syllable of one letter from the rest of the word.

Wrong: man-y, a-gainst, a-long, ston-y.

Split syllables

368. Do not split a syllable.

a. Wrong: exc-ursion, go-ndola, illustr-ate, instr-uction, pun-ctuation.

Right: ex-cursion, gon-dola, illus-trate, in-struction, punc-tuation.

b. Wrong: prostr-ate, pri-nciple, abs-urd, fini-shing, sugge-stion.

Right: pros-trate, prin-ciple, ab-surd, finish-ing, sug-ges-tion.

c. Wrong: nat-ion, conclus-ion, invent-ion, introd-uct-ion, abbr-eviat-ion.

Right: na-tion, conclu-sion, inven-tion, intro-duc-tion, abbre-via-tion.

d. Wrong: diffic-ult, tob-acco, exc-ept, univ-ersity, dislo-dgment.

Right: diffi-cult, to-bacco, ex-cept, uni-versity, dis-lodg-ment.

369. Divide at the point where a prefix or suffix joins the root word, if pronunciation permits. Prefixes and suffixes

Right: be-tween, pre-fix, ante-cedent, con-fine, de-light.

Right: lov-ing, love-ly, judg-ment, invit-ed, Jew-ish, punish-able, strong-er, strong-est.

But note these: extraor-di-nary, prog-ress, prej-u-dice, run-ning, hus-tling, twin-kling, bat-tling.

370. When two consonants come between vowels, divide between the consonants, if pronunciation permits. If the consonant is doubled before a suffix, the second consonant goes with the suffix. (See Rule 369.) Two consonants

Right: remem-ber, advan-tage, dip-lomat (*but* di-plomacy), impor-tant, rub-ber, ab-breviation, oc-casion, ad-dition, af-finity, Rus-sian, expres-sion, omis-sion, com-mit-tee, ex-cel-lent, stop-ping, drop-ping, ship-ping, equip-ping.

371. Divide after a vowel, if pronunciation permits. After a vowel

Right: sepa-rate, particu-lar, ele-mentary, criti-cism.

372. Never divide digraphs. For example, never divide *th* as in *another;* *sh* as in *cushion;* *ph* as in *graphic;* *ng* as in *singing;* *gn* as in *designer;* *tch* as in *wretched;* *gh* as in *doughty*, or silent *gh;* *ck* as in *picket;* *oa* as in *encroaching;* *ai* as in *complainant.* The digraphs *th*, *ch*, etc., not to be divided

Wrong: cat-holic, ras-hness, disc-harge, diap-hragm, gin-gham.

Right: cath-olic, rash-ness, dis-charge, dia-phragm, ging-ham.

Wrong: consig-nment, wat-ching, doug-hty.

Right: consign-ment, watch-ing, dough-ty.

Wrong: bo-at, sa-il, Spa-in.

Right: boat, sail, Spain.

The divisions *post-humous* (See Appendix C), *dis-habille* (See Appendix C), *Lap-ham, nightin-gale, distin-guish, sin-gle, sig-nature,* and *Leg-horn* form no exceptions to the foregoing rule, for in them *th*, *sh*, etc., are not digraphs; they are each pronounced as two distinct sounds.

EXERCISE

Syllabication

Indicate with a hyphen where the following words might be divided at the end of a line.

again, climbed, passed, financier, schoolmaster, diction, decapitate, ready, skipped, occasion, impression, shamed, disappear, particular, convention, coming, fanning, emanate, beginning, education.

ABBREVIATIONS

Generally objectionable

373. Most abbreviations are in bad taste in literary composition of any kind, including letters.

Bad: Last summer I worked for the Chandler Mfg. Co. in Casey, Ill. Casey is on the C. & E. I. R.R.
Improved: Last summer I worked for the Chandler Manufacturing Company in Casey, Illinois. Casey is on the Chicago and Eastern Illinois Railroad.

i.e., *e.g.*, etc.

374. A few abbreviations, such as *i.e.*, *e.g.*, *q.v.*, *viz.*, *etc.*, *A.D.*, *B.C.*, *a.m.*, *p.m.*, etc. are commonly used in good literature.

Note that many abbreviations that are proper when combined with other expressions are improper when standing alone.

Vulgar: I came this p.m.
Right: I came at 10 p.m.

Bad: Let me know the No. of your room.
Right: He lives in room No. 12.

Vulgar: My dear Dr.
Right: My dear Dr. Hart.

Titles

375. Spell out all civil, religious, and military titles except the following: (*a*) Preceding names: Mr., Messrs., Mrs. (French: M., MM., Mmes., Mlle., Mlles.), Dr., St. *Rev.* and *Hon.* are usually abbreviated except in very formal contexts, when they are spelled out and preceded by *the*. (*b*) Following names: Esq., M.D., Sr., Jr., Ph.D., M.A., LL.D., etc.

Right: Professor Wright, President Hall, Captain Jones.
Right: Rev. Henry L. Lake; [or] the Reverend Henry L. Lake.

NOTE. — Never abbreviate titles used without names.

Wrong: We saw our math. prof. this afternoon.
Right: We saw our mathematics professor this afternoon.

376. Spell out Christian names. Christian names

Bad: Chas., Geo., Wm.
Correct: Charles, George, William.

377. Spell out references in the text to volumes, chapters, pages, etc. These words may be abbreviated in footnotes, parenthetical citations, bibliographies, etc. *Vol., ch., p.*, etc.

Correct: I found the passage on page 345.

378. The abbreviations *St.*, *Ave.*, *Ct.*, are sometimes used in business correspondence but should not be used in formal writing or in the addresses of letters of friendship and of formal notes. In writing the name of a company, use *&* only with the abbreviation *Co.*, unless the company uses the symbol in its letterhead and signature. *St., Ave.*, etc.

379. Spell out the names of the months and the days of the week. Months, days

Right: August, February, Monday, etc.

380. Spell out the names of countries, states, etc. Countries, states

Right: United States, New York.

EXERCISE

Correct any errors in abbreviations in the following sentences: Abbreviations

1. They live on the blvd.
2. Col. House was a personal friend of Pres. Wilson.

3. I have worked for the same Co. for ten years.
4. We are going home for Xmas.
5. I was in Calif. in Aug., 1933.
6. Sec. Davis will read the minutes of the last meeting.
7. He read from Act II, Sc. I.
8. The goods will be shipped C.O.D.
9. The date is B.C., not A.D.
10. We climbed Mt. Rainier last summer. After that I resolved to climb no more mts.

NUMBERS

Dates, folios, etc., and house numbers

381. Do not spell out dates, street numbers, page numbers, or numbers of divisions (parts, chapters, paragraphs, sections, rules, etc.) of a book or a document.

Right: On October 13, 1920, I was born at 362 Adams Street. See page 916 of our family Bible.

NOTE. — Ordinal numbers designating days of a month may be either spelled out or represented by figures.

Right: The thirteenth of May fell on Friday.
Right: The 13th of May fell on Friday.

Uniform treatment

382. Treat alike all numbers in a related context. Do not use figures for some and words for others. Editorial or printing style sometimes, among newspapers especially, prescribes that sums higher than a certain maximum shall be put in numerals.

Illogical: We found ten people living in 2 rooms.
Improved: We found ten people living in two rooms.
Possible but inadvisable: He sacrificed two men to save 25.

Isolated numbers

383. Spell out isolated numbers of less than three digits. (Note exceptions in Rule 381.) For sums of money in figures, use the dollar sign ($).

Right: In 1932 four of us managed a ranch of 32,000 acres.

Right: They bought a fifty-pound cheese.
Right: He will be seventy years old today.
Right: His fortune amounts to $72,000.
Right: The hat cost $1.19.

384. Spell out the number in the case of an isolated sum in cents. Isolated sum in cents

Right: The price is ninety cents.

385. Use figures for several numbers occurring together in a related context. Several numbers

Right: My room costs $5 a week and my board $6.50; my contribution to the church is 30 cents; my incidental expenses range from $9.35 to $22.50 a month.

386. In sums of money from one to ten, ciphers are used when there are no fractional amounts. For sums above ten the ciphers should be omitted. Use of .00

Right: The prices were respectively: $7.00, $8.50, and $10.00.
But for uniformity: The prices were respectively: $7.00, $8.50, and $35.00.
Right: It will cost $50 to paint the walls.
Right: He gave me 50 cents on Monday, 75 cents on Tuesday, and 35 cents on Wednesday.

387. It is preferable to spell out a sum used as an adjective. A sum used as an adjective

Right: I sent her a ten-dollar bill.

388. In informal and business correspondence, numbers used as the names of streets (usually numbers above ten) may be expressed in figures followed by *st*, *nd*, *rd*, *d*, or *th*. Numbers as names of streets

Right: 618 98th Street.

389. Do not use numerals at the beginning of a sentence. Spell the numbers out or recast the sentence so as to begin it with another word. Numerals at beginning of sentence

Bad: 1914 was a momentous year.
Right: The year 1914 was momentous.
Right: Nineteen hundred fourteen was a momentous year.

Ages, and hours of the day

390. A number representing a person's age or one designating an hour of the day should nearly always be spelled out.

Right: At twelve o'clock all the children below eight years of age are sent home.

NOTE. — Figures are used with the abbreviations A.M. and P.M.

Right: The train arrives at 3:42 P.M.

Round numbers

391. Round numbers should be spelled out.

Right: I have about three hundred chickens.
Right: I have 293 chickens.

Decimals and per cents

392. Use figures for decimals and percentages.

Right: It rained .62 of an inch.
Right: You will receive 5 per cent of the profits.

Use of *st*, *nd*, etc., with day of the month

393. It is not necessary to use *st*, *nd*, *rd*, *d*, or *th* after a figure designating the day of the month if the year is also designated.

Unnecessary: January 8th, 1927.
Right: January 8, 1927.

Parenthetic repetition of numbers

394. A number that is spelled out should not be repeated in parenthesized figures, except in legal or commercial papers. If the number is repeated, the figures should stand immediately after the spelled-out number or after the word *dollars*, etc., not before the number.

Right: I enclose ten dollars ($10).
Right: I enclose ten (10) dollars.

NOTE. — The figures, not the spelled-out word, should be put within the parentheses.

Wrong: I enclose $10 (ten dollars).
Right: I enclose ten dollars ($10).

EXERCISE

In the following sentences the numbers are all represented by figures. Should some of them be spelled out? If so, give your reason for changing the form. Numbers

1. 20, 30, 40 years ago these were the activities of the farmers in the Middle West.
2. My family moved to the farm in 1930, 4 years after my brother's death.
3. He caught a 40-pound catfish in the river 3 miles from our farm.
4. At 10 o'clock the lights on our corridor are turned off.
5. The round trip fare is 92 cents.
6. Her address 2 years ago was 196 West 9th Street.
7. About 60 people answered the advertisement.
8. The 3rd and 4th grades are to have a spelling match.
9. The original drainage project consisted of about 200 miles of canals 60 feet wide by 5 feet deep. At the present time about 1,500,000 acres have been reclaimed.
10. He paid $30.00 for his new suit.

CAPITALS

395. Capitalize proper nouns in general, including: Proper names

a. Days of the week and the months.

b. Organizations such as political parties, governmental bodies and departments, societies, institutions, clubs, churches, corporations, etc.:

The Socialist Party, the House of Representatives, the Department of Labor, the Red Cross Society, the Home for the Friendless, the Rotary Club, the Methodist Church, Catholics, the Standard Oil Company.

c. Historical events: the Fall of Rome.

d. Historical periods: the Middle Ages, the Renaissance.

e. Documents: the Declaration of Independence.

f. Geographical names: the Azores.

g. Buildings: the Woolworth Building.

h. All words pertaining to Deity:

God the Father, Jesus Christ, the Virgin, a Christian, the Bible, the Holy Book, in His Name.

i. Personifications:

Yet Hope had never lost her youth;
  She did but look through dimmer eyes;
  Or Love but play'd with gracious lies,
Because he felt so fix'd in truth.

— TENNYSON.

Not seasons

396. The words *spring*, *summer*, *midsummer*, *autumn*, *fall*, *winter*, and *midwinter* should not be capitalized.

North, south, etc.

397. *North*, *south*, *east*, *west*, and their various forms (*northwest*, etc.) and derivatives (*northern*, etc.) should not be capitalized except when they designate divisions of the country.

Right: As we sailed north, we saw a ship going west.
Right: The West is prosperous. — The people of the South are migrating westward. — The Northern delegates clashed with the Southern.

Words denoting family relationship

398. Capitalize words denoting family relationship, such as *father*, *mother*, *sister*, only when they are used with the name of a person or as a substitute for it. In the latter usage they are not always capitalized.

Right: I heard that Uncle John had written to Mother.
Right: She accompanied her brother.

Titles of persons

399. Titles of persons should be capitalized when they precede proper names. When used without proper names, titles of governmental officers of high rank should be capitalized; other titles should not.

Right: There go Professor Cox and Colonel Henry. — A certain professor became a colonel in the volunteer

army. — The President and the Postmaster-General sent for the postmaster of our town and the secretary of our society. — There goes A. H. Cox, Professor of Latin.

NOTE. — Academic degrees, when abbreviated, are written with capital letters; when not abbreviated, they are written with either capital letters or small letters.

Right: LL.D., Ph.D., Master of Arts, master of arts.

400. Capitalize *club, company, society, college, high school, railroad, county, river, lake, park, street* or any other common noun when it is made a component part of a proper name; not otherwise. **Common-noun elements of proper names**

Wrong: I went to that College one year.
Right: I went to that college one year.

Wrong: Do you mean Hamilton college?
Right: Do you mean Hamilton College?

NOTE. — Many writers consistently go contrary to this rule. Thus: Bleeker street, Portland county, Pennsylvania railroad, the Saturday club, Wilson school.

401. Capitalize nouns and adjectives of language or race, such as *German, Latin, Indian, Negro,* etc. *Negro* is sometimes and *gypsy* is often written with a small letter, especially when used to designate an individual. Words of race and language

402. Do not capitalize studies unless a particular course is named. Names of studies

Right: I like history and civics.
Right: I am taking History I.

403. Capitalize only the important words of the titles of books, articles, compositions, etc. The unimportant words are the articles (*a, an, the*), conjunctions, and prepositions. Words in literary titles

Right: I read *The Light that Failed* and *A Tale of Two Cities.*

NOTE. — Capitalize both words of a compound noun in a title, but only the first word in compound adjectives, adverbs, etc.

Right: *Walking-Stick Papers.*
Right: *The House on Forty-ninth Street.*

At the beginning of a sentence or quotation

404. Capitalize the first word of a sentence. This rule applies in general to quoted sentences.

Wrong: The conductor cried, "hands off!"
Right: The conductor cried, "Hands off!"

Note, however, that capitals are not used in the following instances:

The part of a sentence following *he said*

a. The part of the quotation following the expression, *he said,* or its equivalent, unless that part is a new sentence.

Wrong: "Hammer on the window," advised the policeman, "Until he gets up."
Right: "Hammer on the window," advised the policeman, "until he gets up." [or] "Hammer on the window," advised the policeman. "He's probably asleep."

He said

b. The expression, *he said,* or its equivalent.

Wrong: "Hammer on the window," Advised the policeman. "He's probably asleep."
Right: "Hammer on the window," advised the policeman. "He's probably asleep."

Quoted sentence with words omitted

c. A quoted sentence from which words are omitted at the beginning.

Right: ". . . the outer passes away, in swift endless changes; the inmost is the same yesterday, today, and forever." — CARLYLE.

Quoted sentence-element

d. A quoted sentence-element incorporated in a sentence.

Wrong: It seemed to be "Without form and void."
Right: It seemed to be "without form and void."

e. An indirect quotation. Indirect quotation

Wrong: He said, "He could not come."
Right: He said he could not come.
Right: He said, "I cannot come."

405. Capitalize the first word of every line of poetry. See the *Right* examples under Rules 360–362. Do not capitalize, however, when part of a line is omitted. At the beginning of lines of poetry

Right:

". . . . . he went, unterrified,
Into the gulf of death; but his clear Sprite
Yet reigns o'er earth; the third among the sons of
light." — SHELLEY.

406. Capitalize the pronoun *I* and the interjection *O*, but not the interjection *oh* except at the beginning of a sentence. *I*, *O*, and *oh*

407. Capitalize the first and last words in the salutation of a letter and only the first word in the complimentary close. Salutation and complimentary close of letters

Wrong: Dear sir:
Right: Dear Sir:

Wrong: Yours Sincerely,
Right: Yours sincerely,

408. Do not capitalize the word following a semicolon. Misuse after a semicolon

Wrong: Send him to the library; His father wants to speak to him.
Right: Send him to the library; his father wants to speak to him.

409. Do not, as a rule, capitalize the word following a colon, unless a complete statement precedes the colon and a long complete statement follows. Capital after a colon

Right: Bring the following articles with you: one pair of heavy shoes, one pair of light shoes, overshoes, a heavy coat, a rain coat, and a pair of woolen blankets.

Right: Here is the old question of campaign funds: If I take a hundred thousand dollars from a group of men representing a particular interest that has a big stake in a certain schedule of the tariff, I take it with the knowledge that those gentlemen will expect me not to forget their interest in that schedule, and that they will take it as an implicit honor that I should see to it that they are not damaged by too great a change in that schedule. — Woodrow Wilson.

Series of short questions in one sentence

410. In a sentence composed of a series of short questions, only the first question need begin with a capital.

Right: What is freedom but machinery? what is population but machinery? what is coal but machinery? what are railroads but machinery? what is wealth but machinery? what are, even, religious organizations but machinery? — Arnold

Exercise

Capitals

What words in the following sentences should be capitalized? Why?

1. He is enrolled in the college of commerce, and is taking economics I.
2. Several thousand chinese lost their lives in the recent flooding of the yangtze river.
3. A novel experiment in american education was announced recently by the yale school of law and the harvard school of business administration.
4. I am writing to sister tonight.
5. Did you know that sister marie has been transferred to a convent in Canada?
6. I have never known the nights here to be so beautiful as I remember them in the north, in the land of the midnight sun.
7. "That's the man," they shouted. "we'd know him anywhere."
8. There sat mr. squirrel begging for nuts.
9. Suddenly through the outer stillness came the sharp cling! cling! cling! of a very different bell.
10. He makes these regional divisions: the east, the old south, the middle west, and the far west.

11. Soon bedlam broke loose, and each broker in his excitement resembled a communist orator at a red may-day picnic.
12. He was a civil war veteran.
13. It was class day — the day when we bequeathed our virtues and vices to the undergraduates in a solemn last will and testament.
14. There is much room for improvement in the american high school.
15. He is a mixture of indian, negro, and mexican.

ITALICS

411. To italicize a word in a manuscript, draw one straight line below it, thus: italicize. Representation in MS.

412. Italicize titles of separate publications such as books, periodicals, pamphlets, newspapers, etc., and also the titles of musical compositions and works of art. Do not italicize the author's name. Italics with titles of books, etc.

Right: Sir Walter Scott's *The Talisman;* the *Atlantic Monthly;* the *New York Times;* Beethoven's *Eroica Symphony;* Da Vinci's *Last Supper.*

NOTE. — It is permissible to enclose titles of separate publications in quotation marks instead of italicizing them; but the simpler and better approved practice is to italicize. Titles of parts of published works are usually enclosed in quotation marks.

413. If the title of a literary, musical, or artistic work begins with *the*, this word should not be omitted, and it should be capitalized and italicized. Titles beginning with *the:* Single works

Right: Do you like Kipling's *The Man Who Was* and Chaminade's *The Silver Ring?*

Right: I felt depressed after reading *The House of Mirth.*

414. An initial *the* in the title of a newspaper or other periodical should not be capitalized or italicized. Periodicals

Right: She found some copies of the *Pall Mall Gazette*, the *Evening Telegraph*, the *Century Magazine*, and the *New York Evening Post*.

Names of ships

415. Italicize names of ships.

Right: I cut the *Hispaniola* from her anchor.

Italics with words discussed

416. When a word is spoken of *as a word*, it is usually italicized. When a word is quoted, it is usually enclosed in quotation marks.

Right: The misuse of *grand*, *awful*, and *nice* is a common fault.
Right: "Intriguing" is now her pet word.

With foreign words

417. Italicize unnaturalized foreign words introduced into an English context.

Right: He is a *bona fide* purchaser.
Right: The scientific name of the May apple is *Podophyllum peltatum*.

Latin words in footnotes

418. Italicize the following Latin words or abbreviations used in reference and in footnotes: *circa*, *c.*, *et al.*, *ibid.*, *idem.*, *infra*, *loc. cit.*, *op. cit.*, *passim*, *sic*, *supra*, *vide*. (Pages 29–30.)

For emphasis

419. Avoid the habit of frequently italicizing words for emphasis; do not emphasize a word in this way unless there is some especially good reason — as, for instance, the fact that obscurity would result from lack of emphasis.

Unnecessary: The curse of this age is *commercialism* coupled with *hypocrisy*.
Improved: The curse of this age is commercialism coupled with hypocrisy.

Italics for emphasis:

Surely young men and women who cannot spell, punctuate, paragraph, formulate their thoughts on paper or even orally, nor grasp the essentials of any subject of college grade, do not *belong* [in college], — unless we are to give up entirely the long-held conception of what a college is or should be. — RICHARD BURTON.

To speak French fluently and idiomatically and with a good accent — or with an idiom and accent which to other rough islanders *seemed* good — was a rather suspect accomplishment, being somehow deemed incompatible with civic worth. — MAX BEERBOHM.

420. Do not italicize for the purpose of calling attention to your humor or irony; this practice is undignified and inartistic. (See Rules 244 and 295 *h*.) **Improper use for marking humor**

Bad: The villain in the play was *charming*.
Right: The villain in the play was charming.

EXERCISES ON MECHANICS

EXERCISE 1

Show how each of the following words may be correctly divided at the end of a line. For example: **Syllabication**

re-mem-ber
in-com-plete

1. *instrumental, distributive, gratification, dissatisfaction, lexicographer, isosceles, retinue, perspicacious, disinterestedness, philologist, maiden, husband, eightieth, despondency, incontrovertibly, amphitheater, rheumatism, changeable.* **Miscellaneous**
2. *abject, acquit, adhere, belie, concur, defer, disagree, educate, excuse, forget, unreal, invite, mistrust, interest, obtain, suburb, supervise, repeat, postmark, provide, embed, unified.* **Prefixes**
3. *driven, loaded, inspector, laughable, payment, hurrying, quickly, selfish, stronger, strongest, clearness, memorize, helpful, listless, chemist.* **Suffixes**
4. *possess, cottage, message, cobbler, lesson, mutton, garrison, parallel, prattle, slipping.* **Doubled consonants**
5. *mother, witchcraft, attachment, clanging, thoroughness, seraphim, checkmate, resignment, triumphant, fleshiness, autochthonous.* **Digraphs**

Exercise 2

Abbreviations, numbers, capitals, italics

Correct in the following sentences any errors in abbreviations, numbers, capitals, and italics. State the reasons for the changes made.

1. He made a survey of Athletics in the Universities and Colleges in the U. S.
2. When grandmother was a girl, things were different.
3. She always adds a P. S. to her letters.
4. Did you consult Edwardes' dictionary of non-classical mythology?
5. Something injured his amour propre when he was traveling in the East last Winter.
6. I spent fifty cents for a pattern, $6.80 for my material, and a dollar and ten cents for trimming; so you see that my dress will cost only $8.40.
7. It is a 10-ton load.
8. 1929 brought us good fortune.
9. "You will surely decide to go," he said, "For you will never have such a chance as this again."
10. After each war we resolve "That these dead shall not have died in vain."
11. Our country entered the war in nineteen hundred and seventeen.
12. You have a hard road ahead: There will be tedious hours of work under an exacting master, perhaps in unpleasant surroundings, and there will be little pay and less honor.
13. The use of the word like as a conjunction is a very common error.
14. My Chemistry and Math. grades were high.
15. The Harvard and Yale are good passenger boats going up and down the Pacific coast.
16. To some southern democrats, all northerners are still black republicans.
17. They discussed the eighteenth amendment.
18. The president of the United States rose to greet the president of our university.
19. The catholic church was powerful in the middle ages.
20. Political Science, history, economics, and spanish have been my favorite subjects.
21. He made his money in the Real Estate business.
22. He caught a large Muskellunge.

PREPARATION OF COPY FOR THE PRINTER AND CORRECTION OF PROOF

421. Manuscript prepared for a publisher or a printer is called "copy." The general directions for the preparation of manuscript given in the chapter on Mechanics (Pages 314–338) should be carefully observed.[1] Copy

Copy should be typewritten on one side only of paper about $8\frac{1}{2} \times 11$ inches in size, in double or triple space, with ample margins on all edges. Sheets should be arranged in their proper order and numbered. The name and address of the writer should be written in an upper corner of the first page.

422. Copy should be prepared exactly as the writer wishes it to appear in print. After it is completed it should be gone over with care to make sure that every detail of arrangement, of spelling, punctuation, paragraphing, capitalizing, etc., is unmistakably clear and consistent throughout. Copy that is not uniform has to be edited, often at the expense of the author, and causes unnecessary delay. Alterations made after copy is in type are usually charged to the author. Complete, consistent, and accurate copy

423. Typographical details are usually left to the editor or publisher, but the author must indicate some of them. Draw one line under matter to be *italicized;* two lines under matter to be printed in SMALL CAPITALS (small caps); three lines under matter to be printed Technical practices

[1] For more detailed information on the preparation of manuscript and the correction of proof than is given in this book, see the *Manual of Style*, University of Chicago Press, 1937; *Style Manual*, Government Printing Office, 1935.

in CAPITALS (caps); and a wavy line under matter to be printed in **boldface.** For italic capitals, draw three lines under the matter and write "italic caps" opposite it in the margin. Quoted matter not em-

Sample of corrected and marked copy

```
     Copy that is not uniform has to be
edited, often at the expense of the
author, and causes unnecessary delay.
Alterations made after copy is in type
are charged usually, to the author. Typo-
graphical details are usually left to the
editor or publisher, but the author must
indicate some of them. draw one line
under matter to be italicized; two lines
under matter to be printed in small capi-
tals (small caps); three lines under mat-
ter to be printed in capitals (caps); and
a wavy line under matter to be printed in
boldface.
```

bodied in a paragraph with other matter is often printed in smaller type or with a wider margin than that of the body of the text. The publisher will usually follow his office practice in this regard, but the author may properly indicate his own preference by extra indention or by using single-space typing, or both, with such quoted matter.

Insertions in the copy

424. If it is necessary to insert new material after the copy is written, this new material should be written on a separate sheet marked "Insert A" and attached to the sheet to which the new material is to be added. On the former, the same words "Insert A" should be written at the point where the insertion is to be made. If several pages of new material are to be inserted at the same point, they should be marked with the number of the page on which the insertion comes and should be marked A, B, C, etc. Thus inserts for page 18 should be marked 18A, 18B, 18C, etc. If pages are to be omitted after the copy has been numbered, the omission may be made clear in this manner: If pages 6–10 are to be omitted, there should be a note at the bottom of page 5 stating "page 11 follows." (For the correct placing of footnotes in copy, see pp. 28–29.)

425. Manuscript should be sent flat, not folded, and never rolled, in a strong covering, either a heavy envelope or substantial wrapping paper, securely tied and sealed. If sent by mail, it requires letter postage. Manuscript weighing more than a few ounces can usually be sent at less expense by express than by mail. It should always be insured. Sending manuscript

426. After the copy is set in type, a proof is taken and corrected by the proofreader of the printer or the publisher. This "galley" proof, with the original copy, is then sent to the author, who makes his corrections in ink in the margin of the proof. The corrections and changes should be indicated by the standard proofreader's marks. (See Rule 428.) If new material is added, it should, if possible, fill one or more complete lines, in order that alteration may be easier; if a substitution is made, it should be of the same length as the original matter. The printer's errors are corrected without charge to the author, who Galley proof should make such corrections and put a circle around them.

Changes from the copy must be paid for by the author. Any necessary alterations must be made in the galley proof; changes in the page proof are very difficult and expensive to make. In no case should alterations in page proof require changes beyond the page on which they occur. The galley proof and copy should be returned to the publisher.

Page proof

427. After the corrections are made, the type is arranged in pages,[1] and page proof is sent to the author with the marked galley proof. In the page proof, the author must be certain (1) that the corrections in the galley proof have been made; (2) that the titles or "folio heads" at the top of the pages are correctly worded and placed; (3) that the pages are correctly numbered; (4) that no lines have been omitted or transposed at the bottom or top of the pages; (5) that footnotes are correctly placed; (6) that no letters or marks of punctuation have been dropped from the end of the lines; and (7) that no words are divided at ends of lines except between syllables. The page proof should be marked "O.K.," if there are no corrections; or "O.K. with corrections," if there are corrections to be made. The page proof with the galley proof should then be returned to the publisher.

[1] The handling of proof here described represents the practice in publishing books, rather than magazine articles.

428. Proofreader's Marks.

Proofreader's marks

♂	Dele, or delete: take it out.
ɑ	Letter reversed—turn.
#	Put in space.
⁀	Close up—no space.
^	Bad spacing; space more evenly.
wf	Wrong font: character of wrong size or style.
tr	Transpose.
¶	¶Make a new paragraph.
□	□Indent; or, put in an em-quad space.
⊏	⊏Carry to the left.
⊐	Carry to the right.
⊓	Elevate.
⊔	Depress.
X	Imperfect type—correct.
⊥	Space shows between words—push down.
//	Straighten crooked line.
‖=	‖Straighten alignment.
stet	Restore or retain words crossed out.
⁀	Print (ae, fi, etc.) as a ligature.
out-see copy	Words are omitted from, or in, copy.
(Qy) or (?)	Query to author: Is this correct?
caps	Put in capitals.
s.c.	Put in SMALL CAPITALS.
lc	Put in LOWER CASE.
rom	Put in roman type.
ital	Put in italic type.
bf	Put in bold face type.

LETTERS

BUSINESS LETTERS

THE PARTS OF THE LETTER

Illustrative letters

429. The following letters illustrate the correct form for business letters. Letter I is a formal business letter from an individual to a firm; letter II is a formal business letter from a firm to an individual on the firm's letterhead; letter III is an informal business letter from a firm to an individual on the firm's letterhead.

LETTER I

Heading

2432 Henderson Avenue
San Diego, California
May 19, 1937

Inside address

Pearson and Harper
864 Market Street
San Francisco, California

Salutation

Gentlemen:

Body

I am enclosing a sample of Chinese brocade. Will you please send me ten yards of this material, and charge the bill to my account with you?

Close

Yours truly,

Signature

Helen Richards

(Mrs. John R. Richards)

Letter II

D. C. HEATH AND COMPANY
PUBLISHERS OF TEXTBOOKS FOR SCHOOLS AND COLLEGES
285 Columbus Avenue — Boston, Massachusetts
D C HEATH AND COMPANY

Heading

January 27, 1937

Professor John W. Stirling
Old Town University
Charleston, Ohio

Inside address

My dear Professor Stirling

Salutation

In response to your letter of January 24, we are sending you by parcel post a copy of A MODERN READER by Lippmann and Nevins. We believe you will find that this anthology of essays, in which the emphasis is laid upon thought rather than creation or esthetics, will meet your requirement. The style of these essays is excellent and the material is modern.

We shall be glad to have you examine this book and to know whether or not it meets your requirements.

Body

Very truly yours

Close

D. C. HEATH AND COMPANY

Ralph G. Brown

Signature

Manager

Title of writer

Copy to A. B. Brown

LETTER III

Heading	THE MARSH CORPORATION STATE AND LAKE STREETS CHICAGO, ILLINOIS
	January 6, 1937
Salutation	Dear Mr. Holmes:
	We certainly appreciate your interest in sending us your mailing list. I must have overlooked acknowledging it in the rush of the holiday season. I am sure that you will forgive me.
Body	We are going to write these people, making mention of some of the things that we think will be of interest.
	In the meantime, I am sending you the current number of Marsh's Business Bulletin. I think that you will be particularly interested in this number, and if you are not already getting this service, you may want to have it come to you regularly.
	Do call again when you are in the city.
Close	Yours very truly, THE MARSH CORPORATION
Signature	G. H. Baldwin
Writer's and stenographer's initials	GHB:DF Vice-president
Inside address	Mr. J. R. Holmes 123 Morse Avenue Cincinnati, Ohio

The Heading

430. The heading, which gives the address of the writer and the date of the letter, is usually placed in the upper right-hand corner of the first page. Present-day usage favors the block style to the indented style. What is important, however, is a consistent practice: if the block style is used, it should be used throughout the heading and throughout the inside address and the salutation. Position

Indented heading:
5743 Dorchester Avenue
Chicago, Illinois
August 27, 1937

Block heading:
5743 Dorchester Avenue
Chicago, Illinois
August 27, 1937

NOTE. — In business letters it is not advisable to drop the heading to the bottom of the letter at the left-hand side of the page. This arrangement, often used in informal personal letters, is too informal for business letters. (For the dropped inside address, see Rule 446.)

431. In printed, lithographed, or engraved letterheads the name of the writer or of the firm and the address are usually placed in the middle of the page; on such stationery the date may be written at the right of the page or in the center under the address. Business letterheads

432. Do not write a part of the heading at the beginning of the letter and a part at the close (see Rule 430); and do not repeat the heading or a part of it at the close when it has been written at the beginning. Separation or repetition of members

Bad:

Cleveland, Ohio
May 1, 1937

. . . .

Yours truly,
Robert Graves
642 Euclid Avenue

Bad:

Cleveland, Ohio
May 1, 1937

. . . .

Yours truly,
Robert Graves

642 Euclid Avenue
Cleveland, Ohio

Right:

642 Euclid Avenue
Cleveland, Ohio
May 1, 1937

. . . .

Yours truly,
Robert Graves

Punctuation

433. Punctuation may be used or may be omitted at the end of the lines of the heading, but care should be taken to follow a consistent practice. (See also Rule 447.) If end-punctuation is used, there should be a comma after *Street*, *Avenue*, etc.; a comma or a period after the state; and a period after the year. Whether there is end-punctuation or not, there should be punctuation within the lines. A comma should be used after the city and after the day of the month, but not between the month and the day. All abbreviations should be followed by periods.

With end-punctuation:

2684 Webster Avenue,
Atlanta, Georgia,
March 10, 1937.

Without end-punctuation:

2684 Webster Avenue
Atlanta, Georgia
March 10, 1937

434. The address should precede the date. Address before date

Right:

Groveport, Ohio
June 4, 1937

435. The address in the heading should be such as would be sufficient for a postal direction. Sufficient address

Right:

212 State Street
Chicago, Illinois

Right:

Route 3
La Salle, Illinois

436. If the address contains a street direction, this should precede the name of the city. Street direction before city

Right:

28 High Street
Columbus, Ohio

437. A house number should be written in Arabic figures and should be preceded by no word or sign. House numbers

Right: 15 H Street; not # 15 H Street, nor Fifteen H Street.

438. Street numbers less than ten are usually spelled out. (See Rule 388.) Numbers of streets

Right: 285 Second Street.
Right: 285 42nd Street.

439. In writing a street direction do not omit *Street, Avenue*, etc. Do not omit *Street*, etc.

Bad: 17 Main.
Right: 17 Main Street.

440. The date should consist of the name (not the number) of the month, the number of the day of the month, and the complete number of the year. The date: Completeness

Inelegant: 3/21/'37.
Right: March 21, 1937.
Right: 21 March, 1937.

Figures, not words

441. All the numbers in the date should be written in Arabic figures, not represented by words. (See Rule 381, but also Rule 475.)

Unnecessary: March the twenty-first, nineteen hundred and thirty-seven.
Right: March 21, 1937.

St, *nd*, etc., not to be used

442. The number of the day should not be followed by *st*, *nd*, *rd*, *d*, or *th*.

Undesirable: March 21st, 1937.
Right: March 21, 1937.

Abbreviations to be avoided

443. Avoid the use of abbreviations in the heading.

Undesirable: Norton, Mass.
Jan. 3, 1937

Preferred: Norton, Massachusetts
January 3, 1937

The Inside Address

Name and address of person written to

444. The inside address contains the name and the address of the person written to. The address should be sufficient for a postal direction. Large and well-known business organizations may not need street addresses; *i.e.*, the Illinois Central Railroad gives its address on its letterhead as Chicago, Illinois, with no street address. When a street address is a part of the mailing address, it is important to have this recorded on letters of which copies are kept.

Position

445. The inside address should be placed at the left-hand side of the page three or four spaces below the last line of the heading. The first line should be flush with the left-hand margin; the rest of the address may also be placed at the margin line (block style) or indented, each line about one-fourth of an inch more than the preceding. Whether the block style or the indented style is used, it should be consistent with the style of the heading.

Right: Henry White and Company
19 West Forty-fourth Street
New York City

Right: Henry White and Company
19 West Forty-fourth Street
New York City

446. Occasionally in business letters not dealing with mercantile transactions and in professional letters, the inside address may be dropped to the bottom of the letter at the left-hand side of the page. This arrangement, more informal than the usual arrangement, tends to make the letter more direct and more personal. (See Rule 430, Note.)

Position in informal business letters

447. Punctuation marks may be used or may be omitted at the end of the lines of the inside address; but care should be taken to follow a consistent practice. If end-punctuation is used, a period should be placed after the last line and commas after the others. Whether there is end-punctuation or not, there should be punctuation within the lines; for example, a comma should be placed between the city and the state. Periods should be used after all abbreviations.

Punctuation

With end-punctuation:
Marshall Field and Company,
State and Madison Streets,
Chicago, Illinois.

Without end-punctuation:
Marshall Field and Company
State and Madison Streets
Chicago, Illinois

Letter to an individual in a firm

448. If, in a letter to a firm, the particular attention of a member of the firm is desired, the following forms may be used:

Right: Messrs. Meade, Brown, and Harrison
843 Fifth Avenue
New York City
New York

Attention of Mr. M. L. Brown
Gentlemen:

Or: Attention: Mr. M. L. Brown
Gentlemen:

Or: Gentlemen: Attention of Mr. M. L. Brown

Name without address

449. Do not write a name alone above the salutation.

Wrong:
Mr. Harvey Myers
My dear Sir:

Right:
Mr. Harvey Myers
Seattle, Washington
My dear Sir:

Omission of title discourteous

450. In the inside address do not omit *Mr.*, or whatever other title is proper, before the name of an individual. Before a firm name composed of individual names, it is correct to write *Messrs.* or to omit the title. *Messrs.* is improper before a name not composed of individual names.

Right: Messrs. Hoyt and Marsh
Chicago, Illinois

Hoyt and Marsh
Chicago, Illinois

Lacking in courtesy and propriety:
J. H. Woolson
Morristown

Right:
Mr. J. H. Woolson
Morristown, New Jersey

451. Avoid the use of abbreviations in the inside address. Names of firms, however, should be written as they appear on the stationery of the firm. Do not abbreviate titles except the following: *Mr.*, *Esq.*, *Messrs.*, *Mrs.*, *Dr.*, *Rev.*, *Hon.* Degrees are abbreviated: *D.D.*, *M.D.*, *Ph.D.*, etc. (See Rule 375.) Abbreviations to be avoided

Not permissible: Heath Pub. Co.
Boston, Massachusetts

Correct: D. C. Heath and Company
Boston, Massachusetts

Correct: Dr. John T. Carver
642 43rd Street
New York City

Note 1. — The long names *United States of America* and *District of Columbia* may be abbreviated respectively to *U. S. A.* and *D. C.* It is permissible in business letters to abbreviate the names of states also; but the better practice is to spell out those names. Abbreviation of the short names *Maine*, *Ohio*, and *Iowa* is objectionable in any letter. Permissible exceptions

Note 2. — The title *Esq.*, a proper substitute for *Mr.*, follows the name. When it is used, no title should precede the name. Use of the title *Esq.*

Wrong: Mr. Ralph Williams, Esq.
Right: Ralph Williams, Esq.

The Salutation

452. The salutation should be written flush with the left-hand margin, and should be placed two or three spaces below the inside address. The salutation is usually followed by a colon. Position and punctuation

Right: Dr. A. L. Holmes
Tower Building
Washington, D. C.

Dear Sir:

453. The salutation should be suited to the person or persons addressed and to the type of letter. Form *a.* When the name of the person addressed is not known:

Usual:
Dear Sir:
Dear Madam:
Gentlemen: (Also correct: Dear Sirs:)
Mesdames: (Also correct: Ladies:)

Formal:
My dear Sir:
My dear Madam:

Very formal:
Sir:
Madam:

b. When the person is addressed by name:
Usual:
Dear Mr. Smith:
Dear Mrs. Harper:
Dear Captain Young:

Formal:
My dear Mr. Smith:

Name alone not permissible

454. Never use a name alone as a salutation.

Bad:
Mr. Percy Clapp:
Will you please inform me . . .
Right:
Dear Mr. Clapp:
Will you please inform me . . .

Abbreviations not to be used

455. In the salutation never use any abbreviation, except *Mr.*, *Mrs.*, and *Dr.* (See Rule 375.)

Bad: My dear Prof. Walker,
Right: My dear Professor Walker,

Bad: Dear Capt. Ayer,
Right: Dear Captain Ayer,

The Body

Position

456. The body of the letter usually begins two spaces below the salutation. Both the block style and the indented style are used. In the block style each paragraph begins flush with the left-hand margin. In the indented style the first paragraph begins about ten or twelve spaces from the left-hand margin, not, however, farther to the right than the end of the salutation; each succeeding paragraph must receive the same indention as the first. If the heading and the inside address are in the block style, either the block or indented style is used in the body. But if the heading and the inside address are in the indented style, the body is indented.

457. The body of a letter is usually single-spaced, with double-spacing between paragraphs. **Spacing**

458. The length of the letter will determine the width of the margins. The shorter the letter, the wider the margins should be. The right and left margins should be as nearly equal as possible. **Margins**

The Complimentary Close

459. The complimentary close should be written on a separate line, about two spaces below the last line of the body of the letter, should stand near the middle of the page, should have only the first word capitalized, and may be followed by a comma. **Position and punctuation**

Note. — Expressions introducing the complimentary close, such as *I am, believe me, good-by,* now used only in very formal letters, should be included in the body of the letter. **Position of preceding words**

Right:

Accept my congratulations upon your new appointment; and believe me

Yours sincerely,

Henry Cobb.

460. The complimentary close, like the salutation, should be appropriate to the person or persons addressed and to the tone of the letter. **Form**

Impersonal, frequently used:
Yours truly
Yours very truly
Very truly yours

Formal, used for persons superior in rank:
Yours respectfully
Respectfully yours
Very respectfully yours

Informal, friendly, personal:
Yours sincerely
Sincerely yours
Cordially yours
Yours faithfully
Faithfully yours

Undesirable closes

461. Do not use any abbreviation, such as *yrs* or *resp'y* in the complimentary close. *And oblige* and *I beg to remain* are not used in modern business letters.

The Signature

Position of the signature

462. The signature is usually placed about two spaces below the complimentary close, and either directly beneath it or two spaces or so to the right.

Form

463. The signature should always be written by hand. In a typewritten letter in which the name of the writer does not appear on the letterhead, the name may be typewritten beneath the written signature or at the left-hand side of the page with the initials of the stenographer. Letters from firms are generally signed with the name of the firm, typewritten, and directly beneath that, in handwriting, the name of the person who is responsible for the letter. Sometimes the writer's official capacity is indicated.

Right: D. C. Heath and Company
Allen Grant Odell
Right: John R. Clark
Business Manager

464. A married woman should sign her own name, not her husband's name preceded by *Mrs.* If she wishes to be addressed in reply as *Mrs.*, she should precede her name by *Mrs.* in parentheses, or write her husband's name preceded by *Mrs.*, all in parentheses, on the line below her signature.. The usual custom is to address a woman as *Miss* if her married status is not indicated. **Women's signatures**

Correct: Very truly yours,
(Mrs.) Mary Osborn Williams

Correct: Very truly yours,
Mary Osborn Williams
(Mrs. John R. Williams)

Correct, but usually unnecessary: Very truly yours,
(Miss) Elizabeth Elliot

465. The following inside and envelope addresses are the forms used in writing officials, dignitaries of the church, etc., whom the writer does not know personally. The frequently used salutation and complimentary close are the formal *Sir:* and *I have the honor to remain, Most respectfully yours,* or the less formal *Dear Sir* and *Believe me, Yours faithfully,*. Upon occasion *the* is omitted before *Honorable* and *Reverend,* and also *Honorable* and *Reverend* are abbreviated to *Hon.* and *Rev.* **Forms for officials, etc.**

President

The President
The White House
Washington, D. C.

Vice-President

The Vice-President
Washington, D. C.

Member of the Cabinet

The Honorable Cordell Hull
Secretary of State
Washington, D. C.

Honorifics

Senator

The Honorable George W. Norris
United States Senate
Washington, D. C.

Representative

The Honorable William B. Bankhead
House of Representatives
Washington, D. C.

Governor

The Honorable Herbert H. Lehman
Governor of New York
Albany, New York

Legislator (State Senator)

The Honorable Thomas V. Smith
State Capitol
Springfield, Illinois

Judge

The Honorable Horace Keene
Judge of the Circuit Court
Courthouse
Memphis, Tennessee

Mayor

The Honorable Fiorello H. LaGuardia
Mayor of New York
City Hall
New York City

Archbishop

The Most Reverend Joseph F. Rummel
Archbishop of New Orleans
New Orleans, Louisiana

Salutation: Most Reverend Sir:
Close: I have the honor to remain,
Your Grace's humble servant,

Bishop

The Right Reverend William Turner
Bishop of Buffalo
Buffalo, New York

Salutation: Right Reverend and dear Sir:

Priest

The Reverend William A. Thomas
Elizabeth
Pennsylvania

Salutation: Reverend and dear Sir:

Protestant minister

The Reverend John Mitchell
Laurel Grove
Ross
California

Vulgarisms, Clichés

466. The following faults, characteristic of ill-educated writers and of writers without good taste, are to be especially avoided in letters: **Vulgarisms, clichés**

a. The omissions of pronouns, articles, and prepositions. **Ellipsis**

Bad: Received your letter of the 6th ult. While very doubtful of the result, will try to carry out your instructions.
Right: I have received your letter of August 6. (See Rule 467.) Though I am very doubtful about the results, I will try to carry out your instructions.

Bad: We enclose check for three dollars.
Right: We enclose a check for three dollars.

Bad: Direct letter care Thomas Cook.
Right: Direct the letter in care of Thomas Cook.

Bad: Mr. H. P. Thurston, Editor *Jenksville Patriot.*
Right: Mr. H. P. Thurston, Editor of the Jenksville *Patriot.*

NOTE. — The omission of *I* is proper in diaries and in letters written in the style of a diary — *i.e.*, intended to present mere hasty memoranda jotted down without any attempt at completeness of form. Thus, Tennyson to his wife: "Slept at Spedding's where I found they expected me. Started this morning 11 a.m. Hay fever atrocious with irritation of railway, nearly drove me crazed, but could not complain, the only other occupant having a curiously split shoe for his better ease . . ." In such letters, clipped expressions harmonize with the context. In a letter that is intended to be complete and regular in form, the omission of *I* and of other grammatically essential words is incongruous and in bad taste. (See Rule 467.)

Yours, your favor

b. Writing *yours, your favor,* or *your esteemed favor* for *your letter.* (See Rule 33.)

Yours received

c. The use of the formula *Yours of the 17th received,* or *Yours of the 17th at hand.* Write a grammatically complete expression, such as *I have your letter of June 17.*

In reply would say

d. The use of the formula *in reply would say* or *will say.* Write a grammatically complete expression, such as *In reply allow me to say.*

I would, will, or can say

e. The use of the formula *I would say, I will say,* or *I can say.* Write *Allow me to say* or *I desire to say,* or else omit any such introduction.

Same

f. The use of the expression *same* or *the same.* Use *it* or *they.* (See *Same* in Appendix A.)

> Bad: Yours of the 3rd at hand, and in reply would say we are at present out of lamps desired but will send same as soon as possible.
>
> Right: Thank you for your order of March 3. The lamps you wish are out of stock at present, but we will send them as soon as possible.

Please

g. The use of the expression *please* alone. Rather write *Will you please.*

Please find enclosed

h. The use of the formula *Please find enclosed.* Write *I enclose.*

($10) ten dollars

i. The use of the formula *($10) dollars* or *ten ($10) dollars.* (See Rule 394.)

Name of city abbreviated

j. The abbreviation of the name of a city; *e.g.,* of *Cincinnati* to *Cin.,* of *Philadelphia* to *Phil.,* or of *New York City* to *N. Y. City.*

k. Monotonously closing all letters with a sentence introduced by a participle, as *Hoping to hear soon . . .*, *Thanking you again . . .* ; or monotonously closing all letters of request with *and oblige.* These old-fashioned endings lack force.

Participial close

and oblige

467. The rule that it is improper to begin the body of a letter with *I*, is nonsense; beginning with *I* is always permissible and often desirable.

The use of *I*

468. The monotonously frequent use of *I* in letters is a common fault that it is well to guard against. But one should not, in order to avoid this fault, commit the worse fault of simply omitting *I;* as *Have not heard from you for a long time. Should think you ought to have written before this.* The noticeably frequent use of *I* is nothing worse than an awkwardness; the ellipsis of *I* is a vulgarism. (See Rule 466 *a*.) As between the two, the awkwardness is preferable. To avoid the repetition of *I*, practice variety of sentence structure, not ellipsis.

Not to be avoided by mere ellipsis

PERSONAL LETTERS

469. The following letter illustrates a usual form for a personal letter. It is a letter from a young English boy to an American woman, a friend of his mother.

Illustrative letter

Dear Miss Pomeroy,

Thank you very much for sending the interesting collection of American folksongs so promptly. They are very entertaining.

My time is now taken up with intensive study for my approaching examination, which begins on Monday. I cannot, therefore, say that I have been exploring Haworth or Harrogate, or that I have flitted across to America to see whether your house is safe. No. But I *can* say that I have been sympathizing with Cicero in his defence of the Roman Republic, and, a minute later, fully approving of J. Caesar's actions in transforming the Republic into an Empire (for I have finished the Cicero-book and am dipping into one on Caesar); I have been considering the reign of Tiberius, as Tacitus describes it; and feeling indignation against the vices rampant in the city of Rome as Juvenal portrays them; and appreciating alike the statesmanship of Pericles (Thucydides' hero), and the valor of Achilles and Patroclos and their heroic actions at Ilium.

It would therefore be useless to write much more. I can only send my thanks, and also my wishes that no flame may touch your house while you are in Italy and that you may enjoy your travels.

Yours most sincerely,

George M. Scott

Haverhill, Surrey
January 10, 1937

Form

470. The form of personal letters varies, depending largely upon the degree of intimacy of the writer and the person written to. On the whole, however, the form follows somewhat that of the business letter.

Heading

471. The heading may be placed at the top of the letter on the right; or it may be placed at the bottom of the letter on the left, the latter being the preferred position today. Frequently the address of the writer is placed at the top right, and the date of the letter at the bottom left. The heading may be reduced to the date only, placed in either position.

Inside address

472. The inside address is omitted in personal letters.

Salutation

473. The salutation, followed by a comma rather than a colon, is suited to the formality or informality of the letter. Salutations with *My* are more formal than those without *My*. The name of the person is always used in the salutation in personal letters, never *Dear Sir* or *Dear Madam.* The salutations *Dear Friend, Friend John,* etc., are out of fashion.

474. The complimentary close and signature are also suited to the formality or informality of the letter. The following complimentary closes are used: *Sincerely yours, Most sincerely yours, Very sincerely yours, Yours sincerely,* etc.; *Cordially yours,* etc.; *Faithfully yours,* etc.; *Gratefully yours,* etc.; *Affectionately yours,* etc.; *Lovingly yours,* etc. **Complimentary close**

FORMAL NOTES

475. Formal notes in the third person should have no heading, no salutation, no complimentary close, no inside address, and no signature. They should be written consistently and solely in the third person; the writer should not refer to himself as *I* or to the addressee as *you.* Except *Mr., Mrs., Messrs.,* and *Dr.,* no abbreviations whatever should be used; and numbers occurring in dates should — unlike those in ordinary letters — be spelled out. For information about other matters, the following examples will suffice: **Solely in third person** **No abbreviations** **Numbers spelled out**

Mrs. Burton requests the pleasure of Miss Irwin's company at dinner on Friday, May the twenty-second, at seven o'clock.
935 Webster Street,
May the third.

Miss Irwin accepts with pleasure Mrs. Burton's invitation to dinner on May the twenty-second.
1720 Princeton Avenue,
May the fourth.

Mr. Matthews regrets that, on account of illness, he is unable to accept Mr. and Mrs. Eliot's invitation for January the fifteenth.
500 Anderson Street,
January the tenth.

Use present tense

Note. — Use the present tense in letters of regret or acceptance.

Wrong: Mr. Smith will be pleased to accept . . .
[The being pleased to accept is present, not future.]
Right: Mr. Smith accepts; [or] Mr. Smith is pleased to accept.

Wrong: . . . regrets that he will be unable to accept . . . [The inability to accept is present, not future.]
Right: . . . regrets that he is unable to accept . . .

THE ENVELOPE

Superscription

476. The form of the address on the envelope is the same as that of the inside address. (See Rules 444–451.) The return address should be placed on the front of the envelope in the upper left-hand corner.

James Swift
463 Ninth Street
Bridgeport, Connecticut

Mr. Thomas Howe
1802 Wendell Drive
Portland, Oregon

The postage stamp

477. The postage stamp should be attached in the upper right-hand corner, right side up, with its edges parallel to the edges of the envelope. A carelessly attached stamp gives the impression of slovenliness.

MECHANICAL DIRECTIONS

Ink, paper, envelopes

478. Business letters are usually typewritten, and personal letters handwritten. Use black or blue-black ink or typewriter ribbon. Use a good quality of paper, white or light-colored. For business letters use a flat sheet $8\frac{1}{2} \times 11$ inches. For personal letters use either a flat sheet about 6×8 inches, or a sheet so folded that it forms a booklet of four pages. Envelopes should always match the paper in color and quality, and should hold the paper easily when it is properly folded.

479. Business letters are usually written on one side of the sheet only. Personal letters are usually written on both sides of the sheet. If a folded sheet of four pages is used, all four pages may be written on. They should be used consecutively, unless only two pages are required, in which case pages one and three may be used. In the folded sheet, the letter should begin on the page with the folded edge to the left. The lines of writing should be at right angles to the fold. Arrangement

480. The writing should begin an inch or two below the top of any page. It is best to keep a blank margin at least half an inch wide at the left side of every page. Rules 339–348 and 139–143 should be observed in letters as well as in other manuscripts. Typewritten letters are usually single spaced, with double spacing between paragraphs. Margins Legibility

481. The following rules in regard to the manner of folding letters and inserting them into envelopes are merely detailed applications of the simple rule of courtesy: Fold and enclose the letter in such a way that the receiver, on taking the letter from the envelope and unfolding it in the natural way, will find the first page turned toward him and the writing right-side up. The fundamental principle underlying folding and enclosing letters

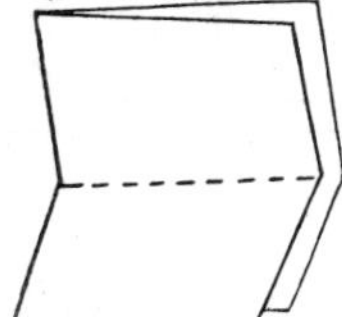

482. A letter on a four-page sheet should be enclosed in an envelope in which it will fit when folded with one horizontal crease through the center. With the letter top-side up, fold the lower half over the upper Folding and enclosing: Four-page sheets

half. Place the letter in the envelope with the horizontal crease at the bottom of the envelope.

Flat sheets of note size

483. A letter written on flat sheets of paper of note size (approximately 6 × 8 inches) may be enclosed —

Envelope of note size

a. In an envelope into which it will fit when folded with one crease running through the center. With the letter top-side up, fold the lower half over the upper half. Place the letter in the envelope with the crease at the bottom, and with the half containing the heading next to the face of the envelope.

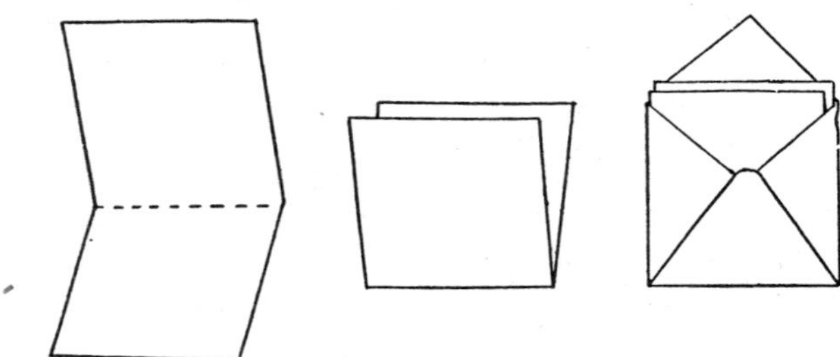

Commercial envelope

b. In an envelope of commercial size (approximately $3\frac{1}{2} \times 6\frac{1}{2}$ inches). In this case, fold the letter into three sections — a central section and two flaps.

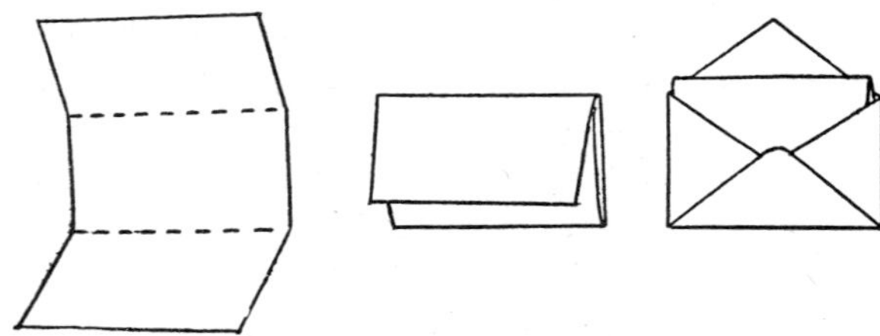

Writing parallel with short sides

(1) Letter in which the lines of writing run parallel with the short sides of the paper. With the letter top-side up, fold up from the bottom about one-third, and fold down from the top about one-fourth. Place the letter in the envelope with the two flaps next to

the back of the envelope, with the upper flap over the lower one, and with the top edge of the letter at the bottom of the envelope.

(2) Letter in which the lines of writing run parallel with the long sides of the paper. With the letter face up and right-side up, fold the right-hand part toward the left about one-third of the distance, and fold the left-hand part toward the right about one-fourth of the distance. Place the letter in the envelope with the flaps next to the back of the envelope, with the left flap on top of the right one, and with the outward edge of the left flap pointing upward.

Writing parallel with long sides

484. A letter written on flat sheets of paper of full commercial size (approximately $8\frac{1}{2} \times 11$ inches) may be enclosed —

Flat sheets of full commercial size

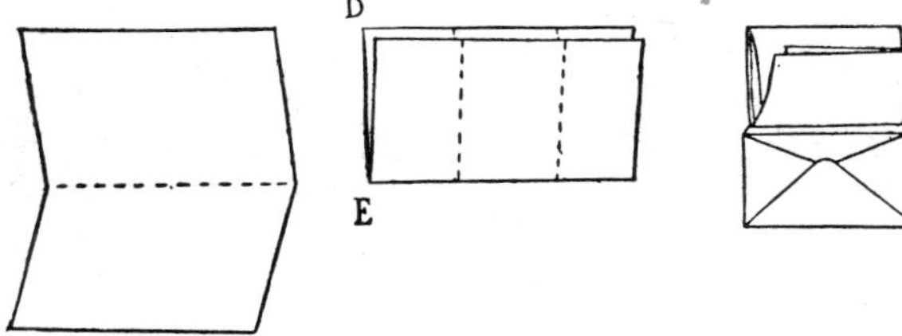

a. In an envelope of commercial size (approximately $3\frac{1}{2} \times 6\frac{1}{2}$ inches). In this case fold the letter into three sections — a central section and two flaps. With the letter top-side up, fold the lower part over the upper part with a horizontal crease running slightly below the center. With the horizontal crease toward you, fold the right-hand part toward the left, about one-third of the distance. Fold the left-hand part toward the right about one-fourth of the distance. Place the letter in the envelope with the two flaps next to the back of the envelope, with the left flap on top of the right one, and with the outward edge of the left flap pointing upward.

Commercial envelope

Official envelope

b. In an envelope of official size (approximately 10 × 4 inches). In this case, it should be folded and enclosed according to the method shown in Rule 483 *b.*

Square envelope

c. In an approximately square envelope. With the letter top-side up, fold the lower half over the upper half evenly; then fold the right half over the left half evenly. Place the letter in the envelope with the vertical crease at the bottom and with the two horizontal creases at the right-hand side of the back of the envelope.

APPENDIX A

MISCELLANEOUS FAULTY EXPRESSIONS

A.D. Means *in the year of the Lord.* Should not, therefore, be appended to the name of a *century.* Should not be appended to a date self-evidently modern. When used, should precede the date and should not be preceded by a preposition.

> Wrong: The sixth century A.D.
> Right: The sixth century after Christ.
> Right: Arminius died A.D. 21.

About. See **At about.**
Accept. See **Except.**
Ad. Colloquial abbreviation for *advertisement.* Write the word in full.
Addicted to, subject to. *Addicted to* means *devoted to persistently,* as to a habit or indulgence. Do not confuse with *subject to,* which means *exposed to some agency.* A man may be *addicted to* opium, but *subject to* attacks of rheumatism.
Affect. Means *to influence;* as *War is almost sure to affect trade seriously.* Is never used as a noun — always as a verb. Often confused with *effect. Effect* (verb) means *to bring to pass;* as *He will effect a reconciliation. Effect* (noun) means *result;* as *The drug had a fatal effect.*
After. Is redundant when used with the past participle.

> Redundant: After having written.
> Right: After writing.

Aggravate. Means *to make worse;* as *The shock aggravated his misery.* In the sense of *provoke, irritate, arouse the evil feelings of,* it is familiar, not literary usage.
All right. Not *alright, allright,* or *all-right.*
All-round. There is no such word as *all-around* recognized by good usage. *All-round* is a colloquialism.
All the. *All the farther, all the higher, all the faster,* or similar expressions should not be used mistakenly for *as far as,* etc. *All the* with an adverb means *by that amount, just so much.*

> Wrong: That was all the farther we went that day.
> Right: That was all the distance we went that day; or, That was as far as we went that day.
> Right: We shall go all the faster for our rest.

Allude. Means *to refer indirectly. Refer* means an open, direct mention. *When he alluded to profiteers, we knew whom he meant.*
Already, all ready. Distinguish *already,* meaning *beforehand,* or *by this time,* from *all ready,* which means *completely ready. The hotel was already full. They were all ready to go.*
Alternative. Strictly, means *choice between two things,* or *one of two things between which choice is possible;* as *The alternative is difficult. One alternative was to jump from the window; the other was to be burned to death.* Expanded in familiar usage to mean a choice between more than two things.

Altogether, all together. *The story is altogether false* [*i.e., completely false*]. *We were all together in the room.*

And etc. Never put *and* before *etc.*

Redundant: Pillows, flags, posters, and etc.
Right: Pillows, flags, posters, etc.

Anent. The use of this synonym of *about* or *concerning* suggests affectation.

Any place, every place, no place, some place. Vulgarisms for *anywhere, everywhere, nowhere, somewhere.* (See Rule 8.)

Anywheres. Dialectal for *anywhere.*

As (1). Should not be used too frequently in the sense of *because.* The conjunctions *for* or *since* may often be advantageously substituted. Where *as* occurs in this sense there should often be no conjunction.

Bad: I want you to come home now as it is time for supper.
Better: I want you to come home now; it is time for supper.

As (2). In negative statements and in questions implying a negative answer, good usage prefers the correlatives *so . . . as* rather than the correlatives *as . . . as.*

Doubtful: The modern nations are not as artistic as the ancient nations were.
Preferable: The modern nations are not so artistic as the ancient nations were.

As (3). Not to be used in place of *that* or *whether. I don't know that* [not *as*] *we can go.*

At about. Prefer *about.*

Redundant: He came at about three o'clock.
Right: He came about three o'clock.

Aught. Means *anything.* The name of the symbol 0 is *naught,* not *aught.*

Auto. A colloquialism for *automobile.* Not yet proper in formal writing.

Avail. *Of no avail* is properly used only with some form of *be;* elsewhere use *to no purpose.*

Unidiomatic: He tried, but of no avail.
Right: He tried, but to no purpose.
Right: His attempt was of no avail.

Awful. Means *inspiring with awe;* as *The awful presence of the king.* Colloquial as epithet of disapproval. Say not *an awful mistake,* but *a serious* or *disastrous mistake;* not *an awful blunder,* but *a ludicrous blunder.*

Badly. Colloquially used for *a great deal* or *very much* with verbs signifying *want or need.*

Wrong: I want badly to see you.
Right: I want very much to see you.

Balance. Colloquial English when used in the sense of *remainder,* except as a balance at the bank. (See **Bank on, Take stock in.**)

Colloquial: One was an Italian; the balance were Greeks.
Right: One was an Italian; the rest (or the others) were Greeks.

Bank on, take stock in. Colloquial in the sense of *rely on, trust in, receive as trustworthy, confidently expect.* (See **Balance.**)

Barbarous, barbaric. *Barbarous* means, in its restricted sense, *cruel; barbaric* is especially related to the barbarian love of noise or show, as *barbaric* music.

Besides. Means *additionally*, or *in addition to.* Not to be confused with *beside,* which is always a preposition, meaning *by the side of;* as *beside* the house.

Between. In its literal sense *between* applies to only two objects, and *among* to more than two; but *between* is often used with more than two objects. "It is still the only word available to express the relation of a thing to many surrounding things severally and individually . . ." NEW ENGLISH DICTIONARY.

Blame . . . on. Crudely used instead of *blame . . . for.*

Crude: You needn't blame it on me.
Right: You needn't blame me for it.

Bunch. Colloquial for *group* or *party.*

But. See **Hardly.**

Calculate. A provincialism for *think, suppose, expect,* or *intend.*

Can. Denotes power or ability. Loosely used to denote permission.

Loose: Can students hand in their theses in manuscript?
Right: May students [or, are students allowed to, or permitted to] hand in their theses in manuscript?

Can't seem. See **Seem.**

Cause. Complete such an expression as *the cause was* with a predicate noun or a noun clause. (See Rule 87.)

Illogical: The cause of his failure was on account of his imprudence.
Right: The cause of his failure was his imprudence; [or] . . . was that he was imprudent.

Certainly. The use of the word *certainly*, as a means of emphasis in relation to matters on which no doubt has been cast, is a colloquialism, and its overuse is monotonous; as in the expressions, *We certainly had a good time. That certainly was a hard examination. I certainly wonder where she bought that hat.*

Characteristic. Means a *distinguishing quality;* as *His chief characteristic is absent-mindedness.* Should not be used without intelligent regard to its meaning.

Bad: One characteristic of my daily life is climbing College Hill.
Right: One incident of my daily life is climbing College Hill.

Charge. Should be combined, when it means *accuse,* not with *of,* but with *with.*

Unidiomatic: They charged him of many crimes.
Idiomatic: They charged him with many crimes.

Claim. Means *to demand as due;* as *I claim the reward.* Colloquial for *assert* or *maintain,* when there is no question of right, title, or advantage.

Colloquial: He claimed that the William Tell story was only a legend.
Right: He asserted that the William Tell story was only a legend.

Coincidence. Means *the occurrence of two events at the same time or in remarkable connection with each other;* as *My forgetting my ticket and Bob's appearance just then with a ticket he didn't need, made a lucky coincidence.* Should not be used to designate a single event.

Company. Colloquial for *companion, escort, guests, visitors.*

Complected. Not to be used for *complexioned.*

Wrong: A light-complected girl.
Right: A light-complexioned girl.

Conscience, consciousness, conscious, conscientiousness. *Conscience* is *the power of making moral distinctions;* not to be confused with *consciousness,* which is simply *the power of being aware of anything. Conscience* is *moral consciousness.* Similarly, distinguish *conscious,* an adjective meaning *aware* or *mentally alert,* and *conscientiousness,* a noun meaning *loyalty to conscience.*

Considerable. A colloquialism when used as a noun.

> Colloquial: He lost considerable in the fire.
> Right: He lost considerable property [or, a good deal of property] in the fire.

Contemplate. Should not be combined with a preposition.

> Bad: He contemplated on [or over] a trip to Alaska.
> Right: He contemplated a trip to Alaska.

Contemptible. Means *worthy of being despised;* as *He is a contemptible sneak.* Not to be confused with *contemptuous,* which means *showing scorn;* as *He made a contemptuous answer.*

Contemptuous. See **Contemptible.**

Continual. Not synonymous with *continuous,* according to modern usage. *Continual* means *occurring in close succession, frequently repeated;* as *Continual hindrances discouraged us. He coughs continually. Continuous* means *without cessation, continuing uninterrupted;* as *Continuous opposition discouraged us. He slept continuously for ten hours.*

Continuous. See **Continual.**

Could of. See **Of.**

Couldn't seem. See **Seem.**

Credible, credulous, creditable. *Credible* means *believable.* Distinguish from *credulous,* meaning *easily imposed on, believing too easily,* and from *creditable,* which means *praiseworthy.*

Criticize. May mean *to censure,* but may mean merely *to pass judgment on,* whether favorable or adverse.

Crowd. Colloquial for *set* or *clique.*

> Colloquial: She does not belong in our crowd.
> Improved: She does not belong in our set.

Cunning. Means *artful, ingenious,* or *giving evidence of art or ingenuity;* as *a cunning intriguer, cunning workmanship.* As *pretty* or *amusing* it is a colloquial Americanism.

Cute. Used in the United States to mean *pretty, vivacious, lively, amusing, dainty, piquant, engaging,* etc.

Data, phenomena, strata. Plural, not singular forms. The singular forms are *datum* (rarely used), *phenomenon,* and *stratum.*

Date. Colloquial for *engagement* or *appointment.* Slang for *person with whom a social engagement is made.*

Deal (1). Should be combined with *with,* not with *on* or *of,* when the intended meaning is *discuss.*

> Unidiomatic: He deals on three subjects.
> Unidiomatic: He deals of three subjects.
> Idiomatic: He deals with three subjects.

Deal (2). Colloquialism for *transaction, agreement,* or *arrangement.*

> Colloquial: He will give us a square deal.
> Improved: He will deal honestly with us.

Demand. Means *to claim* or *call for peremptorily.* The object of this verb should be the thing claimed, never the person from whom the thing is claimed.

> Illogical: Japan demanded Russia to leave Manchuria.
> Right: Japan demanded that Russia leave Manchuria. [The object of *demanded* is the substantive clause *that . . . Manchuria.*]

Depot. Best applied to a building for the deposit of merchandise. To designate a building for the accommodation of passengers, it is better to say *station.*

Different. Usually followed by *from,* but also by *to,* especially colloquially in England, and by *than.* The constructions with *to* and *than* have long literary usage to support them, but are considered incorrect by many. — WEBSTER.

> Doubtful: The method is different than the one that formerly prevailed.
> Improved: The method is different from the one that formerly prevailed.

Disinterested. Means *without self-interest, unselfish;* as *the judge's disinterested performance of his duty.* Not to be confounded with *uninterested,* which means *not interested, indifferent;* as *he seemed uninterested in our proposal.*

Done. An ungrammatical error when used as the past tense of *do,* or as an additional auxiliary indicating past time. Typical illiterate sentences are *He done fine, He done real good,* for *He did well* (see **fine** (1), **real,** and **good**); and *I done lost it,* for *I lost it* or *I have lost it.*

Don't (1). A contraction of *do not.* Therefore ungrammatical when used with a subject in the third person singular. (See Rule 200.)

> Wrong: He don't know.
> Right: He doesn't know.
> Right: I don't know, we don't know, you don't know, and they don't know.

Don't (2). This contraction and other similar ones are suitable for conversation, but not for formal writing.

Doubt (doubtful) whether, that. When the sentence is negative; that is, when there is no doubt, the clause is introduced by *that.* (*That* is preferred to *but that* or *but what.*)

> Right: I do not doubt that he forged the check.

When the sentence is positive; that is, when there is doubt, the clause is usually introduced by *whether. That* is used, however, by some writers when there is a strong negative probability in the subordinate clause.

> Right: I doubt whether he forged the check.
> Accepted: I doubt that he forged the check. [Strong negative probability.]

Dove. Should not be used as the past tense of *dive.* Say *dived.*

Due to. Is an adjective modifier. It should, therefore, modify a substantive, not a verb. It is confused with *owing to, because of, on account of,* which have become prepositions and which, therefore, can introduce phrases modifying verbs. CURME says, "The preposition *due to* is not more incorrect than the preposition *owing to* . . ., but it is not as yet so thoroughly established in the language." *Syntax*, p. 561.

Undesirable: The forces were divided, due to a misunderstanding.
Improved: The forces were divided through [or because of] a misunderstanding.
Improved: The division of the forces was due to a misunderstanding.

Each other. Strictly used as referring to only two, as distinguished from *one another*, which refers to more than two; but the expressions are generally used interchangeably.

Effect. See **Affect.**

Either, neither. Preferably used to designate one of two persons or things; less commonly, one of three or more.

Less common: I asked Leahy, Mahoney, and McGinty, but neither of them was willing.
Preferable: I asked Leahy, Mahoney, and McGinty, but none of them [or . . . no one of them] was willing.

Elegant. Means *excelling in the power to discriminate properly and select properly*, or *giving evidence of such excellence;* as *an elegant gentleman, elegant ornamentation.* Should not be used loosely. Say not *an elegant view*, but a *beautiful view;* not *an elegant game of football*, but *an excellent or a masterly game;* not *an elegant march*, but *a spirited or rousing march;* not *an elegant pie*, but *a delicious pie.* Choose an adjective that expresses your meaning precisely.

Element. Means a *component part;* as *The elements of training are exercise, diet, and regularity.* Should not be used without intelligent regard to its meaning.

Bad: Next, the logs are driven downstream. Great danger besets the lumbermen in this element.
Right: Next, the logs are driven downstream. Great danger besets the lumbermen in this process.

Enormity, enormousness. *Enormity* ordinarily means *outrageous wickedness. Enormousness* means *of abnormal size.*

Enthuse. Colloquial. Use instead *to make*, or *to become enthusiastic.*

Vulgar: He doesn't enthuse me.
Right: He doesn't rouse any enthusiasm in me.

Vulgar: She never enthuses.
Right: She never becomes enthusiastic.

Equally as good. A confusion of two phrases: *equally good* and *just as good as.* Use either of the last mentioned phrases in place of *equally as good.*

Right: Their radio cost much more than ours, but ours is equally good.
Right: Our radio is just as good as when we bought it.

Etc. The use of *etc.* is incongruous in a context intended to be artistic. Use a definite term in place of *etc.* or simply omit *etc.*

Wrong: She was more beautiful, witty, virtuous, etc., than any other lady.
Right: She was more beautiful, witty, virtuous, and loyal than any other lady.
Right: She was more beautiful, witty, and virtuous than any other lady.

In any context, avoid the vague use of *etc.;* use it only to dispense with useless repetition or to represent terms that are entirely obvious.

Every bit. Colloquial for *in every way, quite.*

Every place. See **Any place.**

Every so often. A colloquial expression for *at regular periods or intervals.*

Except (verb) means to *exclude;* as *He alone was excepted from the amnesty. Except* (preposition) means *with the exception* (*i.e., exclusion*) *of;* as *All's lost except honor. Except* is not to be confused with *accept,* which means *to receive.*

Except. Cannot be used as a conjunction.

> Wrong: I cannot go except you go with me.
> Right: I cannot go unless you go with me.

Exceptional, exceptionable. *Exceptional,* which means *unusual,* is to be distinguished from *exceptionable,* which means *objectionable. It was an exceptional offer. Your language is exceptionable.*

Expect. Should not be used for *suppose.*

> Colloquial: I expect it's time for us to go.
> Right: I suppose it's time for us to go.

Extra. Not to be used in the sense of *unusually,* as *an extra fine day.*

Factor. Means *a force or agent coöperating with other forces or agents to produce a certain result;* as *The factors of success are industry and perseverance.* Should not be used without intelligent regard to its meaning.

> Bad: Being ducked in the lake is an inevitable factor in the freshman's experience.
> Right: Being ducked in the lake is an inevitable part of the freshman's experience.

Falls, ways, woods. Plurals, not singulars.

> Wrong: Go a little ways downstream till you come to a falls. Beside it is a woods.
> Right: Go a little way downstream till you come to a fall. Beside it is a wood.
> Right: The falls of the river are close by.

Faze. A colloquialism.

> Bad: You could not faze her by your criticisms.
> Improved: You could not daunt her by your criticisms.

Fellow. A colloquialism when used to mean a *person,* an *individual,* a *beau,* a *sweetheart.*

> Colloquial: Many of the fellows are wearing fur coats.
> Improved: Many of the men are wearing fur coats.

Fine (1). Means *refined, delicate, free from impurity, of excellent quality: fine cutlery, fine dust, fine sense of honor, fine gold.* Loosely used as a general epithet of approval: *a fine fellow, a fine day, a fine ship.*

Fine (2). Colloquial when used to mean *well* or *very well.*

> Colloquial: I feel fine.
> Improved: I feel very well.

Finely. Correctly used as an adverb to mean *in a fine manner, excellently, closely.* Should not be used for *well.*

> Wrong: She is doing finely in her work.
> Correct: She is doing well in her work.

First-rate. May be used as an adjective but colloquially as an adverb.

Right: It is a first-rate building.
Colloquial: He plays tennis first-rate.
Right: He plays tennis very well; [or] He plays a first-rate game of tennis.

Firstly. Most writers prefer *first,* even when followed by *secondly, thirdly,* etc.

Fix (1). Colloquial for *plight, situation,* or *condition.*

Fix (2). Colloquial in the United States for *repair* or *arrange.* The expression *fix up* used in one of these senses is likewise a colloquialism.

Former, latter. Properly used to designate one of two persons or things, not one of three or more. (See **Either, neither.**) For designating one of three or more, say *first, first-named, first-mentioned,* or *last, last-named, last-mentioned.*

Genial, congenial. *Genial* means *cordial and pleasant in manner.* Do not confuse it with *congenial,* which means *suited to one's disposition;* as *a congenial friend, a congenial occupation.*

Gent. A vulgarism for *gentleman.*

Gentleman, lady. Terms properly used to designate persons of refined speech and manners, as distinguished from ill-bred or uncultivated people; the use of them to designate mere sex is objectionable.

Wrong: Saleslady, business gentleman, lady stenographer. — There are lady cabdrivers in Paris. — There are more ladies than gentlemen who play the piano. — Cornell admits ladies, but Williams admits only gentlemen. — Ladies' cloakroom.
Right: Saleswoman, businessman, woman stenographer. — There are woman cabdrivers in Paris. — There are more women than men who play the piano. — Cornell admits women, but Williams admits only men. — Women's cloakroom.

The use of *man* and *woman* need never be shunned; even where *lady* or *gentleman* may be used correctly, *man* or *woman* is equally polite, and is often preferable.

Right: Is your wife a Massachusetts woman? — You are the only woman I know who drives a motor. — Are you the man I met last spring in Denver?

The terms *ladies* and *gentlemen* are used in addressing people in popular assemblies.

Gentleman friend, lady friend. These terms, not in themselves objectionable, have, through the use that has been made of them, become objectionable. Prefer *man friend* (plural: *man friends*) or *gentleman of one's acquaintance, woman friend* (plural: *woman friends*) or *lady of one's acquaintance.*

Get. *Get to* (*go*) is a provincialism for *to contrive, to manage. Get around* is a colloquialism for *to circumvent, to evade. Get next to, get on to, get away with, get across, get left, get a hustle on, get behind* (*to endorse*), *get by with, get over* (*to make clear*), etc., are slang.

Getup. A colloquialism for *style of dress.*

Going on.

Tautological and provincial: How old is he? Sixteen, going on seventeen.
Right: How old is he? Sixteen.

Good. An adjective; should not be used as an adverb meaning *well.*

Wrong: Do it good this time.
Right: Do it well this time.

Got. The perfect tense is colloquial in the sense of *possess*. It is correct in the sense of *obtained*.

> Colloquial: Have you got a knife with you?
> Preferable: Have you a knife with you?
> Right: Have you got what you wanted?

It is also colloquial in the sense of *must*.

> Colloquial: I have got to hurry.
> Preferable: I must hurry.

Gotten. The older form of the past participle of *get*. Still used in the United States, but being replaced by *got*, except in expressions like *ill-gotten gains*.

Grand. Means *on a large scale, imposing;* as *a grand mountain range*. Should not be used loosely. Say not *a grand day*, but *a beautiful* or *brilliant day*.

Grip. Colloquial in the United States for *valise* or *bag*.

Had better, had best, had rather. Entirely grammatical and fully approved by good usage. *Would better, would best,* and *would rather* are not preferable. *Had better* is preferable to *would better; had best* and *would best, had rather* and *would rather* are equally good.

> Correct but undesirable: You would better not stay long.
> Right: You had better not stay long.
> Right: They had best attempt no violence.
> Right: I had rather go than stay.

Had have or **had of.** Often incorrectly used for *had*.

> Incorrect: If he had have [or had of] tried, he would have succeeded.
> Right: If he had tried, he would have succeeded.

Had ought. See **Ought.**

Hardly, scarcely, only, but. Should not be used with a negative.

> Wrong: It was so misty that we couldn't hardly see.
> Right: It was so misty that we could hardly see.
>
> Wrong: For a minute I couldn't scarcely tell where I was.
> Right: For a minute I could scarcely tell where I was.
>
> Wrong: They are not allowed to go only on Saturdays.
> Right: They are allowed to go only on Saturdays.
>
> Wrong: There isn't but one store.
> Right: There is but one store.

Have got. See **Got.**

Heap, heaps. Colloquial for *very much, a great deal, a great many.*

Hear to it. A vulgarism. Say *consent to it*, or *allow it*.

Help. Colloquial in the United States for *a servant, servants,* or *employees.*

Hired girl. Colloquial for *maid* or *servant.*

Home. Properly used as an adverb expressing motion, as *He went home. He is home* is wrong when it means *He is at home*, but right when it means *He has come home.* (See Rule 107.)

Honorable. See **Reverend.**

Hung. With reference to the death penalty, *hanged* is preferred to *hung*.

> Undesirable: He was found guilty and hung.
> Right: He was found guilty and hanged.
> Right: We hung the flag on the balcony.

Hustle. Colloquial in the United States when used intransitively to mean *hasten, hurry,* or *be energetic* or *industrious.* Correctly used with a direct object.

> Colloquial: He hustled the legislation through.
> Improved: He hastened the legislation through.
>
> Colloquial: People were hustling about in confusion.
> Right: People were hurrying about in confusion.
> Right: The police hustled the loiterers from the hall.

Hustler. A colloquialism for *an energetic* or *capable person.*

i.e. Means *that is;* denotes, therefore, that what follows is equivalent to what precedes. Should not be used when what follows is not equivalent to what precedes, or when *that is* will not fit grammatically into the place of *i.e.*

> Right: The act is treated as a capital crime — *i.e.*, a crime punishable by death. [*A crime punishable by death* is equivalent to *a capital crime;* and *that is* may be grammatically substituted for *i.e.*]
> Wrong: I like to read the Bible; *i.e.*, some of the stories in the Old Testament. [*Some of the stories in the Old Testament* is not equivalent to the *Bible.*]
> Wrong: I like some parts of the Bible; *i.e.*, the stories in the Old Testament. [*That is* cannot be grammatically substituted for *i.e.*]
> Right: I like some parts of the Bible — namely, [or *viz.*,] the stories in the Old Testament.
> Right: He had committed lese majesty — *i.e.*, had given an affront to the Emperor. [*Had . . . Emperor* is equivalent to *had . . . majesty* and *that is* may properly be substituted for *i.e.*]

If, whether. *Whether* is preferred after *see, ask, learn, know, doubt,* and the like.

> Acceptable: I don't know if I can.
> Preferable: I don't know whether I can.

Ilk. An archaic adjective meaning *same.* In the expression *of that ilk,* as correctly used, *ilk* is an adjective modifying *estate* understood; *Sir George Urquhart of that ilk* means *Sir George Urquhart of that same (estate) — i.e., Sir George Urquhart of Urquhart.* The use of *ilk* as a noun meaning *kind* is a blunder.

> Wrong: I'm not of her ilk, I'm glad to say.
> Right: I'm not of her sort, I'm glad to say.

In, into. *In* generally used for *place in which* and *into* for *place toward which.*

> Wrong: He went in the bank.
> Right: He went into the bank.
> Right: He was in the bank.

In our midst. See **Midst.**

Incredible, incredulous. The former means *unbelievable;* the latter, *disinclined to believe. He had caught an incredible number of fish, and I was incredulous when he told me.*

Individual. Should not be used indiscriminately for *person.* Properly used to mean *individual person.*

> Right: He made a general address to the class, and also gave special advice to the individuals in the class.
> Loose: He is a tall, gaunt individual.
> Right: He is a tall, gaunt person.

Indulge. Means (*a*) *to treat with forbearance, to humor;* as *She indulges her children* or (*b*) *to put no restraint upon oneself;* as *He indulges in* [*i.e., puts no restraint upon himself in regard to*] *gambling. Indulge in* is often misused for *practice* or *engage in.*

Bad: Practice in surveying is indulged in in the autumn.
Right: Practice in surveying is engaged in [or taken] in the autumn.

Inferior. See **Superior.**

Ingenious, ingenuous. An inventor is *ingenious;* a person of a frank, trusting nature is *ingenuous.*

Inside. Does not require *of* following. Say simply *inside.*

Right: They were trapped inside the walls.

Inside of. A colloquial Americanism for *within,* in time expressions.

Bad: It will disappear inside of a week.
Right: It will disappear within a week.

Instance, instants, incident. *Instance* means *a single occurrence, an example;* as *I will give you an instance of this habit. Instants* means *seconds, moments;* as *She waited several instants before replying. Incidents* are *happenings.*

Just. A colloquialism when used as an intensive.

Bad: I shall be just delighted to come.
Right: I shall be quite delighted to come.

Kind, sort. Are singular, and should therefore be modified by a singular demonstrative adjective.

Incorrect: I don't like those kind [or those sort] of photographs.
Right: I don't like that kind [or that sort] of photographs.

Kind of, sort of (1). A colloquialism when used to modify verbs or adjectives. Say *somewhat, somehow, for some reason, rather,* or *after a fashion.*

Bad: People who kind of chill you . . .
Right: People who somehow chill you . . .

Bad: The man who does nothing but study gets sort of dull.
Right: The man who does nothing but study gets rather dull.

Bad: I kind of felt my way at first.
Right: I felt my way, after a fashion, at first.

Kind of, sort of (2). Should not be followed by *a* or *an.* Confusion of class and individual. Class is needed, not individual.

Inelegant: What kind of a house is it?
Right: What kind of house is it?

Inelegant: It is a sort of a castle.
Right: It is a sort of castle.

Kindly. Misused in business letters.

Inaccurate: I thank you very kindly. [*Implies that the writer is doing a kindness.*]
Right: I thank you very much.
Right: I thank you for your kindness.

Inaccurate: I would kindly ask you to send me your circular. [*Implies that the writer is doing a kindness to the receiver of the letter.*]
Right: Will you kindly [please] send me your circular?

Lady, lady friend. See **Gentleman** and **Gentleman friend.**
Latter. See **Former.**
Lay. Often confounded with *lie.* Remember that *lay* is the causative of *lie; i.e., to lay* means *to cause something to lie.* Remember the principal parts of each verb:

I lie	I lay	I have lain.
I lay	I laid	I have laid.

Right: I lie down every afternoon.
Right: I lay the paper by his plate every morning.
Right: I lay down yesterday after dinner.
Right: I laid the paper by his plate yesterday.
Right: I have lain here for two hours.
Right: I have laid the paper by his plate many times.

Learn. A provincialism when used in the sense of *teach.*

Wrong: He learned us our lessons.
Right: He taught us our lessons.

Leave, let. Contrary to good usage to use *leave* for *let* in these phrases: *to leave be, to leave go.*

Right: Let me be.
Right: Let go of the rope.

Less. Should not be used in place of *fewer. Less* refers especially to degree, value, amount; *fewer* refers especially to number.

Wrong: Less men were hurt this year than last.
Right: Fewer men were hurt this year than last.
Right: You will need less butter with this recipe.

Let. See **Leave.**
Let's. Contraction for *let us.* Should only be used where *let us* can be used.

Wrong: Let's don't leave yet.
Right: Let's not leave yet.

Liable. Means (*a*) *easily susceptible;* as *It is liable to injury;* (*b*) *likely;* as *It is liable to be misunderstood;* (*c*) *legally responsible.* But NOTE: *Liable* is not properly used in the sense of *likely* except in designating an injurious or undesirable event which may befall a person or thing.

Wrong: We are liable to have a clear day tomorrow.
Right: We are likely, etc.
Right: We are liable to have rain before we reach the hard roads.

Like. Should not be used to introduce a clause. Use *as* or *as if.* Best usage also prefers the use of *like* with elliptical clauses in which the predicate or sometimes the subject is to be supplied from the context.

Colloquial: He acted like the rest did.
Right: He acted as the rest did.
Right: He acted like the rest.

Colloquial: I felt like I had done something generous.
Right: I felt as if I had done something generous.
Right: I felt like a philanthropist.

Liked. Should not be compounded with *would* or *should.*

Bad: He would liked to have gone.
Right: He would have liked to go.

Likely. Usually used as an adverb meaning *probably* after *most*, *quite*, *very*, etc.

Right: You are most likely right.

Line. Should not be used loosely or tautologically.

Bad: What line of work are you now doing?
Right: What kind of work are you now doing?

Bad: I am now engaged in the hardware line.
Right: I am now engaged in the hardware business.

Bad: I like anything in the card line.
Right: I like any game of cards.

Bad: Was there anything in the refreshment line?
Right: Were there any refreshments?

Bad: He said a few things in the advice line.
Right: He gave me a little advice; [or] He said a few things by way of advice.

Bad: I'm not very good in the walking line.
Right: I'm not very good at walking.

Bad: He was also famous along the line of literature.
Right: He was also famous in literature.

Bad: The dean said some things along the line of athletics.
Right: The dean said some things about athletics.

Bad: We are planning something in the line of a surprise.
Right: We are planning something by way of surprise.

Bad: Let me tell you something along that line.
Right: Let me tell you something in connection with that subject.

Bad: If he is so weak in physics and chemistry, he needs some tutoring along those lines.
Right: If he is so weak in physics and chemistry, he needs some tutoring in those subjects.

Bad: I need some tacks. Have you anything along that line?
Right: I need some tacks. Have you anything of that sort?

Locate. A colloquialism for *settle*. Correct when used transitively.

Bad: He located in Ohio.
Right: He settled in Ohio.
Right: He located his factory in Lima.

Lose out, win out. Colloquial, not proper except in connection with sports.

Lot, lots, a whole lot. Colloquialisms for *much*, *many*, *a great deal*.

Bad: We had lots of fun on my grandfather's farm.
Right: We had a great deal of fun on my grandfather's farm.

Lovely. Means *lovable* or *inspiring love;* as *a lovely character*. A colloquialism when used loosely. Say not *a lovely time*, but *a pleasant* or *delightful time;* not *a lovely drive*, but *an interesting* or *pleasant drive;* not *a lovely costume*, but *a handsome*, or *dainty*, or *rich*, or *striking*, or *elegant costume*. Avoid especially the expression *perfectly lovely*. Choose the adjective that expresses your meaning definitely.

Luxuriant. Means *of rank* or *vigorous growth*. Not to be confounded with *luxurious*, which is related to indulgence in pleasures of the senses. *A luxurious home*, but *luxuriant vegetation*.

Mad. Means *insane*. Colloquial for *angry*.

May be, maybe. *May be* is a verb form. *Maybe* is an adverb.

Right: He may be there.
Right: Maybe I can go.

May of. See **Of.**

Mean. Means *lowly* or *base.* Colloquial when used to mean *cruel, vicious, unkind,* or *ill-tempered.* Slang when used to mean *excellent* or *formidable;* as *He serves a mean ball.*

Messrs. The plural of *Mr.* Like *Mr., Messrs.* should never be used without a name or names following it.

> Vulgar: Messrs., will you come in? [To say this is like saying *Mister, will you come in?* or *Mrs., I have come.*]
> Right: Gentlemen, will you come in?
> Right: Messrs. Zangwill and Barrie met the Messrs. McCarthy.

Midst. The expressions *our midst, your midst,* and *their midst* preceded by a preposition have been ridiculed and censured by critics. Instead of *in our midst,* many writers prefer *in the midst of us* or *among us.* Instead of *from our midst,* many writers use *from the midst of us* or *from among us,* or substitute for *midst* some nouns such as *neighborhood, community, fellowship,* etc.

Might of. See **Of.**

Miss. Like *Mr., Mrs.,* and *Messrs., Miss,* when used as a title, must always be followed by a name. (See **Messrs.**)

> Vulgar: My dear Miss:
> Right: My dear Madam: [or] My dear Miss Smith:
>
> Vulgar: Miss, will you please bring us our order?
> Improved: Waitress, will you please bring us our order?

Most. Dialectal for *almost.* (See Rule 215.)

Mrs. The combination of *Mrs.* with a husband's title is incorrect. *Mrs.* may be followed only (1) by the husband's surname, (2) by the husband's Christian name (or initials) and surname, or (3) by the woman's Christian name and the husband's surname; the husband's *title,* if stated at all, should be put in another part of the sentence.

> Right: Mrs. Boughton. [1]
> Right: Mrs. John C. Boughton. [2]
> Right: Mrs. Mary Dole. [3]
> Wrong: Mrs. Professor Yates, Mrs. Dr. Fairbanks, Mrs. President Hughes, Mrs. Bishop Ross, Mrs. Rev. Fisher, Mrs. Captain Johnson.
> Right: Mrs. Richard E. Yates; Mrs. Fairbanks, wife of Dr. Fairbanks; Mrs. Louisa Hughes, widow of President Hughes; Mrs. Jeremiah Ross; Mrs. Noah Fisher; Mrs. C. V. Johnson.

Much. See **Very.**

Must of. See **Of.**

Mutual. Incorrect, according to modern usage, in the sense of *shared in common;* for this meaning the proper adjective is *common. Mutual,* properly used, means *reciprocal, interchanged.*

> Wrong: As we conversed, we found that we had several mutual friends in Portland. [The title of Dickens's novel *Our Mutual Friend* is a quotation from some ill-educated persons in the story; it therefore furnishes no good argument for the correctness of the expression *mutual friend.*]
> Right: As we conversed, we found that we had several common friends in Portland.
>
> Wrong: The two men had a mutual interest in sculpture.
> Right: . . . a common interest in sculpture.

Right: They practiced mutual forbearance and aid [*i.e.*, each one helped and bore with the other]. — Their faces showed a mutual hatred [*i.e.*, showed that each hated the other]. — Mutual friendship [*i.e.*, friendship interchanged between two persons]. — Common friendship [*i.e.*, friendship shared by two persons for a third].

Nearly. Often misused for *near*.

Wrong: He came nearly getting hurt.
Right: He came near getting hurt.

Neither. See **Either.**

Nice. Has the primary meaning of *keen* and *precise in discrimination*, or *delicately* or *precisely made;* as *a nice judge of values, a nice distinction in meaning.* It may also mean *pleasant* or *agreeable*, but in this sense it is overused. Prefer adjectives that more exactly express the meaning.

Acceptable	More exact
A nice person.	An agreeable, *or* admirable, *or* conscientious, *or* honorable, *or* kind person.
A nice time.	A pleasant *or* agreeable time.
He is nice to us.	He is kind *or* courteous to us.

No good. A colloquialism when used adjectively. Say *worthless, of no value, useless.*

Colloquial: That can opener is no good.
Improved: That can opener is useless.

No place. See **Any place.**

No use. Colloquial when used adjectively. Say *of no use, useless, of no value*, or *unsuccessful.*

Colloquial: She is no use in the kitchen.
Improved: She is of no use in the kitchen.

Not. A double negative is forbidden by modern usage.

Wrong: I could not find it nowhere.
Right: I could find it nowhere.
Right: I could not find it anywhere.

Notorious. Means *of bad repute;* as *a notorious gambler.* Not to be used for *famous, celebrated,* or *noted.*

Not to exceed. Should not be used except in giving or quoting orders or directions. Often misused for *not more than.*

Right: They were authorized to spend any sum, not to exceed $500,000.
Bad: The trains are composed of not to exceed twenty cars.
Preferred: The trains are composed of not more than twenty cars.

Nowhere near. A colloquialism for *not nearly.*

Colloquial: There is nowhere near enough for all of us.
Improved: There is not nearly enough for all of us.

Nowheres. Dialectal for *nowhere.*

Observance. Means *the act of paying respect or obedience.* Not to be confused with *observation*, which means *the act of inspecting, looking at.*

Right: The observance of Good Friday.
Right: From his observation of the sky, he judged that a storm was approaching.

Observation. See **Observance.**

Of. *Could of, may of, might of, must of, should of,* and *would of* are illiterate corruptions of *could have, may have, might have, must have, should have,* and *would have.*

Off of. *Of* is superfluous.

> Bad: Keep off of the grass.
> Preferred: Keep off the grass.

On the side. Slang for *incidental, collateral, occasional,* or the corresponding adverbs.

> Slang: He makes a great deal of money on the side.
> Improved: He makes a great deal of money in addition to his salary.

Only. See **Hardly.**

Or. Should not be correlated with *neither;* use *nor.*

> Bad: Neither the long Arctic night or any other cause . . .
> Improved: Neither the long Arctic night nor any other cause . . .

Oral. See **Verbal.**

Other times. *Sometimes* is an adverb; *other times* is rarely used as an adverb. Prefer *at other times.*

> Right: Sometimes she is very talkative; at other times she is not.

Ought. The combination of *ought* with *had* is conspicuously bad English.

> Wrong: You hadn't ought to have entered.
> Right: You ought not to have entered.
>
> Wrong: We ought to send, had we not?
> Right: We ought to send, ought we not?

Ought to of. Vulgarism for *ought to have.*

> Vulgar: You ought to of waited.
> Right: You ought to have waited.
> Right: You should have waited.

Out loud. Colloquial expression. Say *aloud.*

Outside of (1). *Of* is superfluous. Say simply *outside.*

> Right: Outside the barn the cattle were shivering.

Outside of (2). *Outside of* should not be used for *aside from, except, besides.*

> Doubtful: Outside of this mistake, it is very good.
> Preferred: Aside from this mistake, it is very good.

Over with. *With* is superfluous.

> Bad: The regatta is over with.
> Improved: The regatta is over.

Overly. Dialectal for *excessively, too, very.*

> Vulgar: I'm not overly anxious.
> Right: I'm not excessively anxious.

Pair, set. Singular, not plural, forms.

> Wrong: Two pair of gloves and three set of chisels.
> Right: Two pairs of gloves and three sets of chisels.

Part. See **Portion.**

Party. Means *a person or group of persons taking part* (*in some transaction*). Incorrect when used to mean simply *person.*

> Right: He was party to the plot.
> Right: The parties to the marriage were both young.
> Wrong: The party who wrote that article must have been a scholar.
> Right: The person who wrote, etc.

Per. Use *per* with Latin words, such as *annum, diem, cent;* not, as a rule, with English words. Avoid the expression *as per;* say *according to.*

> Inelegant: Three dollars per day; one suicide per week; seven robberies per month; $3200 per year; two deaths per thousand; thirteen cents per gallon.
> Right: Three dollars a day [or *per diem*]; one suicide a week; seven robberies a month; $3200 a year [or *per annum*]; two deaths for every thousand; thirteen cents a gallon.

Per cent. It is better to use *per cent* only after a numeral. *Per cent* means literally *by the hundred* and should therefore be used when there is an exact numerical statement. *Percentage* means, loosely, a *part* or *proportion of a whole.* (See Rule 8.)

> Doubtful: A large per cent were Chinese.
> Right: Twenty *per cent* were Chinese.
> Right: A large percentage were Chinese.

The words *per cent* should be used rather than the sign %. In strictly commerical writing, however, the sign is used, but only after numerals. Note that *per cent* is written as two words; *percentage* as one.

Phase. Means *appearance* or *aspect;* as *That phase of the question I haven't considered.* Should not be used without intelligent regard to its meaning.

> Bad: I began to engage in all the different phases of college pleasure.
> Right: I began to engage in all the different kinds of college pleasure.

Phenomena. A plural noun. See **Data.**

Phone. A colloquialism. Not yet proper in formal discourse.

Piano. Should not be used to mean *piano lessons.*

> Colloquial: She is taking piano.
> Improved: She is taking piano lessons.

Piece. A provincialism when used in the sense of *distance* or *short distance.* A colloquialism when used as a verb to mean *to nibble between meals.*

Plan on. *On* is superfluous. Say simply *plan.*

> Bad: We planned on taking a walk.
> Right: We planned taking a walk; [or] We planned to take a walk.

Plenty (1). Dialectal when used as an adjective before a noun. Say *plentiful* or *plenty of.* (See Rule 8.)

> Dialectal: There is plenty wheat.
> Right: Wheat is plentiful.
> Right: There is plenty of wheat.

Plenty (2). Colloquial when used as an adverb meaning *amply, quite.* (See Rule 7.)

> Colloquial: It is plenty good enough.
> Improved: It is quite good enough.

Plenty (3). A provincialism when used with *a.*

Provincial: We always have fruit aplenty.
Improved: We always have plenty of fruit.

Poorly. Colloquialism when used to mean *not well, in poor health.*

Colloquial: She has been poorly for many years.
Improved: She has been in poor health for many years.

Portion. Best used in its restricted sense, as *a proportionate* part **or** share, and distinguished from *part,* the general term. *A portion of the inheritance; a part of the day.*

Postal. An adjective. Inelegant for *postal card.*

Practical. Means *related to actual use,* as opposed to theoretical or ideal. Do not confuse with *practicable,* which means *capable of being put into practice.* A *practical* scheme (*i.e.,* valuable or sensible) may not be *practicable* at the present time.

Prefer. Should be followed by *to, before, above, rather than* in place of *than.*

Unidiomatic: I should prefer going there than anywhere else.
Right: I should prefer going there to going anywhere else.

Proposition. Means *a thing proposed* or *the act of proposing;* as *He made a proposition to sell.* Should not be used without intelligent regard to its meaning. Avoid especially the use of *proposition* for *work* or *task.*

Slang: To sink that shaft was a hard proposition.
Right: To sink that shaft was a hard piece of work.

Bad: The library-buffet car is the most comfortable proposition on wheels.
Right: The library-buffet car is the most comfortable vehicle on wheels.

Proven. An archaic form. Better *proved.*

Put in. A colloquialism for *spend* or *occupy.*

Colloquial: I put in three hours in trying to memorize it.
Right: I spent three hours, etc.

Put in an appearance. A legal phrase. In ordinary writing, say *appear.*

Quality. Means *characteristic* or *trait;* as *The qualities of birch bark are lightness of color, thinness, and smoothness.* Should not be used without intelligent regard to its meaning.

Bad: The social qualities of college life are more in evidence in the winter. (See Rule 30.)
Right: The social activities of college life are more apparent in the winter.

Bad: He gives three qualities of a businessman: Have something to say, say it, and stop talking.
Right: He gives three maxims for a businessman: Have something to say, say it, and stop talking.

Quite. Means (*a*) *wholly;* as *The stream is now quite dried up;* or (*b*) *greatly, very;* as *We could see it quite distinctly.* A colloquialism when used in the sense of *slightly, not very, pretty, rather.*

Colloquial: The room is quite large, but not large enough for anyone to be comfortable in.
Improved: The room is moderately large, but not large enough for anyone to be comfortable in.

Quite a few. Colloquial for *a good many* or *a considerable number.*

Quite a little. Colloquial for *a considerable amount* or *a good deal.*

Raise (1). A provincialism when applied to human beings, in the sense of *rear, bring up.*

Raise (2). Often confounded with *rise.* Remember that *raise* is the causative of *rise; i.e., to raise* means *to cause something to rise.* Therefore *raise* must always have an object. Remember the principal parts of each verb:

I rise	I rose	I have risen.
I raise	I raised	I have raised.

Right: I rise at six o'clock every morning.
Right: I raise flowers for sale.
Right: I rose at six o'clock.
Right: I raised flowers for sale.
Right: I have risen at six o'clock for years.
Right: I have raised flowers for sale for years.

Real. Colloquial when used for *very.* (See Rule 8.)

Colloquial: It is real handsome.
Right: It is very handsome.

Reason. Do not complete such an expression as *the reason is* with (*a*) a *because* clause, (*b*) a *because of* phrase, (*c*) a *due to* phrase, or (*d*) an *on account of* phrase; complete it with a *that* clause. (See Rule 87.)

Illogical: The reason he was offended was because they were arrogant.
Illogical: The reason he was offended was because of their arrogance.
Illogical: The reason he was offended was due to their arrogance.
Illogical: The reason he was offended was on account of their arrogance.
Right: The reason he was offended was that they were arrogant.

Refer. See **Allude.**

Remember of. *Of* is superfluous.

Bad: I remember of meeting him.
Improved: I remember meeting him.

Respectful, respectable, respective. *He was respectful to his elders; a respectable old woman; their respective positions — i.e.*, the positions belonging to each. *Yours respectfully* (not *respectively*) is proper in the complimentary close of a letter.

Reverend, Honorable. Should be preceded by *the,* and should not be followed immediately by a surname. (See Rules 375 and 399.)

Vulgar: Rev. Carter.
Vulgar: The Reverend Carter.
Right: The Reverend Mr. Carter.
Right: The Reverend Amos Carter.
Right: The Reverend Dr. Temple.

Right. Meaning *very, extremely* is now archaic in literary language. In colloquial language it is dialectal, generally used in southern United States.

Dialectal: It is right kind of you to do this.
Improved: It is very kind of you to do this.

Right along. Colloquial. Say *continuously.*

Colloquial: I hear from him right along.
Improved: I hear from him continuously.

Right away, right off. Colloquial. Say *immediately, at once, directly.*
Run. A colloquial Americanism in the sense of *manage* or *operate.*
Said. See **Say.**
Same (1). No longer in good use as a pronoun except in legal documents.

Crude: We will repair the engine and ship same [or the same] to you next week.
Right: We will repair the engine and ship it to you next week.

Inelegant. The principal of the bonds was paid and the same canceled. [See Rule 103 *a.*]
Right: The principal of the bonds was paid and the bonds were canceled.

Same (2). *The same as* should not be used for *in the same way as* or *just as.*

Wrong: The draft is treated the same as a check is treated.
Right: The draft is treated just as a check is treated.

Say (1). Vulgar use of *says* for *said.*

Vulgar: I says to him, "Look out!"
Correct: I said to him, "Look out!"

Vulgar: Yesterday he says to me, "I'll pay you soon."
Correct: Yesterday he said to me, "I'll pay you soon."

Say (2). Should not be used to mean *give orders,* with an infinitive as object.

Colloquial: The guard said to go back.
Right: The guard ordered us [or told us] to go back.

Scarcely. See **Hardly.**
Search. The phrase *in search for* is incorrect; say *in search of.*

Right: The lion goes in search of sheep.
Right: The lion goes on a search for sheep.

Seem. *Can't seem* is illogical. Prefer *seem unable,* or *do not seem able.*
Seldom ever. Now illiterate. Say *very seldom,* or *hardly ever.*
Seldom or ever. A vulgarism. Say *seldom if ever.*
Selection. Means *a thing selected;* as *He played a selection from Wagner.* Should not be used where there is no idea of selecting.

Bad: Our class prophet then read an amusing selection, in which he satirized his classmates.
Right: Our class prophet then read an amusing composition [or skit, or squib, or piece], in which, etc.

Set (1). Often confounded with *sit.* Remember the principal parts of each verb:

I sit	I sat	I have sat.
I set	I set	I have set.

The use of *set* without an object, as expressing mere rest, is a vulgarism; say *sit, stand, lie, rest,* or *is set.*

Wrong: The pole sets firmly in the socket.
Right: The pole is set [or sits] firmly in the socket.

Wrong: The vase sets on the mantel.
Right: The vase stands [or rests] on the mantel.

Wrong: The boat sets lightly on the water.
Right: The boat lies [or rests] lightly on the water.

Setting hen is an idiomatic expression in good usage.

Set (2). *Set* for *sets* (plural). See **Pair.**
Shan't. A colloquialism. A contraction for *shall not.*
Shape. Should not be used loosely to mean *manner, condition, state.*

Wrong: They executed the maneuvers in good shape.
Right: They executed the maneuvers in an expert manner.

Wrong: He is in good shape for the debate.
Right: He is in good condition [or thoroughly prepared] for the debate.

Should of. See **Of.**
Show (1). Colloquial for *play, opera, concert.*
Show (2). A colloquialism for *chance* or *promise.*

Colloquial: The freshman team had an excellent show of winning.
Right: The freshman team had an excellent chance of winning.

Show up. A colloquialism when used intransitively in the sense of *appear, attend, come,* or *be present;* and when used transitively in the sense of *show* or *expose.*
Sight of. *A sight of* is a colloquialism for *much, many, a great deal.*

Colloquial: He left her a sight of money.
Improved: He left her a great deal of money.

Size. Never use *size* as an adjective; say *sized,* or *of size.*

Wrong: The different size dies are sorted.
Right: The different sized dies are sorted.

Wrong: Any size chain will do.
Right: A chain of any size will do.

Snap. A colloquialism when used for *vigor, energy, life, crispness.*
So (1). A colloquialism when used to join coördinate clauses.

Colloquial: They have no garage; so we left the car in the street.
Improved: We left the car in the street because they have no garage.

So (2). Should not be used for *so that.*

Wrong: They strapped it so it would hold.
Right: They strapped it so that it would hold.

So (3). Vague and weak when used as an intensive adverb meaning *very* or *extremely.*

Weak: During the first semester I was so lonely.
Right: During the first semester I was very lonely.

Some (1). A colloquialism when used as an adverb meaning *a little, somewhat.* (See Rule 8.)

Wrong: I worked some last winter.
Right: I did some work last winter.

Wrong: I am some better today.
Right: I am somewhat better today.

Some (2). A colloquialism when used as an intensifying adjective; as *That is some car you are driving.* In formal writing a word conveying the precise meaning should be substituted.
Some place. See **Any place.**
Sort. See **Kind.**
Sort of. See **Kind of.**

Specie. Means *gold* or *silver money*. *Species,* meaning *kind,* has the same form in the singular and the plural.

> Right: The first species is more valuable than the other two species are.

Start. *I started to school in 1918* is wrong, but *I started to school early that morning* is correct. *I started in school in 1918* is correct, though less desirable than *I began to attend school.* In the expressions, *He started in to quarrel,* and *He started up in business,* the *in* and the *up* are superfluous, and should be omitted.

Stop. Means *to cease* or *to cease from motion.* A colloquialism when used in the sense of *stay* or *visit.* Good British usage.

> Right: Are you staying [not *stopping*] with friends?

Strata. A plural noun. See **Data.**

Such (1). When *such* is completed by a relative clause, the relative pronoun of the clause should not be *who, which,* or *that;* it should be ***as*** (see *as* in a dictionary).

> Illogical: I will act under such rules that may be fixed.
> Right: I will act under such rules as may be fixed.
>
> Illogical: All such persons present who consent will rise.
> Right: All such persons present as consent will rise.

Such (2). When *such* is completed by a result clause, this clause should be introduced, not by *so that,* but by *that* alone.

> Illogical: There was such a mist so that we couldn't see.
> Right: There was such a mist that we couldn't see.

Such (3). Avoid the vague and weak use of *such* without a result clause.

> Weak: We had such a good time.
> Right: We had a good time.
> Right: We had a very good time.
> Right: We had such a good time that we did not wish to leave.

Superior, inferior. Should not be limited by a *than* clause, but by a *to* phrase.

> Wrong: It was superior from every point of view than the lathe previously used.
> Right: It was superior from every point of view to the lathe previously used.

Sure. Slang when used for *certainly, indeed, surely,* or an intensive sometimes equal to *yes.*

> Wrong: Will you go? Sure.
> Right: Will you go? Surely [I will go].

Suspicion. Incorrectly used as a verb.

> Wrong: I did not suspicion that he was coming.
> Right: I did not suspect that he was coming.

Swell. Colloquial when used to mean *stylish, smartly dressed, ultrafashionable.* Slang when used to mean *grand, excellent, first-rate.*

Take and. Sometimes used redundantly.

> Redundant: It will stay if you take and put it on right.
> Improved: It will stay if you put it on right.

Take it. Should not be used in introducing an example.

Bad: Take it in Wisconsin, the old-fashioned method of logging is becoming extinct.
Right: In Wisconsin, for example, the old-fashioned method of logging is becoming extinct.

Take sick. Dialectal for *become sick.*
Take stock in. See **Bank on.**
Than, till, until. Often improperly used for *when.* (See Rule 87.) Note, however, that *no sooner* should be followed by a *than* clause.

Illogical: Scarcely had he mounted the wagon than the horse started.
Logical: Scarcely had he mounted the wagon when the horse started.

Illogical: We had hardly got there and put things in order till Jenks came.
Logical: We had hardly got there and put things in order when Jenks came.

Illogical: No sooner had we arrived when the play began.
Logical: No sooner had we arrived than the play began.

That. Colloquial as an adverb. (See **This,** and see Rule 8.)

Colloquial: He went only that far.
Right: He went only so far.

Colloquial: If it is that bad, we must retreat.
Right: If it is so bad [or so bad as that], we must retreat.

Colloquial: I am that tired I could sleep on any bed.
Improved: I am so tired that I could sleep on any bed.

That there. See **This here.**
These here. See **This here.**
This. Colloquial as an adverb. (See **That,** and see Rule 8.)

Colloquial: Having come this far . . .
Right: Having come thus far [or as far as this] . . .

Colloquial: The water hasn't ever before been this high.
Right: The water hasn't ever before been so high as this.

This here, these here, that there, those there. Gross vulgarisms. Say *this, these, that,* or *those.*
Those kind, those sort. See **Kind, sort.**
Those there. See **This here.**
Through. Inelegant when used as in the following sentence:

Wrong: He is through writing.
Right: He has finished writing; [or] He has done writing.

NOTE. — Do not say *is finished* or *is done* in the sense above shown.

Till for *when.* See **Than.**
Too. See **Very.**
Transpire. Means *to give forth* or *to become known;* as *In spite of their efforts at concealment, the secret transpired.* It is used by many writers of good standing to mean *to happen, to occur,* but this usage is disapproved of by many authorities.
Treat. When used to mean *discuss* or *speak of,* it is now usually followed by *of,* not by *on* or *with.*

Doubtful: The author treats on two subjects.
Improved: The author treats of two subjects.

Trend. Means *direction;* as *The rivers of this land have a southern trend.* Should not be used without regard to its proper meaning.

Bad: The egg business is only incidental to the general trend of the store.
Right: The egg business is only incidental to the general business of the store.

Try and. Colloquial for *try to.*

Colloquial: I shall try and get a good position.
Right: I shall try to get a good position.

Tutor. A colloquialism when used in the sense of *being tutored.* Correctly used in the sense of *doing the work of a tutor.*

Colloquial: I tutored in Latin before the examination.
Correct: I was tutored in Latin before the examination.

Ugly. Means *repulsive to the eye.* A provincialism when used to mean *vicious, malicious,* or *ill-tempered.*

Bad: The horse has an ugly temper.
Right: The horse has a vicious temper.

Bad: The conductor acted very ugly.
Right: The conductor acted very discourteously [or uncivilly].

United States. This name should usually be preceded by *the.* Do not write: *We live in United States.*

Until for *when.* See **Than.**

Up. Do not attach a superfluous *up* to verbs.

Bad: He opened up the box and divided the money up among the men.
Improved: He opened the box and divided the money among the men.

Verbal and **oral.** *Oral* is used of the spoken word only. *Verbal,* meaning *in words,* is used especially of transactions which are not committed to writing.

Right: Our exercises are to be oral.
Right: It was only a verbal agreement.

Very, much, and **too** with past participles. A past participle that has not yet become an adjective should not be immediately preceded by *very* or *too,* but by an adverb like *much, greatly, seriously, gravely, sadly, happily, deeply,* or any other appropriate adverb. A past participle that has become an adjective may be preceded by *very* or *too.* Upon occasion opinion may vary as to whether the participle has become an adjective or not.

Idiomatic: I am very much interested in the work. [*Interested* is a past participle.]
Idiomatic: I am too tired to go. [*Tired* is an adjective.]

Note that *too* less often requires an adverb between it and the participle.

Unidiomatic: I am very disgusted.
Idiomatic: I am very much disgusted.
Idiomatic: I am too disgusted for words.

Violin. Should not be used to mean *instruction in violin playing.*

Colloquial: He has just begun violin.
Improved: He has just begun to take violin lessons.

Vocal, voice. Should not be used to mean *vocal lessons.* (See Rule 8.)

Colloquial: Are you keeping on with your vocal?
Colloquial: She is taking voice.

Voice. See **Vocal.**
Wait on. A vulgarism for *wait for.*

Wrong: If I'm not there, don't wait on me.
Right: If I'm not there, don't wait for me.

Want (1). Should not be limited by a clause as in the following sentence:

Wrong: I want you should be happy.
Right: I want you to be happy.

Want (2). *Want in, want out, want through,* etc., are unauthorized localisms.

Vulgar: Do you want in?
Right: Do you want to come in?

Want for. Omit the superfluous *for* after *want.*

Provincial: I want for you to get some water.
Improved: I want you to get some water.

Way (1). Unlicensed abbreviation for *away.*

Wrong: Way up the hill I saw a deer.
Right: Away [or far] up the hill I saw a deer.

Way (2). Should not be used adverbially without a preposition governing it.

Wrong: When he acts that way . . .
Right: When he acts in that way . . .

Wrong: How could a sane man act the way Beals did?
Right: How could a sane man act in the way in which Beals acted? [or, better] . . . act as Beals did?

Ways for *way.* See **Falls.**
Where (1). Often misused for *that* as in the following sentence.

Wrong: I see in this morning's paper where Cronin has been caught.
Right: I see in this morning's paper that Cronin has been caught.

Where (2). Do not use *where to* in the sense of *whither;* omit the *to.*

Bad: Where are you going to?
Improved: Where are you going?

Whether. See **If.**
Which. Should not be used as a relative pronoun in referring to a person.

Wrong: The people which do that are rascals.
Right: The people that do that are rascals.

While. Means (*a*) *during the time in which,* (*b*) *though,* or (*c*) *whereas;* as (*a*) *I played while he sang;* (*b*) *While this may be true, it does not satisfy me;* (*c*) *Yours is in good condition, while mine is quite worn out.* Should not be used loosely without regard to its meaning.

Loose: On one side was a grove, while on the other was a river.
Right: On one side was a grove, on the other a river.

Who. Should not, as a rule, be used in referring to animals; use *which.*
Whose. In modern usage, the possessive case of *who* only, though originally also of *which,* and sometimes so used.

Doubtful: Soon we came to a swamp, on whose bank stood a hunter's cabin.

Preferable: Soon we came to a swamp, on the bank of which stood a hunter's cabin.

Win out. See **Lose out.**

Wire. A colloquialism for *telegraph* or *telegram.* (See Rule 8.)

With. Often vaguely used in place of more exact connectives.

Vague: With the men he has helping him, Parker seems certain to win.

Better: Considering the men he has helping him, Parker seems certain to win.

Without. Should not be used as a conjunction for *except* or *unless.*

Wrong: He will not do it without he has a good opportunity.
Right: He will not do it unless he has a good opportunity.

Woods for *wood.* See **Falls.**

Would better, would best, would rather. Correct, but often used under a misapprehension. See **Had better.**

Would have. Often incorrectly used in *if* clauses instead of *had.*

Wrong: If he would have stood by us, we might have won.
Right: If he had stood by us, we might have won.

Would of. See **Of.**

Write-up. Slang for *a report, a description, an account.*

You was. A vulgarism. *You,* though it may designate one person, is grammatically plural, and its verb must always be plural. Say *You were.*

GENERAL EXERCISES ON THE GLOSSARY

Accept **and** *except*

I. See *Except* in the Glossary. Write the following sentences, filling the blanks with *accept* or *except:* 1. I would —— the offer, —— for my religious scruples. 2. He was the best pianist in Europe; I do not —— even Liszt. 3. Most of the rebels were offered pardon and ——ed it; but the leaders were ——ed from the offer. 4. He burned all the household goods, not ——ing even the heirlooms. 5. Why did you —— Charles from your invitation? He wouldn't have ——ed anyway.

Affect **and** *effect*

II. See *Affect* in the Glossary. Write the following sentences, filling the blanks with *affect* or *effect:* 1. That statement is true, but it does not —— the case. 2. The failure of the bank did not —— his equanimity. 3. The admonition of the dean had a good ——. 4. The generals ——ed a junction, but this action had no —— on the enemy. 5. His brooding ——ed his health. 6. The utmost efforts of his physician could not —— a cure.

Like

III. See *Like* in the Glossary. Complete the following sentences: 1. I wish I could run like ——. 2. If you find him engaged at his gymnastics, like ——. 3. She sat for a long time deep in thought, like ——.

Fill the blanks with *as, as if,* or *like:* 4. Don't act —— a baby. 5. —— all his predecessors, he was despotic. 6. We never quarrel now —— we did when we were boys. 7. He was hanged, just —— a common spy. 8. He was hanged, just —— he had been a common spy. 9. He votes —— his father did. 10. She sings —— she had a cold. 11. He can run —— a race-horse. 12. He can run —— a race-horse runs. 13. He takes severe training —— a man usually does when he is preparing for a prize fight. 14. He takes very severe training —— a prize fighter. 15. She stood —— a statue. 16. She stood —— a statue might have stood. 17. He whimpered, —— a spoiled child, about every little inconvenience. 18. He whined, —— a spoiled child does, at every inconvenience. 19. —— his father did, he saved his money. 20. —— all his predecessors had been, Henry VIII was despotic. 21. We do not quarrel now —— we were still unfriendly. 22. They quarrel constantly, —— boys usually do. 23. They quarrel —— cats and dogs. 24. He was hanged, —— many another spy caught in such an enterprise. 25. He was hanged —— many another spy has been. 26. I vote, —— my father, for the Conservative party. 27. I vote, —— my father did, for the Conservatives. 28. She sings —— a person afflicted with goitre. 29. She sings —— a person with goitre might sing.

IV. Correct the following ungrammatical sentences, stating the reasons for your changes: 1. She sings like she had a cold. 2. They executed him like he had been a common spy. 3. The sky looks like we should have rain. 4. He acts like he was the master of ceremonies. 5. The game isn't played like we used to play it. 6. He counted out the money dexterously, like a bank teller does. 7. These waves roar just like the ocean waves do. 8. She walks clumsily, like a duck waddles. 9. He turns his toes in, like an Indian does. 10. He grew white like he feared the boat would capsize. 11. I felt like I must scream. 12. It seemed like I was in a nightmare. 13. She cried out, like she had been struck. 14. Move your hand just like I move mine. 15. It stretches like a rubber band does.

Real

V. See *Real* in the Glossary. Correct the following sentences: 1. You are real generous. 2. The room is real comfortable. 3. It was a real hard storm. 4. She writes a real pretty hand. 5. I felt real lonesome. 6. She told us a real sad story. 7. Hanksburg is a real pleasant town.

Due to

VI. Study *Due to* in the Glossary. Correct the following sentences: 1. Hamlet treated her rudely due to his mental distraction. 2. Shop work is easy for me due to a natural talent for manual work. 3. Due to someone's carelessness the valve had been left open. 4. Due to bad weather the game is postponed. 5. He refused to buy due to the high price asked. 6. Due to his ignorance of French he misunderstood the letter. 7. I was put in the bow due to my light weight. 8. He had to sell his house due to need of ready money. 9. Due to his long exposure he became sick. 10. I kept warm and comfortable due to my fur coat.

Falls, *ways*, and *woods*

VII. Study *Falls, Ways, Woods* in the Glossary. Correct the following sentences: 1. It is a long ways from here. 2. We carried our boat around a falls. 3. Is there a woods on your farm? 4. This falls is not very high. 5. Walk a little ways with us. 6. He lost himself in a woods. 7. The woods is on fire.

Write three sentences using the expression *a little way,* three using *a long way,* three using *a wood,* three using *the woods are,* three using *the falls were.*

Whose

VIII. Study *Whose* in the Glossary. Correct the following sentences: 1. I sat on the roof, whose slope was not very steep. 2. I selected a cloth whose texture was woven loosely. 3. I perceived a steeple on whose top revolved a gilded vane. 4. It was an antique table, whose legs bore the pineapple decoration. 5. He exhibited a painting in whose execution he had evidently expended much labor. 6. Get some of those matches whose ends are tipped with red. 7. A verb whose subject is a collective noun may properly be in the plural. 8. He lit a fire, whose heat was very comfortable. 9. A chain any of whose links are weak is a weak chain. 10. You sold me a book whose type is too small.

Could of, *may of*, etc. for *could have*, *may have*, etc.

IX. Study *Could of, Should of, Would of, May of, Must of, Might of* in the Glossary. Correct the following sentences: 1. You should of seen me. 2. I would of come if I could of spared the time. 3. He may of lost his way. 4. I might of lost mine, and then I should of lost this pleasure. 5. If I could of seen him, I would of told him. 6. She must of suspected treachery, or she would not of stayed away. 7. If he could of known, the outcome might of been different. 8. I would not of accepted the offer even if I could of named my own price.

Would have and *had have* for *had* in past perfect

X. Study *Had have* and *Would have* in the Glossary. Correct the following sentences: 1. If we would have started back fifteen minutes later, we should probably have perished in the blizzard. 2. If he would have found the way, he would have gone. 3. If I would have known how it would end, I never would have begun. 4. If he would have been at his post, the accident would not have occurred. 5. If the weather would have been colder, the ice would now be safe. 6. If the boat would have tipped only a little more, it would have been swamped. 7. If she would have been a second later, she would have missed the train. 8. If the wind would have been north, the barn would certainly have caught fire. 9. If the bridge would have been properly built, it would not vibrate as it does. 10. If the old gentleman would have caught the boys, they would have repented sorely. 11. If the alarm clock would have been set, you would have waked in time.

You was for *you were*

XI. Study *You was* in the Glossary. Also write the following sentences, filling each blank with a word to indicate past tense: 1. —— you satisfied? 2. You —— generous. 3. You —— content, ——n't you? 4. You —— mistaken. 5. —— you happy, or ——n't you? 6. You —— never pleased. 7. —— you sure? 8. —— you as severe as you —— justified in being? 9. ——n't you sterner than you —— authorized to be? 10. You —— treacherous, you —— deceitful; therefore you —— punished.

Different

XII. Study *Different* in the Glossary. Revise the following sentences: 1. They speak very differently than you speak. 2. Plumbing is entirely different than steam-fitting. 3. This machine is somewhat different than the one I bought. 4. To sail a brig is widely different than to sail a schooner. 5. He is a different man today than he was when you knew him. 6. His purpose is different than I thought it was. 7. My reward was very different than what I deserved. 8. They did it differently then than they do now. 9. Your machinery is different than what I use. 10. Conditions were radically different than what I expected. 11. His character was different, as a matter of fact, than what the historian says it was. 12. You need a different sort of manager than you now have. 13. The state of affairs in Nicaragua is no different than in Bolivia. 14. *The Witching Hour* deals with a different subject than Mr. Thomas, the author, has used hitherto.

Such . . . as

XIII. Study *Such* (1) in the Glossary. Write sentences containing the following expressions: *all such men as hold this belief, such tools as are necessary, such books as I find interesting, such men as seem to be in earnest, such members as desire to dance, all such citizens as love their country, such as are in need of money, for such as keep His covenant, with such fruits as the season afforded, such as prefer horses to motors, such influence as he may have.*

Such . . . that

XIV. Study *Such* (2) in the Glossary. Complete each of the following sentences with a *that* clause: 1. He is such a coward . . . 2. There was such a drought . . . 3. He has such skill . . . 4. There is such a crowd . . . 5. We made such a protest . . . 6. Such a tempest arose . . . 7. He came with such an army . . . 8. She exercised such tact . . . 9. The lawyer displayed such eloquence . . .

Superior and *inferior*

XV. Study *Superior, Inferior* in the Glossary. Complete the following sentences, beginning each added member with a *to* phrase: 1. This method is superior, in the opinion of all who have used it, . . . 2. His style is inferior, so the critics all agree, . . . 3. The team was inferior, both in weight and in experience, . . . 4. This year's class play will be inferior, unless I am much mistaken, . . . 5. The streetcar service here is inferior, however you may regard it, . . . 6. The present system is superior, so far as one can judge, . . . 7. His present situation is superior, so far as salary is concerned, . . .

Prefer and *preferable*

XVI. Study *Prefer* in the Glossary. The "prefer . . . than" fault can be corrected by the substitution of *prefer . . . to* or by the substitution of *prefer . . . rather than.*

> Right: I prefer building to leasing.
> Right: I prefer to build rather than to lease.

Rewrite each of the following sentences twice, correcting in the two ways shown above: 1. I prefer to miss the train than to run for it. 2. Do you prefer to be expelled than to apologize? 3. He preferred to write a letter than to explain in person. 4. I prefer to enter business at once than to go to college. 5. I should much prefer to pay the money than to dispute with you. 6. They prefer to take their ease than to work. 7. She prefers to go to a party than to study her lessons. 8. I preferred to freeze my nose than to be suffocated by the bad air. 9. I prefer to risk the journey alone than to have your company. 10. He preferred to kill the horse than to let it suffer.

Than, till, until

XVII. Study *Than, Till, Until* in the Glossary.

Hardly . . . when

Complete the following sentences, using a *when* clause or a *than* clause as the sense requires: 1. No sooner did the boat touch the wharf . . . 2. The clock had scarcely finished striking . . . 3. Hardly had I seated myself . . . 4. No sooner had Bassanio departed . . . 5. The policeman had no sooner turned his back . . . 6. Our hero had hardly opened his eyes . . . 7. She no sooner reached the bridge . . . 8. Scarcely had the buck emerged from the brush . . . 9. I had hardly laid down the pen . . . 10. No sooner did the King show signs of yielding . . . 11. I no sooner overcome one obstacle . . .

Too and *very* with participles

XVIII. Study *Too, Very* in the Glossary. Correct any unidiomatic sentences. Give your reasons for making or for not making changes. 1. He seemed very moved by the appeal. 2. I am very delighted to hear it. 3. They are too offended to forgive us. 4. He is too injured to walk. 5. I am very grieved by this news. 6. She lay down again, feeling very relieved.

7. We are too involved in this affair to withdraw. 8. You need not feel too discouraged. 9. I don't feel very elated. 10. He can't judge fairly; he is too misled by his prejudices.

MISCELLANEOUS EXERCISES ON THE GLOSSARY

Various errors in diction

Correct any errors in diction that you may find in the following sentences. The standard should be the diction of written discourse. Consult the latest edition of a good dictionary.

1. Do you know the lay of the land? 2. He is laying for a chance to get even. 3. You should not disturb a setting hen. 4. He don't like the set of the coat on the shoulders. 5. If you organize your work, you can get it done all the faster. 6. I can't seem to forget that movie. It sure was a grand one. 7. He is the kind of a fellow who always enthuses about everything. 8. I guess I'll never get to go places. 9. The bunch can't hardly ever get together any more, due to our all being in business now. 10. They aren't putting the blame on the right party.

11. This is all the farther I have read. 12. If he would have done as the doctor said, he might have pulled through. 13. You cannot make him go without he wants to. 14. I started to work when I was eight years old. 15. We could of taken in a show on the way home. 16. She is quite a little better. 17. It don't seem like it's ever going to clear up. 18. I should liked to have seen her. 19. I don't know as I care to go. 20. Less accidents have occurred this year than last.

21. I doubt if he is right. 22. She needs a new coat very badly. 23. That is not along my line. 24. If my father had have been there, he would never have consented. 25. You have nowhere near the right amount. 26. We three shared it between us. 27. You came nearly getting drowned. 28. Sometimes she likes to go and then other times she doesn't. 29. He is the strangest individual that I have ever known. 30. She spent a whole lot of time on that getup.

31. The whole family had mean dispositions and were always quarreling with each other. 32. You couldn't faze her. 33. That much is over with. 34. I had hardly got the door shut than they were at me with questions. 35. This cottage was superior in many ways than the one we had last year. 36. Take it on the home farm, we have never had a complete crop failure. 37. I worked some in the laboratory last night. 38. She took vocal from him. 39. He was very disappointed not to go. 40. She answered me that queer way.

41. Go a ways with me. 42. With all that your father has done for you, you should be willing to help him now. 43. I see where I shall have trouble. 44. Where did he go to? 45. I am real glad to meet you. 46. He was raised on the farm. 47. She raised up and told us what she thought. 48. I've put in a good day's work. 49. They charged him of bribing a witness. 50. You will find this product equally as good.

51. Let's don't leave our car here. 52. I will do the balance of the work tomorrow. 53. I expect considerable was lost in

Various errors in diction

the crash. 54. We have company for supper. 55. I have no doubt but what he will answer your letter. 56. It was very mean of her to refuse to go with you. 57. He was not overly pleased with the prospect. 58. Your parents always want for you to do your best. 59. His family located in Iowa. 60. He passed most all of us in the course.

61. It is perfectly lovely of you to ask me. 62. They have been overly careful with the child's diet. 63. I will kindly request you to mind your own business. 64. I think that he is kind of foolish. 65. Bring your scissors, needles, and etc. 66. The course ends with the fifth century A.D. 67. After having waited for her for several hours, I went home. 68. He is an all-around athlete. 69. We have supper at about six o'clock.

APPENDIX B

A GLOSSARY OF GRAMMATICAL TERMS

Absolute. See **Nominative Absolute.**
Abstract noun. See **Noun.**
Active Voice. See **Voice.**
Adjective. A part of speech used to describe or limit the meaning of a substantive. There are the following kinds:

a. Descriptive: a *true* friend, a *poor* man.
b. Limiting: *a* boy, *an* apple, *the* man.
c. Pronominal:

1. Possessive: *my, his, her, its, our, your, their.*
2. Demonstrative: *this, that, these, those. This* hat, etc.
3. Interrogative: *whose, which, what. Whose* hat? etc.
4. Relative: *whose, which.*

   The man *whose* house was robbed has just returned.

5. Indefinite: *any, each, no, some,* etc.

   Each boy had his own room.

d. Numeral:

1. Cardinal: *one, two, three,* etc.

   Ten students were admitted.

2. Ordinal: *first, second, third,* etc.

   He won the *first* game.

Adjective clause. A clause that modifies a substantive.

The rain *that fell yesterday* was a blessing. [The adjective clause modifies the noun *rain.*]

Adjective clauses are also called **relative clauses.**
Adjunct. A modifier is an adjunct of the sentence-member it modifies; a predicate substantive or adjective is an adjunct of the verb it completes.
Adverb. A part of speech used to modify a verb, an adjective, or another adverb. An adverb answers the questions: *where? when? how? in what manner?* and *to what extent?*

He bowed *politely.* [*Politely* modifies the verb *bowed.*]
A *very* old woman came in. [*Very* modifies the adjective *old.*]
He was *too* much absorbed to listen. [*Too* modifies the adverb *much.*]

Adverbial clause. A clause used to modify a verb, adjective, or adverb.

I will come *if I have any money.* [The adverbial clause modifies the verb *will come.*]
He is greater *than his father was.* [The adverbial clause modifies the adjective *greater.*]
He walked faster *than I did.* [The adverbial clause modifies the adverb *faster.*]

Adverbial objective. A substantive used adverbially.

He walked *two miles.* [Modifies the verb *walked.*]
It is worth *ten cents.* [Modifies the adjective *worth.*]
He walked *two miles* farther. [Modifies the adverb *farther.*]

Antecedent. A word, phrase, or clause to which a pronoun refers.

He who runs may read. [*He* is the antecedent of *who.*]
He is paying my tuition which is more than I had expected. [The clause is the antecedent of *which.*]

Appositive. A substantive attached to another substantive and denoting the same person or thing. A substantive is said to be **in apposition** with the substantive to which it is attached.

George, my hostess's *cousin,* was enjoying his favorite sport — *yachting.* [*Cousin* is in apposition with *George; yachting* is in apposition with *sport.*]

Article. The word *the* is called the **definite article;** the word *a* or *an* is called the **indefinite article.** Articles are adjectives.

Auxiliary. The verbs *be, have, do, shall, will, may, can, must, ought,* with their inflectional forms, when they assist in forming the voices, modes, and tenses of other verbs, are auxiliaries.

I *was* given a message.
He *should* come.
He *has been* gone a week.

Cardinal number. See **Adjective.**

Case. A characteristic of substantives, indicating the relation existing between a substantive and the other words in the sentence. This relation may be shown by an inflectional form of the word or by its position. In English there are three cases, **nominative, possessive** (or **genitive**), **objective** (or **accusative**). In nouns the nominative and objective cases are identical, but in pronouns they are, with the exception of the nominative and objective singular of *it,* distinct. (For the declension of nouns and pronouns, see **Noun** and **Pronoun.**) The subject of a finite verb is in the nominative case. A substantive that shows ownership or origin or a similar relation is in the possessive case. The object of a verb or of a preposition is in the objective case.

My *home* is in Chicago. [*Home* is in the nominative case.]
John's hat is lost. [*John's* is in the possessive case.]
We lived within a *stone's* throw. [*Stone's* is in the possessive case.]
He ate the *pear.* [*Pear* is in the objective case, the object of the verb *ate.*]
She sat on the *bench.* [*Bench* is in the objective case, the object of the preposition *on.*]

Causal conjunction. A conjunction that introduces a statement of cause or reason; *e.g., for, because, since. For* is coördinating; *because* and *since* are subordinating. (See Appendix D.)

Clause. A group of words that is part of a sentence and that contains a subject and a predicate. Clauses that make independent assertions are **independent** (or **principal**) **clauses.** Clauses that are not by themselves complete in meaning are **dependent** (or **subordinate**) **clauses.** Subordinate clauses are used as nouns, adjectives, or adverbs. They are usually introduced by subordinating words. (See Appendix D.)

We heard him when he came in. [*We heard him* is the principal clause; *when he came in* is the subordinate clause.]

That she will be late is certain. [Subordinate clause used as a noun.]
The woman *who spoke to us* is our neighbor. [Subordinate clause used as an adjective.]
He will come *when he is ready*. [Subordinate clause used as an adverb.]

Clauses that play the same part in a sentence, whether they are principal or subordinate, are called **coördinate clauses.**

The bell rang and *everyone stood up*. [Coördinate principal clauses.]
He left *because he did not like the work* and *because the pay was low*. [Coördinate subordinate clauses.]

Climax. A series of assertions or coördinate sentence-elements so arranged that each one is stronger or more impressive than the preceding one. A series of assertions or sentence-elements in which the last element is weaker or less impressive than the preceding elements is an **anticlimax.**

Collective noun. See **Noun.**

Common noun. See **Noun.**

Comparative. See **Comparison.**

Comparison. Inflection of an adjective or adverb to indicate an increasing degree of quality, quantity, or manner. The **positive degree** is the simple form with no comparison indicated.

Their house is *cold*.
The view from their house is *beautiful*.
He was always *fortunate*.

The **comparative degree** indicates that the quality, quantity, or manner is greater or more intense in comparison to some standard.

Their house is *colder* than ours.
The view from their house is *more beautiful* than the one from ours.
He was always *less fortunate* than his brother.

The **superlative degree** indicates that the quality, quantity, or manner is at its greatest or most intense.

Their house is the *coldest* in town.
The view from their house is the *most beautiful* I have ever seen.
He was the *least fortunate* member of his family.

When adjectives have one or two syllables, the comparative degree is usually formed by adding *er* to the positive; and the superlative degree is usually formed by adding *est* to the positive. When adjectives have more than two syllables, the comparative degree is usually formed by placing *more* or *less* before the positive; and the superlative degree is usually formed by placing *most* or *least* before the positive. Some adjectives have irregular comparison; *e.g.*, *good*, *better*, *best*; *bad*, *worse*, *worst*.

Complex sentence. See **Sentence.**

Compound sentence. See **Sentence.**

Concrete noun. See **Noun.**

Conjunction. A part of speech used to connect words, phrases, and clauses. There are the following kinds: (See Appendix D.)

a. **Coördinating**
1. **Pure conjunctions:** *and*, *or*, *but*, *for*.
2. **Correlatives:** *either . . . or*, *neither . . . nor*, etc.
3. **Conjunctive adverbs:** *moreover*, *nevertheless*, *however*, etc.

b. **Subordinating**
1. Conjunctions introducing adjective clauses: *who, which, that.*
2. Conjunctions introducing adverbial clauses: *when, while, where, because, so that,* etc.

Coördinating conjunctions connect sentence-elements that are logically and grammatically equal; *i.e.*, they may connect two subjects or two verbs, or two adjective clauses, etc. Subordinating conjunctions connect subordinate (or dependent) clauses with their principal (or independent) clauses. A conjunction may be distinguished from a preposition by the fact that a preposition must always be followed by a substantive, its object.

He fell *into* the cold water. [*Into* is a preposition followed by the noun *water*, its object.]

He remembered the engagement *when* reminded. [*When* is a conjunction followed by the predicate of an elliptical clause.]

Conjunctive adverb. See **Conjunction.**

Consonant. See **Vowel.**

Construction. The grammatical function performed by any word in a sentence; *e.g.*, in the sentence, *He walks fast*, the construction of *he* is that of the subject of *walks;* the construction of *walks* is that of the predicate of *he;* the construction of *fast* is that of the adverbial modifier of *walks.*

Coördinate. Sentence-elements that are equal in grammatical construction and in meaning are coördinate. In the sentence, *He and she talked long and earnestly, and at last agreed, he* and *she* are coördinate; *talked* and *agreed* are coördinate; *long* and *earnestly* are coördinate; *talked long and earnestly* and *at last agreed* are coördinate.

Coördinate clause. See **Clause.**

Coördinating conjunction. See **Conjunction.**

Copula. A verb, especially a form of the verb *to be*, used to express simply the relationship between the subject and the predicate.

Correlative conjunction. See **Conjunction.**

Declension. See **Inflection.**

Demonstrative adjective. See **Adjective.**

Demonstrative pronoun. See **Pronoun.**

Dependent clause. See **Clause.**

Direct address. A grammatical construction in which a speaker or writer addresses a second person directly.

Mary, wait for me.
Boys, I am coming.

Direct question. See **Direct quotation.**

Direct quotation (or **direct discourse**). Quotation of words exactly as they were spoken or written. A statement of the substance of a quotation without the use of the exact words is **indirect quotation** (or **indirect discourse**). A question directly quoted is a **direct question.** A question indirectly quoted is an **indirect question.**

He said, "I will help." [Direct quotation.]
He said that he would help. [Indirect quotation.]
He asked, "Will you help?" [Direct question.]
He asked whether I would help. [Indirect question.]

Ellipsis. See **Elliptical expression.**

Elliptical expression. An expression that is grammatically incomplete, but one the meaning of which is clear because the omitted words are implied.

> Elliptical: Please come here.
> Complete: Will you please come here?
>
> Elliptical: If possible, bring your drawings along.
> Complete: If it is possible, will you bring your drawings along.

Factitive adjective. An adjective denoting a quality or state produced by the action of a verb on an object. In the sentence, *It will make you strong, strong* is a factitive adjective.

Finite verb. Any verb form that may be used as the predicate of a sentence. Infinitives, gerunds, and participles are not finite verbs.

Future tense. See **Tense.**

Future perfect tense. See **Tense.**

Gerund. A verb form ending in *ing* and used as a noun. It should be distinguished from the present participle, which also ends in *ing* but is used as an adjective. (See **Participle.**) A gerund may fulfill the principal functions of a noun:

> Subject of a verb: Fishing is tiresome.
> Object of a verb: I hate fishing.
> Object of a preposition: I have an aversion to fishing.
> Predicate noun: What I most detest is fishing.
> Appositive: That detestable sport, fishing, I cannot endure.
> Absolute noun: Fishing being my aversion, let's not fish.

Like a noun, the gerund may be modified by an adjective. In the sentence, *We were tired of his long-winded preaching, his* and *long-winded* modify the gerund *preaching*.

Since a gerund is a verb form, it may take an object and be modified by an adverb.

> He disapproved of our taking luggage with us. [*Luggage* is the object of the gerund *taking*.]
> Our success depends upon his acting promptly. [*Promptly* is an adverb modifying the gerund *acting*.]

Gerund phrase. See **Phrase.**

Govern. To require a particular case or mode; as a transitive verb governs the objective case.

Grammar. The science that deals with (*a*) the classification of words according to the functions they perform in a sentence (see **Parts of Speech**); (*b*) the inflection of words (see **Inflection**); (*c*) the relations of words to one another in a sentence (see **Syntax**).

Indefinite pronoun. See **Pronoun.**

Indicative. See **Mode.**

Indirect question. See **Direct quotation.**

Indirect quotation. See **Direct quotation.**

Infinitive. That form of the verb usually preceded by *to*. *To* is called the **sign of the infinitive.** The sign *to* is often omitted, especially after the auxiliaries *do, can, shall, will, may, must,* etc., as in the sentence, *I can go*.

The infinitive has two tenses, present and perfect, and, if the verb is transitive, both active and passive voices. For these forms see the conjugation of the verb, page 418.

The infinitive, since it is a verb form, can have a subject, can take an object, and can be modified by an adverb.

We asked her to come. [*Her* is the subject of *to come.*]
They think it to be him. [*Him* is the predicate complement of *to be.*]
We hope to hear soon. [*Soon* is the adverbial modifier of *to hear.*]

The infinitive may be used as a noun:

To meet her is a pleasure. [Subject.]
His chief delight is *to tease her.* [Predicate nominative.]
He wished *to see the dog.* [Object of verb.]
He was about *to speak.* [Object of preposition.]

The infinitive may be used as an adjective:

He gave me a book *to read.* [Modifies the noun *book.*]
He is *to be congratulated.* [Predicate adjective.]

The infinitive may be used as an adverb:

We waited *to see you.* [Modifies the verb *waited.*]
We are able *to help.* [Modifies the adjective *able.*]
He is old enough *to travel alone.* [Modifies the adverb *enough.*]

Infinitive sign. See **Infinitive.**

Inflection. A change in the form of a word to show a change in the meaning. Substantives may be inflected to show case, person, number, and gender. Verbs are inflected to indicate mode, tense, voice, person, and number. Adjectives and adverbs are inflected to show comparison. The inflection of substantives is called **declension**; that of verbs **conjugation**; that of adjectives and adverbs **comparison.**

Intensive pronoun. The pronouns *myself, thyself, himself, herself, itself, ourselves, yourself, yourselves, themselves, oneself,* when they are used in apposition, are called intensives because they serve to intensify or emphasize the substantives that they are used with; *e.g., I myself will do it. He saw the bishop himself.* When one of these words is used as the object of a verb and designates the same person or thing as the subject of that verb, it is called a **reflexive pronoun**; *e.g., I hurt myself. They benefit themselves.*

Interjection. A part of speech that expresses emotion and that has no grammatical relation with the rest of the sentence; *e.g., oh, alas, ha, ah, hello, hurrah.*

Interrogative adjective. See **Adjective.**

Interrogative pronoun. See **Pronoun.**

Intransitive. See **Verb.**

Mode (Mood). The form of the verb that indicates the manner of the action. There are three principal modes: the indicative, the imperative, and the subjunctive.

The **indicative mode** is used to state a fact or to ask a question.

The wind is blowing.
Is it raining?

The **imperative mode** is used to express a command or an urgent request.

Do it immediately.
Please answer the telephone.

The **subjunctive mode** is used to express a wish, a supposition, a doubt, an exhortation, a concession, a condition contrary to fact. The subjunctive mode is being largely replaced by the indicative.

Wish: I wish that I *were* able to help you.
Wish: *Were* I only able to help you.

Supposition: We can go provided he *consent*. [The indicative would be more commonly used here.]
Improbability: If he *be* so cruel as that — I cannot believe that he is — then we must be ready to fight. [The indicative would also be used here.]
Exhortation: Heaven *forbid!*
Concession: Although he *be* the richest man in town, he will give nothing. [The indicative would also be used here.]
Condition contrary to fact: If she *were* younger, she would understand.

The **potential mode** is a term used by some grammarians to denote the verb forms expressing possibility, liberty, power, etc. This mode is formed by the auxiliaries *can, may, could, would, should, must, might* with the infinitive without *to; e.g., He can speak French.*

Modifier. See **Modify.**

Modify. To describe or limit the meaning of a word or group of words. In the sentence, *I dislike sour oranges*, the word *sour* describes the word *oranges; i.e.*, it modifies it. In the sentence, *Call softly, softly* describes or modifies *call.* A word that describes or limits the meaning of a word or group of words is called a **modifier.** The modifiers of substantives are adjectives (including participles), adjective phrases, adjective clauses, appositives, and substantives in the possessive case. The modifiers of adjectives, verbs, and adverbs are adverbs, adverbial phrases, adverbial clauses, and adverbial objectives.

Nominative. See **Case.**

Nominative absolute. A construction consisting of a substantive in the nominative case and a participle used to express time, cause, or circumstances of an action. This construction is called absolute because it is independent of the rest of the sentence, although it is in effect an adverbial modifier.

The water having receded, the people returned to their homes.
We did not go to the city, *the concert having been postponed.*

Nominative of address (Vocative substantive). See **Direct address.**

Noun. A part of speech, the name of a person, place, thing, or idea.

There are the following kinds:

A **common noun** is the name that is applied in common to all the members of a group of persons, places, things, or ideas; *e.g., man, village, book, courage.* Common nouns are not usually capitalized.

A **proper noun** or **proper name** is the name of a particular person, place, or thing; *e.g., Theodore Roosevelt, Chicago, Domesday Book, Revolutionary War.* Proper nouns are capitalized.

A **collective noun** is the name of a group or class considered as a unit; *e.g., flock, class, group, crowd, gang.*

A **concrete noun** is the name of something that can be perceived by any one of the senses; *e.g., tree, sugar, perfume, shriek, velvet.*

An **abstract noun** is the name of a quality or general idea; *e.g., strength, love, bravery.*

A noun may be used as:

Subject of a verb: The *boy* came.
Object of a verb or verbal: She cut her *hand.* We wish to see *her.*
Object of a preposition: He stood near the *tree.*
Predicate substantive: He is my *cousin.*

Appositive: Mr. Hall, *my friend*, met us at the train.
Nominative of address: *John*, come here.
An adjective: The *winter* wind was bitter.
An adverb: We waited five *minutes*.

The declension of nouns is shown in the following table:

	Singular	*Plural*
Nom.	boy	boys
Poss. (*Gen.*)	boy's	boys'
Obj. (*Acc.*)	boy	boys
Nom.	man	men
Poss. (*Gen.*)	man's	men's
Obj. (*Acc.*)	man	men

Number. A substantive that names only one person or thing is singular in number; *e.g.*, *boy*, *boy's*, *it*, *its;* one naming two or more persons or things is plural in number; *e.g.*, *boys*, *boys'*, *they*, *theirs*. (For the forms of singular and plural numbers of typical nouns and pronouns, see the declensions under **Noun** and **Pronoun.**) The verb form properly used with a singular subject is in the singular number; *e.g.*, *He comes here often.* The form used with a plural subject is in the plural number; *e.g.*, *They come here often.* (For the forms of singular and plural numbers of a typical verb, see the conjugation of a verb on pp. 415–418.)

Object. The object of a verb is the person or thing that receives the action of the verb. It answers the question *what* or *whom*. The object may be a word, a phrase, or a clause:

We saw *the eclipse*. [Word.]
I like *to play the piano*. [Infinitive phrase.]
Did you know *that he used to live in Mexico?* [Clause.]

The **direct object** of a verb is the person or thing that is directly affected by the action of the verb.

I asked a *question*.
He struck a *note* on the piano.

The **indirect object** of a verb is the person or thing indirectly affected by the action of the verb. The indirect object can usually be made the object of the prepositions *for* or *to*.

I built *my wife* a house. [I built a house *for my wife*.]
I wrote *him* a letter. [I wrote a letter *to him*.]

Regarding the object of a preposition, see **Preposition.**

Objective (**accusative**). See **Case.**

Ordinal number. See **Adjective.**

Objective complement. Either a noun or an adjective that completes the predicate by telling something about the direct object.

They called him a *fool*. [Noun.]
I like my coffee *hot*. [Adjective.]

Part of speech. The classification of words according to the special function that they perform in a sentence. In English there are eight parts of speech: nouns, pronouns, verbs, adjectives, adverbs, prepositions, conjunctions, interjections.

Participle. A verbal adjective. English verbs have three participles: present, past, and past perfect. The present participle ends in *ing; e.g.*, *eating, running.* The past participle ends in *ed, d, t, en, n,* or is formed by a vowel change; *e.g., stopped, told, slept, fallen, known, sung.* The past perfect participle is formed of *having* plus the past participle. If the verb is transitive, there are both active and passive participles. (For these forms see the conjugation of the verb, p. 418.)

Since a participle is a verbal adjective, it has the characteristics of both a verb and an adjective. Like an adjective, it modifies a substantive:

> The *inquiring* reporter stopped him.
> *Encouraged* by his help, we shall continue the work.
> *Having* just *returned* from my vacation, I had not heard of the accident.

Like a verb the participle may take a direct or an indirect object and may be modified by an adverb.

> Wishing *us success*, he drove away. [*Us* is an indirect object, *success* a direct object, of the participle *wishing*.]
> Stumbling *awkwardly*, he came into the room. [*Awkwardly* is an adverb modifying the participle *stumbling*.]

Passive. See **Voice.**
Past tense. See **Tense.**
Past perfect tense. See **Tense.**
Perfect. See **Tense.**
Person. That characteristic of words, shown by their form, which indicates the speaker (**first person**), the person spoken to (**second person**), and the person spoken of (**third person**). Only personal pronouns and verbs change their form to show a change in person:

> First person: I am
> Second person: You are
> Third person: He is

(For the declension of personal pronouns, see **Pronoun;** for the conjugation of a verb, see pp. 415–418.) Nouns are regarded to be in the third person.

Personal pronoun. See **Pronoun.**
Phrase. In a strict grammatical sense a phrase is a group of words without a subject and predicate, and used as a single part of speech: as a substantive, verb, adjective, or adverb. There are the following kinds:

a. **Prepositional phrase** consisting of a preposition and its object with or without modifiers. It is used as an adjective or an adverb.

> The woman *in the large chair* is the secretary of the club. [Adjective.]
> I went *with her*. [Adverb.]

b. **Participial phrase** consisting of a participle and its object and modifiers. It is used as an adjective.

> We saw a large bull *coming toward us*. [Adjective.]

c. **Gerund phrase** consisting of a gerund and its object and modifiers. It is used as a substantive.

> *Walking through the woods at night* was very exciting. [Substantive.]

d. **Infinitive phrase** consisting of an infinitive and its subject, object, and modifiers. It is used as a substantive, adjective, or adverb.

To see is *to believe.* [Substantive.]
He gave us ten dollars *to spend on our trip.* [Adjective.]
His strange conduct is not easy *to explain.* [Adverb.]

e. **Verb phrase** consisting of one or more auxiliaries and a principal verb. It is regarded as a verb unit.

I *have been gone* ten years.
You *should have waited* for him.

Plural. See **Number.**
Possessive adjective. See **Adjective.**
Possessive (genitive) case. See **Case.**
Predicate. A word or group of words, in a sentence, that makes a statement about the subject. Thus in the sentence, *John drove the car, drove* is the predicate, for it tells what the subject *John* did. The predicate contains a finite verb, either a simple verb or a verb phrase; *e.g., went, have gone.* It may have a direct and an indirect object, a predicate substantive or adjective, an objective complement, and adverbial modifiers. See **Object, Predicate complement, Objective complement, Adverb, Adverbial clause, Adverbial objective.**
Predicate adjective. See **Predicate complement.**
Predicate complement. A substantive or adjective completing the meaning of a copulative verb. (See **Copula.**) The predicate substantive is also called the **predicate nominative.**

Predicate substantive: He is *a carpenter.*
Predicate adjective: She is *very young.*

Predicate nominative. See **Predicate complement.**
Predicate substantive. See **Predicate complement.**
Predication. Any group of words consisting of a subject and predicate, whether a simple sentence or a clause.
Preposition. A part of speech that shows the relation between a substantive and another word in the sentence; *e.g., in, on, into, toward, from, for, against, of, between, with, without, within, before, behind, under, over, above, among, at, by, around, about, through,* etc. In English many words are both prepositions and adverbs, their classification depending upon their use. If they are followed by a substantive that with them forms a unit, they are prepositions; if they are not, they are adverbs. Prepositions require substantives to complete their meaning; adverbs do not.

He stood *behind* the chair. [Preposition.]
He walked *behind.* [Adverb.]
He is *in* the bank. [Preposition.]
He came *in* while we were there. [Adverb.]

Prepositional phrase. See **Phrase.**
Present tense. See **Tense.**
Principal clause. See **Clause.**
Principal parts. The forms of any verb from which other forms may be derived. They are (*a*) the present infinitive, (*b*) the past first person singular, and (*c*) the past participle (see **Verb**); *e.g., flee, fled, fled; choose, chose, chosen; love, loved, loved.*
Principal verb. A verb not used as an **auxiliary.** The auxiliaries themselves may be used as principal verbs.

I *have written* ten letters. [*Written* is the principal verb; *have* is the auxiliary.]
I *have* ten letters. [*Have* is the principal verb.]

Pronoun. A part of speech, a word used instead of a noun. Pronouns may be classified as follows:

a. **Personal:** *I, thou, you, he, she, it,* and their inflectional forms. (See **declension** below.)

I listened to *her*.

b. **Demonstrative:** *this, that, these, those.*

This is my favorite book.

c. **Interrogative:** *who, which, what.*

Who can answer this question?

d. **Relative:** *who, which, that,* and the compounds *whoever,* etc.

The house *that* they bought was built many years ago. (See **declension** below.)

e. **Indefinite:** *any, anyone, some, someone, no one, nobody,* etc.

Everyone is invited.

f. **Reflexive:** *myself, yourself,* etc.

I did it *myself.*

g. **Intensive:** *myself, yourself,* etc.

He *himself* is to blame.

h. **Reciprocal:** *each other, one another.*

They blamed *each other.*

DECLENSION OF PRONOUNS

PERSONAL

	Singular	*Plural*
Nom.	I	we
Poss. (*Gen.*)	my, mine	our, ours
Obj. (*Acc.*)	me	us
Nom.	you	you
Poss. (*Gen.*)	your	your, yours
Obj. (*Acc.*)	you	you
Nom.	he	they
Poss. (*Gen.*)	his	their, theirs
Obj. (*Acc.*)	him	them
Nom.	she	they
Poss. (*Gen.*)	her, hers	their, theirs
Obj. (*Acc.*)	her	them
Nom.	it	they
Poss. (*Gen.*)	its	their, theirs
Obj. (*Acc.*)	it	them

RELATIVE

Nom.	who	who
Poss. (*Gen.*)	whose	whose
Obj. (*Acc.*)	whom	whom

Proper name. See **Noun.**
Proper noun. See **Noun.**

Reflexive pronoun. See **Intensive pronoun.**
Relative adjective. See **Adjective.**
Relative clause. See **Adjective clause.**
Relative pronoun. See **Pronoun.**
Sentence. A group of words containing a subject and a predicate and expressing a complete thought. There are the following kinds:

a. Structure

1. A **simple sentence** contains only one clause, which must be independent (or principal); the subject and the predicate may be either simple or compound.

The wind blew all day. [Simple subject and predicate.]
The wind and rain beat at our door. [Compound subject; simple predicate.]

2. A **compound sentence** contains two or more independent (or principal) clauses, but no dependent (or subordinate) clauses.

The bell rang, and in a minute the children were out of the school.

3. A **complex sentence** contains only one independent (or principal) clause and one or more dependent (or subordinate) clauses.

When we came home, we found the door unlocked.

4. A **compound-complex sentence** contains two or more independent (or principal) clauses, and one or more dependent (or subordinate) clauses.

The signal was given, and there was a deafening roar as the three motors burst into their song of power.

b. Thought

1. A **declarative sentence** makes a statement.

The boy closed the door.

2. An **interrogative sentence** asks a question.

Is the door closed?

3. An **imperative sentence** expresses a command.

Close the door.

4. An **exclamatory sentence** expresses strong feeling.

What a glorious view you have!

Sentence-element. Any part of a sentence, either a word or a group of words.
Sign of the infinitive. See **Infinitive.**
Simple conjunction. See **Conjunction.**
Simple sentence. See **Sentence.**
Singular. See **Number.**
Subject. A word or group of words naming the person, place, thing, or idea about which something is said. Thus in the sentence, *John went away*, *John* is the subject, for it is about him that something is said. The subject of a sentence is either a noun or a pronoun or a group of words used as a noun.

The girl wrote a letter. [Noun.]
That you will be promoted is certain. [Clause.]

The **simple subject** is a noun or pronoun. The **complete subject** is the simple subject and its modifiers.

The trees have grown well. [*Trees* is the simple subject.]
The young trees that we planted last year have grown well. [*The young trees that we planted last year* is the complete subject.]

Subjunctive. See **Mode.**
Subordinate clause. See **Clause.**
Substantive. Any word or group of words used as a noun. It may be a noun, a pronoun, a clause, an infinitive, or a gerund.

The *house* is painted white. [Noun.]
I am going. [Pronoun.]
I saw *that she was hurt.* [A clause used as the object of the verb *saw.*]
We had planned *to meet her here.* [Infinitive phrase used as the object of the verb *planned.*]
Meeting her here was a part of our plan. [Gerund phrase used as the subject of the verb *was.*]

See also **Noun** and **Pronoun.**

Substantive clause. A clause used as a noun. It may be used in the following ways:

Subject of a verb: *That he is a scholar* is certain.
Object of a verb: I know *that he is a scholar.*
Object of a preposition: There is no doubt as to *whether he is a scholar.*
Predicate substantive: The truth is *that he is a scholar.*
Appositive: This is certain — *that he is a scholar.*
Adverbial substantive: I am sure *that he is a scholar.*
Absolute substantive: *Granted that he is a scholar*, he may yet be mistaken.

Superlative. See **Comparison.**
Syntax. Deals with the relationship of words to each other in a sentence. Thus in the sentence, *We saw him yesterday*, the syntax of the words is as follows: *we* is the subject of the verb *saw; saw* is the predicate of the pronoun *we; him* is the object of the verb *saw; yesterday* is an adverb modifying the verb *saw.* Syntax and inflection are the two main divisions of grammar. (See **Inflection.**)
Tense. A characteristic of verbs shown by different forms that indicate the time of the action. There are six tenses: the present tense, the past tense, the future tense, the perfect (present perfect) tense, the past perfect tense, and the future perfect tense. (The tenses of a typical verb are shown on pp. 415–418.)
Transitive. See **Verb.**
Verb. A part of speech used to assert an action, a condition, or state.

He hit the ball. [*Hit* expresses action.]
He is poor. [*Is* expresses condition or state.]

There are these kinds:

a. A **transitive verb** requires a direct object to complete its meaning; *i.e.*, it must be followed by a word that answers the question *whom* or *what.* In the sentence, *The girl wrote the letter*, *wrote* is a transitive verb because it requires the direct object *letter* to complete its meaning.

b. An **intransitive verb** does not require an object to complete its meaning. In the sentence, *The girl ran down the hill*, *ran* is intransitive because it does not require an object to complete its meaning.

(For other characteristics of verbs, see **Mode, Number, Person, Tense, Voice.** For the conjugation of a typical verb, see pp. 415–418.)

Vocative substantive (**nominative of address**). A substantive used in direct address. See **Direct address.**

Voice. A characteristic of verbs. A verb is in the **active voice** when its subject is the doer of the act. A verb is in the **passive voice** when its subject is acted upon.

Active voice: I rang the bell. [The subject *I* did the act of *ringing.*]
Passive voice: The bell was rung by me. [The subject *bell* was acted upon by *me.*]

With one exception all the passive forms of any verb are composed of the several forms of the auxiliary *to be* and the past participle of the principal verb; the one exception is the past participle itself. See the conjugation on pages 415–418. Only transitive verbs can have a passive voice.

Vowels. The letters *a, e, i, o,* and *u* are vowels. The letters *b, c, d, f, g, h, j, k, l, m, n, p, q, r, s, t, v, x,* and *z* are consonants. *W* when used as in *weak,* and *y* when used as in *young* are consonants; *w* when used as in *how,* and *y* when used as in *try* are vowels.

CONJUGATION OF THE VERB **TO TAKE**

Principal Parts: **take, took, taken**

	ACTIVE VOICE		PASSIVE VOICE	
	Indicative mode			
	Singular	Plural	Singular	Plural
Present tense	SIMPLE			
	1. I take	we take	1. I am taken	we are taken
	2. you do take	you take	2. you are taken	you are taken
	3. he does take	they take	3. he is taken	they are taken
	EMPHATIC			
	1. I do take	we do take		
	2. you do take	you do take		
	3. he does take	they do take		
	PROGRESSIVE			
	1. I am taking	we are taking		
	2. you are taking	you are taking		
	3. he is taking	they are taking		
Past tense	SIMPLE			
	1. I took	we took	1. I was taken	we were taken
	2. you took	you took	2. you were taken	you were taken
	3. he took	they took	3. he was taken	they were taken
	EMPHATIC			
	1. I did take	we did take		
	2. you did take	you did take		
	3. he did take	they did take		
	PROGRESSIVE			
	1. I was taking	we were taking		
	2. you were taking	you were taking		
	3. he was taking	they were taking		
Future tense	SIMPLE			
	1. I shall (will) take	we shall (will) take	I shall (will) be taken, etc.	
	2. you will (shall) take	you will (shall) take		
	3. he will (shall) take	they will (shall) take		
	PROGRESSIVE			
	I shall (will) be taking, etc.			
Perfect tense	SIMPLE			
	1. I have taken	we have taken	I have been taken, etc.	
	2. you have taken	you have taken		
	3. he has taken	they have taken		
	PROGRESSIVE			
	I have been taking, etc.			

	ACTIVE VOICE		PASSIVE VOICE
	Indicative mode — continued		
	SINGULAR	PLURAL	
PAST PERFECT TENSE	SIMPLE 1. I had taken 2. you had taken 3. he had taken PROGRESSIVE I had been taking, etc.	 we had taken you had taken they had taken	I had been taken, etc.
FUTURE PERFECT TENSE	SIMPLE I shall (will) have taken, etc. PROGRESSIVE I shall (will) have been taking, etc.		I shall (will) have been taken, etc.

Subjunctive mode

	ACTIVE SINGULAR	ACTIVE PLURAL	PASSIVE SINGULAR	PASSIVE PLURAL
PRESENT TENSE	SIMPLE 1. if I take 2. if you take 3. if he take EMPHATIC 1. if I do take 2. if you do take 3. if he do take PROGRESSIVE 1. if I be taking 2. if you be taking 3. if he be taking	 if we take if you take if they take if we do take if you do take if they do take if we be taking if you be taking if they be taking	1. if I be taken 2. if you be taken 3. if he be taken	if we be taken if you be taken if they be taken
PAST TENSE	SIMPLE 1. if I took 2. if you took 3. if he took EMPHATIC 1. if I did take 2. if you did take 3. if he did take PROGRESSIVE 1. if I were taking 2. if you were taking 3. if he were taking	 if we took if you took if they took if we did take if you did take if they did take if we were taking if you were taking if they were taking	1. if I were taken 2. if you were taken 3. if he were taken	if we were taken if you were taken if they were taken

	ACTIVE VOICE	PASSIVE VOICE

Subjunctive mode — continued

FUTURE TENSE	[The future subjunctive is exactly like the future indicative.]
PERFECT TENSE	[The perfect subjunctive is exactly like the perfect indicative.]
PAST PERFECT TENSE	[The past perfect subjunctive is exactly like the past perfect indicative.]
FUTURE PERFECT TENSE	[The future perfect subjunctive is exactly like the future perfect indicative.]

Potential mode

	SINGULAR	PLURAL	
PRESENT TENSE	SIMPLE 1. I may *or* can take 2. you may *or* can take 3. he may *or* can take	 we may *or* can take you may *or* can take they may *or* can take	I may *or* can be taken, etc.
	PROGRESSIVE I may *or* can be taking, etc.		
PAST TENSE	SIMPLE 1. I might *or* could take 2. you might *or* could take 3. he might *or* could take	 we might *or* could take you might *or* could take they might *or* could take	I might *or* could be taken, etc.
	PROGRESSIVE I might *or* could be taking, etc.		
PERFECT TENSE	SIMPLE I may *or* can have taken, etc. PROGRESSIVE I may *or* can have been taking, etc.		I may *or* can have been taken, etc.

	ACTIVE VOICE	PASSIVE VOICE
	Potential mode — continued	
PAST PERFECT TENSE	SIMPLE I might *or* could have taken, etc. PROGRESSIVE I might *or* could have been taking, etc.	I might *or* could have been taken, etc.
	Imperative mode	
	SIMPLE: take EMPHATIC: do take PROGRESSIVE: be taking	be taken
	Infinitive mode	
PRESENT TENSE	SIMPLE INFINITIVE: to take PROGRESSIVE INFINITIVE: to be taking GERUND: taking	INFINITIVE: to be taken GERUND: being taken
PERFECT TENSE	SIMPLE INFINITIVE: to have taken PROGRESSIVE INFINITIVE: to have been taking GERUND: having taken	INFINITIVE: to have been taken GERUND: having been taken
	Participial mode, or *participles*	
PRESENT TENSE	taking	being taken
PAST TENSE	[There is no past participle in the active voice.]	taken
PERFECT TENSE	SIMPLE: having taken PROGRESSIVE: having been taking	having been taken

APPENDIX C

ENUNCIATION AND PRONUNCIATION

ENUNCIATION

Enunciate distinctly. Because of hasty and careless speech, words are run together, and as a consequence letters are slurred, changed, or completely lost. **Distinct enunciation**

Words are often run together with the consequent mispronunciation or loss of letters: **Words run together**

arncha, cudja, cudntcha, didja, didncha, doncha, getcha, gotcha, havncha, wudja, woncha, gimme, gonna, gotta, hafta, wanta.

Vowels are often not distinctly enunciated, usually being reduced to short *i* or short *u*, as in the following words: **Vowels reduced to short *i* or *u***

Word	*Careless enunciation*
college	collige
cabbage	cabbige
instead	instid
can	cin
get	git
just	jist
it	ut
of	uv
from	frum
because	becuz
was	wuz
analysis	analusus
nobody, somebody	nobuddy, somebuddy
basement	basemunt
judgment	judgmunt
American	Uhmurucun
climate	climut

The letters italicized in the following words are often dropped: **Letters dropped**

bein*g*	temper*a*ment	slep*t*
doin*g*	w*h*ich (hwich)	clo*th*es

goin*g*	while (hwile)	cru*e*l
seein*g*	white (hwite)	auxil*i*ary
somethin*g*	when (hwen)	fact*o*ry
accident*al*ly	what (hwat)	bound*a*ry
re*al*ly	as*ked*	lab*o*ratory
gener*al*ly	kep*t*	lib*r*ary
fin*al*ly	stric*t*	Feb*r*uary
us*u*ally	nex*t*	ar*c*tic
prob*ab*ly	fac*ts*	univers*i*ty
authori*ta*tively	ac*ts*	gover*n*ment
artist*ical*ly	lif*ts*	reco*g*nize
consider*a*ble	contradic*ts*	car*a*mel
vi*o*lent	subjec*t*	per*h*aps
stud*e*nt	objec*t*	po*e*m
diff*e*rent	crep*t*	pum*p*kin

PRONUNCIATION

A List of Words Often Mispronounced

The accentual and diacritical marks in the following list of words are not intended to give an exhaustive description of the pronunciation of each word, but only to point out common errors. The following diacritical marks are used:

ă as in *at*
ā as in *mate*
ǡ as in *chaotic*
ä as in *arm*
ȧ as in *ask*
â as in *care*
ĕ as in *men*
ē as in *see*
ė̄ as in the first syllable of *event*
ẽ as in *fern*
ĭ as in *tin*
ī as in *wine*
ŏ as in *lot*
ō as in *host*
ȱ as in *obey*
ŏ̊ as in *soft*
ô as in *orb*
ŭ as in *bun*
ū as in *use*
ū̇ as in *unite*
ụ as in *bull*
ũ as in *urn*
ü as in *menu*
o͞o as in *tool*
o͝o as in *foot*
ou as in *thou*
t͜u as in *nature*
zh as in *azure*

	Word	*Correct pronunciation*
Words often accented on the wrong syllable	absolutely	ab′solutely
	acumen	a cū′men
	admirable	ad′mirable

Word	*Correct pronunciation*
adult (noun)	a dult′
adult (adjective)	a dult′ *or* ad′ult
adversary	ad′ver sa ry
albumen	al bu′men
alias	ā lias
ancestral	an ses′tral
applicable	ap′plicable
apropos	ăp′rō pō′
brigand	brĭg′and
choleric	kŏl′eric
comparable	com′par a ble
condolence	con dō′lence
contrary	con′tra ry
conversant	con′ver sant (*occasionally* con ver′sant)
cuckoo	kŏŏk′ōō
deficit	def′i cit
despicable	des′picable
detour	de tour′
dirigible	dir′i ji ble
discharge	dis charge′
elevated	el′e vat ed
entire	en tire′
evidently	ev′i dent ly
exquisite	ex′quisite
formidable	for′midable
gondola	gon′dola
grimace	gri māce′
guardian	guard′i an
hospitable	hos′pitable, *British* hospit′-able
impious	im′pĭ ous
incognito	in cog′nito
incomparable	in com′parable
industry	in′dustry
inevitable	in ev′itable
inquiry	in quī′ry
interesting	in′teresting
inventory	in′ventory
irreparable	ir rep′arable
lamentable	lam′entable
maintenance	main′tenance

	Word	*Correct pronunciation*
	mischievous	mis′chie vous
	municipal	mu nis′i pal
	orchestra	or′chestra
	orchestral	or kes′ tral
	piquant	pē′kant
	positively	pos′i tive ly
	precedence (priority)	prē cēd′ence
	precedent (noun)	prĕs′e dent
	precedent (adjective)	prē cēd′ent
	preferable	pref′erable
	recall (noun)	re call′ *or* re′call
	recall (verb)	re call′
	reputable	rep′utable
	robust	ro bust′
	superfluous	su per′fluous
	theater	the′a ter
	vagary	vȧ gā′ry *or* vȧ gâr′y
Words in which certain vowels are often mispronounced	accurate	accūrate
	aviator	ā′vi a tor
	Basil	Băz′il
	because	bekôz
	biographical	bīographical
	bouquet	bōō kā′
	catch	cătch (not "cĕtch")
	chock-full	Pronounced as spelled; not "chuck-full."
	choler	kŏl′er
	clique	klēk
	coupé	kōō pā′
	coupon	kōō′pon
	creek	krēk
	culinary	kū′linary
	data	dā′ta (not "dat ta")
	deaf	dĕf
	demise	dē mīz′
	describe	dē scribe′
	destruction	dē struc′tion
	directly	di rect′ly
	experiment	ex pĕr′iment (not "ex pĭr-iment"
	faucet	faw′set

Word	*Correct pronunciation*
garrulous	găr′ū lŭs *or* găr o͝o lŭs (not "gär yu lous")
genealogy	jĕn e ălogy *or* jē ne ălogy (not "-ology")
genuine	jen u ĭn (not "-īn")
ghoul	go͞ol
gratis	grā tis
hearth	härth
heinous	hā nous
heroine	her′oĭne
historian	his tō′ ri an
hoof	ho͞of
hypocrisy	hĭ poc′ri sy
ignoramus	ig no rā′mus
Italian	Ĭ tal yan (not "Ī-")
joust	jŭst *or* jo͞ost
literature	lit er a tūre (not "-toor")
mineralogy	min er ăl ogy (not "-ology")
naked	nā ked (not "nĕkked")
nape	nāp
Pall Mall	Pĕl Mĕl
panegyric	pan e jĭr ic *or* pan e jĕr ic
pathos	pā thos
penalize	pē′nal ize
percolator	per kō la′tor (not "perkyu-")
premise (noun)	prĕm′iss
premise (verb)	prē mīz′
pretty	prĭt y
programme	prō′grăm (not "-grum")
pronunciation	pro nun si a shun (not "pronown-")
quay	kē
radiator	rā′di a tor
regular	reg yu lar
reservoir	res′er vwôr
rinse	Pronounced as spelled; not "rense."
roily	Pronounced as spelled; not "rī ly."
roof	ro͞of
root	ro͞ot
route	ro͞ot (preferred)

	Word	*Correct pronunciation*
	Russian	Rŭsh′an (not "Rōōsh-")
	saucy	sô′sĭ
	since	sĭnce (not "sĕnse")
	sleek	slēk
	slough (noun, *mire*)	slou
	slough (noun, *cast skin*)	slŭf
	slough (verb)	slŭf
	status	stā tus
	suite	swēt (not "sōōt")
	tassel	tăs″l
	trow	trō
	ultimatum	ul ti mā tum
	verbatim	ver bā′tim
	wrestle	rĕs″l (not "răs″l")
	xylophone	zī lophone
	zoölogy	zō ŏl ogy (not "zōō-")
Words in which certain consonants are often mispronounced	archipelago	ar ki pel′a go
	banquet	bang′quet
	bequeath	The *th* is pronounced as in *thus.*
	cello	chel′o
	chaise	shāz
	chasm	kăsm
	English	ing′glish
	flaccid	flak′sid (See Rule 327, note.)
	handkerchief	hang′ker chief
	has (as in *has to*)	hăz (not "hăss")
	have (as in *have to*)	hăv (not "hăf")
	partner	Pronounced as spelled; not "pard ner."
	schism	sizm
	turgid	tur jid (See Rule 327, note.)
	used (as in *used to*)	ūzd (not "ūst")
	with	The *th* is pronounced as in *thus.*
Words to which an additional sound is often incorrectly added	across	a kros (not "a krost")
	aëroplane	ā′ẽr oplane (not "air′ĭ o-")
	almond	ä′mund *or* ăm′und
	athlete	ath′lete
	athletic	ath let′ic
	attacked	a tackt′ (not "a tack′ted")

Word	*Correct pronunciation*
buoy	bwoi *or* boi
casualty	caz′u al ty (not "-al′i ty")
cerement	sēr ment
column	kol um (not "-yum")
disastrous	dis as trous (not "-terous")
electoral	e lec to ral (not "ri al")
elm	*one syllable*
enthusiasm	en thū zi asm
film	*one syllable*
grievous	grēv′ous
height	hīt (not "hīth")
helm	*one syllable*
hindrance	hin drans (not "-der ans")
lightning (noun)	līt ning (not "līt en ing")
mischievous	mis′chēv ous
often	of en
poignant	poin′yănt *or* poi′nănt
remembrance	re mem brans (not "-ber-ans")
salmon	săm un
specialty	spesh′al ti (not "spesh i al-i ti")
umbrella	um brel la (not "um ber-el la")
wash	wŏsh (not "wôrsh")
watch	wŏtch (not "wôrch")

Words often mispronounced in various ways

Word	*Correct pronunciation*
ad infinitum	ad in fi nī′tum
bourgeois	bo͞or zhwȧ′
débris	dā′ brē′
début	dā bü′ *or* dě bū′
dishabille	dĭs ȧ bēl′ *or* děz ȧ bēl′
dishevel	di shev′el
dramatis personæ	drăm′a tis per sō′nē
finis	fī′nĭs
foyer (of a theater)	fwä′yā′ *or* foy′er
gaol	jāl
irrelevant	Pronounced as spelled; not "irrevelant."
larynx	lăr′inx *or* lā′rinx (not "lar nix")
mauve	mōv (not "mawv")

Word	*Correct pronunciation*
naive	nȧ ēv′
posthumous	pŏs′t͟u mŭs
rendezvous	rän de vo͞o *or* rĕn de vo͞o
sarsaparilla	sär sa pa ril la (not "săss-parilla")
sough	sŭf *or* sou
vaudeville	vōd′vĭl *or* vô dẽ vĭl
viz. (*or* viz)	An arbitrary sign for the Latin word *videlicet* (pronounced vĭ dĕl′i sĕt). In reading *viz.* aloud, say either "videlicet" or "namely" (the English equivalent of *videlicet*); do not say "vizz."

Variation in the sound of *o*

Throughout the United States there is considerable variation in the pronunciation of *o* as illustrated in the following words. The pronunciation varies from the *o* in lŏck, hŏt, nŏt, to the *a* in fäther, to the *o* in sŏ̊ft, to the *o* in ôrb. The pronunciation of these words with the full sound of *o* as in ôrb is generally considered to be a fault.[1]

bŏg	bŏ̊ss
dŏff	Bŏ̊ston
fŏg	cŏ̊ffee
fŏreign	dŏ̊g
frŏg	gŏ̊ne
gŏd	lŏ̊ng
hŏg	ŏ̊ff
tŏrrid	ŏ̊ffer
	ŏ̊ffice
	ŏ̊fficer
	ŏ̊ften
	scŏ̊ff
	sŏ̊ng
	tŏ̊ngs
	wrŏ̊ng

[1] The diacritical marks are those given in Webster (second, 1934 edition). In most instances the dictionary indicates a variation in pronunciation.

Variation in the sound of long *u*

Throughout the United States there is considerable variation in the pronunciation of long *u*. The pronunciation varies from yōō to ĭōō to ōō. The yōō or ĭōō sound, wherever possible, is often considered more elegant than the ōō sound.

Words in which yōō or ĭōō occurs without much variation:

avenue	pure
beauty	union
cube	usurp
ewe	use, abuse, misuse
feud	you
few	youth

Words in which there is variation from yōō to ĭōō to ōō. The pronunciation ōō is often criticized and ridiculed, yet it is widely used.

assume, presume, resume	new
dew, due	numerous
duke	suit
duty	student
educated	supreme
enthusiasm	tune
lute	

Words in which the *y* sound is now completely silent in standard speech. Note that the *u* follows *r* in these words.

brew	prune
crew	rule
drew	shrew
fruit	threw
grew	true

APPENDIX D

CONNECTIVES

Connectives as an aid to coherence

1. The following list of transitional words and phrases may aid in gaining coherence within the sentence and within the paragraph. Inexperienced writers often fail to make clear the precise relationship of their ideas either because they fail to use connectives or because they use the wrong ones. Their vocabulary of transitional words is limited to a small group, such as *and, but, so.* Connectives should, of course, not be overused; the relationship in the thought may be so clear that transitional words are not necessary.

Connectives and punctuation

2. A study of connectives may also be an aid to the understanding of the rules of punctuation. (See Rules 64, 247, 268.) The grossest errors in punctuation are due to the writer's failure to recognize the relative rank of the parts of a sentence. He must be able to distinguish between independent and subordinate parts, and to recognize coördinate relationship. Transitional words indicate to the reader whether parts of a sentence are independent or subordinate, and whether they are coördinate with one another. (The following lists are in no way complete.)

TRANSITIONAL WORDS WITHIN THE SENTENCE

Connectives within the sentence (i) coördinating words

3. I. Coördinating words (Most of these coördinating words may also be used between sentences.)

A. Classification according to meaning

1. Addition: *and, further, furthermore, besides, also, moreover, likewise, nor* (*and not*), *too, again, and then, finally, next.*
2. Contrast: *but, however, yet, and yet, still, nevertheless, notwithstanding, on the contrary, on the other hand.*
3. Result: *therefore, hence, consequently, so, accordingly, thereupon, thus, wherefore, then.*
4. Alternation: *or, nor, otherwise, else, either . . . or, neither . . . nor, as . . . so, both . . . and, not only . . . but also, the one . . . the other, on the one hand . . . on the other hand.*
5. Cause: *for.*
6. Repetition, exemplification, intensification: *in fact, indeed, in other words, that is, namely, for instance, for example, thus.*

B. Grammatical classification
1. Pure conjunctions: *and, but, for, or, neither, nor.*
2. Correlatives: *either . . . or, neither . . . nor, as . . . so, both . . . and, not only . . . but also, the one . . . the other, on the one hand . . . on the other hand.*
3. Conjunctive adverbs: *further, furthermore, besides, also, moreover, likewise, again, then, finally, however, yet, still, nevertheless, notwithstanding, therefore, hence, consequently, so, accordingly, thereupon, thus, wherefore, indeed, namely.* The phrases *on the contrary, on the other hand,* etc., are used as conjunctive adverbs.

NOTE. — It is possible for a conjunctive adverb to connect parts that are not coördinate.

Right: Although it was stormy, *yet* we decided to go.
Right: If you follow the directions carefully, *then* you will have no trouble.

4. II. Subordinating words

(ii) Subordinating words

A. Relative pronouns: *who, which, what, that, as.*
B. Subordinating conjunctions
1. Time: *when, whenever, while, before, after, until, till, since, as soon as, as long as, as often as, now, now that, prior to, once.*
2. Place: *where, wherever, whence, whencesoever, whither, whithersoever, whereto.*
3. Cause: *because, as, since, inasmuch as, seeing that, now that, owing to the fact that.*
4. Purpose: *that, so that, in order that, lest, for the purpose that.*
5. Degree or comparison: *as, than, more than, rather than, as . . . as, not so . . . as, such . . . as, just as . . . so.*
6. Condition: *if, so, unless, on condition that, provided that, supposing, in case that, but that, so that.*
7. Concession: *though, although, even if, no matter how.*
8. Result: *that, so that, so . . . that, such . . . that, and so, but that, such that.*
9. Manner: *as, as if, as though.*

TRANSITIONAL WORDS WITHIN THE PARAGRAPH

Connectives within the paragraph

5. (Transitional words within the sentence may be used to link sentences together. (See p. 428.) These words will not be repeated here.)
1. Addition: *in addition to what has been said; more than this; equally important; another point to be considered;* etc.

2. Contrast: *in contrast to this; at the same time; for all that; after all; although this may be true;* etc.
3. Comparison: *similarly; likewise.*
4. Result: *since this is true; under these circumstances; under these conditions; it follows that;* etc.
5. Purpose: *for this purpose; with this end in view;* etc.
6. Repetition, exemplification, intensification: *to be sure; as I have said; in other words; in the same way; in short; that is to say; as has been noted;* etc.
7. Abatement: *to be sure; I admit; there is, to be sure, an exception; perhaps; it may be.*
8. Time: *at length; after a lapse of time; after a few days; in the meantime; meanwhile; immediately;* etc.
9. Place: *on the opposite side; near by; adjacent to; yonder; beyond;* etc.
10. Series: *first; second; third;* etc.
11. Reference to a word or group of words in a preceding sentence: *he; she; it;* etc.; *this; that;* etc.; *in this manner; in this way; thus;* etc.

MISUSE OF COÖRDINATING WORDS

And and *but*

6. Distinguish between *and* and *but.* Note carefully whether the statements are in the same line of thought or are in opposition.

Wrong: After I finished high school, I wanted to work in my uncle's shop, and my father wanted me to go to college.
Right: After I finished high school, I wanted to work in my uncle's shop, but my father wanted me to go to college.

But

7. Be certain that *but* connects statements that are really adversative.

Illogical: For an examination, a student cannot review all of the work covered, but he must have the ability to select the most important points in the course and concentrate on them.
Right: For an examination, a student cannot review all of the work covered, but he should select the most important points in the course and concentrate on them.

Illogical: In vain we begged her to stay at home, but she was determined to go.
Right: We begged her to stay at home, but she was determined to go.

Illogical: The complaints have come not from the faculty, but they have come from the students.
Right: The complaints have come not from the faculty, but from the students.

Illogical: He was impetuous and self-confident, but always courageous.
Right: He was impetuous and self-confident and always courageous.

For and *because*

8. Do not confuse *for* and *because.* The *for*-clause gives the reason for the belief in a statement; the *because*-clause gives the reason for the statement.

Wrong: They did not come yesterday because I met the train.
Right: They did not come yesterday, for I met the train. (The writer's reason for knowing that they did not come.)
Right: I was absent from class yesterday because I had not done the assigned reading. (Either *for* or *because* may be used in this sentence. *Because* states explicitly an immediate cause or reason felt to be closely related to the principal clause; *for* is less explicit and introduces a statement felt to be relatively independent.)

9. The use of *so* to express sequence or result is best limited to informal writing. (See Rule 55.) *Therefore, wherefore, consequently, accordingly, so, then,* all denote a succession usually causal, but they differ in these respects: *therefore* is the most formal and is used in strict reasoning; *consequently* is used in close logical sequence; *accordingly* is less formal and does not indicate so close a logical sequence as *therefore* and *consequently; so* and *then* are the least formal of all and do not necessarily imply a close causal sequence. *So*

Right: The teaching of law as a profession should no more be irrational than the teaching of it as part of a liberal education or as a preparation for law studies. The case method, therefore, falls short and is slavish if it stops in each instance with the first case in a series. — WOODROW WILSON.
Right: From still earlier centuries had come down an inordinate fondness for allegorizing everything on which allegory could lay its hands. And so there sprang up the Bestiaries, amazing compilations of beasts, and birds, and fishes, endowed with qualities they never had, and allegorized into types of sacred things. — J. L. LOWES.

10. Be certain that *that is, that is to say, i.e.,* introduce material that is the equivalent of or the explanation of what precedes rather than the correction of it. *That is, that is to say*

Wrong: I have asked all of the class to come; that is, all that I could reach by telephone.
Right: I have asked all of the class to come; at least, all that I could reach by telephone.

Right: He makes frequent use of feminine rhyme; that is, a rhyme in which two syllables, one accented and one unaccented, occur at the end of each line.

MISUSE OF SUBORDINATING WORDS

11. Do not use *as* for *that* or *whether; as if* for *that; so as* for *so that.* Misuse of subordinating words: *as*

Wrong: I don't know as I am going.
Right: I don't know that I am going; [or] I don't know whether I am going.

Awkward: It seems as if he ought to do his share.
Improved: It seems that he ought to do his share.

Wrong: We went early so as we could see the parade.
Right: We went early so that we could see the parade.

As and *since* used ambiguously

12. Make certain that *as* and *since* are not used ambiguously. They may express both time and cause.

Ambiguous: Since she has been ill, we have been very much worried about her.
Clear: We have been very much worried about her because she has been ill; [or] since her illness, we have been very much worried about her.

Because, since, as

13. Distinguish between *because, since, as. Because* gives an immediate cause or reason; *since* is less formal and more incidental than *because; as* gives a reason even more incidental than *since.* The *since-* and *as-*clauses often begin their sentences. The conjunctions *for, because, since,* are often to be preferred to *as* to express cause.

Right: I returned the book because it was due.
Right: Since you are ready, we may as well go.
Right: As we have gone thus far, we might as well go farther.

But what for *but that, that*

14. Do not use *but what* for *but that* or *that.*

Wrong: I do not know but what I had better go to see her.
Right: I do not know but that I had better go to see her.

Wrong: I have no doubt but what she would like to go.
Right: I have no doubt that she would like to go.

Except for *unless*

15. Do not use *except* for *unless.*

Wrong: I will not send it except I hear from you.
Right: I will not send it unless I hear from you.

How for *that*

16. Do not use *how* for *that.*

Wrong: I had heard how it was possible to reach there in two days.
Right: I had heard that it was possible to reach there in two days.

If for *though, and* or *but*

17. Do not use *if* for *though, and,* or *but.*

Undesirable: She is a good teacher, if somewhat abrupt.
Right: She is a good teacher, though somewhat abrupt.
Right: She is a good teacher, but somewhat abrupt.

If for *whether*

18. Do not use *if* for *whether* to introduce a noun clause used as the object of a verb.

Wrong: Please let me know if you received the check. (Do not let me know if you did not receive it.)
Right: Please let me know whether you received the check.

Like for *as, as if, as though*

19. Do not use *like* (a preposition) for *as* or *as if, as though* (conjunctions), to express manner. *Like* with an incomplete clause is commonly used in colloquial speech, but it is best avoided in a formal style.

Wrong: He acted like he had made a great mistake.
Right: He acted as though he had made a great mistake.

Colloquial: He took to his father's business like a duck to water.
Formally correct: He took to his father's business as a duck to water.

20. Do not use *so* for *so that* to express purpose. *So* for *so that*

Wrong: We went early so we could see the parade.
Right: We went early so that we could see the parade.

21. Do not use *than* for *when.* *Than* for *when*

Wrong: We had hardly started than she began to cry.
Right: We had hardly started when she began to cry.

22. *That* is generally used to introduce a restrictive clause and *which,* a non-restrictive clause. (See Rule 259 *a.*) *That* and *which*

Right: Stories that deal with crime are not suitable for children.
Right: Those stories, which deal with crime, are not suitable for children.

23. Do not use *until* for *when.* *Until* for *when*

Wrong: He had been gone only a few minutes until a high school friend of mine came in.
Right: He had been gone only a few minutes when a high school friend of mine came in.

24. Do not use *when* for *although* or *even though, because, that,* or *whereupon.* *When*

Bad: When they granted all her requests, she was not satisfied.
Right: Even though they granted all her requests, she was not satisfied.

Bad: We were worried when he had not written.
Right: We were worried because he had not written.

Bad: It was at this time in my life when I most appreciated giving to my friends the things they desired.
Right: It was at this time in my life that I most appreciated giving, etc.

Bad: She tore the letter open and read it hastily; when she ran from the room.
Right: She tore the letter open and read it hastily; whereupon she ran from the room.

25. *When* indicates a point in time; *while,* a duration of time. *When* and *while*

Wrong: She was working every possible moment when her classmates were loafing.
Right: She was working every possible moment while her classmates were loafing.
Right: She was working when we went to see her yesterday.

26. Do not use *where* for *that.* *Where* for *that*

Wrong: I saw in the paper where a man had been arrested for forgery.
Right: I saw in the paper that a man had been arrested for forgery.

27. *While* may mean (1) *during the time that,* (2) *at the same time that,* (3) *although.* Avoid the loose use of *while.* *While*

Misleading: She read to the children while I sang to them.
Clear: She read to the children and I sang to them.

Vague: While she was the most popular girl on the campus, she held no office.
Clear: Although she was the most popular girl on the campus, she held no office.

Vague: Mary enjoyed going to dances and parties while her sister preferred to stay at home.
Clear: Mary enjoyed going to dances and parties but her sister preferred to stay at home.

Right: She read to me while I sewed.
Right: I lived with them while I was in college.

Who, which, that

28. Use the relative pronoun *who* to refer to persons, *which* to animals and inanimate objects, *that* to persons, animals, and inanimate objects.

Without for *unless*

29. Do not use *without* for *unless.*

Wrong: It would be foolish to start without we know whether the mountain passes are open.
Right: It would be foolish to start unless we know whether the mountain passes are open.
Right: It would be foolish to start without knowing whether the mountain passes are open.

INDEX

[Boldface numbers refer to sections or rules; other numbers refer to pages.]